D1459288

Prospective Community Studies in Developing Countries

The International Union for the Scientific Study of Population Problems was set up in 1928, with Dr Raymond Pearl as President. At that time the Union's main purpose was to promote international scientific co-operation to study the various aspects of population problems, through national committees and through its members themselves. In 1947 the International Union for the Scientific Study of Population (IUSSP) was reconstituted into its present form.

It expanded its activities to:

- stimulate research on population
- develop interest in demographic matters among governments, national and international organizations, scientific bodies, and the general public
- foster relations between people involved in population studies
- disseminate scientific knowledge on population

The principal ways through which the IUSSP currently achieves its aims are:

- organization of worldwide or regional conferences
- operations of Scientific Committees under the auspices of the Council
- organization of training courses
- publication of conference proceedings and committee reports.

Demography can be defined by its field of study and its analytical methods. Accordingly, it can be regarded as the scientific study of human populations primarily with respect to their size, their structure, and their development. For reasons which are related to the history of the discipline, the demographic method is essentially inductive: progress in knowledge results from the improvement of observation, the sophistication of measurement methods, and the search for regularities and stable factors leading to the formulation of explanatory models. In conclusion, the three objectives of demographic analysis are to describe, measure, and analyse.

International Studies in Demography is the outcome of an agreement concluded by the IUSSP and the Oxford University Press. The joint series is expected to reflect the broad range of the Union's activities and, in the first instance, will be based on the seminars organized by the Union. The Editorial Board of the series is comprised of:

Prospective Community Studies in Developing Countries

Edited by

Monica Das Gupta, Peter Aaby, Michel Garenne, and Gilles Pison

CLARENDON PRESS · OXFORD

1997

Oxford University Press, Great Clarendon Street, Oxford OX2 6DP

Oxford New York
Athens Auckland Bangkok Bogota Bombay
Buenos Aires Calcutta Cape Town Dar es Salaam
Delhi Florence Hong Kong Istanbul Karachi
Kuala Lumpur Madras Madrid Melbourne
Mexico City Nairobi Paris Singapore
Taipei Tokyo Toronto Warsaw
and associated companies in
Berlin Ibadan

Oxford is a trade mark of Oxford University Press

Published in the United States by
Oxford University Press Inc., New York

British Library Cataloguing in Publication Data
Data available

Library of Congress Cataloging in Publication Data
Data available

ISBN 0-19-829209-0

1 3 5 7 9 10 8 6 4 2

Typeset by Best-set Typesetter Ltd, Hong Kong
Printed in Great Britain by Biddles Ltd, Guildford & King's Lynn

Contents

III   Africa

List of Contributors

PETER AABY Statens Serum Institute, Department of Epidemiology, Danish Epidemiology Science Centre, Copenhagen, Denmark

KHAWAJA M. A. AZIZ International Centre for Diarrhoeal Disease Research, Dhaka, Bangladesh

GRETCHEN BERGGREN and WARREN BERGGREN World Relief, Wheaton, Il., USA

PIERRE CANTRELLE Institut Santé et Développement, Paris, France

MONICA DAS GUPTA Harvard University, Center of Population and Development Studies, Cambridge, Mass., USA

ANNABEL DESGRÉES DU LOÛ Laboratoire d'Anthropologie, Musée de l'Homme, Paris, France

CECILE DE SWEEMER CRDI, BP, Dakar, Senegal

MICHEL GARENNE Harvard University, Center of Population and Development Studies, Cambridge, Mass., USA

EDDY GENECE Département de la Santé Publique et de la Population, Port-au-Prince, Haiti

MIGUEL A. GUZMÁN Louisana State University, Medical Center, Dept. of Pathology, New Orleans, Louisiana, USA

SIDNEY L. KARK and EMILY KARK Beit Hakeren, Jerusalem, Israel

EMILIA KOUMANS IES Officer, Center for Disease Control, Atlanta, GA, USA

ANDRÉ LANGANEY Laboratoire d'Anthropologie, Musée de l'Homme, Paris, France

HENRI MENAGER University of Illinois, School of Public Health, Chicago, Il., USA

W. HENRY MOSLEY Johns Hopkins University, School of Hygiene and Public Health, Department of Population Dynamics Baltimore, Maryland, USA

ALEX S. MULLER Academic Medical Centre, University of Amsterdam, Amsterdam, The Netherlands

OMONDI-ODHIAMBO Medical Research Centre, Kenya Medical Research Institute, Nairobi, Kenya

GILLES PISON Laboratoire d'Anthropologie, Musée de l'Homme, Paris, France

NEVIN S. SCRIMSHAW Harvard University, Center of Population and Development Studies, Cambridge, Mass., USA

CARL E. TAYLOR Johns Hopkins University, School of Hygiene and Public Health, Department of International Health, Baltimore, Md, USA

STEPHEN M. TOLLMAN University of the Witwatersrand, Department of Community Health, Health Systems Development Unit, Johannesburg, Republic of South Africa

JEROEN K. VAN GINNEKEN Netherlands International Demographic Institute, The Hague, The Netherlands

JOHN B. WYON Harvard School of Public Health, Department of Population and International Health, Boston, Mass., USA

Introduction

MICHEL GARENNE, MONICA DAS GUPTA, GILLES PISON, AND PETER AABY

Background

The idea of a systematic prospective study of a community to understand basic processes of births, diseases, and deaths started with the development of Public Health, Epidemiology, and Demography as major subjects of scientific research at the beginning of the twentieth century. The Pellagra Study (1916–21) is usually quoted as the first scientific prospective study of a community, in the cotton mill villages of South Carolina. It was designed to study the etiology of pellagra, a nutritional disorder, and was based on a comprehensive follow-up of a deprived Southern community. About twenty years ago, Kessler and Levin (1970) published a book summarizing experiences on prospective studies of communities conducted in the USA. The book presents ten studies conducted in American communities, covering a wide range of issues: comprehensive studies of diseases, epidemiological surveys of specific diseases, social surveys, psychiatric surveys, and three national health surveys which had some common features with the local studies. Most of these studies were of medium or long duration, the record being the Washington County Study in Maryland, which has been going on for some sixty years.

A recent paper by Mosley (1989) summarizes those experiences and provides a perspective for similar endeavours conducted in developing countries. The first documented prospective demographic community study conducted in a so-called developing country is probably the Yang-Tse River Valley Study conducted in China in the 1930s (Chiao, Thompson, and Chen 1938). Another little-known study was conducted in Guanabara, in Brazil in the 1940s. Many other prospective community studies were started after the Second World War, mostly in Africa and Asia. Some of them were of relatively short duration, others are still going on, as exemplified in this book. The Appendix in this book gives an idea of the wide variety of studies conducted in developing countries, variety in size, duration, and research focus. Closely related to the more demographic studies were the studies of health systems that Carl Taylor presents in this book (Chapter 1). Here again China was a pioneer, with the work of C. C. Chen and J. Grant in the 1930s, followed by the work of Sidney Kark in South Africa, which is presented here by Steve Tollman (Chapter 9).

Many of us who had spent many years in the field studying the health and

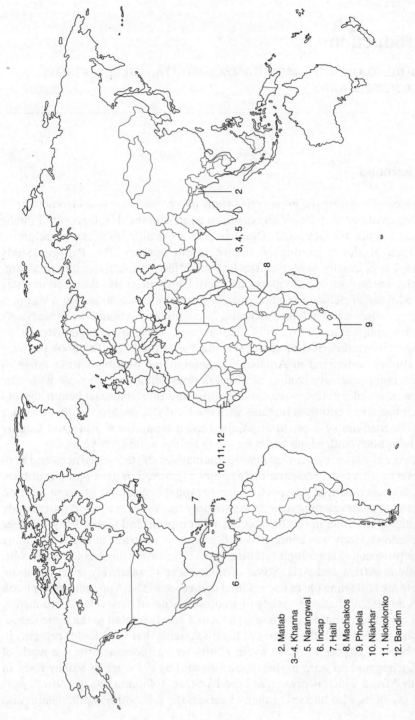

Location of the prospective community studies

2. Matlab
3–4. Khanna
5. Narangwal
6. Incap
7. Haiti
8. Machakos
9. Pholela
10. Niakhar
11. Niokolonko
12. Bandim

the dynamics of populations of developing countries felt the need to exchange their experiences with their colleagues. The International Union for the Scientific Study of Population (IUSSP) and the French Institute for Scientific Research Overseas (ORSTOM) jointly organized a seminar in order to review those experiences in developing countries and to bring together the senior generation of pioneers with the younger researchers who are now conducting or starting fieldwork. This meeting was extraordinarily rich in the exchange of experiences and in the discussion of the various scientific, technical, ethical, and political aspects of these researches. This book presents most of the papers presented at the seminar, which constitute only a small sample of the many studies conducted in developing countries since 1950 (see the Appendix). We decided that a more thorough account of some of the key studies was more important than a detailed account of all these valuable researches.

The chapters in this volume are reflective accounts of a type of research which has been fundamental to many major innovations in methods of data collection as well as in analytical perspectives. We were fortunate to be able to have such critical information on some of the most innovative field studies written up by the people who actually designed and conducted them. The main purpose of this volume is to bring together a great deal of information that is otherwise extremely difficult to locate, on how key prospective studies were carried out, and what were their most important findings. Such information is currently difficult to access because it is published in a diverse range of journals and books, often in obscure and ancient publications and reports. Moreover, some of the studies did not specifically describe their methodologies in a systematic fashion. For these reasons, we did not specifically request fresh data analysis for this volume. The findings presented here relate primarily to health and mortality, as this is the substantive theme which is common to all the studies, and the central focus of inquiry of most of the studies.

Vocabulary

These studies are often called 'Population Laboratories' or 'Population Observatories', but we have preferred the expression 'Prospective Community Studies' for several reasons. First, the word 'laboratory' usually refers to some kind of experiment, which is normally foreign to the scientific study of human communities. Second, the word 'observatory' refers to some kind of idealistic, impartial observation of phenomena, which would be almost impossible and probably unethical, and which does not account for the very interventionist attitude of most researchers, or at least for some kind of 'participant observation'. The common denominator of these scientific *studies* is to be *prospective*, implying a follow-up for several years, and based on a sizeable *community* in order to cumulate enough person-years of experience to ensure statistical significance. As a rule of thumb, a total of 100,000 person-years cumulated over time, for instance a population of 20,000 persons followed for five years, provides a large body of data of demographic and public health interest. However, this number is only indicative of sample sizes required where moderate or high levels of morbidity and mortality prevail: where these levels are lower, larger samples may be required. Smaller studies such as the Keneba Study are as valuable as larger ones like Matlab. A more comprehensive account of the range in size and duration of such studies is given in the Appendix.

Overview of the Studies

This collection of papers presents a wide variety of situations. The variety starts with the objectives: some of the studies have almost a single focus, such as Mlomp and Bandafassi, others have led to a wide variety of researches, ranging from very biomedical studies to anthropological, epidemiological, and demographic researches, such as Matlab. This variety of objectives is reflected in a wide variety of methods, size of endeavour, financial means, scale of interventions, and the like. In this respect, Matlab appears as the industrial giant of the prospective community studies, with hundreds of full-time employees, enormous research output, and now more than thirty years of continuous research work (see Chapter 2 by Aziz and Mosley). By contrast, Bandafassi is more of a craft industry, with one part-time researcher and a correspondingly more limited focus (see Chapter 11 by Pison, Desgrées du Loû, and Langaney).

The papers also offer a wide variety of styles. Although precise guidelines and a typical plan for this book were given to all the authors, they were not necessarily followed closely. The editors felt that it was more important to respect the choices and the style of each author in order to give a fair account of each study.

Research Focuses

Across the many topics studied, health topics are dominant. Many of the largest studies have undertaken research on vaccines, tropical diseases, and other diseases that are among the leading causes of death in these populations, in particular diarrhoeal diseases and cholera, acute respiratory infections, malaria, measles, whooping cough, and tetanus, as well as on nutrition. Another set of favoured topics range around family planning and fertility control. Some of the studies have attempted a more comprehensive study of health systems and health interventions (see Chapter 5 by Taylor and De Sweemer and Chapter 7 by Berggren *et al.*). Other dimensions of population dynamics are less often studied, e.g. nuptiality and the family, migration, and interactions with socio-economic development, although they have been studied thoroughly in the more demographic undertakings, a good example being Khanna-II (see Chapter 4 by Das Gupta).

The frequency of the topics most often studied can be found in the Appendix. It seems that over time the priorities shifted from family planning towards health and disease processes. The so-called 'population problem' was the focus of the original Khanna Study. However, the same Khanna Study is now better known for its contribution to understanding health and diseases than for its contribution to family planning. The Narangwal Study developed its research on health systems with a more holistic approach, where family planning services were seen as an integral part of the health system and not merely a tool to reduce population pressure. In the Matlab Study, the main focus had the opposite evolution, and expanded from research on diseases and vaccines to research on home delivery of family planning services. Nevertheless, health is still the major component of research in Matlab, and the number of publications on health topics far outnumbers the number of publications on family planning.

Impetus

In the history of these studies, it is amazing to see that most owe their birth and their survival to the strong will of a single individual. Only a few were started by an institution *per se* in order to conduct a long-term prospective study. In fact, virtually no institution will commit itself to a long-term comprehensive study of a population. Most of the studies reviewed started by an initial project and were later continued thanks to the commitment of the leading researcher. Funds had to be raised step by step, usually from different donors. In this sense, they are real research enterprises.

Through their experiences, these leaders built real schools of thought, which have dominated the field for several decades. In Chapter 1, Carl Taylor reminds us how John Grant, a pioneer on health systems, influenced some of the US studies (Eastern District), a Chinese study (DingXian), the Singur Study (India), and the Narangwal Study (India). John Gordon, a pioneer epidemiologist, was seminal in the Khanna Study in India (see Chapter 3 by Wyon), the Guatemala Study (see Chapter 6 by Scrimshaw and Guzmán), and the Haiti Study (see Chapter 7 by Berggren *et al.*). Gordon also trained Carl Taylor, who became the leader of the Narangwal Study (Chapter 5). Closely related to the Harvard school is the Johns Hopkins school, where Henry Mosley played a leading role, in particular in Matlab (Chapter 2). The British school in Africa was influenced by the work of Ian MacGregor in the village of Keneba, where researchers have been working continuously since 1949, and by the work of Brian Greenwood, who is leading the studies in Farafennie. Unfortunately, this school is not represented in this book, nor is the British/Australian school working in Papua New Guinea. The South African school started with Dr H. S. Gear, who installed Sidney Kark in Pholela (Chapter 9). His nephew, John Gear, is involved in the most recent Agincourt Study with Steve Tollman. The French school was started by Pierre Cantrelle, and most of the francophone researchers working in the field have been trained by him in Niakhar, including Michel Garenne and Gilles Pison (Chapters 10 and 11).

Of course, other studies were started independently from these leading schools—Machakos, for instance, and some of the Indian and Thai studies. However, there have been many connections between the studies. Jim Phillips, trained in Matlab, has been leading the extension project in Bangladesh and has been influential in the Indramayu project run by Budi Utomo and Christine Costello in Indonesia and more recently in a new study in Ghana. Michel Garenne is participating in the Nouna Study in collaboration with Heidelberg University as well as in the Agincourt Project with the Department of Community Medicine of the Witwatersrand University in Johannesburg.

Methodology

In all the studies, the *demographic surveillance system* (DSS) is the basis on which everything else is built. Stephen Tollman, Sidney Kark, and Emily Kark (Chapter 9) remind us that the key concept here is the community as an object of study as opposed to the individual who is investigated in clinical studies. The diagnosis of the health status or of the demographic problem is a community diagnosis, not an individual case. The measure is the prevalence of the condition in the population, not whether or not the person has the condition. Therefore, some of the solutions to problems are also based on the community, its own recognition of the problems, its commitment to solve them, and its active participation. Other problems depend more for their solution on research and intervention coming from outside the community, such as, for example, measles vaccination.

Most of the studies started by a full-scale census, on which the continuous recording of demographic and epidemiological events is built. Vital events are collected at various intervals, ranging from high frequencies of visits to households (once every one or two weeks, or monthly) to low frequency (once a year). Similarly, full-scale censuses are conducted either frequently, once a year as in Niakhar or Bandafassi, or occasionally, once every seven to ten years, as in Matlab, as it is done in national populations.

A key methodological issue is the handling of residence status and migration. In general, people have relied upon some kind of explicit *de jure* definition of residence, for instance at least six months in the same household (Matlab). Others have used a *de facto* definition, at least for some of the epidemiological studies (Machakos). Attempts have been made to compare the values of the two approaches in Machakos.

Another important methodological and practical issue has been the organization of computer files. In this respect the most flexible approach is to use a combination of a single fixed identification number for each individual and an address number, which can be variable over time with changing residence of individuals. Most studies now use some kind of relational database for handling their files and most now use primarily microcomputers, with the exception of very large data sets, as in Matlab. Microcomputers made data analysis much cheaper and much more efficient than ever before.

Many studies have used some kind of *verbal autopsy* in order to estimate the frequency of causes of death, a key information for diagnosis and for the evaluation of interventions. They have been extensively used in the earliest studies, such as the Khanna Study, the Keneba Study, and especially the Narangwal Study, where they seem to have been baptized with this curious and expressive name. Here again there have been a variety of approaches, from very simple interviews with the family, as in the earlier years in Niakhar, to structured questionnaires as in the later years in Niakhar and detailed discussion of the case by several physicians as in Narangwal.

Most of the projects undertook multidisciplinary research. In fact, health needs to be understood not only as a biomedical process but also as a social process. The dynamics of multidisciplinary research depends very much upon the personality of the team leader and the existence of a real democratic and scientific atmosphere. As soon as these conditions are no longer met, the dynamics of the research usually collapses. Authentic multidisciplinary research may be the greatest asset but also the greatest challenge of prospective community studies, as of other research endeavours. It can often be most successfully conducted when key researchers have training in more than one discipline themselves, allowing for easy cross-fertilization of ideas.

Ethical Issues

The continuous follow-up of a population raises several ethical issues. The quality of the relationship with the population under study is the key factor of success and longevity of prospective studies. The necessity of a continuous recording of events and of comprehensive computer files raises difficult issues of confidentiality and privacy. They seem to have been handled adequately so far by the projects, though they are rarely explicit in the papers presented in this volume. Some of the authors mention the many problems they had, in particular how to deal with negative rumours against the project, which often arise from interpersonal problems amongst project personnel.

More complex are the issues related to interventions. Most of those projects were deeply concerned with issues of equity and sustainability, as exemplified in the Haiti Study (Chapter 7). However, there is a trade-off between research and interventions. What will the project provide to the population? How to provide services that will be sustainable in the long run? If this is not done, there is a danger of facing a difficult situation when the project is over. How to answer to the pressing demand from the population, especially in the difficult conditions of rural tropical Africa? How to provide health services without affecting precisely the object of study? There is here the ethical dilemma of saving an individual at one point in time versus conducting non-interventionist research which may save far more lives in the long run. These issues have been addressed in the projects aimed at improving health services, such as Narangwal, and were especially critically addressed in the first phase of the Keneba Study.

Another issue related to clinical trials, which are often conducted in similar settings, is that of informed consent. How to explain what is a randomized controlled trial to an illiterate population? How to explain the risk of side-effects to people? What must be the relationship of the research team with the local political institutions and organizations and sometimes the international organizations and the donor agencies? If these issues are not typical of prospective community studies, they often occur and have to be addressed in a proper ethical framework.

Institutional and Financial Support

The successful functioning of prospective community studies requires locally strong institutional support, and a linkage with a major academic research institution. Most of the studies had such a double support group, although some lacked the academic linkage, important for ensuring the quality of the publication and their international diffusion. Carl Taylor reminds us that one strong linkage is enough and that multiple linkages can be more confusing than profitable.

Because these studies have a multiyear time frame, it is critical for them to have some continuity of financial support to ensure that the project can be completed. Continuous financial support is probably the most difficult condition to fulfil and some researchers have had to fight virtually year by year to get proper support for their projects. The situation became more critical in the recent years, owing to the economic crisis in the West and to the competition with the many other projects and studies. A basic support from the core institution and a variety of other sources for specific projects seems to be the most secure way of ensuring continuity.

The active participation of local institutions is critical for success and sustainability, as well as the link with a major academic institution. Most of the major prospective studies have both forms of collaboration, though how active the collaboration is with local institutions varies from study to study. The

Matlab Study, which is clearly an international project, can also largely be considered a local institution. The Narangwal Study was conducted in close collaboration with Indian institutions, as was Machakos in Kenya. The Niakhar Study began as a project of the Census Bureau of Senegal, and became more international only later. The Khanna-II Study was conducted entirely out of an Indian institution, as was also the case with the Pholela Study in South Africa.

Local research capacity-building is one of the major assets of prospective community studies. The Matlab Study is probably the best example of this, as it has been in the field for decades, during which numerous researchers from Bangladesh and elsewhere have been trained to be scientific leaders in their own settings.

Political Aspects

In several cases, international or local politics interfered with the development of the study. This was the case in Pholela, South Africa, when the National Party came into power (Chapter 9), in DingXian when the Japanese invaded China (Chapter 1), and in Narangwal, India, at the time of the independence of Bangladesh (Chapter 5). Sometimes, negative findings resulting from the research were the source of the exclusion of researchers, such as in Niakhar, Senegal. Rumours spread by the press may be deleterious and are difficult to control, as exemplified by the case of Matlab (Chapter 2).

Comparison with Standard One-Shot Surveys

Prospective community studies have very different strengths and weaknesses from standard one-shot surveys. The greatest strength of standard surveys is that they can be conducted on national populations, whereas community studies are highly localized. However, prospective studies enable innovative investigation of kinds that are not possible in the context of standard surveys, and this is their greatest strength. Some of the most salient points of comparison are discussed here.

Scope for innovative research

The scope for doing innovative research while undertaking a prospective community study is enormous because it allows for serendipity and feedback during the study itself. As the results of data already collected are analysed, the researchers are in a position to formulate entirely new hypotheses and test them in the next round of data collection. This follows from the possibility of the researchers having direct contact with the study population and being able to feed their observations back into questionnaire design and analysis. There is an iterative process also between what the researchers observe in the field and the formulation of hypotheses to test. The chapters in this volume abound with examples of innovative research done as a result of this serendipitous process.

One of the best examples of such research is the finding on weanling diarrhoea in the Khanna Study. The stated objective of the study was to test the effect of intensive contraceptive service delivery, but in the course of monitoring births and deaths in the population the authors found that child deaths were high during the second half of the first year and the second year of life, which was out of line with the pattern prevailing in the developed world. Investigating this further, they discovered that the deaths peaked at the time of weaning. The interaction of infections acquired at this time with malnutrition seemed to be the cause of this excess mortality.

These results had enormous impact on formulating policies for improving child survival around the world. However, over a decade elapsed before the findings were translated into policy. The results were published during the 1960s and also widely circulated in a World Health Organization report of 1968. Eventually they were translated into policy by UNICEF in its child survival programme, which has now become a routine part of child survival programmes in the developing world.

Another example of new hypotheses being formulated during prospective fieldwork is the question of which categories of children in the Khanna-II Study are at especially high risk of dying. Field observation suggested entirely new approaches to this question. One of the new findings was that child deaths are highly concentrated amongst a small proportion of families. The policy implication of this would be to focus health services more actively on this small subset of families rather than spread them evenly through the population as is usually done. Large reductions in child mortality could be achieved through this cost-effective method.

The fact of following up a population over time enables certain kinds of research to be done much more effectively in a prospective community study. A good example of this is the measles vaccine trials in the studies in Senegal, Bissau, and Haiti reported in this volume. It was only because deaths were monitored prospectively in these studies that it was possible to find that high-titre measles vaccines were unsafe compared to low-titre ones. Previous routine trials of the high-titre vaccine had not noticed this effect. This has had important and immediate policy implications. The investigation of measles epidemics in Bissau is yet another example of the value of serendipitous research, throwing up entirely new insights into the impact of primary versus secondary infection, and how the effect differs by gender. Aaby (Chapter 12) explains how he went from surprise to surprise when investigating measles epidemics in Bissau.

Evaluation

It is not possible to evaluate prospective community studies as one might in the case of such standard surveys as the Demographic and Health surveys. In these, the objectives are decided at the outset and the subsequent implementation is little responsive to local circumstances and research questions. It is then relatively easy to ask whether the data were collected as intended and the analysis done along the lines foreseen when drawing up the questionnaires.

By contrast, the serendipitous nature of community-based prospective studies allows the researchers to respond to questions raised by field observation and to digress from the initial objectives of the study. As described above in the case of weanling diarrhoea and the malnutrition-infection syndrome, these digressions have often yielded the most seminal findings.

Unlike the Demographic and Health surveys, which design a questionnaire at headquarters and have it canvassed in the field, prospective community studies have a complex iterative process in their design and conduct. Involving long-term research on the same people, these studies also have to be responsive to local exigencies and circumstances. This is another reason why they cannot be evaluated at the face value of the original study protocol, but have to be evaluated in terms of the value of the results which emerge from them.

Costs

Prospective community studies are expensive compared with routine surveys. Instead of being visited once, a population is visited repeatedly, and this raises the costs of data collection. The advantage of course is that it is possible thoroughly to train and motivate the fieldworkers to collect very high-quality data through the duration of the study, and that it is possible to provide high-quality supervision of data collection and processing.

Just how expensive a study is obviously depends on prevailing wage rates and the frequency of data collection. With weekly visits to each household, the annual costs in the Niakhar Study in Senegal was estimated at about $300,000 per year for 25,000 people under study. This was slightly higher than the per capita cost in the Matlab study because local salaries were higher. The Niakhar costs include the salaries of fieldworkers, supervisors, and physicians, cars and travel to the field, data-coding and -entry, computer facilities, and salaries of research assistants. However, they do not include the salaries and travel of expatriate researchers and the cost of offices in Dakar.

A less sophisticated system, relying on less frequent observation, would obviously cost much less. Given the costs of these enterprises, it is critical to think carefully about the optimum frequency of observation and the optimum size of study population. The costs are dramatically reduced when local salaries are low: for example, the total cost of data collection and processing in the Khanna-II Study was only $400,000 for a four-year prospective study of 18,000 people. This was partly because no expatriate salaries were involved, and partly because households were visited only once a month.

An important feature of prospective community studies is that the marginal cost of any supplementary study is very small. Since the staff are already in place and are visiting the households in any case, adding a module to the questionnaire is simple and inexpensive. The data from the module can be analysed in conjunction with all the other information already available on the household. This enormously increases the research potential of these prospective studies.

Time-scale

The time-scale of these studies is very wide. A study like Khanna-I took about three years to organize, and six years in the field. The fieldwork period was followed by a period of publication lasting about ten years which culminated in the writing of a comprehensive book. About twenty years elapsed between the conception of the study (1951) and the publication of the book (1971). This is a normal time-scale of a very well-planned, relatively short, and well-organized study. For some of the researchers, this has been the work of their life. The Narangwal Study started in 1965 and the book was published in 1983, eighteen years later. In Machakos a delay of fourteen years occurred between the beginning of the study in the field (1970) and the publication of the book (1984). Of course, most of the results were available to decision-makers long before the final publication through interim reports and various publications in scientific journals. In the case of the Khanna and the INCAP studies, the main findings on the synergistic effect between nutrition and infection were put into use long after they were published, as mentioned above. Major undertakings such as these prospective community studies have a life expectancy of fifteen to twenty years. In this respect, they differ markedly from other epidemiological, anthropological, or demographic studies of much shorter average duration.

Most of the projects that lasted for long periods, say more than ten years, undertook major changes in their focus and scope. For instance, in Matlab the emphasis shifted from cholera vaccine trials to family planning. In Keneba, the focus changed from malaria to nutrition. In Niakhar, the main activities shifted from the collection of precise demographic data towards health interventions and vaccine trials. Changes in subjects requiring study and in sources of funding are also an important component of these evolutions.

Generalizability of results

One concern that people may have about prospective community studies conducted by medical professionals is that they may select locations which have especially high prevalence of diseases which they wish to study. This is clearly the case with the Matlab Study, which was situated in an area with high levels of endemic cholera. This was specifically set up as a cholera research laboratory, however, and the majority of studies have not selected their sites on this basis. For those studies with a more demographic focus, the main issue is to have enough births and deaths in the population. Given the high levels of morbidity and mortality in most developing-country settings until very recently, most researchers are not faced with the possibility of shortage of events to study.

Another concern regarding community studies is how representative of a wider population are their results. Phenomena that can be shown in a given population need to be replicated in other sites to test their validity. In fact, replicating results found in one site is the most common approach used in epidemiology and public health research, such as vaccine trials and new drugs trials. Many of the results discussed in this volume gained international recognition only years after the first finding. The problem of generalizability, then, can be resolved satisfactorily.

Legacy

The legacy of the prospective community studies is truly outstanding. First, they are the *locus* where new ideas and new approaches are developed. Many of the important findings related to tropical public health and demography come from these studies. To quote a few earlier classics: the synergistic effect between infection and malnutrition; the concept of weaning diarrhoea; the interactions between breast-feeding, child mortality, and fertility; the age pattern of mortality in South Asia (the second-year death rate) and in West Africa; the effect of tetanus toxoid immunization of the mother on survival of the child; various estimates of vaccine efficacy or other health interventions such as antibiotics, vitamin A supplementation, oral rehydration therapy, antimalarial chemotherapy, the treatment of acute lower respiratory infections, the effect of impregnated bednets; child-fostering; death-clustering; selective gender discrimination, etc. Second, their importance does not diminish with time. On the contrary, they seem to have a negative discount rate, that is their value increases with time as the applications of the research become more widely understood.

Among the studies that stopped more than twenty years ago, the Khanna Study is still widely quoted and the Narangwal Study remains the classic in the field. Most of the current projects on integrated health services are trying to apply the ideas developed in Narangwal more than twenty years ago. The ongoing studies are extremely active and remain the source of the most exciting debates in the demographic and epidemiological literature for developing countries.

Several of these studies were at the heart of the debate about infection and malnutrition. The three authors of the classic study on the synergistic effect of malnutrition and infection participated in the Khanna Study, the Narangwal Study, and the INCAP Study. The INCAP Study and the Narangwal Study provided the first convincing evidence of the impact that proper health services and food supplementation can have on child survival. In both cases, the impact was found to be dramatic, despite the poor socio-economic environment. These findings on the impact of health interventions have not only important and immediate implications for policy, but they also shed light on the more academic debate on the mortality decline. In this respect, it appears that large reductions in mortality can be achieved either by improving nutritional status or by providing preventive and curative health services. Although health services seem to have a more immediate and a more direct effect, large gains can also be made by improving nutrition. The synergistic effect between nutrition and infection appears here as extremely important. It can work either way: either as a 'road to death' when malnutrition succeeds and/or precedes infection, or as a 'road to health' when better nutrition reduces the severity of diseases which in turn permits the child to grow healthily. There are good arguments to suggest that historically both nutrition and control of morbidity have worked in a synergistic way to pave the road towards better health for all.

The debate on vaccines, their efficacy, and their impact on child survival has been fuelled by results from the studies in Haiti, Matlab, Niakhar, Machakos, and Bissau. In particular, vaccinations against tetanus, measles, and whooping cough were found to have a major impact on mortality. The Haiti Study was instrumental in demonstrating the effect of tetanus toxoid immunization during pregnancy in order to protect the new-born child from neonatal tetanus. A finding that high-titre measles vaccines were associated with mortality amongst a significant proportion of children showed that other measles vaccines were safer to use. This finding emerged from studies in Niakhar, Bissau and Haiti (see Chapter 10 by Garenne and Cantrelle and Chapter 12 by Aaby). This important finding has probably saved the lives of millions of children who would otherwise have been vaccinated with high-titre vaccines. This underlines the importance of long-term prospective data collection within the same community.

A lesson from all these studies is the importance of working closely with the population in order to improve its health. Community participation is seen by all the authors as a key factor in the success of their projects and their interventions, as opposed to the more classic vertical programmes. Several studies document the effect of home delivery of health services, in particular of family-planning services. This direct interaction with the population has an effect on how the population perceives diseases and health processes and certainly increases its awareness of health issues and of the potential to increase survival chances. For instance, the Haiti project shows how research and services contribute to each other.

Prospective community studies have demonstrated clearly how biological and social processes are intertwined. A number of results on the behavioural determinants of health emerged from these studies. For example, we learned a great deal about the gender bias in South Asia from the studies in Khanna and Matlab. Death-clustering, a new area of research in the field of demography and child survival, also originated in Khanna-II. The Haiti Study showed that marriage patterns, child-fostering, and migration are also major determinants of health: indications of this emerge from cross-sectional studies, but could be explored convincingly only with the use of prospectively collected data.

Most of these studies focus on the health of children below the age of 5. In most of the study sites, deaths in this age-group accounted for more than half of the deaths of all ages combined. In comparison, little research has been conducted on the health of young adults, with the exception of maternal mortality. With the emergence of AIDS and the re-emergence of other sexually transmitted diseases and of tuberculosis, there is a renewed interest in the health of young adults. The Pholela Study, which was conducted in a more economically advanced country, addressed these issues and showed how much could be gained by working closely with the community.

Although relatively costly and time-consuming, there is no doubt that these studies were worth undertaking and are worth pursuing. Their legacy certainly shows them to be extremely worth-while research enterprises, as our basic knowledge of health processes would be far more deficient if they had not been undertaken. Much knowledge which has become standard input to understanding health processes and to policy-making would never have come without these longitudinal studies. They provided a scientifically documented rationale for many health interventions, which otherwise may not have been made or been based on inadequate information.

References

Chiao, C. M., Thompson, W. S., and Chen, D. T. (1938), *An Experiment in the Registration of Vital Statistics in China*, Scripps Foundation for Research in Population Problems, Oxford, Oh.

Kesler, I. I., and Levin, M. L. (1970), *The Community as an Epidemiologic Laboratory: A Case-Book in Community Studies*, Johns Hopkins Press, Baltimore.

Mosley, W. H. (1989), 'Population Laboratories for Community Health Research', Population Council, Working Paper 21.

Part I

Asia

1 Origins of Longitudinal Community-Based Studies

CARL E. TAYLOR

Some of the most important advances in improving understanding of health and family planning have come from longitudinal community-based studies. The underlying principle is that the unit studied is not an individual but a whole population. With population-based approaches, causal and associated variables can be examined both quantitatively and qualitatively in natural circumstances.

Convergence of field experience in longitudinal community-based studies has evolved from three distinct disciplines: epidemiology, demography, and health systems research. For more systematic use of these methods it seems desirable to synthesize what has been learned. In this paper the historical contributions of the three disciplines are briefly described. Because of the demonstrated potential for community-based studies in improving primary health-care services, some general principles are defined to guide future efforts.

1.1 Field Studies of Specific Diseases

Some of the earliest longitudinal community-based studies are among the classics of epidemiology. The methodology was to follow a health problem over time as it appeared among a group of people, and make inferences about causation. For example, Snow's monograph on cholera (Snow 1936) is considered one of the best early models of what epidemiology can do. The most famous part of Snow's monograph describes a study where he traced the case-by-case evolution of a cholera epidemic in the Broad Street area of London. From patterns of water use he concluded that transmission was from the Broad Street pump and applied the control intervention that has edified generations of epidemiology students—he took the handle off the pump. Other epidemiological studies of infectious diseases such as Budd on typhoid (Budd 1874) and Panum on measles (Panum 1940) made retrospective analyses of transmission patterns during epidemics in defined populations. The classic studies of Goldberger on pellagra (Goldberger 1964) were important in developing methodology. In the southern regions of the USA he identified populations with high prevalence of pellagra which were followed carefully to demonstrate that the cause was not an infection but a nutritional deficiency which could be controlled by diet.

Among the many field studies of specific diseases, some of the technically most precise were on geographically localized diseases such as malaria, schistosomiasis, filariasis, and onchocerciasis. Epidemiology, as the diagnostic discipline of public health, should guide practical control procedures once causation has been defined. Shoe-leather epidemiology is the term applied to the systematic process of investigating frequency, distribution, and factors influencing the occurrence of a health problem as part of making a community diagnosis.

1.2 Prospective Community Studies

The next development in methodology was to shift the focus from a disease to an entire population. The concept of laboratory experimentation was expanded and combinations of multiple health problems in an area were followed over time. One of the first most consistently productive such study areas has been Washington county, Maryland where the Johns Hopkins School of Hygiene and Public Health has maintained meticulous data-gathering for more than sixty years. The natural history of several diseases has been traced and correlated with multiple socio-economic and behavioural variables. Among prospective studies focusing on cardiovascular diseases, noteworthy examples are those at Framingham, Massachusetts and Karelia, Finland. Epidemiological understanding of multicausality has been helped by the ability to assign quantitative estimates to risk factors.

The term 'prospective community studies' is proposed for field research in which a population is followed longitudinally with systematic data-gathering over time. For example, an individual is either pregnant or not pregnant, but a normal population is usually about 2–4 per cent pregnant. Or, a variety of clinical tests can diagnose if an individual has asymptomatic infection or disease, with fluctuating rates depending on local variables. Causation can be inferred by using controls or comparison groups.

An outstanding example of applying scientific principles in a longitudinal field laboratory is the Matlab Project in Bangladesh which is described in Chapter 2. The study area was set up originally for phase-three clinical trials of cholera vaccine but was then used for other research projects, such as very productive demographic and family-planning research. A cholera treatment facility ensured widespread public support and co-operation.

1.3 Studies of Population Dynamics

The term 'population laboratory' has been used to describe field sites which demographers use to study population dynamics. A classic example is the

ORSTOM experience in rural Senegal, where Pierre Cantrelle and his colleagues have, over a period of thirty years, followed population groups ranging up to 35,000 in size (see Chapter 11). Many similar efforts include those of Linton, who, with support from USAID, started a series of population laboratories which were productive as long as external support was available, and of Frederiksen (1971), who·coined the term 'epidemographic studies'. With demography focusing on denominators and epidemiology on numerators, a natural bridging follows when both disciplines meet in fieldwork.

One of the most productive early population studies was the Khanna project of Wyon and Gordon (1971), described in Chapter 3. They tested the impact of simple family-planning methods on population growth. The basic methodology was epidemiological, since it was designed by Dr John Gordon, an epidemiologist. It reversed the sequence described above in the case of the Matlab project, in that a population laboratory produced definitive studies of the epidemiology of 'weanling diarrhoea', the number-one cause of death in most of the world's villages, and neonatal tetanus, the fourth cause of death among children in the Punjab. It led to longitudinal field studies of synergism between malnutrition and infections at INCAP in Guatemala (Chapter 6) and at Narangwal just twenty-five miles from Khanna (Chapter 5).

1.4 Health Systems Research on Primary Health Care

Community-based studies obviously contribute to finding solutions after the causes of health problems have been defined. Health systems research is a relatively new discipline which often uses community-based studies.

The origins of the worldwide primary health-care movement can be traced directly to the DingXian project organized by Drs John B. Grant and C. C. Chen in the early 1930s (Seipp 1963). Since there is no chapter on this classic study in this volume it will be described briefly here. DingXian (TingHsien) is a rural county 100 miles south-west of Beijing which had about 400,000 population when the project started around 1930. Dr Jimmy W. C. Yen and a group of professors from Nanjing and Beijing moved to these villages to start the Rural Reconstruction Movement. During the 1920s and 1930s over 60 million Chinese peasants were taught to read and write in the Mass Education Movement. The DingXian project was designed to gather practical information for newspapers, magazines, and books being published for the new literates. It developed a fourfold programme for mass education, community organization, agriculture and village industry, and health and family planning, based on the work of 'farmer scholars' specifically trained to promote action in each of the four subject areas in every village.

A new pattern in comprehensive health care, emphasizing prevention, was evolved in which people were empowered to provide their own health services at an annual per capita cost of less than US 15 cents (without adjusting for inflation). Some of the first data on health conditions in rural China and the framework for what became Mao's barefoot doctor movement came from this study. It was the first demonstration in the world that primary health care can be provided under conditions of extreme poverty by teaching community health workers to care for their neighbours. We are still trying fully to implement the ideas developed at DingXian. Some principles taken from Grant's collected papers based also on his work in India, Eastern Europe, and Puerto Rico (Seipp 1963) are:

1. The use of medical knowledge and efficiency of health protection depends chiefly on social organization and horizontal integration rather than separate, single-purpose programmes.
2. Organizations
    - Rural reconstruction must be based on the primary ecological unit of Chinese society, which is the village.
    - The community should express its own needs and interests rather than priorities being 'superimposed by some idealist'.
    - Leadership should be local.
    - The largest item in the cost of reconstruction is personnel; both men and women can be encouraged to volunteer services in various community activities under routine supervision by more qualified personnel.
    - In the pilot demonstration area, health care must be self-supporting so as to provide a baseline of economic practicability of what can be widely duplicated in the region.
3. Process
    - Rural reconstruction should bring 'power' to the community.
    - As a first step, the village worker and health-centre auxiliary should do a village survey of present status and needs.
    - A village council of six to eight persons should be formed in working relation to existing power groups and it should eventually be granted statutory status. This council should mobilize the people to eliminate poverty, disease, and ignorance. Administration must be decentralized and liberalized.
    - Successful replication of findings from a pilot demonstration area requires large-scale training with established vocational and professional training institutions using the demonstration area for field training.
4. University Teaching Health Centres
    - The area served should conform to an existing administrative unit of the government, is representative of the state, and large enough to make services economical, usually consisting of about 500,000 people.
    - The service budget should be covered by health services, and teach-

ing and research costs by the university. Functional responsibility should be similarly divided.

- Personnel should be jointly approved by services and the university, and hold joint appointments.
- An advisory board for the teaching health centre should have representation from the community, health services, and the university. There should be an executive group representing each field of activity which should deal with administrative routines, budgeting, and policy.
- Manuals for routine procedures should be prepared by responsible university departments, with all procedures being greatly simplified.
- The teaching health centre should be adjacent to the teaching medical centre and should be considered equivalent to the teaching hospital. It should serve as the planning and research laboratory for regional health services.

The DingXian experience led to second-generation field projects in several countries. Particularly important were Kark's projects in the 1940s in Pholela in South Africa, described by Tollman in Chapter 9. Even though the imposition of apartheid terminated this project, the ideas developed led to similar field studies by Kark in Israel, where the basic principles of Community-Oriented Primary Care (COPC) were first defined. These ideas were then applied in the USA by South African colleagues of Kark, who greatly influenced efforts to rationalize health care in a system known for its disorganization.

Other second-generation studies developed in other parts of the world. Hydrick in Indonesia (Hydrick 1937) demonstrated the potential of using village health workers to improve health. Recent observations suggest that the rapid spread of primary care through the Posyandu programme in Java may have been most effective and rapid in areas around Jogjakarta where Hydrick originally worked (Hull 1989). Other Rockefeller staff members, such as Jacocks, developed adaptations based on Grant's health-centre approach in Sri Lanka, where there has been remarkable reduction in mortality and fertility even with continued extreme poverty. The Rockefeller Foundation programme in Kerala had similar long-term impact.

Grant became dean of the Calcutta Institute of Hygiene and Public Health, where he stimulated similar rural and urban projects, notably at Singur in Bengal. Grant was also joint secretary of the Bhore Committee and he included primary health-care concepts in what has been the basic blueprint for India's health development. With the support of the Rockefeller Foundation, demonstration health centres were developed in many states in India, including Najafgarh near Delhi, Sarojininagar near Lucknow, and so on.

The Rockefeller Foundation undertook a major programme in the 1930s to develop demonstration health centres in many developing countries. The process was influenced by efforts to eradicate hookworm in the southern USA in the 1920s. The main benefit of these extensive field activities was to start county health departments to provide services to poor rural populations. In developing countries the demonstration health centres were located close to the capital cities in order to have maximum influence on policy. Funding was phased so that after five years the health centre would be completely supported by the country. Staff were trained in the USA and a complete local health-care team was organized with clearly defined roles. In the 1950s and 1960s I visited many of these demonstration centres in countries such as Yugoslavia, Turkey, Thailand, Indonesia, Japan, Peru, and so on. Almost universally, one of the first things officials did after the Rockefeller support terminated was to pull the highly trained staff into the health ministry to apply the new rural health-care methods to the whole country. This set the basic pattern for health care in many developing countries. My visits, twenty or more years after the projects, showed that the demonstration health centres were still faithfully maintaining many of the original routines with considerable pride in health conditions which were better than in neighbouring villages. Health and hygienic improvements in homes had persisted, while those requiring community action such as public pumps or latrines tended not to have been maintained.

A late example of a second-generation project was the Narangwal project (Kielmann, Taylor *et al.* 1983), described in Chapter 5, in which I was able to benefit from the direct advice of both John Grant and John Gordon. The momentum for field demonstration and research projects has accelerated in the past decade. In India there are now hundreds of rural health projects, mostly run by academic institutions or non-governmental organizations. In most countries, much of the innovation in health care comes from such projects. However, government efforts to extend findings to national services have had limited success. The efforts to reach people in greatest need and the flexibility in problem-solving at the local level, which make a special project successful, tend to be lost as bureaucracies take over national expansion. In an increasing number of countries, primary health-care programmes have integrated health and family-planning services which have produced a synergistic and dramatic decline in both mortality and fertility. A landmark event was the Alma Ata Conference on Primary Health Care in 1978 sponsored by WHO and UNICEF.

1.5 General Principles

Based on the accumulation of experience from the previous studies, I have attempted to synthesize some fundamental principles for organizing a prospective community-based study site to promote primary health care.

1. The area covered by a prospective community-based study site should include all basic government services, which usually means choosing a whole district or county of between 200,000 to 500,000 people. To prevent study fatigue, individual projects and training activities can then be moved around in the area.

2. Sustainable improvement of health depends on social organization based on a health centre. Each such centre should take responsibility for a defined population. A major responsibility of the health unit is to assist communities and families to take responsibility for their own health care. Two components are needed for effective community participation. There should be a committee of local decision-makers representing all groups, including especially the poor and women. There should also be a designated community health worker for liaison with health services and to provide simple health care. This person should be locally supported. Priority should be given to prevention of disease, instead of permitting curative care to crowd out preventive activities, with the poor not receiving either.

3. Complete registration of all households is essential to facilitate data collection about community problems and priorities and for equitable distribution. Data should be limited to items which are actually used. Data-gathering should involve collaboration by health workers and the people to promote community empowerment and increase awareness of local needs and resources.

4. Analyses of data for community diagnosis should be done jointly by community decision-makers and health workers to define the three or four most serious problems in an area and agree on priorities for incremental action. Discussion of possible interventions should start by defining local patterns of causation. Standard combinations of interventions should be in accordance with local conditions, desires, and cultural constraints, with joint decisions being made about how resources and responsibility will be shared.

5. By identifying the families in the community among whom priority health problems are concentrated, health workers can help to target social action. Dialogue between health workers and the community should focus on the need for equity. The few indicators chosen specifically for Surveillance for Equity (Taylor 1992) should be simple enough to be understood by the average person in the community. Once local problems are publicly identified, it is difficult for local leaders to ignore the people in greatest need and continue the usual channelling of benefits to their friends and supporters. The district health service can set standards requiring communities to achieve measurable indicators which can be achieved only by giving priority to the most needy families. Data for transmission upward will then mean something, because they are action-oriented rather than routine data that are never used. Selected information appropriately analysed helps to adapt policy, regulations, and allocation of resources in a cyclic process.

6. Implementation should start by training everyone in new roles that are defined in community dialogue with the health system. Reallocating roles among established health workers is necessary but difficult, because they usually resist any change in their sense of identity, and claim that new methods and roles will reduce quality of services. The training should demonstrate that new methods will make their work easier and more effective. Each person should be trained for clearly defined tasks, and workloads should be balanced. Responsibilities of community workers can be increased greatly if the training is incremental and repetitive with adequate supportive supervision.

7. Continuing improvement in the quality of care and sustainability depend on a regular two-way feedback which adapts for cultural acceptance, improves access in geographic and socio-economic terms, flexibly adjusts services to changing conditions, ensures a fair framework for self-financing, strengthens communication channels for behaviour change, and regularly evaluates new ideas for pragmatic results. Action should follow promptly when surveillance uncovers a problem. Clusters of problems can be corrected by packaging integrated interventions, such as using maternal and child health as a normal entry-point for family planning. The relationship between the health system and the community is fragile, and time is needed to build mutual trust.

8. The process of adapting care to local conditions is usually too complex for the average community health unit to do on its own. Regional patterns can, however, be worked out in a prospective community study site and then a systematic process of extension can reach throughout a region where conditions are similar. To work out regional models, field collaboration is needed between health officials, academic specialists with expertise in health systems research, and community decision-makers. They can determine causal factors responsible for the local mix of nutrition and health problems, agree on priorities, and sequence the implementation of sharing costs, roles, training, supervision, and general management. This regional process is not a one-time effort but a continuing responsibility of both health services and academic specialists that requires careful nurturing of local capacity. Every training institution should assume responsibility for a prospective community study site. Groups of people from adjacent counties or districts should be brought to the prospective community study site to help them adapt procedures to their own conditions. They need to convince themselves from seeing programmes in action that they can make the needed changes in their own activities. The process is incremental, but not necessarily slow. The prospective community study site can also be part of a network for national surveillance and demonstration of sustainable implementation which will facilitate improvement in national policies and programmes. This general process is described in a monograph of sustainable human development published by the Environment Section of UNICEF (Taylor-Ide and Taylor 1995) for the 1995 World Summit on Social Development in Copenhagen.

1.6 Summary

Many of the basic principles and methods of epidemiology were developed in early community-based studies. It is only a little more than sixty years since the first prospective population-based studies and early health systems research in whole populations were done to find ways to improve health and nutrition and to observe factors influencing population growth. The three disciplines of epidemiology, demography, and health systems research are now coming together in potentially synergistic activities. Most of the prospective community-based study sites that have continued for a long period have eventually been used for multiple purposes. Practical programmes can be built on that synergy.

References

Budd, W. (1874/1931), *Typhoid Fever*, repr. for American Public Health Association, Grady Press, New York.

Frederiksen, H. S. (1971), *Epidemographic Surveillance: A Symposium*, Monograph 13 of Carolina Population Center, University of North Carolina, Chapel Hill, NC.

Goldberger, J. (1964), *Goldberger on Pellagra*, Louisiana State University Press, Baton Rouge, La.

Hull, T. (1989), 'The Hygiene Program in the Netherlands East Indies: Roots of Primary Health Care in Indonesia', in Paul Cohen and John Purcal (eds.), *Political Economy of Primary Health Care in Southeast Asia*, Australian Development Studies Network, Canberra.

Hydrick, J. L. (1937), *Intensive Rural Hygiene Work and Public Health Education of Netherlands*, Dept. of Public Health Services, Java, Indonesia.

Kessler, I. I., and Levin, M. L. (1970), *The Community as an Epidemiological Laboratory: A Casebook of Community Studies*, Baltimore and London, John Hopkins Press.

Kielmann, A., Taylor, C. E., DeSweemer, C., Parker, R. L., Chernichovsky, D., Reinke, W. A., Uberoi, I. S., Kakar, D. N., Masih, N., and Sarma, R. S. S. (1983), *Child and Maternal Health Services in Rural India—The Narangwal Experiment*, i. *Integrated Nutrition and Health Care*; ii. *Integrated Family Planning and Health Care*, World Bank Research Publication, Johns Hopkins University Press, Baltimore.

Panum, P. L. (1940), *Panum on Measles*, repr. by American Public Health Association, Washington, DC.

Seipp, C. (1963), *Health Care for the Community*, Selected Papers of Dr John B. Grant, Johns Hopkins University Press, Baltimore.

Snow, J. (1936), *Snow on Cholera*, repr. of two Papers, OUP, London.

Taylor, C. E. (1992), Surveillance for Equity, *International Journal of Epidemiology*, 2: 1043–9.

Taylor-Ide, D., and Taylor, C. E. (1995), *Community Based Sustainable Human Development—A Proposal for Going to Scale With Self-Reliant Social Development*, UNICEF Environment Section, New York.

WHO and UNICEF (1978), *Primary Health Care*, Report of the International Conference at Alma-Ata, World Health Organization, Geneva.

Wyon, J. B., and Gordon, J. E. (1971), *The Khanna Study*, Harvard University Press, Cambridge, Mass.

2 The History, Methodology, and Main Findings of the Matlab Project in Bangladesh

K. M. A. AZIZ AND W. HENRY MOSLEY

2.1 Introduction

The Matlab population is the largest population under continuous surveillance in the world. The project was established in 1963 by the Pakistan–SEATO Cholera Research Laboratory (PSCRL), the predecessor of the International Centre for Diarrhoeal Disease Research, Bangladesh (ICDDR,B) for the purpose of field-testing cholera vaccines. The organization of the Matlab field operations was driven from the outset by rigid technical and ethical requirements for the implementation of prospective double-blind, controlled vaccine field trials. These high scientific standards have been applied to field operations in Matlab ever since.

Over 300 national and international scientists have been involved directly or indirectly in research projects in Matlab over the past three decades. The range, breadth, and depth of the research projects encompassing diarrhoeal diseases, health services, population, nutrition, and maternal and child health cannot even be simply listed in this short paper. Fortunately, in 1990, the ICDDR,B produced a well-indexed and abstracted *Annotated Bibliography of ICDDR,B Studies in Matlab, Bangladesh* which provides citations of the 567 papers and publications produced to date for scholars needing detailed information about the work carried out there (Habte and Strong 1990).

This chapter will highlight major elements in the design and implementation of Matlab field operations and related data-management issues. These will be discussed in the context of the technical requirements for some of the major research projects that were carried out in the Matlab area. Major attention will be given to the establishment and evolution of the demographic surveillance system (DSS), as this provides the foundation for all other field research projects. In addition, some operational issues related to a number of specialized prospective research projects will be briefly noted, particularly those that involve intensive in-depth study of sub-populations using a variety of measuring instruments from the biomedical and social sciences. This chapter will not deal with the technical issues surrounding computer management of large complex databases being generated by the DSS, for which interested parties will need to communicate directly with the ICDDR,B.

2.2 Rationale for the Initial Research Objective

The Pakistan–SEATO Cholera Research Laboratory was established in Dhaka, East Pakistan (now Bangladesh), in 1960 to develop, improve, and demonstrate measures for the prevention and eventual eradication of cholera (Habte and Strong 1990). An essential component of this programme was the conduct of controlled field trials of cholera vaccines. At the time, it was recognized that field trials of cholera vaccines required certain conditions: cholera had to be endemic; all villages in the area had to be accessible so that long-term, follow-up studies could be undertaken; rapid treatment for cholera had to be readily available at all times; there had to be laboratory facilities for positive identification of cholera in patients with diarrhoea; and the studies had to be scientifically designed, with vaccine recipients properly randomized. These conditions were essential, as only microbiologically proven cholera cases could be considered in the protective efficacy of a vaccine.

2.3 Site Selection

In 1963, the Director of the PSCRL, Abram Benenson, together with Robert Oseasohn and M. Fahimuddin, made numerous trips by boat to find a suitable location for the planned cholera vaccine field trials (Oseasohn, Benenson, and Fahimuddin 1965). Initially some villages in Bhola, then in Barisal District, which were well known for annual cholera incidence, were thought to be a possible site of the study. Matlab was subsequently considered because it was known to be the second highest cholera endemic area after Bhola. It was a low-lying area criss-crossed by several rivers and canals, facilitating access, and it was densely populated, which meant field work could be comparatively efficient. Compared to Bhola, this area was located at a distance that would allow investigators from Dhaka to make a round trip within a day (Figure 2.1). In addition, a census of the villages in the Matlab area had been taken during the smallpox eradication campaign in 1961, and the household census cards were still available and easily updated.

2.3 Research Design for Vaccine Field Trials

Because the annual incidence of cholera in an endemic population is relatively low (about 3/1,000), statistical requirements mandate large populations for vaccine field trials if a protective efficacy greater than 50 per cent is to be established with any degree of confidence. Even larger populations are required if the subject of the trial is only a subgroup (e.g. children under 15).

The design of a controlled field trial of a cholera vaccine involves taking a complete census in the villages under study and assigning an identifying census

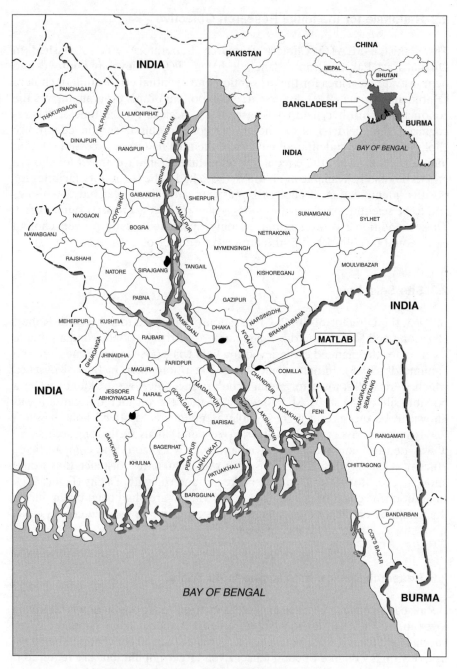

Fig. 2.1. Map of Bangladesh showing the Matlab study area

Table 2.1. Elements in the design and implementation of a cholera vaccine field trial

---

A. Preconditions

Endemic cholera must be present.

Study population size must be large enough to detect a significant effect of a cholera vaccine in reducing the incidence of cholera-associated diarrhoea episodes.

B. Elements in the design and implementation

Baseline census—to assign individual identifying numbers.

Provision of each individual and household with census record card.

Random allocation of cholera vaccine(s) and control vaccine (by code letter) to individuals listed in census books.

'Double-blind' administration of assigned vaccines and recording in census book.

Daily house-to-house surveillance for all severe diarrhoeal episodes. (Home visits recorded daily on household census card.)

Rectal swab culture of all moderate diarrhoea at home with daily shipment to laboratory.

Immediate rapid transport (speed boats) of severe diarrhoea cases to research treatment centre.

All field surveillance, clinical, and laboratory records identified by individual census number to link records for data analysis.

Vaccine code broken at end of study to analyse per cent reduction in cholera case rate among cholera vaccine recipients as compared to control group.

---

number to every individual (Table 2.1). The vaccine to be tested and a control vaccine (usually a typhoid vaccine or tetanus toxoid) are coded and randomly assigned to individuals in the census books. The vaccines are then administered by vaccine teams going house to house, locating recipients by census number, and giving them the assigned vaccine. In a 'double-blind' study, neither the vaccinator nor the recipient knows which is the cholera and which is the control vaccine. In order to detect all cholera cases, fieldworkers must visit every household regularly to make inquiries about the occurrence of acute diarrhoeal illnesses and to obtain rectal swab cultures.

Whenever a field trial is initiated in a new population (as was the case for the first four field trials initiated between 1963 and 1968), *daily* surveillance is critical to the study design for ethical as well as scientific reasons. The acute diarrhoea of cholera can be fatal in a few hours without treatment; since death is an unacceptable outcome in any research, a field hospital in a central location with 24-hour speed-boat ambulance service was essential to provide rapid treatment for all severe, acute diarrhoeal cases detected. In the early years, daily home visits were necessary, as people were not accustomed to taking cholera cases to hospitals, since in their experience severe cases were always fatal.

All records from the field, the hospital, and the laboratory are linked by the individual census number of each case. These linked records are then analysed to assess the protective efficacy of the vaccine.

The major cholera vaccine trials conducted in Matlab were:

1963–4: The first carefully controlled field trial of an injectable cholera vaccine tested a very high-potency whole-cell vaccine and found that it gave significant protection for about two years (Oseasohn, Benenson, and Fahimuddin 1965).

1964–5: A second trial of the same vaccine showed that it was only effective for about eighteen months after vaccination. Concurrently, a test of a vaccine based on the endotoxin of the Ogawa serotype produced some immunity but only for about a year (Benenson *et al.* 1968).

1966–9: The effects of one and two doses of a standard cholera vaccine, given to children below 14, were tested and showed that children aged 0 to 4 years benefited from two doses (Mosley *et al.* 1969). Annual booster doses were also beneficial, but the effects were short-lived (Mosley *et al.* 1972).

1968–9: Testing monovalent Inaba and Ogawa vaccines seemed to show that immunity depended on the development of serotype-specific immunity, although this was later questioned (Mosley *et al.* 1970).

1974–5: After several years of vaccine development in the USA and the UK which resulted in an injectable cholera toxoid vaccine, the largest field trial to date was carried out involving some 93,000 recipients; unfortunately, it gave only 40 per cent protection which lasted about three months (Curlin *et al.* 1978).

1985–9: Given the poor success with injectable vaccines, researchers developed an oral vaccine based on a part of the cholera toxin (B-subunit) that produces intestinal immunity but no disease. After ten years of research, two orally administered vaccines—one a combination of killed whole cholera cells with the B-subunit of cholera toxin, and the other the killed whole cells alone—were ready for field testing. Over a five-month period in 1985, some 63,000 people received three doses of one of the vaccines or a placebo. Both vaccines provided 57 per cent protection after two years; some protection extended to the third year, but children below 5 had a lower rate of protection (Clemens *et al.* 1988).

2.4 The Study Population: Demographic Landmarks

As noted above, the selection of the study area, the determination of the population size, and the structure and organization of field surveillance activities were defined by the requirements of the first four vaccine field trials between

1963 and 1968 which successively expanded the study area (Demographic Surveillance System 1978). In subsequent years, the surveillance system was modified and the population size adjusted for demographic and other considerations. These developments are described below and summarized in Table 2.2.

The first of the cholera vaccine field trials of PSCRL was launched in twenty-three villages with a population of 27,629. In 1964 the field trial area was expanded to include an additional thirty-five villages with a population of 32,548. The trial area was further expanded in 1966 to cover an additional

Table 2.2. Demographic landmarks in Matlab, Bangladesh, 1963–92

Year	Event	No. of villages	Population	Covered by household surveillance[b]	
				Villages	Populations
1963[a]	New census	23	27,629	(23	28,000)[c]
1964[a]	New census	+35	32,548	(58	62,000)[c]
1966[a]	Recensus 1963–4 pop.	58 }	111,748	132	112,000
	New census	+74 }			
1968[a]	New census	+101	109,402	233	226,000
1970	Update 1966 census	132	−124,642	233	245,000
1974[a]	Recensus all	233	274,979	233	277,000
1975	*Contraceptive distribution project*				
	Treatment villages	*150*	*140,000*		
	Control villages	*83*	*136,000*		
1977	Reduce study area	−84	−105,000	149	174,000
1977	*Family planning—Health service project*[d]				
	Treatment villages	*70*	*89,000*		
	Control villages	*79*	*85,000*		
1978	Update 1974 census	149	174,443	149	174,500
1982	Update 1978 census	149	−187,574	149	188,000
1984[a]	Population estimate			149	193,000
1992	Population estimate			149	206,000

[a] Years cholera vaccine trials were initiated.
[b] Frequency of household surveillance: 1963–70 daily; 1970–1 irregular (war); 1972–4 every 1–2 days (?); 1974–8 every 2–3 days; 1978 onwards fortnightly.
[c] From 1963 to 1965 only diarrhoea/cholera surveillance was carried out. Demographic surveillance began in 1966.
[d] In some publications this project is referred to as the Maternal and Child Health–Family Planning project (MCH–FP).

seventy-four villages. The total population of 111,748 in 132 villages was later referred to as the old trial area (OTA). Beginning in May 1966 following the census, a regular registration of births, deaths, and migrations was initiated in the 132 villages (Aziz *et al.* 1967; Mosley *et al.* 1968; Demographic Surveillance System 1978). This continuous (daily) monitoring of vital events generated data of a very high standard, as these demographic events could be independently verified by supervisory staff, and thus served as a means of checking on the quality of the daily diarrhoea surveillance activities.

To obtain another population for a new vaccine trial, the area was further expanded in 1968 by the addition of 101 villages covering a population of over 109,402. This population was referred to as the new trial area (NTA). Daily demographic surveillance now covered 226,000 in 233 villages. In 1974, in preparation for the toxoid vaccine field trial, the entire population of the surveillance area was re-enumerated, showing 276,984 in the 233 villages (Ruzicka and Chowdhury 1978). In October 1975 a household Contraceptive Distribution Project (CDP) was initiated in one-half of the total population, i.e. 150 villages, while the remaining half in eighty-three villages was considered as the control population (Huber and Khan 1979; Rahman *et al.* 1980).

Economic constraints at the ICDDR,B led to a major modification in the field structure and programme activities in October 1977 with a reduction in surveillance area. Eighty-four villages with about 105,000 people were excluded, while 149 villages with 173,443 people were retained (Becker, Razzaque, and Sarder 1982). The Maternal and Child Health–Family Planning and Health Services Project (MCH-FP)[1] was then launched in seventy villages with a population of 89,000, and the remaining seventy-nine villages with 85,000 persons were considered as a comparison area (Bhatia *et al.* 1980). Figure 2.2 shows the 233 villages covered from 1968 to 1977, while Figure 2.3 shows the 149 villages divided into MCH–FP and comparison areas.

2.5 The Demographic Surveillance System[2]

The demographic surveillance system (DSS) consists of registration of births, deaths, marriages, divorces, in- and out-migrations, and internal movements (Demographic Surveillance System 1978). There are also periodic censuses taken along with socio-economic information of the study population. The censuses were carried out on the basis of a *de jure* count. The following sections describe the censuses and the demographic surveillance with reference

[1] The Maternal and Child Health–Family Planning Health Services project (MCH–FP) is referred to in some publications as the Family Planning Health Services project (FPHS). In this paper both names will be used interchangeably.

[2] This section is taken from an unpublished paper being prepared by Abdur Razzaque (personal communication, 1991).

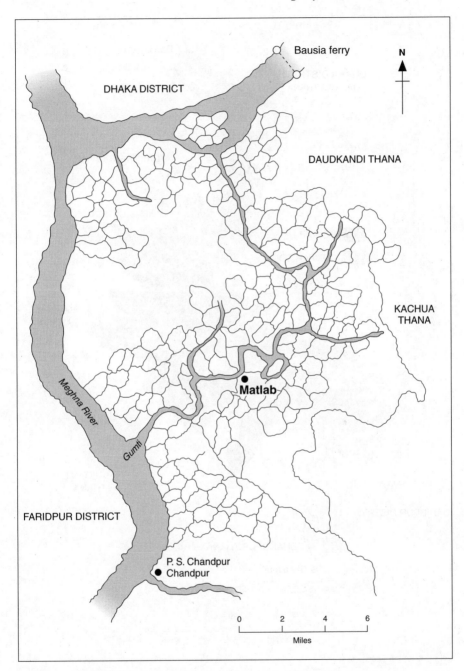

Fig. 2.2. Matlab area showing villages of demographic surveillance system, 1977
Source: ICDDR,B

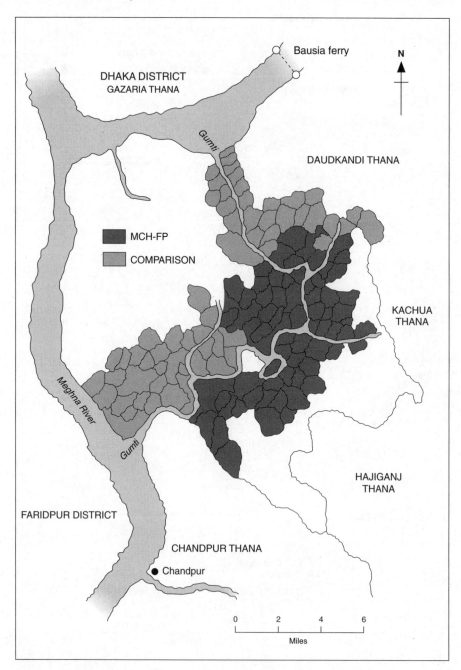

Fig. 2.3. Matlab area showing villages of demographic surveillance system (DSS), 1978

Source: ICDDR,B

to the changes over time. Special note is made of the numbering system, since this relates to the many cohort (record linkage) studies that have been done with the Matlab data over the years. Over the years these data have been managed with increasing sophistication resulting from the frequent updating of the ICDDR,B computer facilities. In 1986 an IBM mainframe System 4361 was installed, and new software is being developed to establish a relational dynamic database.

2.5.1 Census of the old trial area, 1966

Residents of each household were listed by assigning an eight-digit identification number. The identification number consisted of two parts: the first three digits identified the village and the last five digits identified an individual within a village, e.g. the first individual in village V12 would be V12-00001. In each village, the individual numbers started from unity and were continuous household by household until the whole village was covered.

After the completion of the census, three copies of typed census volumes were prepared: one for fieldworkers, one for the Matlab office, and one for the Dhaka office. After receiving the volume, fieldworkers issued a family register for every household. Family registers of a *bari* (mostly contiguously located patrilineal households around a common courtyard) were placed together in one household to use during surveillance.

2.5.2 Demographic surveillance of the old trial area, 1966–70

The demographic surveillance in this period was limited to registration of births, deaths, and migration into or out of the study area. The cause of death is based on verbal reports by relatives of the deceased which were classified into nine to twenty-seven categories at different times over the ensuing years. The cause of death reporting in Matlab is extensively reviewed by Zimicki *et al.* (1985).

The numbering system in the 1966 census, while satisfactory for the vaccine trial, proved deficient for demographic studies. For example, a live birth occurring after the census was given the mother's identification number followed by a letter. If the mother's number was V01-00100, the baby was assigned V01-00100/A. An identification number assigned to an in-migrant joining an existing household required adding a letter to the number of the last member in the household. In-migrants creating new households were assigned numbers following the last identification number in the village. If the last number in the village was V01-00200, the in-migrants were assigned numbers V01-00201, V01-00202, and so on. Change of place of residence within the DSS area was not recorded as an event until 1982, but remarks were noted in the census volumes of new and old residence. A registered person changing residence always retained his/her original identification number.

2.5.3 Census of new trial area, 1968

Because the identification numbers introduced in the 1966 census were difficult to handle during surveillance, a modified number consisting of three parts was introduced: the first three digits identified the village, the next four digits identified the household, and the last two digits identified the individuals within a household beginning with the head. This census included relationship to household head, occupation, total times married, and current marital status.

2.5.4 Recensus of the old trial area, 1970

The census procedures and the numbering system were the same as those that followed in the NTA census in 1968. Additional socio-economic information, such as education, was collected in this census.

2.5.5 Census of the entire DSS area (OTA and NTA), 1974

The census procedures and assigning of identification numbers were the same as in the NTA census of 1968 and the OTA census of 1970. After the census of 1974, minor modifications were made in assigning identification numbers to newborns and in-migrants in an existing household. Registration of marriages and divorces was introduced for the first time in January 1975. By this time the demographic surveillance system (DSS) was put on a more systematic foundation and the first of a regular series of annual DSS Reports began to be produced.

2.5.6 Contraction of DSS area and census update, 1978

In August 1977 the DSS area was reduced to 149 villages. At this time the population database was again updated by verifying computer printouts of the 1974 census adjusted for births and deaths with the actual situation in the field.

2.5.7 Census of DSS area, 1982

During this census dual numbering was introduced for the first time. This was particularly advantageous for tracking persons who changed residences. As noted above, the DSS census number identified the location at the time of enumeration and was nine digits: the first three digits for village, the middle four digits for household, and the last two digits for the individual in a household. The new 'registration number' was ten digits and would be permanent for an individual. The first digit showed in what period the individual was included in the DSS. Anyone who was enumerated on or before 31 June 1982 had 1 in the first column and the remaining nine digits were the 1974 census number. Provision was made for recording both a current location and the permanent registration numbers on forms. If there was a birth or an in-migrant (new) in an existing household, he/she was assigned a current location number (village and household were identical with the other members but individual number followed the last member in the household) and his/her current number was converted to the permanent registration number by adding 2 at the beginning. If a registered individual moved from one village to another within the surveillance area, he/she would be assigned a new current location identification number but his/her permanent registration number would be retained.

2.6 Field Staff Selection and Management

The administrative structure for management of the field staff was hierarchical. This structure was developed taking into account the social, cultural, and logistic conditions and constraints existing in the Matlab area. Over the eighteen years that the field surveillance activities have been in existence, only one fundamental reorganization in the field activities has been introduced. This occurred in 1977–8 when the Maternal and Child Health–Family Planning Operations Research project was initiated (Bhatia *et al.* 1980).

Table 2.3 shows the staffing and organization of the field surveillance activities from the year 1968, when the population laboratory had reached 240,000. In fact, essentially this same structure existed in the twenty-three villages in the study area from the inception of the project in 1963. As a rule, the senior supervisor has been a university graduate with a social science major, while the next level of supervision was managed by individuals with at least two years of post-high-school training in sanitary inspection or the equivalent. Generally, these persons were experienced professionals from the Ministry of Health or the military. These senior-level staff were recruited nationally and usually did not come from the Matlab area.

The field assistants (later health assistants) were all recruited locally from the Matlab area. Persons at this level require a minimum of high school graduation or its equivalent, and are responsible for recording all vital events and other activities in the field area. Cultural constraints required that all of these workers be male so that they had the personal mobility required by the project. These men, however, could not go freely into any village home if the women's husbands were not present, because of the conservative customs of this Islamic society. Consequently, in every village at least one mature woman (locally called a *dai*) was recruited to escort the field assistant or other field staff through her village. Typically, this was a poor illiterate widow past childbearing age, who had the freedom of mobility required for the work.

As noted in Table 2.3, until 1977 the daily or every two-or-three-day household surveillance for births, deaths, and episodes of diarrhoea was carried out by the *dai*. Her work area was assigned so that she could make an inquiry in every household within about two or three hours. Acute diarrhoeal episodes

Table 2.3. Staffing and administrative organization of field surveillance activities, Matlab 1968 to present

Surveillance worker	Number	Average population per worker	Visitation cycle
a. 1968–74			
Field surveillance supervisor	2	120,000	random
Sanitary inspector	14	17,000	monthly
Field assistant	50	4,800	weekly
Dai (female worker)	300	800	daily
b. 1974–7			
Supervisor	1	280,000	random
Field surveillance assistant	3	93,000	random
Senior field assistant	4	70,000	4 months
Field assistant	16	17,500	1 month
Dai	290	900	2–3 days
c. 1978–			
Senior field research officer	1	159,000	random
Field research officer	3	53,200	random
Senior health assistant	6	26,600	2–3 months
Health assistant	12	13,300	monthly
Community health worker	80/30[a]	1,000/2,700[a]	weekly

[a] From 1978 the area was divided into the Family Planning–Health Service Area with 80 community health workers (CHWs) and the control area with 30 CHWs. The populations were similar, but intensity of coverage was very different (see text).

were reported daily to the field assistant for examination and rectal swab culture. Until 1974 the field assistant visited each house weekly, and from 1974–7 monthly. He registered vital events, and updated and signed the household census card. The sanitary inspector (later designated senior field assistant) had a systematic schedule to visit every household monthly (later at four-month intervals) and confirm vital events and check the visitation schedule on the household census card.

The fundamental organizational change initiated in 1977 was the replacement of the large number of illiterate *dais* with a smaller number of younger married women with high school education and designated as community health workers. This was done for three reasons: first, the design of the MCH–FP project required that household visits to motivate mothers to practise contraception and to teach them about maternal and child care be done by young married women who themselves were practising contraception (Simmons *et al.* 1988); second, by 1977 there was a sufficient pool of educated young married women in the Matlab area available for this work to make recruitment feasible; third, over the preceding decade, the tumultuous political and economic changes, including the liberation war and famine, had initiated a social transformation which made it more acceptable for young married women to take up this kind of work.

As noted in Table 2.3, there were 110 of these community health workers unequally divided between the two halves of the surveillance area as required by the MCH–FP project design. The eighty fieldworkers in the MCH–FP project area carried with them a record book which had a detailed record-keeping system (RKS) for routinely monitoring the contraceptive use and reproductive status (pregnancy, breastfeeding, lactational amenorrhoea, etc.) of each woman in her area (Bhatia 1982). This specialized record-keeping system was maintained independently of the data collection by the demographic surveillance system. It is worth noting that these eighty community health workers in the MCH–FP area additionally received technical supervision from four female welfare visitors who had received two years of paramedical training after their secondary school education (Bhatia 1981).

2.7 Changes in the Study Objectives Over Time

Until the mid-1970s the research agenda in the Matlab area was limited to the field testing of new technologies (e.g. vaccines) or carrying out basic research on diarrhoeal diseases, nutrition, and the dynamics of population change. In 1975 there was a major shift in research strategy with the initiation of the Contraceptive Distribution Project (CDP) (Huber and Khan 1979). The CDP and its successor, the Family Planning Health Services project (FPHS), moved the ICDDR,B in 1977 for the first time into population-based intervention studies which required behavioural changes in the village women to produce a sustained demographic impact (Rahman *et al.* 1979). At the outset, the strategy with the CDP project was strictly top-down, using existing field staff to make contraceptive commodities (initially pills and condoms, later injections) available house to house. Subsequently, the FPHS project, which took a more client-oriented approach, began offering a wider range of contraceptives (IUDs and sterilization were added) with medical back-up and, over the years, additional MCH services (Phillips *et al.* 1984a; DeGraff *et al.* 1986). Still, as will be noted below, up to 1991 the programme strategy has been essentially top-down, with little effort to institutionalize these programmes within the communities (Phillips *et al.* 1988).

2.8 Organization and Operation of the Contraceptive Distribution Project and the Family Planning Health Services Project

When the CDP first started in 1975, its area comprised 233 villages with an estimated population of 260,000 in the Matlab DSS area. The CDP involved free distribution of oral pills and condoms on a house-to-house basis to half the population of the DSS area; the other half of the DSS area served as a comparison group. One hundred and fifty-four of the existing female village workers (*dais*) were briefly trained to work as distributors and depot-holders of the two contraceptives (Rahman *et al.* 1979). The initial results of the CDP were encouraging. Within three months following the initial mass distribution, the percentage of married women of reproductive age currently using contraceptives, mainly oral pills, rose from a baseline level of 1 per cent to about 18 per cent at three months. However, only about one-third of the acceptors sustained use for even one year (Rahman *et al.* 1980). The resulting demographic impact of the programme was only temporary, and largely limited to older women (Stinson *et al.* 1982).

In late 1977, the modified programme, known as the FPHS project, replaced the *dais* with a cadre of eighty female village workers (FVW) who were backed up by strong supportive supervision and technical staff to provide a full range of contraceptives and selected MCH services in seventy villages (Bhatia *et al.* 1980). This modified FPHS project is still in operation. The FVWs were locally recruited, all of them being literate, young married women. They initially received two weeks' training in human reproduction and fertility control technology, followed by two weeks of closely supervised field training (Bhatia 1981). Subsequently, in weekly sessions, they were gradually given additional training in maternal and child nutrition, tetanus toxoid immunization, and oral rehydration for diarrhoea.

Each FVW currently serves a population of about 1,000 (or about 200 families) and almost all of them reside in the village or the area where they work. A group of twenty FVWs is assigned to a subcentre staffed by a full-time paramedic, which provides routine maternal and child health services, IUD services, menstrual regulation services, and referral support. Work routines require each FVW to visit all currently married women of reproductive age in her area fortnightly, and provide conventional contraceptives (condom and oral pill) and DMPA injections at the house of the client. The project has one female physician who does regular rounds in the field and provides professional support to a central sterilization clinic in the Matlab headquarters (Phillips *et al.* 1984*b*).

The plan of the FPHS project was to incrementally assign comprehensive Maternal and Child Health–Family Planning (MCH–FP) duties to the FVW: general family planning services, comprehensive immunization services, antenatal and postnatal care, nutritional education, and treatment of diarrhoeal diseases. The development of the project proceeded from general training of FVWs to a gradual introduction of all these duties.

The effect of the MCH–FP project was a prompt rise in contraceptive use-prevalence rates, which went up to 32 per cent in the first year. The project maintained this use-prevalence rate for five years; since 1983 the prevalence had again risen, reaching almost 50 per cent in recent years. Figure 2.4 shows

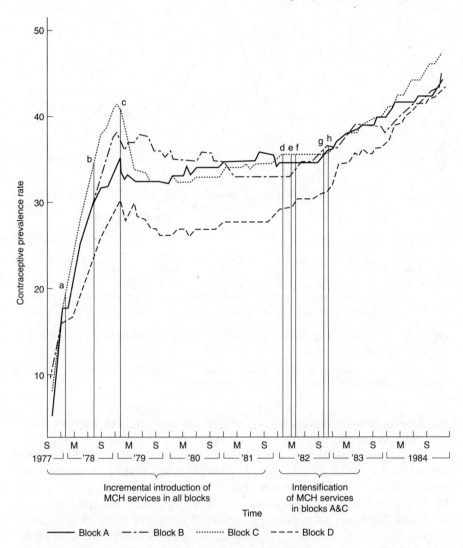

Fig. 2.4. Time-trend in contraceptive use prevalence in four service areas of the Family Planning–Health Services Project, 1977–1984

Note: All blocks had family planning services; Blocks A and C also had intensive maternal/child health-care services, and Blocks B and D had limited maternal/child health-care services. Services are represented as follows: a = IUD insertion; b = tetanus vaccine to pregnant women; c = oral rehydration therapy; d = tetanus vaccine to all women in Blocks A and C; e = measles vaccine in Blocks A and C; f = IUD home insertion; g = antenatal care in Blocks A and C; h = training of traditional birth attendants in Blocks A and C. On the X-axis (Time), M is March and S is September.
[a]Family planning services were introduced in October 1977.

Source: Reproduced with the permission of the Population Council from Deborah S. DeGraff *et al*., 'Integrating Health Services into an MCH–FP Program in Matlab, Bangladesh: An Analytical Update', *Studies in Family Planning*, 17(5): 231

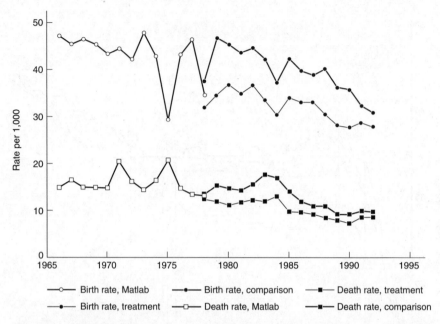

Fig. 2.5. Birth and death rates, Matlab, 1966–1978; treatment and comparison areas, 1978–1992

Sources: Annual publications of the Demographic Surveillance System, International Centre for Diarrhoeal Disease Research, Bangladesh

the time trend in contraceptive acceptance and the timing of introduction of other interventions from 1977 to 1987 (DeGraff *et al.* 1986).

An analysis of the demographic impact of the project showed that by 1979 fertility in the MCH–FP area was 25 per cent lower than in the comparison area (Phillips *et al.* 1982). Recent analysis of the DSS data suggests that the MCH–FP project is having significant impact on infant and child mortality (D'Souza 1986) and on maternal mortality (Fauveau *et al.* 1988). The demographic trends in the Matlab project from 1967 to 1987 are illustrated in Figure 2.5, which shows the impact of FPHS project since 1978 on fertility and mortality (Menken and Phillips 1990).

2.9 Human Relations

The Matlab project from the outset had an unwritten understanding with the community members according to which it was ready to treat cholera patients promptly once the patients from the community were brought to the field hospital. Until the early 1970s, all diarrhoea patients were carried by project ambulance boats to the field hospital at Matlab for prompt attention by the physician. The dramatic life-saving treatment of cholera, which is evident to everyone, has been a key factor in building and maintaining an excellent rapport between the project and the community. The Matlab Field Hospital provides free treatment to all members of the community suffering from diarrhoeal diseases, whether they occur within or outside the surveillance area. The number of in-patients served from 1963 to 1988 was 204,388 (Habte and Strong 1990).

The Matlab project has produced a change in the belief system of the people. The strikingly positive outcome of cholera treatment experienced by thousands of cholera patients over the years has effectively jolted their beliefs in the roles of the goddess *Ola* as well as *Kali* among Hindus and the role of the spirit *Oba* among Muslims in triggering the onset of cholera. The Hindus of Matlab no longer specifically worship the goddess *Ola* and give offerings (*bhog*) to the goddess *Kali* to spare them from attacks of cholera. Muslims also do not commission the services of the *Phakir* (religious healer) to drive away the spirit of *Ola* that brings cholera to the community. A change in deeprooted beliefs usually takes a long time with evidence demonstrating miraculous results repeated in numerous cases. Since the long-term intensive biomedical efforts were concentrated in Matlab Upazila and its neighbourhood only, the changes in beliefs indicated above have remained confined to this area.

The support of the field hospital to the diarrhoea-stricken community members led to a lasting bond of friendship between the project and the people which over the years enabled researchers successfully to undertake many investigations. These include cholera vaccine trials, research on oral rehydration therapy (ORT), clinical research which included studies on drug trials, search for pathogens, bringing diagnostic tools closer to the field, and indepth epidemiological and population studies. This is not to say that difficulties were not encountered from time to time. Some of these will be highlighted below.

2.9.1 Management problems encountered

A major source of low morale among the field staff is insecurity about their jobs, because they are always working on time-limited projects and they lack information on future activities. In general, field staff are not aware of projects under development where they have an opportunity for involvement. Coupled with this, lack of communication between different levels of workers and worry of the continuation of the Matlab project can lead to breakdown of morale. Staff awaiting with uncertainty for project assignments may express jealousy towards staff members who are assigned to well-funded projects. And then selection for long-term versus short-term assignments can create tensions among staff. Finally, as with any organization offering opportunities for employment, relatives and others can create pressure on the project administration for positions.

2.9.2 Public relations problems

Popular magazines and newspapers often published stories about the Matlab project. This provided information throughout Bangladesh to medical professionals, teachers, students, and other élites. Unfortunately, sometimes these reports criticized or misrepresented the activities of the ICDDR,B based on local sources of information about what was happening in the various field programmes. Misrepresentations included such activities as administering injectable and oral vaccines; mass (finger-stick) blood collections; sample surveys collecting such specimens as rectal swab cultures, urine, or breastmilk; and contraceptive field studies involving injectables, IUDs, different oral contraceptives, or surgical sterilization. In the early years of the project, too often insufficient attention was given to the press until some misleading story had already been published. Presently, far more attention is given to effective public relations to communicate the programmes and activities of the ICDDR,B.

2.9.3 Community relations

Many project activities created misunderstandings among the villagers in the Matlab area that considerably hampered the fieldwork and often required extensive effort to rectify. The implementation of the vaccine trials, because they involved such a massive direct intervention into these conservative communities, typically generated many rumours that had to be countered. The adverse reactions in the village were undoubtedly compounded by the fact that the vaccine teams used sophisticated jet injectors rather than more familiar syringes and needles to administer vaccines. Furthermore, the minor side-effects related to the immunization procedure (fainting, local pain, low-grade fever) at times created a sense of panic in the communities. Examples of rumours were that the vaccine was actually a family-planning injection or that the population was being used as guinea-pigs for experimentation with a completely new drug only tried before on animals.

Many studies involved the collection of blood specimens, typically a single drop by finger prick, but some studies required intravenous blood collection. (For example, see McCormack *et al.* 1969.) Because blood is considered a highly valuable item, when IV blood collections were done many people believed that the project was selling their blood in Dhaka. Even finger-prick blood collections would create concern among many individuals, as the prevailing belief was that the amount of blood in the body was fixed and even the loss of one drop could result in a permanent loss of strength. Because there was insufficient feedback to the community about the reasons for taking blood samples repeatedly, there was tension on a continuing basis.

Over the years there were multiple in-depth longitudinal studies of communities involving repeated questioning and specimen collection to study the epidemiology of diarrhoeal diseases or the dynamics of birth intervals. Not surprisingly, many of the questions were considered sensitive by the community, which led to embarrassment and reluctance to respond. For example, the epidemiological studies pursued questions on personal habits including defecation practices, personal hygiene, and food preparation, all of which were considered private matters (Spira *et al.* 1980; Black *et al.* 1982*a*). The intensive routine demographic data could also generate hostility when questions were asked about foetal wastage, stillbirths, conceptions among unmarried women, induced abortion, self-arranged marriages, and divorce (Aziz 1978; Demographic Surveillance System 1978). Some problem also arose with studies of the dynamics of fertility requiring monthly urine collection which would detect extramarital pregnancy and induced abortion, both of which were socially sensitive subjects (Becker and Chowdhury 1983; Fauveau and Blanchet 1989). Furthermore, there was reluctance in providing information on matters considered very private, such as menstrual cycles and sexual behaviour (Ruzicka and Bhatia 1982; Huffman *et al.* 1987*a,b*).

The in-depth investigations referred to above were undertaken only after the project had been in operation for five or ten years, or more. By that time, the field staff had gained a great deal of rapport and credibility with the people. This was facilitated by the development of interpersonal communication skills among project staff over the years. Usually they would build up a 'fictive' kinship relationship with individuals, so that it would be appropriate to engage in personal discussions about sensitive issues (Aziz 1979).

It was not until the development of the MCH–FP project in 1977, which employed young married women from the community who themselves used contraception to counsel women about family planning and child care, that the project actually developed a cadre of field staff for the explicit purpose of effective communication with the community (Bhatia *et al.* 1980; Phillips *et al.* 1988; Simmons *et al.* 1988). The design of this project followed an in-depth analysis of the preceding CDP project which had been implemented in 1975 by the pre-existing field staff. That analysis revealed that the *dais* who were asked to distribute oral contraceptives house-to-house had no credibility in the community for this purpose both because they lacked any personal experience with contraception and because they were typically poor and from the lower social classes (Rahman *et al.* 1978, 1980).

2.9.4 Government relationships

From 1966 to 1989, the headquarters of the Matlab project were located on the premises of the Matlab Government Rural Health Centre. Occasionally, the lack of sufficient space within the same building created some tension between the project and government staff members. To minimize this problem, special administrative contacts were sometimes required between the Matlab project staff and the Health Ministry officials of the government of Bangladesh. In February 1990, the Matlab project, now named the Matlab Health and Research Centre, was moved from the Government Upazila[3] Health Complex to a newly constructed two-storey Health Complex building of its own.

In 1982, the MCH–FP Extension Project was established to test the ways in which the successful components of Matlab could be transferred to the government services programme (Phillips *et al.* 1984*b*). In addition to Matlab, the Extension Project has field sites in two other *upazilas* in rural Bangladesh: Sirajgonj in Sirajgonj District and Abhoynagar in Jessore District. Service delivery in these areas remains the responsibility of the government, with the role of Matlab project staff limited to research and counterpart support.

2.10 Legacy

Population surveillance continues in Matlab; the last chapter has not yet been written, and the impact of the project is not yet final. A few broad generalizations can be derived from the project as a whole, with selected studies noted for appropriate illustration.

Work in Matlab has had a profound impact on health and population policy worldwide. While the cholera vaccine trials in the 1960s and 1970s failed to produce an effective vaccine, they did lead to a recognition that the international quarantine regulations of the World Health Organization requiring travellers to receive cholera vaccine were ineffective (Mosley *et al.* 1972). Consequently, these requirements were eliminated, saving millions of people around the world the inconvenience, pain, and cost of a useless procedure. In terms of demonstrating the practical utility of oral rehydration therapy, the first large-scale hospital-based study was carried out in the Matlab treatment centre in 1968, while the first major investigation of alternative approaches to home-based therapy was tested in the field in the mid-1970s (Cash *et al.* 1970; Chen *et al.* 1980). In the area of family planning, the CDP and its successor, the FPHS project initiated in 1977, provided conclusive documentation of the effectiveness of household distribution of contraceptives in impoverished populations (Phillips *et al.* 1982). It also demonstrated the standards of service delivery required to sustain a demographic impact (Simmons, Phillips, and Rahman 1984; Phillips *et al.* 1988).

The scientific contributions of the Matlab project to the basic understanding of the complex interrelationships between biological and social factors in determining the levels of health and fertility in poor developing-country populations are incalculable. In the area of diarrhoeal diseases, fieldwork in Matlab has tremendously expanded the knowledge of the multiple etiologic agents of these diseases, the spectrum of illnesses they produced, the biological and social factors underpinning their transmission in households and communities, their consequences for survival, growth, and development, and the relative effectiveness of alternative intervention strategies (Black *et al.* 1982*a,b*; 1984*a,b*). In the case of fertility, longitudinal studies in Matlab have provided detailed knowledge about the determinants of natural fertility and birth intervals, including the biological and social factors related to breastfeeding, lactational amenorrhoea, coital frequency, fecundity, and foetal wastage (Chowdhury and Becker 1981; Huffman *et al.* 1987*a,b*; John, Menken, and Chowdhury 1987; Ford *et al.* 1989).

The maintenance of a demographic surveillance system for almost three decades has permitted an extraordinary range of studies that would otherwise have been practically impossible through any other approach. For example, studies in Matlab have documented the demographic impact of natural and man-made disasters including famine and war (Chen and Chowdhury 1977; Bairagi 1986; Razzaque 1989). High-quality nutrition studies require knowledge of the exact chronological age of the study subjects which can only be obtained reliably through an ongoing registration system. The work in Matlab has not only contributed fundamentally to our knowledge of the determinants of growth of infants and children, but more recently, researchers have begun to look at the interrelationships between adolescent growth, nutrition, menarche, and child-bearing (Bairagi 1986; Riley, Huffman, and Chowdhury 1989).

The design of the DSS permitting record linkage of vital events provides multiple opportunities for long-term cohort studies. This system has been exploited to answer many questions, including the interrelationships between infant mortality and fertility, the social and economic determinants of child survival, the levels and determinants of maternal mortality, and the demographic impact of immunization programmes (Swenson 1978; D'Souza and Bhuiya 1982; Koenig *et al.* 1988; Koenig, Fauveau, and Wojtyniak 1989). The Matlab DSS, with its database, has also provided the opportunity for the development and validation of methodologies for demographic data collection (Chowdhury 1977; Becker and Mahmud 1984).

Another important contribution of the Matlab project that should not be overlooked is its role in training scores of scientists in Bangladesh and around the world. This training has not only been in the field in Matlab but also through the availability of data from the DSS to many leading universities around the world. This contribution to the development of a pool of scientists with critical skills in studying developing-country health and population problems is perhaps one of the most important contributions of the ICDDR,B in general and the Matlab project in particular.

References

Aziz, K. M. A. (1978), 'Marriage Practices in a Rural Area of Bangladesh', *Journal of Indian Anthropological Society*, 13(1): 29–40.

——(1979), *Kinship in Bangladesh*, International Centre for Diarrhoeal Disease Research, Dhaka, Bangladesh.

——and Mosley, W. H., Fahimuddin, M., McCormack, W. M., and Islam, M. S. (1967), 'Present Trends of Birth and Death in Rural East Pakistan: A Preliminary Report', *Pakistan Journal of Family Planning*, 1(1): 35–40.

Bairagi R. (1986), 'Food Crisis, Nutrition, and Female Children in Rural Bangladesh', *Population and Development Review*, 12(2): 307–15.

——(1987), 'A Comparison of Five Anthropometric Indices for Identifying Factors of Malnutrition', *American Journal of Epidemiology*, 126(2): 258–67.

Becker, S., and Chowdhury, A. (1983), 'Determinants of Natural Fertility in Matlab, Bangladesh', Office of Women in International Development, Michigan State University, East Lansing, Mich. (Working Papers on Women in International Development, 40).

——and Mahmud, S. (1984), 'A Validation Study of Backward and Forward Pregnancy Histories in Matlab, Bangladesh', International Statistical Institute, Voorburg (WFS Scientific Reports, 52).

——Razzaque, A., and Sarder, A. M. (1982), 'Demographic Surveillance System: Matlab. V. 8 Census Update, 1978', International Centre for Diarrhoeal Disease Research, Dhaka, Bangladesh (ICDDR,B Scientific Report, 55).

Benenson, A. S., Mosley, W. H., Fahimuddin, M., and Oseasohn, R. O. (1986), 'Cholera Vaccine Field Trials in East Pakistan: 2. Effectiveness in the Field', *Bulletin of World Health Organization*, 38(3): 359–72.

Bhatia S. (1981), 'Tranining Community Health Workers in Rural Bangladesh', *World Health Forum*, 2(4): 491–5.

——(1982), 'Contraceptive Intentions and Subsequent Behavior in Rural Bangladesh', *Studies in Family Planning*, 13(1): 24–31.

——Mosley, W. H., Faruque A. S. G., and Chakraborty, J. (1980), 'The Matlab Family Planning–Health Services Project', *Studies in Family Planning*, 11(6): 202–12.

Black, R. E., Brown, K. H., and Becker, S. (1984a), 'Effects of Diarrhoea Associated with Specific Enteropathogens on the Growth of Children in Rural Bangladesh', *Pediatrics*, 73(6): 799–805.

————(1984b), 'Malnutrition is a Determining Factor in Diarrheal Duration, but not Incidence, among Young Children in a Longitudinal Study in Rural Bangladesh', *American Journal of Clinical Nutrition*, 39(1): 87–94.

————Alim, A. R. M. A., and Merson M. H. (1982a), 'Contamination of Weaning Foods and Transmission of Enterotoxigenic *Escherichia coli* Diarrhoea in Children in Rural Bangladesh', *Transactions of the Royal Society of Tropical Medicine and Hygiene*, 76(2): 259–64.

————and Yunus, M. (1982b), 'Longitudinal Studies of Infectious Diseases and Physical Growth of Children in Rural Bangladesh. 1. Patterns of Morbidity', *American Journal of Epidemiology*, 115(3): 305–14.

Cash, R. A., Nalin, D. R., Rochat, R., Reller, L. B., Haque, Z. A., and Rahman, A. S. M. M. (1970), 'A clinical trial of oral therapy in rural cholera-treatment centre', *American Journal of Tropical Medicine and Hygiene*, 19(4): 653–6.

Chen, L. C., and Chowdhury, A. K. M. A. (1977), 'The Dynamics of Contemporary Famine', in *Proceedings of the International Population Conference, Mexico, 1977,* i, International Union for the Scientific Study of Population, Liège, 1977: 409–26.

——Black, R. E., Sarder, A. M., Merson, M. H., Bhatia, S., Yunus, M., and Chakraborty, J. (1980), 'Village-Based Distribution of Oral Rehydration Therapy Packets in Bangladesh', *American Journal of Tropical Medicine and Hygiene,* 29(2): 285–90.

Chowdhury, A. K. M. A. (1977), 'Double-Round Survey on Pregnancy Prevalence and Estimate of Traditional Fertility Rates', in *Proceedings of the International Population Conference, Mexico, 8–13 August 1977,* iii, International Union for the Scientific Study of Population, Liège, 1977: 327–48.

——and Becker, S. (1981), 'Determinants of Natural Fertility Study. V. 1. Methods and Descriptive Tables for the Prospective Study 1975–1978', International Centre for Diarrhoeal Disease Research, Dhaka, Bangladesh (ICDDR,B Scientific Report, 48).

Clemens, J. D., Sack, D. A., Harris J. R., Chakraborty, J., Khan, M. R., Stanton, B. F., Ali, M., Ahmed, F., Yunus, M., Kay, B. A., Khan, M. U., Rao, M. R., Svennerholm, A.-M., and Holmgren, J. (1988), 'Impact of B Subunit Killed Whole-Cell and Killed Whole-Cell-Only Oral Vaccines against Cholera upon Treated Diarrhoeal Illness and Mortality in an Area Endemic for Cholera', *Lancet,* 1: 1375–9.

Curlin, G. T., Levine, R. J., Ahmed, A., Aziz, K. M. A., Rahman, A. S. M. M., and Verwey, W. F. (1978), 'Immunological Aspects of a Cholera Toxoid Field Trial in Bangladesh', Cholera Research Laboratory, Dhaka (CRL Scientific Report, 8).

DeGraff, D. S., Phillips, J. F., Simmons, R., and Chakraborty, J. (1986), 'Integrating Health Services into an MCH–FP Program in Matlab, Bangladesh: An Analytical Update', *Studies in Family Planning,* 17(5): 228–34.

'Demographic Surveillance System–Matlab V. 1. Methods and procedures' (1978), Cholera Research Laboratory, Dhaka (CRL Scientific Report, 9).

D'Souza, S. (1986), 'Mortality Structure in Matlab (Bangladesh) and the Effect of Selected Health Interventions', in *Determinants of Mortality Change and Differentials in Developing Countries: The Five-Country Case Study Project,* United Nations Department of International Economic and Social Affairs, New York (*Population Studies,* 94: 117–44).

——and Bhuiya, A. (1982), 'Socioeconomic Mortality Differentials in a Rural Area of Bangladesh', *Population and Development Review,* 8(4): 753–69.

Fauveau, V., and Blanchet, T. (1989), 'Deaths from Injuries and Induced Abortion among Rural Bangladeshi Women', *Social Science and Medicine,* 29(9): 1121–7.

——Koenig, M. A., Wojtyniak, B., and Chakraborty, J. (1988), 'Impact of a Family Planning and Health Services Programme on Adult Female Mortality', *Health Policy and Planning,* 3(4): 271–9.

Ford, K., Huffman, S. L., Chowdhury, A. K. M. A., Becker, S., Allen, H., and Menken, J. (1989), 'Birth-Interval Dynamics in Rural Bangladesh and Maternal Weight', *Demography,* 26(3): 425–37.

Habte, D., and Strong, M. (1990) (eds.), *Annotated Bibliography of ICDDR,B Studies in Matlab, Bangladesh,* ICDDR,B, Dhaka, Bangladesh.

Huber, D. H., and Khan, A. R. (1979), 'Contraceptive Distribution in Bangladesh Villages: The Initial Impact', *Studies in Family Planning,* 10(6/9): 246–53.

Huffman, S. L., Chowdhury, A., Allen, H., and Nahar, L. (1987*a*), 'Suckling Patterns and Post-Partum Amenorrhoea in Bangladesh', *Journal of Biosocial Science,* 19(2): 171–9.

——Ford, K., Allen, H. A., Jr., and Streble, P. (1987*b*), 'Nutrition and Fertility in Bangladesh: Breastfeeding and Post-Partum Amenorrhoea', *Population Studies*, 41(3): 447–62.

John, A. M., Menken, J. A., and Chowdhury, A. K. M. A. (1987), 'The Effects of Breast-feeding and Nutrition on Fecundability in Rural Bangladesh: A Hazards-Model Analysis', *Population Studies*, 41(3): 433–6.

Koenig, M. A., Fauveau, V., and Wojtyniak, B. (1989), 'Potential Reductions in Infant and Child Mortality through Immunization Programmes: Evidence from Matlab, Bangladesh', in *Proceedings of the XXIst International Population Conference, New Delhi*, IUSSP, New Delhi, pp. 433–48.

——————Chowdhury, A. I., Chakraborty, J., and Khan, M. A. (1988), 'Maternal Mortality in Matlab, Bangladesh: 1976–85', *Studies in Family Planning*, 19(2): 69–80.

McCormack, W. M., Islam, M. S., Fahimuddin, M., and Mosley, W. H. (1969), 'A Community Study of Inapparent Cholera Infections', *American Journal of Epidemiology*, 89(6): 658–64.

Menken, J., and Phillips, J. F. (1990), 'Population Change in a Rural Area of Bangladesh, 1967–87', *Annals of the American Academy of Political and Social Science*, 510: 87–101.

Mosley, W. H., Chowdhury, A. K. M. A., Aziz, K. M. A., Islam, S., and Fahimuddin, M. (1968), 'Demographic Studies in Rural East Pakistan: Preliminary Analysis of the Results of Daily Registration of Births, Deaths and Migrations in 132 Villages in the Cholera Vaccine Field Trial Area in Comilla District, East Pakistan, May 1966–April 1967', SEATO Cholera Research Laboratory, Dhaka, Pakistan.

——McCormack, W. M., Fahimuddin, M., Aziz, K. M. A., Rahman, A. S. M. M., Chowdhury, A. K. M. A., Martin, A. R., Feeley, J. C., and Phillips, R. A. (1969), 'Report of the 1966–67 Cholera Vaccine Field Trial in Rural East Pakistan. 1. Study Design and Results of the First Year of Observation', *Bulletin of World Health Organization*, 40(2): 177–85.

——Woodward, W. E., Aziz, K. M. A., Rahman, A. S. M. M., Chowdhury, A. K. M. A., Ahmed, A., and Feeley, J. C. (1970), 'The 1968–1969 Cholera-Vaccine Field Trial in Rural East Pakistan: Effectiveness of Monovalent Ogawa and Inaba Antigen, with Comparative Results of Serological and Animal Protection Tests', *Journal of Infectious Diseases*, 121(supp.): S1–S9.

——Aziz, K. M. A., Rahman, A. S. M. M., Chowdhury, A. K. M. A., Ahmed, A., and Fahimuddin, M. (1972), 'Report of the 1966–67 Cholera-Vaccine Trial in Rural East Pakistan. 4. Five Years of Observation with a Practical Assessment of the Role of a Cholera Vaccine in Cholera Control Programmes', *Bulletin of World Health Organization* 47(2): 229–38.

Oseasohn, R. O., Benenson, A. S., and Fahimuddin, M. (1965), 'Field Trial of Cholera Vaccine in Rural East Pakistan: First Year of Observation', *Lancet*, 1: 450–3.

Phillips, J. F., Stinson, W. S., Bhatia, S., Rahman, M., and Chakraborty, J. (1982), 'The Demographic Impact of the Family Planning–Health Services Project in Matlab, Bangladesh', *Studies in Family Planning*, 13(5): 131–40.

——————Chakraborty, J., and Chowdhury, A. I. (1984*a*), 'Integrating Health Services into an MCH-FP Program: Lessons from Matlab, Bangladesh', *Studies in Family Planning*, 15(4): 153–61.

——————Simmons, G. B., and Yunus, M. (1984*b*), 'Transferring Health and Family Planning Service Innovations to the Public Sector: An Experiment in Organization Development in Bangladesh', *Studies in Family Planning*, 15(2): 62–73.

———Koenig, M. A., and Chakraborty, J. (1988), 'Determinants of Reproductive Change in a Traditional Society: Evidence from Matlab, Bangladesh', *Studies in Family Planning*, 19(6): 313–34.

Rahman, M. (1984), 'Determinants of Areal Variations in Contraceptive Practice in Bangladesh', PhD. dissertation, Australian National University, Canberra.

——Osteria, T., Chakraborty, J., Huber, D. H., and Mosley, W. H. (1978), 'A Study of the Field Worker Performance in the Matlab Contraceptive Distribution Project', Cholera Research Laboratory, Dhaka (CRL Working Paper, 5).

——Mosley, W. H., Khan, A. R., Chowdhury, A. I., and Chakraborty, J. (1979), 'The Matlab Contraceptive Distribution Project', International Centre for Diarrhoeal Disease Research, Dhaka, Bangladesh (ICDDR,B Scientific Report, 32).

————————(1980), 'Contraceptive Distribution in Bangladesh: Some Lessons Learned', *Studies in Family Planning*, 11(6): 191–201.

Razzaque, A. (1989), 'Sociodemographic Differentials in Mortality during the 1974–75 Famine in a Rural Area of Bangladesh', *Journal of Biosocial Science*, 21(1): 13–22.

Riley, A. P., Huffman, S. L., and Chowdhury, A. K. M. (1989), 'Age at Menarche and Postmenarcheal Growth in Rural Bangladesh Females', *Annals of Human Biology*, 16(4): 347–60.

Roy, S. K., Chowdhury, A. K. M. A., and Rahaman, M. M. (1983), 'Excess Mortality among Children Discharged from Hospital after Treatment for Diarrhoea in Rural Bangladesh', *British Medical Journal*, 287:1097–9.

Ruzicka, L. T., and Bhatia, S. (1982), 'Coital Frequency and Sexual Abstinence in Rural Bangladesh', *Journal of Biosocial Science*, 14(4): 397–420.

——and Chowdhury, A. K. M. A. (1978), 'Demographic Surveillance System—Matlab. V. 2 Census, 1974', Cholera Research Laboratory, Dhaka (CRL Scientific Report, 10).

Simmons, R., Phillips, J. F., and Rahman, M. (1984), 'Strengthening Government Health and Family Planning Programs: Findings from an Action Research Project in Rural Bangladesh', *Studies in Family Planning*, 15(5): 212–21.

——Bagee, L., Koenig, M. A., and Phillips, J. F. (1988), 'Beyond Supply: The Importance of Female Family Planning Workers in Rural Bangladesh', *Studies in Family Planning*, 19(1): 29–38.

Spira, W. M., Khan, M. U., Saeed, Y. A., and Satter, M. A. (1980), 'Microbiological Surveillance of Intra-Neighbourhood El Tor Cholera Transmission in Rural Bangladesh', *Bulletin of World Health Organization*, 58(5): 731–40.

Stinson, Wayne, S., Phillips, J., Rahman, M., and Chakraborty, J. (1982), 'The Demographic Impact of Contraceptive Distribution Project in Matlab, Bangladesh', *Studies in Family Planning*, 13(5): 141–8.

Swenson, I. (1978), 'Early Childhood Survivorship Related to the Subsequent Interpregnancy Interval and Outcome of the Subsequent Pregnancy', *Tropical Pediatrics*, 24(3): 103–6.

Zimicki, S., Nahar, L., Sarder, A. M., and D'Souza, S. (1985), 'Demographic Surveillance System–Matlab. V. 13. Cause of Death Reporting in Matlab. Source Book of Cause-Specific Mortality Rates, 1975–1981', International Centre for Diarrhoeal Disease Research, Bangladesh, Dhaka (ICDDR,B Scientific Report, 63).

3 Determinants of Rates of Early Childhood Sickness and Death, and of Long Birth Intervals: *Evidence from the Khanna Study, Rural Punjab, India, 1954–1969*

JOHN B. WYON

3.1 Introduction

3.1.1 Longitudinal community health research

This chapter reports selected findings from a longitudinal study of community-based rates of deaths, sicknesses, and birth intervals in eleven villages of the Punjab, India. These findings were the result of broader studies of births, deaths, migrations, and population dynamics, and a test of birth-control methods villagers could use on their own to cause lower birth rates in some village communities.

In 1951 John E. Gordon responded to worldwide concern with rapid growth of populations. He agreed to direct a test of the capacity of birth-control methods to reduce the birth rate of a rural population in India.[1] To him, all inhabitants of a village defined the obvious population unit. During the subsequent seven years from April 1953 to March 1960 a field staff conducted observations by monthly visits to all homes in eleven villages near Khanna in the Punjab. In 1969 a small staff conducted a six-month follow-up study in all households of the same villages.

Gordon affirmed that (*a*) the intent of the birth-control programme was to reduce problems arising from rapid population growth, and (*b*) that no detailed, accurate knowledge then existed from rural communities in India (or anywhere else) on the three demographic dimensions of their population growth—the community-based rates of birth, death, and migrations. Even less was known about their determinants. He also believed that the determinants of these rates influence each other.

Gordon judged regular home visits in the villages hosting the birth-control

The request from the IUSSP Committee on Anthropological Demography to prepare a paper for a seminar in Senegal in 1991 provided an effective stimulus to work on this material once again.
[1] By agreement with the Government of India the selected birth-control methods did not require the intervention of a physician; virtually no physicians were practising medicine in rural India. The methods were: rhythm, withdrawal, salt solution on a cotton pad, contraceptive paste on a cotton pad, and foaming contraceptive vaginal tablets.

programme to be the best way to provide couples with assured access to birth-control methods. This would also best enable the study staff to detect virtually all the numerator events needed to measure the demographic rates of birth, death, and migration. An annual census would provide the accurate denominators necessary to measure the levels and changes in the conventional demographic rates, and to investigate their determinants.

These considerations settled the longitudinal, community-based principles of the project design. Gordon's many field experiences studying epidemics in peacetime and during the Second World War supplied confidence in the proposed field method.[2] It seems Gordon perceived clearly in the early 1950s the enormous value of longitudinal data for measuring rates and risks of the incidents of sickness, death, birth, and migration.

3.1.2 Other longitudinal community health researches contemporary with the Khanna Study

In 1950 Dr Clarence Gamble, later founder of the Pathfinder Fund to promote birth control worldwide, read an article by Carl E. Taylor in the *Atlantic Monthly* on the possible reception of a birth-control programme in India. This aroused Gamble's interest and he requested Gordon to conduct a field trial of the capacity of a programme for birth control to reduce the birth rate.

In 1951, while John Gordon was developing ideas for what became the Khanna Study, he was also working with two of his former graduate students, Carl E. Taylor and Nevin S. Scrimshaw. Taylor had come from India to work with Gordon; his doctoral thesis was on the synergism and antagonism between nutrition and infection (Taylor and Gordon 1953). Scrimshaw arrived from Guatemala; he published a paper with Taylor and Gordon (Scrimshaw, Taylor, and Gordon 1959) on interactions between nutrition and infection, later expanded into a World Health Organization Monograph (Scrimshaw, Taylor, and Gordon 1968).

Taylor soon returned to India to start, at the Christian Medical College, Ludhiana, Punjab, the first Department in Asia of Social and Preventive Medicine. As Director of Gordon's project up to 1954 Taylor made the contacts leading to the selection of the town of Khanna as the project base. Scrimshaw returned to Guatemala to head the Institute of Nutrition for Central America and Panama (INCAP).

---

[2] John Gordon was Professor of Epidemiology at the Harvard School of Public Health. He had already used a longitudinal, community-based approach to study an epidemic of scarlet fever in Romania in the 1930s. During the Second World War he was Chief of Preventive Medicine for all US forces in the European theatre of operations. His fundamental assigned task was to learn the nature and determinants of epidemics of communicable diseases, and then to apply the new understanding to preventive and curative programmes (Gordon 1948). However, he applied conventional epidemiologic approaches and methods to develop and apply non-communicable disease epidemiology. In those days, this was regarded as impossible. Now, non-communicable disease epidemiology is taken for granted.

Throughout the period of fieldwork at Khanna, Gordon spent two months each year at INCAP, consulting with Scrimshaw and his colleagues as they developed the Three Villages Study of the effect of nutrition supplements and of medical care on young child mortality (Scrimshaw *et al.* 1969), and at least one month at Khanna. While Taylor developed his ideas over many years for the Narangwal study (Taylor and De Sweemer, Chapter 5, this volume), located 30 miles from Khanna, he was in close touch with Gordon and Scrimshaw.

Gordon was also directing studies on the epidemiology of intestinal infections in the Arctic (Gordon and Babbott 1959). These activities complemented the discoveries at Khanna and in Guatemala that diarrhoea was locally the single commonest preventable cause of death, and that the diarrhoea deaths were concentrated in the first two years of life. Subsequently malnutrition has turned out to be a worldwide major determinant of the deaths within poor communities of young children suffering intestinal, respiratory, and other infections.

3.2 Project Designs: the Context, and Field Method

3.2.1 Project design

John Gordon applied an ecologic approach to public-health research and practices. During 1950 and 1951 Gordon and Taylor considered the proposed field study in India, known later as the Khanna Study. They gave attention to the human and non-human ecologic components of the human communities they proposed to study. Taylor had lived in India from infancy through high school. His missionary parents regularly took him camping with them as they worked in rural areas. He in turn took John Gordon to camp for a week just outside a Punjab village as part of the field reconnaissance for the Khanna Study. They sought a rounded understanding of the determinants of the demographic features of the communities the fieldworkers would study. This required studies of the demographic, biological, economic, and social facets of the community ecosystems through long-term, prospective field observations in defined communities.

Taylor and I first met in 1949 as medical missionaries in India. We found a common interest in the health problems of rural people. In 1951 Taylor suggested that Gordon should talk with me; we met in Calcutta. Gordon invited me to become field director of an Indian field staff I was to appoint. I spent the academic year 1952–3 earning my Master of Public Health degree with Gordon. During the next three months we made a detailed design of the future study. Retrospective library studies supplied the essential historical perspective (Gordon, Ingalls, and Wyon 1954; Wyon and Gordon 1971). The Government of India Ministry of Health, the Rockefeller Foundation, and later the Indian Council of Medical Research, supported the field work. From 1953 to

1960 an Advisory Committee of senior scientists in India and officials of the Central and Punjab Health Ministries guided the project.

In September 1953 I joined Taylor at Ludhiana. With Taylor's support I explored the local area, made numerous contacts, located Helen Gideon, a Punjabi physician, and Senior Health Visitor Balwant Kaur to become the prime supporting field staff. I visited related field projects in India, and selected as project headquarters the town of Khanna 25 miles from Ludhiana.

A full year of library study, progressive development of preliminary fieldwork over two years, and the contributions of three capable senior Punjabi technical staff members, enabled several advanced features before the definitive study began in April 1956. A nine-month exploratory study in one village (June 1954 to March 1955), and a one-year pilot study in two other villages, occupied most of the time needed to develop these insights in the field. The function of the exploratory study was not only to learn field method, but also to explore acceptability of the birth-control methods. The pilot study included a test village (with a birth-control programme), and a scientific control village (no birth control); and then came the definitive study to measure changes in the birth rate (April 1955 to March 1960). The exploratory study was conducted in one village of 1,100 persons; the pilot study in two villages of about 1,350 persons each; and the definitive study in seven villages for the test group (8,000 persons), and the scientific control in four villages (4,000 persons). On the basis of lessons learned about acceptance and effectiveness of birth control during the exploratory and pilot studies, the definitive study was planned to last four years. Fieldwork ended in May 1960. In 1969 a small staff visited all families in the same villages for the follow-up study (January to June).

The national census and economic data available in 1953 were sufficient to make the case that the population dynamics of rural district of Ludhiana in the Punjab, India, reasonably represents other districts in India. However, we selected the villages for study mainly on the basis of criteria necessary to fulfil the requirements of the project design. These criteria were: well-separated clusters of test and control villages, and accessibility during all seasons. Within those limits we selected less developed villages, least involved in industry and commerce, removed from towns, main roads, and railway stations. At the end of the study we examined the demographic features of the study villages among themselves as a group, and compared them with the same features of rural Ludhiana District as a whole. The study village populations and the district populations turned out to be remarkably similar in terms of the demographic characteristics for which data were available (Wyon and Gordon 1971: 91–8).

3.2.2 Context

In Punjab villages the houses cluster closely. One mile or more in all directions separates each village from its neighbouring villages. Only as we came to know these people did we recognize the intensity of the bonds binding individuals with their village. At the same time, individuals are loyal members of their extended family. Moreover, each family is loyal to the families of its fellow caste and *gotra* (clan within caste) groups living in their own and other villages and in towns up to many miles away.

The social groupings of families by caste reflect beliefs deeply held in India about social position in the society as determined by birth. Hindus believe that their personal actions in previous lives determine the caste into which each child is born. The caste name describes the particular service the caste group gives to the village. Each village community requires the services of the castes represented locally; no person from another caste may perform those particular services. That work is their birthright, duty, and their source of livelihood and identity. Examples are: priest, farmer, carpenter, leather worker, and many more. The different caste groups, living and working together in one village, supply the necessary skills the traditional agricultural economy requires.

All villagers recognize the caste groups in their own village. In all study villages, farmers composed 50 per cent of the caste groups, leather workers (who were also considered agricultural workers) composed 25 per cent, and the remainder were a few families from most of the remaining twenty caste groups found in all the eleven villages put together. The rates of birth, death, and migration of these main caste groups scattered among several villages differed considerably among the castes. Nevertheless, differences in vital rates among populations of whole village communities were minor. The explanation of the apparent contradiction lies in the constant proportion of families by caste in each village. Apart from a few commuters to local small towns, virtually all adult men in these village communities plied some trade which aided farming; the name of their caste described their trade. Women did not work beyond the village lands.

Winters were cold, close to freezing; summers were hot and desiccating; during the humid, hot monsoon season it was difficult to move around in the mud; children and even adults tended to defecate near their homes instead of farther away. Seasonal differences in death rates from infections and malnutrition might well be marked.

3.2.3 Field method

Field method and data-recording are described in detail in the book by Wyon and Gordon (1971).

The main dependence was on original data collected through direct field interview by a staff of Punjabi men and women. This conforms to the established cultural custom that, outside the family, men talk to men and women to women. During the first months of the study, senior staff members acted as local village fieldworkers, to learn by personal experience what they later taught and supervised during the pilot and definitive studies. We found that one fieldworker could work successfully with about 1,500 persons, 300 families; never in more than three villages; and never two fieldworkers in the same village. Physicians acted as fieldworkers in two small villages. The same physicians supervised the other fieldworkers, spending roughly a night each week with their field staff to support their work. The irregular hours were compensated by a long weekend each month.

During the definitive field study the staff included two assistant field directors, both physicians; one male and four female physicians; a senior health visitor; and nineteen field staff, mostly married couples, resident in their appointed villages. There were also statistical, administrative, and ancillary staffs. Male staff visited husbands, usually at their place of work; female staff visited wives at home. Our relations with the village communities rested on the agreement that they were hosts; we were their guests. In time the fieldworkers became part of their community. A prime quality of all fieldworkers was the ability to listen and learn.

Initial visits to villages selected for the field study were the task of the field director and a senior Punjabi colleague. Once the village leaders had decided to take part in the study, the regular staff constructed a calendar of local events, based on information from older village residents on the history of the community. The calendar was useful in estimating dates of birth, marriage, or other vital events among a largely illiterate population. The basis for identification of individuals and for the annual census was a map of houses and a list of households. The distinction between residents and non-residents was based on a minimum of six months' residence in the village. This helped in the accurate measurement of age-specific birth and death rates.

Monthly home visits were the principal source of information on population dynamics. Each week the staff also collected from volunteer informants a report of births, deaths, and migrations, supplementing information from the village watchman's[3] official records and their own observations. An annual census supplied accurate denominators for the various demographic and epidemiologic rates, and served as a check for missing or incorrect records.

Record cards were stored by village and household number in packs according to the different studies, each distinguished by its individual colour. The basis for the record system was a family record card containing the names and identification numbers of all family members. Each form had a syllabus of instructions on its use. Cross-reference of births and deaths from one form to another was simplified by assigning a serial number to each birth and death in registers kept for the purpose. A longitudinal visual record of the progressively unfolding process of family building was coded on to a register using the information collected at monthly interviews with wives and husbands. The Record of Death (Figure 3.1) illustrates some of these principles.

Forms to record interviews at monthly visits were printed and bound into books with space for recording twelve interviews each for 120 persons. Extra

[3] From Moghul times each village has had its watchman. He records crimes, epidemics, deaths, and births. Being illiterate, the watchman asks others in the village to register his findings.

RECORD OF DEATH

Disease Code No .... Group Code No ....

1. .... Village   2. Sr. No ....   3. H. Hold No ....

2. IDENTIFICATION

4. Name ....   5. s/o, d/o, w/o, wid/o ....
6. Head of h. hold ....   7. Retn. of (4) to head of household ....
8. Caste ....   9. Age ....   10. Marital Status ....
11. Usual residence ....   12. Informant ....
13. s/o, d/o, w/o, wid/o ....   14. Retn. of Infmt. to deceased ....

3. CAUSE OF DEATH

1. Date of death 19   2. Place of death..................................

3. Symptoms and duration ....
....
....
....
....
....

4. Clinical signs and Lab. Tests ....
....
....
....

5. Medical Care, by and duration :–

	(1) None	(2) Siana	(3) Charmer	(4) Saint
Unqualified	(5) Vaid	(6) Hakim	(7) Dispenser	(8) Other (Specify)
Qualified :	(9) Doctor	(10) Dispenser	(11) Other (Specify)	

6. Cause of death according to informant ....

7. Cause of death according to chowkidar ....

8. Diagnosis of cause of death.

I

		Approximate interval between onset and death
Disease or condition directly leading to death	(a)...	....
	due to (or as a consequence of)	
Antecedent causes	(b)...	....
	due to (or as a consequence of)	
Morbid conditions, if any, giving rise to the above cause, stating the underlying condition last	(c)...	....

II

Other significant conditions contributing to the death, but not related to the disease or condition causing it.
....
....

9. Reliability of diagnosis.   1. Certain   2. Doubtful   3. Unknown

10. Remarks :

Signature of worker ....   Date ....

I.H.L.P.S. Form No. 21.
10th January 1958.

Fig. 3.1.   Record of Death (front and back of card)

Source: Wyon and Gordon 1971

sheets for field notes were included at each end of the book. During the whole study only one field notebook was lost. To minimize the risk of loss of records each fieldworker had a wooden box which contained all the records of the fieldworker's area of responsibility. The box slid into a metal container for transport and storage. Once a year the field staff checked all their records to be sure that none was missing. Most data could be replaced by reinterviewing.

During the first two years of fieldwork, the staff recognized the need for five special studies: on medical diagnosis of causes of all deaths; on medical care in fatal cases; on obstetric practices; on sicknesses and child feeding among children born during the time-span of the project; and on the epidemiology of accidental traumatic injuries in the scientific control villages of the birth-control study.

As a particular stage of the study got under way, preliminary and periodic analyses of results began. This aided the staff to make full use of acquired experience to improve methods and procedures and to perfect record forms. Definitive analysis of the collected data from the study was planned late in 1959; analyses and reporting were completed in Boston in 1971. Most of the work in Boston was completed using IBM cards; electronic computers became available only after most of the work was done. Gordon and I maintained direction of the project from its design in 1953 to the final published report in 1971.

The key features of the fieldwork were (1) that the populations of whole villages were the primary unit of observation, and (2) that the monthly visits to families enabled the staff to build up accurate prospective data on vital events and sicknesses, to offer birth-control and to record birth-control practices, and to record the reproductive events of conception, pregnancy, termination of pregnancy, breast feeding, postpartum amenorrhoea, and migrations. Key features of data analysis were the use of cohort analyses and applications of the life-table method, thanks to Robert G. Potter Jr. (Potter *et al.* 1965*b*).

3.3 Major Findings

3.3.1 High death rates in the second year of life

Seven years after it had started, fieldwork on the Khanna Study proper ceased in 1960. During six months in 1969 a small staff conducted follow-up visits to each family in the same eleven villages. Up to 1971, publications of national age-specific death rates of young children in developing countries were essentially confined to neonatal (less than 28 days), postneonatal (28 to 365 days), and infant (0–365 days) deaths per 1,000 live births per year; and possibly deaths of children 1–4 years (12 to 59 months) per 1,000 children of the same ages (estimated from decennial or less frequent census); and 0–4 years. Most were dependent on unreliable data for their numerators, and equally on more unreliable data for their denominators. Retrospective studies and surveys supplemented analyses of vital data and censuses. Few, if any, field studies in developed countries had explored age-specific child death rates much more deeply. Credible data from developing countries on age-specific and cause-specific death rates were even harder to find. Hospital data lacked credible denominators, but were often the best available source on causes of deaths.

Nevertheless we do have some evidence from the Europe of ninety years ago. In 1901 the infant mortality rate in Spain was estimated at 183 per 1,000 live births, and the second-year death rate was 110 per 1,000 children. The corresponding data from Sweden, indicated that infant mortality there in 1901 was 91 per 1,000 live births (15 in 1963), and the second-year death rate was still up at 25 (0.9 in 1963). The declines in these mortality and death rates from 1901 to 1963 in the two countries give some idea of what may be happening in many developing countries now (Gordon, Wyon, and Ascoli 1967).

By 1960 many developed countries were publishing reported deaths per 1,000 population (the denominators estimated from decennial census) by single-year age-groups up to the fifth year of life. But analyses of these child death rates apparently gave public health practitioners little indication that they might learn something of value by attending to age-specific death rates in more detail than the neonatal, postneonatal, infant (neonatal + postneonatal), and the next four years by single years.

The data given in the remainder of this section are documented in Wyon and Gordon (1971) where not otherwise specified.

The next two paragraphs compare government data on death rates from the Punjab using for numerators the standard records of deaths, by age; and for the denominators either the records of live births (as the denominators of infant mortality), or census estimates by age for denominators of age-specific death rates past the first year.

Three facts are particularly striking about death rates in the Punjab between 1881 and 1921: (1) up to 1921, the crude death rate exceeded the crude birth rate in eleven of those forty years, the major epidemics being plague, smallpox, and influenza; (2) after 1921, the crude death rate declined from about 35 per 1,000 to 15 by 1955, no major epidemics occurring; and (3) the infant death rate declined more slowly. In 1901 the annual infant mortality rate in the Punjab was about 234 deaths per 1,000 live births, and the death rate from 1–5 years was 66 per 1,000 children.

Comparing the 1956–9 single-year death rates for the first 5 years of life in the study population with the 1951 US rates: the first-year death rate was 187 in the Punjab and 27 in the USA (seven times); the second-year death rate in the Punjab was 73, about thirty times the US rate. By the third year of life the Punjab rate was only 23, and thereafter declined rapidly. By comparison, the US single-year death rates after the first year were negligible.

Now we examine findings from the Khanna Study on death rates by age,

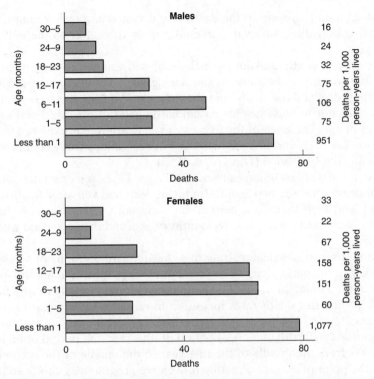

Fig. 3.2. Estimated deaths and death rates from a cohort of live-born children of 1,000 live births, each sex (deaths per 1,000 person-years of specified age by sex and by ages to 36 months, test and control A. villages, 1955–1959)

Source: Wyon and Gordon 1971

but the denominators are age-specific summations of child life in the specific age-groups. The bars in Figure 3.2 represent the estimated numbers of children from a cohort of 1,000 live births dying during the given age- and sex-groups. The column to the right gives the corresponding age-specific death rates per 1,000 person-years lived.

Among 1,000 female children born alive, 79 died in the first month of their life. Their death rate was just over 1,000 per 1,000 person-years lived, but half of them survived less than one week.[4] During the next 5 months of life the death rate declined by two-thirds, and 20 more of the original 1,000 liveborns died. But during the combined 6–11 and 12–17 month age-groups the death rate more than doubled, and about 126 more of the 1,000 liveborns died. By

---

[4] In this case denominators of death rates are derived by summing person-years lived, not persons assumed to live most of a year. When death rates are very high, many individuals live only a few days or weeks. It takes several persons to contribute one person-year to the denominator.

the 18–23 month age-group the death rate declined and only 22 more of the original cohort died. Survival increased rapidly thereafter to the end of the third year.

Age-specific death rates among males followed a similar pattern; male infant mortality was much the same as the female; male deaths for the 1–5 month age group declined markedly, and then increased during the next 12 months of life, but not to such heights as among females; it also declined after 18 months of age. The issue of the excess female death rate is explored in Wyon and Gordon 1971, and is a major focus in Das Gupta's study of mortality in the same villages 1984–6 (Das Gupta 1987).

One important fact emerges from these data. There is a dramatic fall in the risk of death after the first month (in fact it declines even after the first week of life), and then there is a marked high mortality risk period of about 12 months of child life, from 6 to 18 months of age, and then a second sustained decline.

These observations demonstrate that the standard divisions of age-specific mortality in the early years of life did not correspond to the ages of risks of death in the Punjab in the 1950s. Death rates declined rapidly during the first month of life. But death rates measured in terms of the standard neonatal, postneonatal, and 1–4 year death rates do not reflect the crucial age period of high mortality after the neonatal period. In this case, the period of high mortality was from the middle of the first year to the middle of the second year. From the point of view of directing preventive programmes, this is an important difference between the whole postneonatal period and the whole second year.

3.3.2 Infections and malnutrition as causes of death in the first two years of life

Acute diarrhoeal disease was the single most frequent ascribed cause of death in the study villages during the three calendar years 1957–9. Out of the 615 deaths at all ages, 68 persons (11 per cent) died with acute diarrhoeal disease; and the majority (59 per cent) of these were children in their first 2 years of life. Acute diarrhoea was also a significant cause of death of the 20 per cent of deaths to persons over 65 years old.

In this experience, virtually all mothers breast-fed their infants, and most started to wean them from the breast during the period of high mortality, ages 6–18 months. Acute diarrhoeal disease was almost universal, and it was the commonest cause of death at those ages. Gordon coined the term *weanling diarrhoea* to describe this epidemiologic syndrome among humans beings. Weanling diarrhoea is well known to pig, sheep, and cattle farmers.

In their paper on weanling diarrhoea, Gordon, Chitkara, and Wyon (1963) define weaning as the transition from breast- or bottle-feeding to mixed diet. The paper profusely documents the high rates of disease and death from diarrhoea early this century in North America and Western Europe; its worldwide distribution today; the many different kinds of bacteria and viruses causing the disease; its severity among malnourished children; and its association with unhygienic bottle-feeding. In the villages of the Khanna Study mothers used bottles exclusively only when they could not breast-feed; all wholly bottle-fed children died.

Findings from the Khanna Study on the relationship of child-feeding to acute diarrhoeal disease and the deaths of children are based on the prospective study of four annual village birth cohorts of infants, 775 for the first year of life, 462 for the second year of life, etc. (Gordon, Chitkara, and Wyon 1963). Later we shall examine the death rates at the same ages from all causes, and from all eleven villages.

We observed death rates from diarrhoea per 1,000 children per year during the age periods 0–5, 6–11, 12–17, and 18–23 months. They were: 21, 54, 35, and 7 respectively. Deaths from diarrhoea as the percentage of deaths from all causes from another data set for the same age periods were 13, 42, 46, and 17. The lowest rates of cases of acute diarrhoeal disease in the first two years of life were 800 and the highest 3,500 cases per 1,000 children per year (see note 4). Among wholly breast-fed children of 0–5 months the diarrhoea rate was 1,500 per child per year, rising to 1,800 by 9 months and declining to 1,000 by 24 months. Virtually every child suffered multiple attacks.

During the first 3 months, 71 per cent of breast-fed children received only breast milk, and more than one-half during the second quarter year. By 12 months the proportion subsisting wholly on a milk diet, breast and other, was declining rapidly as solid foods were added. Few children depended only on breast milk well into their second year. Many mothers recognized that their children had more diarrhoea after they started supplementing the breast milk, particularly with solid food.

We now move from the clear evidence that when breast-fed children start solid food they have more frequent attacks of diarrhoea to explore how the death rate changes, as age advances, but also by medically diagnosed causes.

We followed 779 newborn infants for up to 2 years of age. Each month the staff recorded sicknesses in the previous month, and feeding practices as one or more of: breast milk, other milk, and solid food. For analytic purposes we assigned all the children, at each trimester of life, to one of the five categories of child-feeding: breast milk given, and solid food given, or withheld; no breast milk given, but solid food given, or withheld; and no food. Figure 3.3 is reproduced from Wyon and Gordon (1971). The bars represent age-specific death rates. Numerators and denominators are given for each bar. In Figure 3.2, the first-month death rate is high because it includes deaths related to pregnancy and childbirth, but in the second trimester the death rate is low. In Figure 3.3 the higher death rates in the third-to-sixth trimesters correspond to the high death rates from 6 to 18 months of age in Figure 3.2. The lower death rates

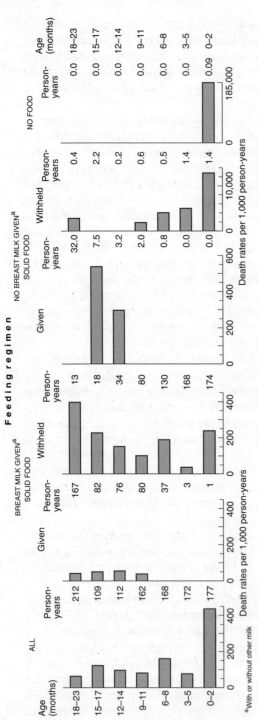

Fig. 3.3. Age-specific death rates by trimesters of life from birth to two years, deaths and causes of death, by feeding regimen: Test II and Control A. villages, except Gowadhi, 1955–1960

Note: Death rates: deaths per 1,000 person-years at each trimester of life; feeding regimens: combinations of breast milk and solid food, or no food; causes of death: diarrhoea and other causes; these children were observed by the cohort method; starting with 779 live births each trimester of life of the children was assigned to that category of feeding regimen applying when the trimester ended, or just before the child died or migrated.

Source: Wyon and Gordon 1971

after age 18 months are clear in both figures. The drop in death rates after 18 months is for both sexes in Figure 3.3, and is not quite as dramatic as the drop in the case of females in Figure 3.2, but the same pattern is clear.

The data given in Figure 3.3 reveal that, among breast-fed children less than 6 months old, few received any solid food (see the columns on person-years). So we cannot compare death rates of children of those ages receiving and not receiving solid food.

We now examine the column 'Breast milk given'. This heading is subdivided into two sets of age-specific groups distinguishing whether supplementary solid food was given or withheld. At each age period one person-year corresponds to at least four children, each spending one-quarter of a year or less in that age-group. The numbers in these two columns tell us that, in the first age-group, 0–2 months, four or more children (one person-year) received breast milk and solid food; but 174 person-years (696 children) received only breast milk, and solid food was withheld. As our eye moves up these two person-years columns we can see children progressively shift from the (withheld) column to the (given) column. The bars indicate the death rates at each age. The lower section of Figure 3.3 gives the numbers of deaths at each age-group, from diarrhoea and from other causes.

When we look closely at the third trimester, 6–8 months of age, some striking findings appear. There were no deaths among the 37 person-years of experience contributed by the approximately 148 children who were receiving breast and solid food during that age-span, whereas, from the 130 person-years of experience contributed by at least 520 children receiving breast milk but no solid food, twenty-four children died. And only ten out of these twenty-four deaths were diagnosed as from diarrhoea.

In the 6–8 month age-span only 22 per cent of the mothers had started to supplement their breast milk with solid food. Between 9 and 11 months, one-half of the mothers had started solid food. But even by the age-group 18–23 months, 8 per cent of the children on breast milk were still not receiving solid food.

From age 6 to 23 months overall, the death rate for each group was three times or more among the children receiving breast milk, but no solid food, as compared with those receiving breast milk and solid food; and we have evidence that they were dying of the same diseases.

These findings suggest increasing calorie deficiency of breast-fed children as they pass through their second trimester of life. Mortality mounted as age advanced if mothers delayed supplementing their breast milk. Breast-fed children were all receiving the prime quality protein-rich food of their mother's own milk; but the children receiving supplemental solid food were also receiving additional calories from cereals, and possibly from milk products.

Chavez and Martinez in Mexico (1982) have shown that lactating mothers just about double the quantity of breast milk they produce from birth to six months later, but then the quantity declines. By this time, most children who are solely breast-fed have doubled their weight, and therefore have doubled their daily requirement for calories. Moreover, this is about the time the infants are starting to use their muscles more and to put anything within reach into their mouths. It appears that increasing calorie malnutrition and increased infection strike together at just about the same age-span of 4–9 months.

The three right-hand columns of Figure 3.3 refer solely to non-breast-fed children. The data in these columns indicate the following: only twenty children were bottle-fed from birth; all eventually died. By the 12–14 month trimester the children of fourteen mothers (3.2 person-years) had ceased breast-feeding, and one child died. During the next trimester the children of at least thirty mothers (7.5 person-years) were no longer breast-feeding, and four died. By the age span 18–23 months 128+ mothers were no longer breast-feeding, but they were giving solid food and none of their children died. Moving back to the breast-fed children, at the same age-group 52+ mothers were still breast-feeding, but were not giving solid food and five of their children died, while 668+ mothers were breast-feeding and giving solid food and only six of these children died.

These observations strongly suggest the following: up to 6 months of age, breast milk generally supplies the protein and the calories infants need to stay alive and grow; we have already noted that by 6 months the risk of death starts increasing. The evidence we are now reviewing strongly suggests that, about 4–6 months after birth, breast milk no longer supplies the necessary quantity of energy. Breast milk supplies the highest-quality proteins, but these foods are burned up if alternative sources of energy are not supplied, and therefore increasing proportions of children die from common infections, particularly from diarrhoea in the Punjab. Even though the introduction of solid food seems to provide opportunities for more infections causing more diarrhoea, we have strong evidence that the risk of death is much reduced among breast-fed children whose mothers supplement their milk with solid food.

If these conclusions on the biology of infections, with and without serious malnutrition, are correct, then it follows that the behaviour of mothers who fail to start supplementing their breast milk at least by the time their children are 6 months of age increasingly place their children at risk of death from common infections such as diarrhoea, pneumonia, and measles.

3.3.3 The most frequent, preventable causes of death among preschool children

Policy-makers and practitioners undertaking to maintain and improve the health of specific populations have only limited resources to serve the needs of the publics or communities who employ them. For these practitioners one foremost question is: what are the most frequent, serious, and preventable conditions affecting the communities? Death is one of these serious conditions.

Many deaths are preventable, particularly within poor communities. Here we have elected to explore what kinds of preschool children (under 5-years old) in the villages of the Khanna Study were dying of what preventable conditions in the late 1950s. Table 3.1 displays some of the relevant age- and cause-specific, but not sex-specific risks of death.

We now discuss how the field staff detected fatal events, and how they determined causes of the deaths. Seven physicians, including the field director, were

Table 3.1. Deaths and death rates per 1,000[a] per year by age and by cause, all deaths of children less than 5 years old in 11 Punjab villages, India, 1957–9

Cause of death	Age-group					
	0–27 days	28 days– 11 mos.	0–11 mos.	12–23 mos.	24–35 mos.	1–4 yrs.
1. *Pregnancy and immaturity*						
Immaturity	20.0	10.7	30.7	0	0	0
Birth injuries	20.0	0.7	20.7	0	0	0
Infections of newborn	4.3	0	4.3	0	0	0
Congenital malformns.	2.1	1.4	3.6	0	0	0
	46.4	12.8	59.3	0	0	0
2. *Infections preventable by immunization*						
Tetanus	20.7	0.7	21.4	0	0	0
Measles	0	5.7	5.7	7.7	0.9	2.3
Whooping cough	0	0	0	4.3	0.9	1.4
	20.7	6.4	27.1	12.0	1.8	3.7
3. *Other infections with malnutrition*						
Diarrhoea	0	27.8	27.8	21.5	2.8	6.4
Pneumonia and bronchitis	0	10.7	10.7	4.3	2.8	2.1
Tuberculosis	0	2.1	2.1	6.0	0.9	1.8
Typhoid	0	2.8	2.8	4.3	0.9	3.2
	0	43.4	43.4	36.1	7.4	12.6
4. *Other*	2.8	13.6	16.4	14.6	8.3	7.3
5. *Unknown*	3.6	6.4	9.9	9.5	3.7	3.7
Totals (Rates)	73.5	82.7	156.2	72.2	21.3	27.4
Deaths, Total *615* all causes	103	116	219	84	23	120

[a] From age 0–11 months, per 1,000 live births; from age 12 months per 1,000 population of the age-group.

Source: Wyon and Gordon 1971.

among the field staff during the definitive study. The Punjab Government Health Ministry seconded Dr Sohan Singh from his former post of Medical Officer of Health for Ludhiana District to be Assistant Field Director of the Khanna Study. He undertook to organize a study of the cause of every death in the eleven study villages. With his colleagues he developed the Record of Death (Figure 3.1); he trained his fellow physicians to use the same terms for symptoms and signs. As soon as one of the field staff heard of a death, a project physician visited the family and took a medical history of the fatal illness. The project physicians together went over the histories of recent deaths and decided whether or not any further information was desirable; if so, they conducted another interview with the relatives. In many cases one of the project physicians had seen the deceased before death. Dr Sohan Singh and two of his colleagues made the final diagnosis of cause of death.

The categories of deaths by cause given in Table 3.1 take into consideration the analyses of deaths by age and by the feeding regimens we have discussed above. When categorizing causes of death, the personal characteristic of age is one useful way to identify groups of persons more or less likely to die. The previous sections have identified accurately ages within the preschool years when the risk of death is particularly high. This table retains the more classical age divisions. It also considers the perinatal period, an important category so far not given attention. We are now seeking to identify preventable medical conditions common in the high-mortality age-groups, and what leads to these concentrations.

One important group of deaths is preventable by immunization procedures. These include tetanus of the newborn, a highly fatal infection preventable by immunizing women at least four months before they deliver their baby. Immunization of young children can also prevent measles and whooping cough, two other prominent infections causing deaths in the Khanna Study villages.

In most developing countries the common, non-immunizable infections of diarrhoea and pneumonia as determined by medical practitioners are easily the most frequently recognized causes of deaths of preschool children. In the villages under the Khanna Study the commonest was diarrhoea, followed by pneumonias. Measles, tetanus of the newborn, and whooping cough were also important. However, according to Dr Sohan Singh and his colleagues, malnutrition did not appear, even as a contributing category. A major reason was that we had decided not to attempt to weigh babies for fear that it would cause alarm among the mothers and families. We therefore had no sound way to recognize malnourished children. Yet we have just presented strong epidemiologic evidence that malnutrition played a major part in determining which children who were sick with one of the common infections would live or die. For our present purposes we have therefore developed a category of infections with malnutrition.

With the above diagnostic categories in mind we display in Table 3.1 information on the deaths of preschool children according to the age-groups 0–27 days, 28 days to 11 months, 0–11, 11–23, and 24–35 months, and 1–4 years. Within those age-groups we have distributed death rates per 1,000 live births for deaths in the first year of life, and thereafter per 1,000 persons of the age-group. The death rates are then distributed according to the groups of causes of death just discussed: Group 1, *Pregnancy and Obstetric*: immaturity, birth injuries, infections of the newborn, and congenital malformation; Group 2, *Infections Preventable by Immunization:* tetanus, measles, and whooping cough; Group 3, *Other Infections with Malnutrition:* diarrhoea, pneumonia and bronchitis, tuberculosis, typhoid; Group 4, *Other*; Group 5, *Unknown*; and *Totals*. A group on diseases of maturity has been omitted because here we are concerned only with preschool children.

Causes of deaths in the Group 1 category arise during pregnancy and delivery. They accounted for 63 per cent of deaths in the first 28 days of life. Deaths from some of these determinants continued into succeeding months, particularly immaturity. They contributed 15 per cent of postneonatal deaths, and 38 per cent of infant (first-year) deaths. When deaths from tetanus of the newborn are included in this age-group, as they should be, then 91 per cent of deaths in the first 28 days and 51 per cent of all deaths in the first year of life arose during pregnancy and soon after delivery. Tetanus spores deposited in or at the umbilical stump cause tetanus of the newborn.

None of our staff was present at any but a few of the births. Diagnosis of immaturity by low birth weight therefore depended on impressions from the mother and relatives gathered by a woman physician after the infant had died. The criteria for the diagnosis of immaturity boiled down to small baby. The diagnosis of birth injuries reflected a difficult labour and evidence that the child was paralysed, cyanotic (blue), or unable to suck. Infections of the newborn included skin and umbilical infections.

Noteworthy is the absence of diarrhoea and pneumonia as diagnosed causes of death in the first 28 days of life. This indicates the generally good state of nutrition of the mothers and the successful establishment of breast-feeding.

Group 2 deaths are those preventable by immunization. Deaths from these causes in the first year of life were dominated by tetanus with 15 per cent of all deaths in the first year of life when the infant mortality rate was 156 deaths per 1,000 live births, with occasional incidence of measles. Measles and whooping cough were important diseases in the early years, but they caused only 4 per cent of deaths in the first year of life, 17 per cent in the second year of life when the overall death rate was 72 per 1,000, and 14 per cent in the years 1–4 when the death rate was 27.4.

Group 3 deaths were the most frequent causes of death after the first month of life. Diarrhoea dominated during the postneonatal period (i.e. mostly 6–11 months) and in the second year (i.e. mostly 12–17 months). Pneumonia was the second cause of death, but much less frequently than diarrhoea until the third year of life, when the whole death rate was only 21.3 per 1,000 as distinct from 156 in the first and 72 in the second year of life.

These observations on death rates attributable to identified causes exclude Group 4 deaths from other causes, and Group 5 deaths from unknown causes, in the numerators of proportions ascribed to all causes. The bias from these unknowns is probably towards underestimating the proportions of deaths preventable.

These observations are amplified in a series of publications by Gordon, Singh, and Wyon (1961*a,b*, 1963, and 1965) and by Singh, Gordon, and Wyon (1962) on illnesses and deaths; and on obstetric practices by Gideon (1961) and by Gordon, Gideon, and Wyon (1964, 1965*a,b,c*).

3.3.4 Determinants of long birth intervals

During the exploratory phase of the Khanna Study we took pregnancy histories. Some women claimed they had natural spacing between their births; and indeed many reported birth intervals of two or three years. If this were generally true, the crude birth rate should be relatively low. We expected an annual crude birth rate of 45 or so per 1,000 population. After five years of fieldwork we knew for sure that it was 38. We established early on that all women were breast-feeding for two years or more if the infant survived; we wondered if either long postpartum amenorrhoea (indicating little or no ovulation) or abstinence from coitus was lengthening birth intervals. A significant period of months after delivery without ovulation or coitus would imply that the birth control would only lengthen that part of a birth interval when the couple had resumed coitus and the wife was normally ovulating and therefore fertile.

The best possible answers to these considerations on the determinants of birth intervals were crucial for determining what population size and what duration of the definitive study would make possible a definitive measurement of an effect of the birth-control programme on the birth rate of the test villages. By that time we had decided to base the birth-control programme on monthly visits to couples to make sure they had good access to birth-control methods. Our questions about determinants of birth intervals made clear that we should also use the monthly home visits to record whether or not, in the past month, the woman had been lactating and had menstruated, and if not to follow her weekly until she either menstruated or proved to have ceased menstruating.

In the exploratory study the women declined to answer regular inquiries about coitus; but through retrospective histories we found that postpartum abstinence from coitus averaged about four months. Postpartum amenorrhoea was considerably longer.

As the pilot study got under way in 1955 we sought guidance on how to address these issues. We found that Robert G. Potter Jr., at the Office of Population Research at Princeton University, had been studying determinants of birth intervals. He told us that from a variety of sources—genealogies, parish records, and special field studies—it had been found that, in societies practising little or no birth control, average birth intervals range from barely more than two years to nearly three years. Lactation was believed to play a fundamental role in this large variation from group to group. For want of direct data, the relative importance of several factors contributing to the variations remained vague (Potter 1963).

Potter had been following two ideas. The first idea was the hypothesis of Henry (1961) and others that interpregnancy intervals are usefully divided into two components: the period of postpartum amenorrhoea, from delivery to the first postpartum menstruation; the other component was the menstruating interval from the first postpartum menstruation to the next conception. The second idea was that of using the life-table method as then applied to measuring survival of cancer patients. Potter recognized the potential value of this method for measuring other intervals of time starting with a defined event. The components of birth intervals were but one example.

As Potter listened to our request, he realized that we were already proposing to collect the data needed to document the lengths of birth intervals, and their components. Moreover, he thought that we would be able to observe the effect on the length of postpartum amenorrhoea when the deaths of children terminated their mother's lactation. He used the data we had in hand from observations in two villages for about ten months on length of postpartum amenorrhoea and menstruating intervals, and on the acceptance and effectiveness of birth control, to estimate the size of the population required, and the duration of the project's birth-control programme, to obtain reliable measurements of its effect on the birth rate. We implemented his suggestions to observe a test population of 8,000 persons and a scientific control of 4,000, for four years.

By 1962 all the data from the Khanna Study on postpartum amenorrhoea and menstruating intervals and deaths of children had been coded on to IBM cards and Potter could begin to direct the data analyses using his concepts and methods.

The Khanna Study provides a broad scope of prospective as well as retrospective data with completed interpregnancy histories for approximately 1,300 out of 1,800 couples. The 500 excluded from the sample for lack of data were distributed by age much like the 1,300 selected (Potter *et al.* 1965a).

Potter distinguished three types of interpregnancy intervals: Entirely Prospective Intervals begin with birth and end with conception within the period of prospective observations; Truncated Prospective intervals start with a birth of known date, but were truncated by out-migration, by death of either parent, or by the end of the study. Partly or Entirely Retrospective intervals started with a birth on a date not clearly established. This throws into doubt the measurement of the length of amenorrhoea and lactation.

Six pieces of information were available for each Entirely Prospective Interval: (1) total length; (2) length of postpartum amenorrhoea; (3) length of menstruating interval; (4) length of lactation: (5) outcome of previous delivery; (6) survival of the last child born. Corresponding data were available for prospective portions of Truncated Prospective Intervals.

The distributions of durations of postpartum amenorrhoea, menstruating intervals, and lactation from Entirely Prospective Intervals are given in Figure 3.4. These are biased to short intervals that fitted into the prospective observations. When the previous pregnancy ended in a miscarriage or stillbirth, there was no lactation and postpartum amenorrhoea was short. In such cases interpregnancy duration depended almost entirely on the length of the menstruating interval. The same was true when the infant died in the first month. Roughly one-half of all Entirely Prospective Intervals were of this type, and most were six months or shorter.

When the infant survived longer than a month, the picture changed drastically. The rates of increase of postpartum amenorrhoea and menstruating

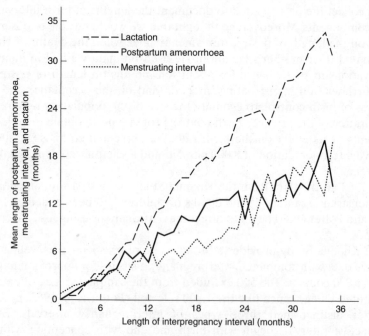

Fig. 3.4. Mean lengths of postpartum amenorrhoea, menstruating interval, and lactation, by length of interpregnancy interval, for 604 entirely prospective intervals following live birth

Source: Potter *et al.* 1965

interval as interpregnancy intervals lengthen are roughly equal. After thirty months generalization is impossible, owing to the small number of cases.

To overcome the biases of Entirely Prospective Intervals Potter combined them with Truncated Prospective Intervals using the life-table technique. The numbers of cases are now materially increased. The proportion of wives who menstruated during the first month after delivery is first calculated. Next, among those amenorrhoeic during the first month, the proportion who resumed menstruation during the second month is computed. More generally, among those amenorrhoeic during the (*n*-1)th month, the proportion who resumed menstruation in the *n*th month is calculated. A diminishing number of women contributed experience to these successive, conditional, monthly probabilities of resuming menstruation. By taking accumulative products of these probabilities, one obtains the likelihood of being in amenorrhoea during the *n*th month after delivery. The same principles apply to determining probabilities of women still lactating and not yet pregnant.

Results are clear and striking—see Figures 3.5 and 3.6. Menstruation returned promptly after delivery of a child who died soon after birth or was stillborn; one-half of the women menstruated within six weeks, and more than

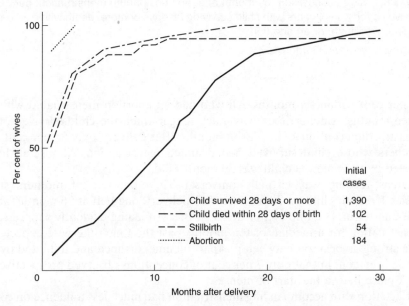

Fig. 3.5. Wives who resumed menses (terminating postpartum amenorrhoea) by month after delivery; per cent of wives aged 15–44 years with child surviving 28 days or more, death within 28 days of birth, a stillbirth, or an abortion; test and control villages 1956–1959.

Source: Wyon and Gordon 1971

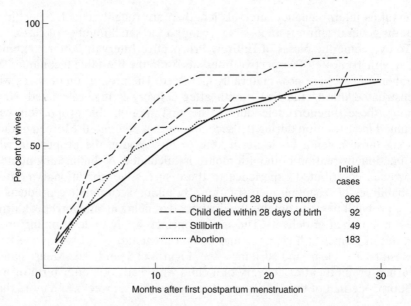

Fig. 3.6. Wives conceiving, by month after first postpartum menstruation; per cent of wives aged 15–44 years with child surviving 28 days or more, death within 28 days of birth, a stillbirth, or an abortion

Source: Wyon and Gordon 1971

80 per cent within six months. All who had an abortion menstruated within three months. Amenorrhoea was much longer when the child survived and breastfeeding continued; by eleven months after delivery, only 55 per cent of mothers whose child survived had resumed menstruation. Almost all had started by the time the child was 30 months old.

Breast-feeding was virtually universal. Three-quarters of mothers still breast-fed their children 20 months after delivery, one-half at 26 months, and one-quarter at 33 months after delivery. Breast-feeding evidently suppressed menstruation for a median of ten months past the time otherwise expected. The strong association between postpartum amenorrhoea and inhibited ovulation is evident in that only 7 per cent of conceptions observed prospectively took place before the start of menses.

Lactation with accompanying menstruation had much less influence on conception. Figure 3.6 presents data on menstruating intervals from the same four groups of wives as Figure 3.5. Differences are small. Women whose live-born child died during the neonatal period conceived more promptly than any other group, although the small number (92) of deaths precludes statistical significance.

Age of wife influenced lactation, interpregnancy, and menstruating intervals.

Wives whose child survived at least one month were grouped into those above and below 30 years. A year after delivery 8 per cent of the older group and 13 per cent of the younger group were pregnant and had stopped breast-feeding. Also, by a year after delivery 62 per cent of the younger group but only 47 per cent of the older group had started menstruating. Once menstruation had resumed, wives of both groups conceived at about the same rate for the next six months. Thereafter the older group lagged. The mean menstruating interval was ten months for the younger group and thirteen months for the older. While use of birth control, including infrequent coitus or unreported induced abortion, could explain longer menstruating intervals, it would have had little effect on length of postpartum amenorrhoea. Contraceptive practice was in fact associated with longer menstruating intervals, especially among those over 30 years. Evidence on postpartum abstinence from coitus was difficult to elicit; two small surveys suggested abstinence from two to five months.

Two technical advances provided unique information on birth intervals. One advance was the field method of monthly home visits at which staff collected data on deliveries, lactation, menstruations, birth-control practices, and survival of the latest birth; the other was to apply the life-table method to analysis of these prospective data on the determinants of birth intervals.

In this experience live birth intervals averaged thirty-one months. Breast-feeding was universal and often extended well into pregnancy. Under the influence of lactation, amenorrhoea extended to a median of eleven months. Together with menstruating intervals of a median of ten months after resumption of menses and nine months for pregnancy, these findings accounted for the observed mean birth intervals of thirty-one months, along with an allowance of about two months for pregnancy wastage (Potter *et al.* 1965*b*).

3.4 Conclusions

The Khanna Study supplied the first data from developing countries clearly identifying:

- diarrhoea and pneumonia as the major immediate causes of death in the first 2 or 3 years of life;
- a clear relation between non-supplementation with solid food (cereals and lentils) of breast-fed children above 6 months of age and increased mortality; this indicates that breast-fed children beyond 6 months of age who do not receive supplementary calories burn up the protein in breast milk to supply the calories; this observation is intuitively contrary to the equally clear observation that mothers are aware that, by supplying solid food, their child is likely to have more diarrhoea;

- the concept of *weanling diarrhoea* (Gordon, Chitkara, and Wyon 1963);
- tetanus of the newborn as an easily diagnosed, but often missed, major cause of death;
- diseases for which immunization procedures are available as a cause of less than 20 per cent of all under-5-year deaths;
- the clear sex preference for males, issuing into the high death rates for females, particularly in early childhood;
- long breast-feeding, extending birth intervals by about ten months;
- a strong effect on the birth rate from delayed marriage of women.

These observations provide clear and easily testable hypotheses on the most important determinants of preventable deaths at other places and times. Many of them have now proved to have broad applications among poor societies. They constitute foundations for major parts of the child survival policies of UNICEF, USAID, etc., widely adopted in developed countries, but very rarely with acknowledgement of their original source.

The Khanna Study also provided the first demonstration in the public-health field of the power of longitudinal observations of events through regular home visits to all members of defined communities, and of valuable results by applying cohort and life-table techniques of data analysis.

The ecological approach encouraged a search for determinants of findings in physical, biological, and behavioural features of the village communities and their environment.

These results from the Khanna Study provided an important foundation for subsequent practices of longitudinal community health research and practice. Examples are the work of Scrimshaw and Guzmán (Chapter 6, this volume), Kielman *et al.* (1983), Taylor and de Sweemer (Chapter 5, this volume), at Narangwal in India; the Berggrens (Chapter 7, this volume), in Haiti and elsewhere; Aziz and Mosley (Chapter 2, this volume), at the International Center for Diarrhoeal Disease Research, Bangladesh; and Ofoso-Amaah and Neumann (1979) at the Danfa Project in Ghana. The Andean Rural Health Care Programme in Bolivia is now applying the principles to primary health-care programmes (Perry and Sandavold 1993).

We have a few regrets about the study. One is that we did not weigh and measure children from birth to 5 years to follow their growth and development. By way of explanation: we felt that the process might interfere with the primary purpose of the project, to test the effect of birth control on birth rates; also, the techniques of field anthropometry were still in their infancy. Secondly, the extended time from seven years in the field to ten years of analysis, interpreting and reporting the data, discouraged applications of the findings in India and elsewhere. Thirdly, our inability to arrange for data-processing, analysis, and interpretation to be carried out in India further inhibited interest on the part of the Health Ministries and academics in India.

References

Aziz, K. M. A., and Mosley W. H. (1997), 'The History, Methodology and Main Findings of the Matlab Project in Bangladesh', in M. Das Gupta et al. (eds.), *Prospective Community Studies in Developing Countries*, OUP, Oxford.

Berggren, G., and Berggren, W. (1997), 'Longitudinal Community Health Care for Equity and Accountability in Primary Health Care in Haiti,' in M. Das Gupta et al. (eds.), *Prospective Community Studies in Developing Countries*, OUP, Oxford.

Chavez, A., and Martinez, C. (1982), *Growing up in a Developing Country. A Bioecologic Study of the Development of Children from Poor Peasant Families in Mexico*, Institute of Nutrition of Central America and Panama, originally published as *Nutricion y Desarollo Infantil* by Nueva Editorial Interamericana S.A. de C.V., Mexico, 1979.

Gideon, H. (1961), 'A Baby is Born in the Punjab', *American Anthropologist*, 64: 1220–34.

Das Gupta, M. (1987), 'Selective Discrimination against Female Children in Rural Punjab, India', *Population and Development Review*, 13: 77–100.

Gordon, J. E. (1948), 'The Strategic and Tactical Influence of Disease, World War II', *American Journal of Medical Science*, 215: 311–26.

——and Babbott, Jr., F. L. (1959), 'Acute Intestinal Infection in Alaska', *Public Health Reports*, 74(1): 49–54.

——Chitkara, I. D., and Wyon, J. B. (1963), 'Weanling Diarrhea', *American Journal of Medical Science*, 245: 345–77.

——Gideon, H., and Wyon, J. B. (1964), 'Childbirth in Rural Punjab, India', *American Journal of Medical Science*, 247: 3424–62.

————(1965*a*), 'Complications of Childbirth and Illnesses during the Puerperium in 862 Punjab Village Women: A Field Study', *Journal of Obstetrics and Gynaecology (India)*, 15: 159–67.

————(1965*b*), 'Midwifery Practices in Rural Punjab, India', *American Journal of Obstetrics and Gynaecology*, 93: 734–42.

————(1965*c*), 'A Field Study of Illnesses during Pregnancy, their Management and Prenatal Care in Punjab Villages', *Indian Pediatrics*, 2: 330–5.

——Ingalls, T. H., and Wyon, J. B. (1954), 'Public Health as a Demographic Influence', *American Journal of Medical Science*, 227: 326–57.

——Singh, S., and Wyon, J. B. (1961*a*), 'A Field Study of Deaths and Causes of Deaths in Rural Populations of the Punjab, India', *American Journal of Medical Science*, 241: 359–82.

————(1961*b*), 'Death Rates and Causes of Death in Punjab Villages', *Indian Journal of Medical Research*, 49: 568–94.

————(1963), 'Demographic Characteristics of Deaths in Eleven Punjab Villages', *Indian Journal of Medical Research*, 51: 304–12.

————(1965), 'Causes of Death at Different Ages, by Sex, and by Season, in a Rural Population of the Punjab, 1957–1959, a Field Study', *Indian Journal of Medical Research*, 53: 906–17.

——Wyon, J. B., and Ascoli, W. (1967), 'The Second Year Death Rate in Less Developed Countries', *American Journal of Medical Science*, 254(3): 357–80.

Henry, L. (1961), 'La Fécondité naturelle: Observation-théorie-résultats', *Population*, 16: 633–4.

80   *Wyon*

Kielman, A. A., Taylor, C. E., DeSweemer, C., Parker, R. L., Chernichovsky, D., Reinke, W. A., Uberoi, I. S., Kakar, D. N., Masih, N., and Sharma, R. S. S. (1983), *The Narangwal Experiment*: i. *Integrated Nutrition and Health Care*; and ii. *Malnutrition, Infection, Growth and Development: The Narangwal Experience*, Johns Hopkins University Press for the World Bank, Baltimore.

Ofoso-Amaah, S., and Neumann, A. K. (1979), *The Danfa Project*, University of Ghana Medical School, Dept. of Community Health and UCLA School of Public Health, Division of Population, Family and International Health, Los Angeles, Calif.

Perry, H., and Sandavold, I. (1993), 'Routine systematic home visitation as a strategy for improving access to services and program effectiveness: lessons from Bolivia and the US', in R. Morgan and R. Raus (eds.), *Global Learning for Health*, National Council for International Health, Washington, pp. 175–85.

Potter, R. G. (1963), 'Birth Intervals: Structure and Change', *Population Studies*, 17: 160–2.

Potter, R. G., Jr., New, M. L., Wyon, J. B., and Gordon, J. E. (1965a), 'Applications of Field Studies to Research on the Physiology of Human Reproduction: Lactation and its Effects upon Birth Intervals in Eleven Punjab Villages, India', in M. C. Sheps and J. C. Ridley (eds.), *Public Health and Population Change*, University of Pittsburgh Press, Pittsburgh.

——Wyon, J. B., Parker, N., and Gordon, J. E. (1965b), 'A Case Study of Birth Interval Dynamics', *Population Studies*, 19: 81–96.

Scrimshaw, N. S., and Guzmán, M. (1997), 'A Comparison of Supplementary Feeding and Medical Care of Preschool Children in Guatemala, 1959–64', in M. Das Gupta et al. (eds.), *Prospective Community Studies in Developing Countries*, OUP, Oxford.

——Taylor, C. E., and Gordon, J. E. (1959), 'Interactions of Nutrition and Infection', *American Journal of Medical Science*, 237(3): 367–403.

—————(1968), *Interactions of Nutrition and Infection*, World Health Monograph Series 57, World Health Organization, Geneva.

——Behar, M., Guzmán, M. A., and Gordon, J. E. (1969), 'Nutrition and Infection Field Study in Guatemalan Villages 1959–1964. IX. An Evaluation of Medical, Social and Public Health Benefits, with Suggestions for Future Field Study', *Archives of Environmental Health*, 18: 216–34.

Singh, S., Gordon, J. E., and Wyon, J. B. (1962), 'Medical Care in Fatal Illnesses of a Rural Punjab Population: Some Social, Biological and Cultural Factors and their Ecological Implications', *Indian Journal of Medical Research*, 50: 865–80.

Taylor, C. E., and Gordon, J. E. (1953), 'Synergism and Antagonism in Mass Disease in Man', *American Journal of Medical Science*, 225: 320–44.

Wyon, J. B., and Gordon, J. E. (1971), *The Khanna Study: Population Problems in the Rural Punjab*, Harvard University Press, Cambridge, Mass.

4 Methodology and Main Findings on Child Survival of the Khanna Restudy, 1984–1988

MONICA DAS GUPTA

4.1 Background and Objectives of the Study

This chapter describes the restudy carried out in the eleven villages of Ludhiana District of Punjab State, India, which were originally studied in the Khanna Study by John Gordon and John Wyon in the 1950s (see preceding chapter). The main objective of this restudy was to study the demographic transition taking place in this society, with a focus on the interrelationships between social and demographic change in this society in the process of transition. Thus this study is more rooted in the social sciences than in epidemiology and the medical sciences, as are most of the other major longitudinal studies conducted in developing countries.

India is in the midst of its demographic transition, with overall levels of fertility and mortality rates falling steadily. There are significant regional differences in this process, however, with Northern and Central India lagging far behind the rest of the country in terms of pace of the decline. The position of Punjab as an island of early demographic transition in this region makes it especially important to study from the point of view of learning what might be done to accelerate the transition in the rest of the region.

Punjab is thus intrinsically an interesting location to study. There are also practical reasons which make it a particularly good setting for such a study. First, there is the unusual situation of having a detailed demographic baseline against which to measure subsequent changes, over the long gap of thirty years between the 1950s and the 1980s. Secondly, my own experience of conducting a study of social and demographic processes in a village in the neighbouring region of Haryana made for an easy understanding of the society and previous experience of how to conduct both qualitative and survey-based fieldwork in this region. Punjab and Haryana have a great deal in common both culturally and economically, and indeed were separated administratively only as recently as 1966.

With a tentative plan for a restudy in mind, I asked John Wyon how he felt about such a study. His response was very encouraging. He said that John Gordon was no longer alive, that he himself had no plans to conduct any further research in Khanna, and that having read my previous work he felt very enthusiastic about the prospect of my doing a restudy of these villages. Throughout the study he has provided a great deal of support in many ways.

The study was conducted by the National Council of Applied Economic Research, New Delhi, and funded by the International Development Research Centre, Canada. The support of both these institutions was critical for the study. Unlike the other studies in this volume, most of which were run out of major developed country academic institutions, this study was developed and run entirely in a developing country.

4.2 Data Collection in the 1984–8 Restudy

Although the objectives of this study were quite different from those of the original 1950's study, the framework of the data-collection process had much in common. As in the original study, there was an initial baseline study, followed by three and a half years of prospective study of births and deaths, and ending with a final census.

The details of the data collection were, of course, quite different, as would be expected given the different disciplinary backgrounds and preoccupations of the principal researchers involved in the two studies. John Gordon was an epidemiologist, and John Wyon a medical doctor. The main objective of their study was to test epidemiological methods in the design and implementation of family-planning programmes. Their own research interests led them to study health issues, in which they made some pathbreaking contributions to the understanding of the factors underlying the high child mortality rates then prevailing in many developing countries. I am a social anthropologist and demographer by training, and therefore focus more on the social and behavioural factors associated with demographic processes.

The restudy consisted of both survey-based as well as qualitative data collection. The qualitative data collection was essentially anthropological in nature, involving participant observation, and structured as well as unstructured conversations with people in the study villages. The quantitative data collection is simpler to describe in exact terms, and was as follows:

1. Mapping and listing of all the households in the study villages. These households were matched with those of the 1950's study. As is commonly found in restudies in rural India, we found that almost all households were still present. There was considerable out-migration of individual men from the households, sometimes accompanied by their wives and children, but the others in the original family were still present in the village.

2. A complete census was taken of the households, including details of individuals' occupation and information on the household's ownership of land, cattle, and other major assets. This information was used to construct an estimate of household income, based on estimated agricultural and non-

agricultural income. The total population of the study villages was above 18,000 people.

3. A complete pregnancy history was collected on all women aged 15–59 (around 3,250 women).

4. This was followed by a prospective study of pregnancies, births, and child deaths of women who were recorded in the maternity history as being currently married, and neither sterilized nor menopausal (around 1,800 women). These women were visited once a month during the prospective study, i.e. for approximately three and a half years.

5. During the prospective study period, several smaller studies were also carried out in a random sample of households from six of the study villages. These included studies of morbidity, income and consumption, the intra-household allocation of food and other resources, and old-age support.

6. At the end of the prospective study, a final census was carried out of all the households in the study villages, including information on births, deaths, and migration during the intercensal period 1984–8.

The design of the questionnaires benefited from several kinds of input. My own previous experience with designing questionnaires and canvassing them in Haryana provided the basic framework and approach to the questionnaire design. An important professional input came from my colleagues at the National Council of Applied Economic Research, who have enormous experience of conducting large-scale surveys. Important inputs also came from others with experience of field studies, notably Lincoln Chen, who had conducted prospective demographic studies in Matlab, Bangladesh, and Shireen Jejeebhoy, who had done a field study in Maharashtra. A different, but extremely important, kind of input was provided by the field staff and the respondents during the pre-testing of the questionnaires. After the pre-test, they gave their comments on the questionnaire and suggestions for improving the design of specific questions or the flow of the questions.

4.3 The Conduct of the Field Study

A field office was opened in the town of Khanna, which has easy access to the study villages, and after which the original study was named. For most of the study's duration, this was a buffalo-shed, consisting of a brick construction of two rooms and a covered open space in front, surrounded by a vegetable field. Punjab being as developed as it is, this buffalo-shed had an electric connection, so it was possible to install fans and to work quite comfortably with plenty of fresh air and open space around. Towards the end of the study, with questionnaires piling up all around us, the office was moved to the larger space of a house in Khanna. The field office was headed throughout by B. L. Joshi of the National Council of Applied Economic Research.

The field staff were all recruited locally. They were mostly from the surrounding villages or from Khanna itself, and were therefore very familiar with the kind of rural households they would interview. Since levels of education are high in Punjab but employment opportunities are limited, it was possible to choose amongst many highly educated candidates in recruiting the field staff. Most of the fieldwork was conducted by women field staff. At the beginning, we recruited men as well as women, but found that the men had a tendency to be aggressive and abrupt in their interviewing technique, and had difficulty absorbing the concept of building a long-term friendly relationship with the respondents which is essential for any study involving repeated visits to households over a long period of time. The women had excellent interpersonal skills, and took much pride in doing their work meticulously. Women field staff also have the flexibility of being able to interview women to collect information, including information on personal matters, as well as interview men to collect economic and other information.

As already mentioned, the field interviewers were involved in the final stages of questionnaire design. In addition to the help in terms of improving the questionnaire, this also meant that they thoroughly understood the logic and objectives of the questionnaire. The process of training the interviewers began with going over the questionnaire to be canvassed, discussing each question thoroughly. This was followed by trying to canvass the questionnaire with each other. When they felt confident with it, they tried it out on respondents from villages not falling within the study. This was done until they were fluent in asking and recording the answers for a given questionnaire. If a particular field interviewer made mistakes or showed other signs of difficulty in collecting data, she was retrained until she could work confidently again.

The women went in pairs to do their interviews. This had several advantages. First, it made the women feel more secure in entering households. Besides, it greatly reduced the stress of starting off and carrying out the interview, because there were two minds at work. One woman would keep up a smooth flow of conversation with the respondent, asking the questions as she went. This made the interview situation much more pleasant for the respondent, whose train of thought is otherwise interrupted by having to wait for the interviewer to record the answer. The other interviewer could concentrate on recording the answer correctly, using the correct codes (we used precoded questionnaires as far as possible). Focusing on the recording alone, she was also able to detect inconsistencies in some of the answers and ask for clarification.

At the end of the day, the questionnaires were handed over to the staff in the Khanna office, who checked them manually within the next day or two for inconsistencies. Any inconsistencies or missing information found were sent back to the field to be corrected. After this the data were entered on the computer and given a final cleaning. By this stage, most of the inconsistencies found were in data entry rather than in data collection. The emphasis throughout was on making the respondent correct inconsistencies in the data rather than our making arbitrary judgements at the data-editing stage.

The field staff came to the field office in the morning, from where they were taken to the study villages by taxi, and dropped back every evening. This made it easy for them to form pairs for their work, and ensured that they arrived fresh without having spent much of their energy simply on reaching the field site. The quality and speed of data collection were much enhanced by this. The number of field staff varied according to the volume of work at different phases of the study. At the peak, thirty-six field staff were engaged in data collection and editing.

The people in the study villages were also extremely helpful to the staff. In each village, households took turns in offering their premises for the field staff to rest during the day, make some tea for themselves, and eat the lunch they had brought along. People were also extremely co-operative in responding to the questionnaires through the long years of the study, keeping the levels of non-response very low. This was, of course, a tribute to the interpersonal skills of the field staff. It was also due to the villagers' long experience of being surveyed and the benefits of being surveyed. They are routinely surveyed for various purposes: by staff from the Education Department trying to track the school-going population, by the national census-takers, by the Health Department workers looking for cases of malaria, etc. They are quite aware that co-operation in a survey is voluntary. Their long experience with development initiatives and with being surveyed has also made them aware that surveys are beneficial to them in a general long-term sense, without necessarily offering an immediate benefit. These conditions make data collection far simpler and also less ethically complicated than in less advantaged settings.

The ethical problems of studying health issues without providing health care were also substantially reduced by the fact that free public-health facilities as well as private facilities are well within geographical and economic reach of the population. We offered some help with transportation if required and distributed analgesics and other simple medicines. We were not in a position to offer direct medical care, since no medical personnel were on the staff of the project. Biomedical scientists were consulted at the time of preparing the questionnaires and during the analysis, but were not directly involved in the project as the study focused on the behavioural rather than the purely biomedical aspects of fertility and mortality.

The co-operation of the people in the study villages made not only for low levels of non-response, but also for high quality of data collection. Inaccuracies of response were reduced by willingness to participate in the study. Another very important factor was the repetition of questions in the prospective survey. After only a short exposure to prospective data collection, respondents became able to answer our questions with dramatically reduced need for probing and cross-checking, because they became familiar with the kinds of questions asked.

The local authorities were also very co-operative. Much of the study took place during the most difficult years of political upheaval in Punjab. Heavy security was imposed on the roads and at the airport, and the trains had the mail vans placed in front to minimize human casualties if the line was blown up and the train derailed. Ludhiana District was one of the quieter districts, but nevertheless curfews were imposed for long stretches of time. We were given permission to travel during the curfew so that the study could continue uninterrupted.

4.4 Main Findings on Child Survival

The study focused on both fertility and mortality. Since the thrust of this volume is on health and mortality, only the main results of the analysis of mortality are discussed here. The analysis of fertility behaviour and of nutritional status are presented elsewhere (Das Gupta 1994, 1995a,b). The main new findings with regard to child survival coming out of this study so far relate to two issues: the concentration of excess female child mortality on girls of higher birth order, and the tendency for child deaths to cluster disproportionately amongst a small proportion of families.

For analysing child mortality, we relied heavily on the retrospective data collection. As described below, the prospective data yielded important results which could not have been collected retrospectively. However, given the low fertility and mortality rates prevalent in Punjab in the 1980s, there was a total of only 1,520 births during the entire prospective study period and a correspondingly low number of child deaths. Thus, whenever the analysis required the data to be disaggregated by age of mother and other characteristics, we used the much larger number of observations in the retrospective data set to obtain the required sample size. This problem would not arise in settings which were less advanced in the demographic transition.

4.4.1 Parity and excess female child mortality

Parents have two separate sets of goals with regard to child-bearing: one relates to the total number of children desired, while the other relates to the desired sex composition of children. Given the strong son preference in this society, this makes for greater unwantedness of higher-birth-order daughters, who are produced when parents are trying to fulfil their targeted number of sons.

Strong son preference is reflected in women's statements about the number of children of each sex that they would like to have. On average, younger women in the study villages would like to have less than two sons and half a daughter each. Educated women would like to have fewer children of each sex.

Table 4.1. Infant and child mortality rates (deaths per 1,000 live births) by age at death, Khanna 1965–84, Khanna 1957–9, and Matlab Thana, Bangladesh, 1974–7

	Age at death (months)[a]					
	<1	1–11	0–11	12–23	24–59	0–59
Khanna, 1965–84						
Males	50.7	27.1	77.7	9.4	8.2	95.3
Females	43.0	51.3	94.3	18.5	12.6	125.4
Total	47.0	38.6	85.6	13.8	10.3	109.6
Male/female	1.18	0.53	0.82	0.51	0.65	0.76[b]
Khanna, 1957–59[c]						
Total	73.5	82.7	156.2	72.2[d]		
Male/female			0.86	0.44[d]		
Matlab Thana, 1974–77[e]						
Total	73.0	58.2	131.2			
Male/female	1.16	0.82	1.00			

[a] Female mortality is probably higher than estimated here, because the sex ratio at birth indicates that female live births are underreported by approximately 5%. Many of these females are likely to have died, perhaps at early ages.
[b] The male/female ratio in the 0–4 year mortality rate in Khanna, 1965–84, is similar to that for Punjab State, 1971–5 and 1975–80 (Dyson 1987).
[c] From Gordon *et al.* 1965.
[d] Rate calculated per 1,000 population in that age-group.
[e] Matlab Project, Matlab Thana, Bangladesh; see D'Souza and Chen 1980.

Source: Das Gupta 1987.

An examination of differences in neonatal and postneonatal mortality by sex clearly reveals that behavioural factors raise the mortality rates of female children. During the neonatal period, when biological factors predominate amongst the causes of death, male mortality is higher than female mortality (Table 4.1). After the first month of life, environmental and care-related factors that are susceptible to societal manipulation come into play. Between 1 and 23 months, when a large proportion of total childhood deaths takes place, female mortality is nearly twice that of males. Results from the Matlab Study in Bangladesh (D'Souza and Chen 1980) show a similar male/female ratio of neonatal mortality, but in postneonatal mortality the excess mortality of girls is lower than in Punjab.

The excess female child mortality is in fact concentrated amongst a small subset of female children. This is revealed in sharper focus when sex differentials in child mortality are analysed by the number of living children of that sex at the time of birth of the indexed child (Figure 4.1). A greatly mitigated version of this effect can also be seen amongst boys. The data show that boys

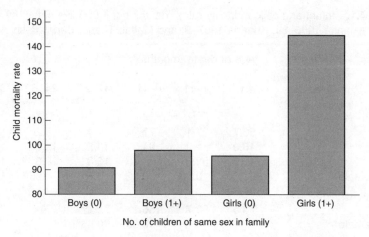

Fig. 4.1. Sex differentials in child mortality by parity, rural Punjab (women aged 15–59)

Source: Based on Das Gupta 1987, table 4

born when the mother already has one or more surviving sons have slightly higher child mortality than boys born to mothers with no surviving sons. Girls born to mothers with no surviving children have child mortality rates that fall between the two rates for the boys. However, there is a sudden jump in the mortality of girls born to mothers who already have one or more surviving daughters. This subset of girls experiences 53 per cent higher mortality than the other children combined. This clearly indicates that neglect is applied selectively amongst female children. The extent of conscious and voluntary behaviour required to do this is far greater than would necessarily be involved in a generalized discrimination against females.

It appears that, as fertility declines, the trend is for the gap in mortality between higher-birth-order girls and their other siblings to increase. Fertility is lower amongst younger cohorts of women than older ones, and lower amongst educated women than uneducated ones. This is clearly reflected in sharpened mortality of higher-birth-order girls as compared with their other siblings. Amongst older women (aged 30–59), this subset of daughters has 45 per cent higher mortality than their siblings, a gap which increases to 71 per cent amongst the children of younger women. Uneducated women have approximately 32 per cent higher mortality for this subset of daughters than for their other children, while for educated women the mortality of these girls is about 136 per cent higher than that of their other siblings. A remarkable feature of this table is that, while there has been substantial decline in the child mortality experienced by younger and more educated women, this benefit is experienced only by sons and by firstborn daughters: the mortality level of higher-birth-order daughters remains almost unchanged. Through a better

Table 4.2. Male/female ratios of expenditure on children's clothing and medicine, by age of child and by landownership status, Khanna, 1984–5

Item	No. of observations[a]	Clothing	Medicine
Age of child (years)			
0 (0–1)[b]	321	1.38	2.34
1–4	1,270	1.37	0.93
0–4	1,591	1.36	1.21
Landownership status[c]			
Landless	985	1.58	1.55
Landed	606	1.34	1.10

Note: The ratios were obtained by dividing the amount spent on boys by the amount spent on girls.

[a] Since each household was visited six times, the average number of children observed would be about one-sixth of the number of observations given here.

[b] The age group '0' includes some observations of children aged 12–23 months, because data were collected every 2 months over a 12-month period. Therefore children aged '0' (i.e. 0–11 months) at the beginning of this study were aged 12–23 months at the end of the study. Children born during the study were included as age '0'.

[c] For children aged 0–4 years combined.

Source: Das Gupta 1987.

ability to manipulate both their fertility and their children's survival, younger women and educated women are better equipped than others to achieve the family size and sex composition that they desire.

These results suggest that it may be difficult to detect what particular forms of 'neglect' lead to this excess mortality, because neglect resulting in death is applied highly selectively to a subgroup of girls. It is perfectly possible that, even within this subgroup of girls, only a limited proportion is subject to such neglect. In principle, it would be possible to achieve an imbalanced sex ratio by denying one crucial input such as health care once only to a small proportion of girls in the total population.

Despite measurement difficulties, this study did find evidence of differential care of boys and girls. The data on medical care show that more than twice as much was spent on boys than on girls in their first year of life (Table 4.2). It is possible that this ratio is somewhat exaggerated by random differences in illness encountered, but the magnitude of the gap suggests a large difference between boys and girls in this sphere.

The data on the allocation of food (Table 4.3) show that, although infant boys and girls are roughly similar in caloric intake, girls are given more cereals while boys are given more milk and fats with their cereal. It is not clear that

Table 4.3. Male/female ratios of food consumption per child, Khanna, 1984–5

Age of child (years)	No. of observations[a]	Cereals	Milk	Fats	Sugars	Total calories
Male/female ratios based on total children in the sample[b]						
0 (0–1)[c]	270	0.76	1.09	1.22	0.98	0.95
1–4	1,115	1.06	1.05	1.09	1.03	1.05
0–4	1,385	1.01	1.05	1.07	1.01	1.02
Male/female ratios based on chidren who had all meals at home on the days of observation						
0 (0–1)[c]	261	0.75	1.07	1.07	0.97	0.94
1–4	1,086	1.06	1.04	1.10	1.03	1.05
0–4	1,347	1.01	1.04	1.07	1.01	1.02
Male/female ratios of food consumed at home, by children who ate partly at home and partly outside the home on the days of observation						
0–1	9	0.76	2.69	7.00	1.11	4.82
0–4	38	0.95	1.77	1.24	1.11	1.22
Male/female ratios by landownership of household, based on children who had all meals at home on the days of observation						
Landless[d]	885	1.00	1.07	1.19	0.99	1.02
Landed[d]	462	1.04	1.06	1.03	1.07	1.06

[a] See note [a] to Table 4.6.
[b] Including 38 children who ate partly outside the home on the days of observation.
[c] See note [b] to Table 4.6.
[d] For children aged 0–4 years combined.

Source: Das Gupta 1987.

this would necessarily cause much excess female mortality, but it is certainly the case that milk and fats are the highly valued (and high-cost) foods of this society, apart from their high nutritional quality. On days when children ate partly at home and partly away, it seems that greater efforts were made to ensure that boys got their usual amount of milk and fats within the house even if they are away for some of the day, while girls were allowed to go without. Once again, this is more suggestive of differential care than suggestive of a factor likely to result in differential mortality.

This study suggests that relative female deprivation in medical care may be more important than that in nutrition in accounting for sex differentials in mortality. This seems to be suggested also by other studies in South Asia showing similar results. Both the original Khanna Study (Wyon and Gordon 1971) and the Matlab data from Bangladesh (Chen *et al.* 1981) show more pronounced sex differentials in medical care than in nutrition.

Table 4.4. Distribution of child deaths amongst women aged 40–9; using the binomial model

		No. of deaths			
		0	1	2	3+
% of mothers:	Observed	62.54	21.53	9.74	6.19
	Expected	52.63	34.24	10.65	2.48
	O-E	9.91	−12.71	−0.91	3.71
% of deaths:	Observed	—	33.95	30.70	35.35
	Expected	—	54.05	33.63	12.32
	O-E	—	−20.10	−2.93	23.03

Note: (chi-square = 170.2655; $p < 0.0000$).

Source: Das Gupta 1996*c*.

4.4.2 Child death-clustering

There is very strong evidence that child deaths tend to 'cluster' in families. Amongst women at the end of their reproductive life—that is, aged 40–9—63 per cent experienced no child deaths, and 16 per cent of the women experienced multiple child loss and accounted for 66 per cent of all child deaths (Table 4.4). Comparing this to the expected distribution of deaths if they were randomly distributed according to the binomial model, we find that the negative deviance is concentrated amongst those with three or more child deaths. Less than 4 per cent of women fall into this category than would be expected in a binomial distribution, and they account for 23 per cent of total child deaths. Thus nearly a quarter of child deaths are attributable to being born into a 'high-risk' family. Tables 4.5 and 4.6 show that, at all stages of childhood, the probability of a child's dying is significantly increased if the child has siblings who died in childhood.[1]

We tested for 'death-clustering' in analysing child mortality because, in an anthropological study preceding this larger-scale study, the author noticed that deaths tended to cluster in some families. It was also apparent from extensive participant observation that the women who had experienced multiple child deaths were often also less resourceful and organized in caring for their currently living children and in running the household. Moreover, they were far less able than other women to describe the circumstances and the causes of their children's deaths. This suggested that they were poor at making effective

---

[1] This finding would not be surprising to medical practitioners, who view a previous history of child loss as a high-risk factor, just as they do with a previous history of other medical factors. However, this clustering is not common knowledge amongst social scientists.

Table 4.5. Maximum likelihood estimates of the logit model of child death at various ages, Khanna 1984

	Age at death (months)											
	(1) 0		(2) 1–11		(3) 12–59		(4) 0–11		(5) 0–59		(6) 0–59	
Explanatory variable	Coeff.	t-value	Coeff.	t-value	Coeff.	t-value	Coeff.	t-value	Coeff.	t-value	Coeff.	t-value
Child has siblings who died below age 5	0.375	3.407**	−0.169	1.254	0.150	1.985*	0.206	1.662*	0.216	2.986**		
Child-care factors												
Rehydration in case of diarrhoea	−0.642	3.874**	−0.380	2.142*	−0.249	1.978*	−0.621	3.926**	−0.504	4.232**		
BCG immunization			−1.524	7.166**	−0.454	5.742**	−1.992	10.189**	−1.405	16.006**		
Prenatal tetanus immunization	−0.187	1.670*	−0.149	1.381	−0.059	0.732	−0.177	1.871*	−0.014	0.169		
Mother's education and autonomy												
Mother's years of schooling	0.007	0.312	−0.001	0.057	−0.029	1.292	0.018	0.997	0.013	0.918	−0.023	2.177*
Husband decides what to cook	0.160	0.599	0.317	1.391	0.184	0.744	0.284	1.091	0.506	2.661**	0.494	3.057**
Sanitation and hygiene												
Mother does not always use soap after toilet	0.044	0.334	0.014	0.134	0.165	2.241*	−0.041	0.382	0.008	0.116	−0.304	0.626
Open source of drinking-water	0.323	1.400	−0.310	0.848	0.140	0.822	0.191	0.936	0.087	0.495	0.021	0.174
Toddlers use toilet	−0.630	1.621	−0.284	0.744	−0.626	1.217	−0.509	1.457	−0.091	0.498	−0.013	0.113

	(1)		(2)		(3)		(4)		(5)		(6)	
	coef.	t	coef.	t	coef.	t	coef.	t	coef.	t	coef.	t
Biological factors												
Preceding birth interval less than 18 months	0.167	1.070	0.256	1.993*	0.109	1.245	0.192	1.462	0.217	2.405**	0.265	3.564**
Succeeding birth interval less than 18 months			0.371	2.979**	0.221	2.234*	0.647	6.356**	0.601	7.647**	0.667	9.705**
Household social and economic status												
High caste	−0.156	1.023	0.096	0.609	−0.223	2.428**	−0.004	0.030	−0.098	1.072	−0.204	3.023**
Income per head	0.312	3.155**	0.155	1.721	0.103	2.153*	0.246	2.998**	0.054	1.737	0.054	2.305*
Size of landholding	−0.000	0.926	−0.001	1.555	−0.000	0.381	−0.000	1.067	0.000	0.475	0.000	0.030
Television owned (media exposure)	−0.707	1.346	0.310	1.136	0.070	0.332	−0.035	0.103	−0.007	0.031	0.025	0.185
Child is female	−0.094	0.740	0.306	2.937**	0.405	4.627**	0.037	0.351	0.114	1.722*	0.139	2.672**
Constant	−3.278	4.188	−2.214	3.087	−2.228	6.119	−2.161	3.303	−0.651	2.434	−1.603	8.660
N	2,920		2,920		2,924		2,920		2,924		2,924	
$\log_e (H)$	−468.326		−341.028		−413.146		−548.294		−826.902		−1,041.423	

Notes: This is based on children born before the survey in 1984. Columns (1), (2), and (4) are based on children born 1–7 years before the survey, and Columns (3), (5), and (6) are based on children born 5–11 years before the survey.

[a] The coefficients for this variable are very small, because the variable is defined in very small units.

* Significant at 5% level; ** significant at 1% level.

The one-way test was used on all the variables except income per head and land.

Source: Das Gupta 1990.

Table 4.6. Maximum likelihood estimates of the logit model of child death at various ages, Khanna 1984–7

	Age at death (months)					
	(1) 0		(2) 1–11		(3) 0–11	
Explanatory variable	Coeff.	t value	Coeff.	t value	Coeff.	t value
Child has siblings who died below age 5	0.052	0.415	0.380	4.124**	0.249	1.942*
Child-care factors						
Rehydration in case of diarrhoea	−0.056	0.171	−0.349	1.445	−0.212	0.813
Child is bottle-fed	−1.423	5.765**	0.461	2.629**	−0.746	3.828**
Boiled water during first month	−0.792	1.908**	0.126	1.311	−0.139	0.777
Physician/nurse attended delivery	−0.189	1.488	−0.077	0.884	−0.123	1.441
Mother's education and autonomy						
Mother's years of schooling	−0.037	1.849*	0.052	3.792**	−0.047	3.012**
Husband decides what to cook	−1.857	0.965	0.193	0.752	−0.168	0.548
Delivery in husband's home	0.244	1.773*	0.144	1.231	0.205	2.029*
Sanitation and hygiene						
Delivery in husband's home	0.244	1.773*	0.144	1.231	0.205	2.029*
Baby's first wraps clean	−0.085	0.271	−2.211	0.930	−0.169	0.584
Biological factors						
Inadequate breast-milk during first month of life	2.027	8.153**	0.358	2.374**	1.505	7.400**
Low birth weight	0.782	2.967**	0.452	1.982*	0.674	3.808**
Duration of labour less than 18 hours	−0.390	2.323*	0.646	0.555	−0.021	0.160
Household social and economic status						
Income per head	−0.057	1.104	−0.082	1.600	−0.077	2.167*
Child is female	0.145	1.187	0.400	2.513**	0.292	2.688**
Constant	−1.799	3.623	−2.186	4.042	−1.388	3.764
N	1,187		1,187		1,187	
log$_e$ (H)	−87.970		−110.808		−177.049	

Notes: This is based on children born during the prospective study, 1984–7, omitting those born less than one year before the study ended.
* Significant at 5% level; ** significant at 1% level.
The one-way test was used on all variables except income per head.

Source: Das Gupta 1990.

home diagnoses of their children's symptoms and at taking active steps to help them. After all, effective health care for a child requires (i) taking the nutritional, hygienic, and other measures necessary to prevent morbidity; (ii) if morbidity occurs, handling it such as to end the episode rapidly; (iii) knowing when the child needs a doctor's help; (iv) locating high-quality medical care (from a highly varied menu, in most developing-country situations), and (v) co-operating effectively with the doctor in curing the child. In all societies, the large majority of illness episodes are handled within the home. Less resourceful care-givers have an obvious disadvantage compared with others.

The analysis shows that the 'death-clustering' variable remains statistically significant even after controlling for several biological factors such as low birthweight, protracted deliveries, lactational failure; several dimensions of household social and economic status; and the child's sex. The death-clustering variable holds even after controlling for maternal education, and for the child-care variables. However, as has already been mentioned, it is very difficult to do more than obtain a few (largely indirect) quantifiable observations on the quality of child care: these variables inevitably represent a far less comprehensive and concrete picture of child care than do the biological and socio-economic variables in their own spheres.

It is apparent that death-clustering within families cannot be adequately explained by these biological and socio-economic factors, and that a large part of the explanation must lie elsewhere. Some of the explanation may lie in genetic frailty or other factors not included in the present analysis. However, the qualitative analysis, as already discussed, strongly suggests that parental abilities play an important role in this phenomenon.

Measuring the quality of child care is inherently far more difficult than in the case of the more biological factors. Nevertheless an attempt was made in this study to include some child-care-related variables, and they proved to be highly significantly related to child survival:

1. The question of encouraging diarrhoeal children to drink plenty of water related to the mother's general practice with her children, and not to the specific child. This question was supposed to evaluate the mother's ability to cope with the common threat of diarrhoea, and perhaps by extension other common illnesses as well. The data show that this variable strongly influences survival at every stage of childhood.[2]

2. The question of whether the child was immunized was also intended to assess the parents' knowledge and utilization of modern medical care. It cannot be interpreted as influencing child survival in a direct sense, because available childhood immunizations (DPT, polio, and BCG[3]) do not protect

---

[2] In Table 4.2 the effect of this variable is no longer significant, presumably because of the inclusion of several variables more specifically related to the child's health (such as giving boiled water) and other aspects of hygiene and child care.

[3] Measles vaccination began to be introduced widely in the public-health service only towards the end of the study.

against the important causes of death in this area. However, receiving or not receiving immunization is an indicator of the quality of health care received by the child. Having an infant immunized requires a considerable degree of active participation on the part of the parents, in knowing and remembering when to have the child immunized, and in being convinced enough of the benefits of modern health care to put up with the distressing side-effects (fever with DPT, an unpleasant boil with BCG) of immunization, for the sake of the less tangible benefits of preventive health care. The coefficients and *t*-values associated with this variable are artificially raised because of the inherent bias in measuring this variable.[4] But even allowing for this, Table 4.5 shows that the immunized children have much higher chances of survival than the rest.

3. The variable on the mother's immunization against tetanus is specific to the child in question, as it refers to the pregnancy leading to this birth. It significantly reduces mortality in the first month of life, the time when children are most susceptible to neonatal tetanus. The relationship is also likely to be partly due to the fact that women who have received some prenatal care are also more likely to receive other forms of prenatal care and generally higher quality care at the time of delivery.

4. As expected, if the water given to a child in the first month of life is boiled, this significantly reduces neonatal mortality. Again, this factor's influence is likely to be partly direct by avoiding water-borne infections, and partly indirect in that it reflects more widely on the quality of child-care practices. The presence of a doctor or nurse at the time of delivery falls short of having a statistically significant impact on improving neonatal survival. This is easily understood if one takes into account the fact that the great majority of deliveries in this area take place at home with the help of midwives (with the exception of some of the more educated women), and the help of doctors and nurses is usually sought only if there are major complications.

5. The mother's personal hygiene (as reflected in frequency in the use of soap) is significantly related to child survival as would be expected at 12–59 months of life, i.e. the age-group in which child mortality is most easily prevented by improved behavioural and environmental factors. The toddler toileting-hygiene variable related to how free the toddler was in choosing a place for toileting, and its lack of association with mortality is probably accounted for by the fact that mothers are usually quick to clean up their toddlers' messes.

Of the two variables pertaining to hygiene at the time of birth, the cleanliness of the mattress on which the delivery took place significantly influenced neonatal mortality. This is only partly because of the direct effect of an unhygienic bed. It is also partly because the small proportion of households which

---

[4] This variable has the problem that by definition a child cannot be immunized unless it survives. Most immunization shots are given through the first year of life. To minimize the inherent bias, the BCG vaccine was used, as this is given in one shot, normally in the first month of life.

deliberately choose to use an old dirty mattress for the delivery (on the grounds that it will have to be thrown away anyway after the delivery) are also likely to be unhygienic and careless in other ways at the time of delivery. The cleanliness of the baby's first wrap was not significant, possibly because of the inclusion of the previous variable.

Maternal education improves child survival through complex mechanisms, as has been extensively reviewed in Ware (1984). Amongst other things, it raises people's skills and self-confidence, increases their exposure to sources of information, and alters the way in which others respond to the person. It also works through increasing female autonomy (Caldwell 1979). In this society, as in some other strongly patrilineal societies, a woman's autonomy is lowest when she is a young married woman. She has a considerable measure of autonomy in her parents' village and once again in her husband's village when she is older, but a young bride is severely constrained by belonging to the bottom of her husband's household's authority structure. Perversely, this point of the life cycle overlaps with a woman's peak child-bearing years, so a woman wields the least authority when it is the most important for her children's health. Education helps to smooth out this trough in the life cycle. Educated women are conceded more authority in the household even when they are young brides, and their views are taken more seriously by their husbands and others.

Maternal education is not significantly related to child survival until the child-care variables are omitted from the equation (Table 4.5, col. 6). This clearly indicates that maternal education improves child-care practices, and that this is one of the major pathways through which it helps reduce child mortality. The data suggest that education improves the mother's basic child-care skills, her domestic management of ill health, efforts at preventive care, and use of modern medical services. In Table 4.6, which is based on the prospective study, maternal education has a significant negative influence on child mortality even after controlling for many details of prenatal and postnatal care which capture some of the influence of education. Both Tables 4.5 and 4.6 show that maternal education has a significant influence on child survival independent of the household's social and economic status.

The influence of the women's autonomy variables on child survival is clearly evident, despite the fact that it is very difficult to obtain meaningful measures of women's autonomy. In Table 4.5, low decision-making power is positively and significantly related to child mortality overall (0–59 months). In Table 4.6, this variable is insignificant in its relationship to infant mortality, being replaced by an alternative and more immediately relevant measure of the mother's autonomy (place of birth). When the birth takes place in the husband's home (as opposed to the woman's natal home or a hospital or clinic), there is a significant increase in the probability of dying, especially in the first month of life. This result clearly implies that, when women have greater decision-making power in the household, their children's health is better ensured. Since women are relatively free in their natal home, it is easy for them to ask for help if they feel that they or their baby are having difficulties. By contrast, in their husband's home they are more constrained and, even if they ask for help, this request is likely to be mediated by the judgement of the mother-in-law or other in-laws. Even if the woman is normally able to seek help on her own, it is especially difficult for her to do so during the customary forty-day period of seclusion and rest after a birth. This is why the impact of this variable is greatest in the first month of life, which is also the most vulnerable period for the infant.

An interesting confirmation of the 'parental-competence' hypothesis comes from Spence *et al.*'s (1954) study in Newcastle upon Tyne. This classic community-based study came to the conclusion that some 14 per cent of the mothers were 'unsatisfactory mothers'.[5] The authors examined the nature of the 'unsatisfactory' care, and concluded that it 'is reflected in lack of cleanliness, inadequate clothing, defective or capricious feeding, unsatisfactory arrangements for sleeping . . . the neglect or infrequent use of the infant welfare centres, and supplementary vitamins' (ibid. 127). The children of these mothers had higher rates of infection, hospitalization, and accidents than the other children, but they appear not to have suffered from much higher death rates because the doctors intervened actively at early stages and hospitalization was easily arranged when required. The study understandably found it hard to quantify the concomitants of 'unsatisfactory mothering'. It mentions that the familial characteristics of these 'unsatisfactory mothers' included 'unhappy and unstable family relations, poor maternal health, and in a minority . . . the unemployment of the father' (ibid. 127). To convey a fuller impression of the meaning of 'unsatisfactory mothering', the authors present case-studies of mothers of different levels of 'satisfactoriness', trying to describe the 'utterly incapable mothers' and 'those mothers who order their lives and their homes with superb excellence and wisdom' (ibid. 120). These case-studies highlight the important influence on child health of the mother's basic abilities and competence in managing the household and child care (ibid. 121–5). These observations are reminiscent of those made above regarding maternal competence in the study region.

The study data suggest that death-clustering is attributable in considerable measure to the basic abilities and personality characteristics of the mother or other primary care-giver. Poor abilities may be exacerbated by factors such as ill health and familial stress. They are improved by education, because educa-

---

[5] Maternal rather than paternal competence is of greater relevance to child health, because of the common observation that mothers are the primary care-givers for their children, even in households dominated by mothers-in-law or households where the husband and wife share some domestic responsibilities. This is why maternal education and autonomy are commonly found to be more closely related to child survival than their paternal counterparts. The term 'maternal incompetence' has not been used in this chapter, to avoid giving the impression that it is the mother's 'fault'.

tion enhances abilities in a variety of ways and also increases exposure to available health-care information. 'Incompetent' parents take poorer care of their children, are slower to recognize and respond effectively to their needs, and consequently experience child loss. The children of these families are more likely than others to be subject to the negative feedback syndrome of becoming frail due to poor feeding patterns and repeated infections, and being more severely affected by a disease. This is compounded by the parents being poorer at handling illness episodes in terms of home-based care and ensuring timely intervention from high-quality medical personnel.

When levels of mortality (and also fertility) decline, people become less exposed to experiencing multiple child loss, even though their level of competence in child care may remain unchanged. In this situation the less competent parents may lose one child or none at all. However, their children's health will continue to be adversely affected, as the Newcastle study shows, unless their child-care skills are improved.

These findings have clear implications for our understanding of the dynamics of child health and policies to improve child health. It is clearly necessary but not sufficient for this purpose to ensure adequate nutrition and availability of health services. In order to maximize the influence of these favourable conditions on child health, it is necessary to enable people to deal more effectively with their own health care. The data show clearly that the quality of care a child receives strongly affects its survival chances. Maternal education has a strong influence on child mortality, and the present analysis strongly supports the view that increasing female education is one of the most effective ways of reducing child mortality.

The results indicate a considerable potential for reducing child mortality by focusing on high-risk households. Substantial reductions in child mortality can be achieved using the simplest possible information for targeting families for extra attention. In this sample, for example, if health workers had used the first death as a marker for targeting intervention and had been successful at preventing all subsequent deaths, they would have reduced child mortality by 66 per cent. It would clearly be highly cost effective to focus health-care resources more specifically on the subset of families who are at high risk of losing children.

4.5 Conclusions

The Khanna restudy gave rise to some new understanding of the nature and causes of high risk of child mortality. First, it showed that a child's survival chances are strongly influenced by the way in which a particular birth fits in with the parents' goals regarding the number and sex composition of children in their family. Secondly, it showed that there is considerable heterogeneity between families in child loss, with a small proportion of families being

especially prone to losing their children, even after controlling for several biological and socio-economic factors which influence child survival. These two
findings have led to a number of researches exploring these hypotheses using
data from other settings such as Bangladesh (Muhuri and Preston 1991), Latin
America (Curtis *et al.* 1993; Guo 1993), and Senegal (Ronsmans 1993).

References

Caldwell, John (1979), 'Education as a Factor in Mortality Decline: An Examination of
Nigerian Data', *Population Studies*, 33: 395–413.
——Reddy, P. H., and Caldwell, Pat (1983), 'The Social Component of Mortality
Decline: An Investigation in South India Employing Alternative Methodologies',
Population Studies, 37: 185–205.
Chen, Lincoln C., Huq, Emdadul, and D'Souza, Stan (1981), 'Sex Bias in the Family
Allocation of Food and Health Care in Rural Bangladesh', *Population and Devel-
opment Review*, 7(1): 55–70.
Curtis, Sian L., Diamond, I., and McDonald, J. W. (1993), 'Birth Interval and Family
Effects on Postneonatal Mortality in Brazil', *Demography*, 30: 33–43.
Das Gupta, Monica (1987), 'Selective Discrimination against Female Children in Rural
Punjab, India', *Population and Development Review*, 13(1): 77–100.
——(1990), 'Death Clustering, Mother's Education and the Determinants of Child
Mortality in Rural Punjab, India', *Population Studies*, 44(3): 489–505.
——(1994), 'What Motivates Fertility Decline? A Case Study from Punjab, India', in
B. Egero and M. Hammarskjold (eds.), *Understanding Reproductive Change*, Lund
University Press, Lund.
——(1995a), 'Fertility Decline in Punjab, India: Parallels with Historical Europe',
Population Studies, 49(3): 481–500.
——(1995b), 'Lifecourse Perspectives on Women's Autonomy and Health Outcomes',
American Anthropologist, 97(3): 481–91.
——(1995c), 'Socio-Economic Status and Clustering of Child Deaths in Rural Punjab',
Harvard University Center for Population and Development Studies, Working Paper
95.08.
D'Souza, Stan, and Chen, L. C. (1980), 'Sex Differentials in Mortality in Rural
Bangladesh', *Population and Development Review*, 6(2): 257–70.
Guo, Guang (1993), 'Use of Sibling Data to Estimate Family Mortality Effects in
Guatemala', *Demography*, 30: 15–32.
Muhuri, Pradip K., and Preston, S. H. (1991), 'Mortality Differentials by Sex in
Bangladesh', *Population and Development Review*, 17: 415–34.
Ronsmans, Carine (1993), 'The Clustering of Child Deaths in Rural Senegalese Fami-
lies', Ph.D. dissertation, Harvard University.
Spence, J., Walton, W. S., Miller, F. J. W., and Court, S. D. M. (1954), *A Thousand Fami-
lies in Newcastle upon Tyne*, London.
Ware, Helen (1984), 'Effects of Maternal Education, Women's Roles and Child Care
on Child Mortality', in W. H. Mosley and L. C. Chen (eds.), *Child Survival: Strategies
for Research*, suppl. to *Population and Development Review*, 10.
Wyon, John B., and Gordon, J. E. (1971), *The Khanna Study*, Harvard University Press,
Cambridge, Mass.

5 Lessons from Narangwal about Primary Health Care, Family Planning, and Nutrition

CARL E. TAYLOR AND CECILE DE SWEEMER

5.1 Narangwal Project Background

Narangwal was the base for longitudinal field research that contributed to international understanding of how primary health care, family planning, and nutrition services can be provided for village people. For about thirteen years, the Rural Health Research Centre of the Indian Council of Medical Research and Johns Hopkins University's Department of International Health was located in Narangwal, a village with a population of about 1,800 located in Ludhiana District of the Indian Punjab. The project worked in twenty-six villages with a population of 35,000 distributed according to a controlled experimental design in three community development blocks with a population of over 300,000.

5.2 Setting of Health Care in the Rural Punjab

During the period of the Narangwal studies, the Punjab experienced dramatic social and economic change. Ludhiana District was one of the main centres of the Green Revolution of the 1960s, and, within five years, agricultural production doubled. Sudden affluence produced dramatic social change. Insatiable demand for education led to primary schools in every village and high schools and rural colleges within easy transportation range.

Rapid economic progress in the villages produced secondary improvement in patterns of health care. Starting in the 1950s the government promoted rural health services in community development blocks serving about 100,000 people. Each block had a primary health centre with at least one doctor and forty to fifty auxiliaries. Sub-centres served a population of about 5,000 and were staffed by an auxiliary nurse midwife (ANM). All services were supposed to be free, but the tremendous increase in government health personnel left little money for drugs and supplies. Filling out over thirty forms a month took up as much as 45 per cent of working time as documented in work-sampling studies (Johns Hopkins University 1976).

5.3 Origins of the Narangwal Research Project

The Narangwal project grew out of prolonged and intimate involvement in the life and problems of village India. A sequence of research projects, starting in 1961, were based at the Narangwal Rural Health Research Centre. The first project was a five-year study of the rural orientation of physicians (Takulia *et al.* 1976; Taylor *et al.* 1976). Indian social scientists lived in the teaching health centres of seven medical colleges in the major regions of India and administered a battery of tests and questionnaires to 1,300 interns at the beginning and end of their two-to-three-month rural rotation in a teaching health centre. A major conclusion was that doctors will never be able to provide most of the services for village India but that care will have to be provided by auxiliaries. Their responsibilties should be focused more on supporting the work of auxiliaries and in caring for curative and preventative problems referred to them. Doctors create dependency rather than the self-reliance that will empower village people to solve their own problems. The second research project studied indigenous practitioners and the beliefs of village people about diet and disease in six of the teaching health centres used for the internship studies.

The next research project was to develop a functional analysis methodology to balance needs and resources for primary health care (Johns Hopkins University 1976) and to optimize roles and relationships within the health team. A package of modules streamlined methods of work sampling, patient flow analysis, interviewing, records analysis, household surveys, and cost accounting.

The two action research projects summarized in this chapter were conducted from 1969 to 1973. The underlying concern was to study integration of the fragmented services for categorical programmes that had been imposed by international funding agencies so they could trace the flow of their dollars. Outside money developed separate hierarchies of staff which national health services were eventually not able to fund. The categorical workers tended to resist integration of services because they were trained to think that they were special and deserved the incentives associated with foreign funding. The findings about how services could be integrated became important in conceptualizing what became the worldwide primary health-care movement at the Alma Ata World Conference in 1978.

One project focused on integration of maternal and child health services (MCH) with family planning (FP). International funding agencies had been insisting on vertical family-planning programmes and that funds not be diverted to reducing mortality. This essentially destroyed beginning efforts to develop MCH services. When opposition developed to top-down population control, in a symbolic gesture, a little MCH was added to family planning. The main activity in India became the organization of mass family-planning camps, first for IUDs, which produced a phenomenal backlash because of complications, and then for vasectomies and tubectomies. Large investments in mass communications and financial incentives to encourage sterilizations have had minimal demographic effect because people tended not to get sterilized until they had had several sons.

In the late 1960s we thought that decision-makers would soon realize that sterilization was not going to meet the need. It seemed important to learn how to influence determinants of sustainable motivation for other family-planning methods, including the two-way interactions between family planning and health services. Growing evidence indicated that family planning improved the health of mothers and children. It seemed reasonable that health services could also improve family-planning utilization, along with long-term trends such as the better education of women. The possibility of shortening the demographically important lag between declines in mortality and fertility rates needed to be tested. Integration might promote acceptability, convenience, credibility, and access for village people and also improve logistics and reduce duplication in services.

Study was needed of less tangible attitudinal influences. Postpartum programmes had demonstrated that motivation was especially high after a birth. It seemed worth while also to test the child-survival hypothesis that motivation to practise family planning might be increased by improving child health. It seemed important to gather data on 'insurance motivation' or parents' feelings that they should have extra children because some might die. Our working hypothesis was that reduction in child mortality might be an important although not essential means of promoting a decrease in fertility in situations with high fertility and mortality. In 1965 the Health Minister, requested us to do systematic studies of integrated health and family-planning services. The Ministry of Health delegated responsibility for oversight to the Indian Council of Medical Research.

The second major action research was on the integration of services to control infections and improve nutrition in weaning-age children. We had co-authored the basic WHO monograph defining the synergistic interactions between malnutrition and infections (Scrimshaw, Taylor, and Gordon 1968). Throughout history and around the world, the leading cause of death, disease, and retarded growth and development in children has been synergism between nutritional deficiencies and common childhood infections (Taylor, Kielmann, and De Sweemer 1978). Children in developing countries may have up to 160 days of illness each year, with three or four episodes of diarrhoea and four or five severe respiratory infections (Scrimshaw *et al.* 1967; Scrimshaw, Taylor, and Gordon 1968; Mata, Urrutia, and Lechtig 1971). Nutritional deficits in early life delay physical and mental growth (Klein *et al.* 1976). Nutritional demands are highest during the rapid growth of early childhood. Infectious diseases are relatively uncommon during breast-feeding while the child is protected by passively acquired maternal antibodies and minimal exposure to infections. As the baby becomes mobile and takes foods in addition to breast-feeding, infections appear at a time of high nutritional demand (Scrimshaw, Taylor, and Gordon 1968). Infections increase nutritional requirements and malnutrition predisposes to infections.

Research thinking had to be reoriented, since the usual epidemiological field study tends to focus on single problems. The only ethical way of studying these multiple combinations of health problems in human populations is to identify groups with high prevalence of both malnutrition and common infections and observe what happens with selective reduction in each type of condition. A prospective experimental design with selective interventions would involve allocation of villages to experimental groups through open discussion with local leaders and the populations to be studied.

When the Narangwal Population and Nutrition projects were developed, few previous projects had conducted population-based, longitudinal action research. The most notable example in India was the Khanna project conducted some ten years earlier about twenty-six miles from Narangwal (Wyon and Gordon 1971). They measured the impact of family planning alone, using foam tablets, as compared with two control groups, but did not measure interactions with health care. Much was learned about the social forces influencing family planning and health conditions. At Narangwal , there was a great deal of carry-over of methods and field procedures from Khanna.

Similarly, another earlier project from which we learned much at Narangwal was the INCAP project on nutrition and infections in Guatemala (Scrimshaw *et al.* 1967). The main design difference was that we had more villages in each experimental group and included a group of villages to test the synergistic effects of combined nutrition and infection interventions.

5.4 Objectives of Research Projects

Two parallel sets of objectives were defined: (i) to test in a controlled experimental design, the impact of various combinations of health, family planning, and nutrition interventions in total village populations; and (ii) to understand how health, family planning, and nutrition interventions can be integrated in practical packages for national programmes.

The scientific testing of hypotheses in a controlled research design seemed at first to be incompatible with the need to evolve service packages. The functional analysis methodology that we had developed earlier (Johns Hopkins University 1976), however, permitted input–output–outcome analysis and provided quantitative data for cost-effectiveness comparison of specific interventions. A practical concern of government officials was that all interventions should fit the severe economic and administrative constraints of national services. An evolutionary approach was used to define the content of service packages in order to put a 'price tag' on each package. Rapid feedback from sequential testing of cost effectiveness and opinions of fieldworkers and villagers contributed to progressive improvement of services. Major components of service packages remained constant, even though the process of implementation changed.

5.5 Experimental Design, Principles, and Methods

The experimental design shown in Figure 5.1 illustrates the eight groups of villages that received specific packages of services. In the family-planning project the five groups of about four villages each received combinations of family

Health and nutrition project

	No nutritional services	Nutritional services provided
NO HEALTH CARE	CONTN 3 villages (2,800)	NUT 2 villages (2,300)
HEALTH CARE PROVIDED	HC 2 villages (2,800)	*NUTHC 3 villages (4,900)

Key:
NUT — Nutrition care
HC — Health care
NUTHC — Nutrition and health care
CONTN — Control-nutrition project

Health and population project

FAMILY-PLANNING SERVICES

	No women's health services	Women's health services provided	No family planning services
NO CHILDREN'S HEALTH SERVICES	FPEd 4 villages (5,500)	FPWS 4 villages (5,000)	CONTP 4 villages (5,400)
CHILDREN'S HEALTH SERVICES PROVIDED	*FPCC 3 villages (4,900)	FPWSCC 4 villages (6,300)	

Key:
FPED — Family-planning services and education
FPWS — Family-planning and women's services
FPCC — Family-planning and children's services
FPWSCC — Family-planning, women's and children's services
CONTP — Control-population project

*Overlapping cluster of villages in both experiments

Fig. 5.1. Experimental design showing distribution of villages in experimental groups

planning (FP), women's services (WS), and child care (CC). The five groups were: FP + WS + CC, FP + WS, FP + CC, FP Education (FP Ed.), and a control population. In the nutrition project there were four groups of villages in which services focused on children under 3. One group averaging 190 children received nutritional care (NUT), a second group averaging 170 children received infection control (HC), the third group averaging 340 children received both, and the fourth group averaging 420 children was a nutrition control. One group overlapped in both projects serving as FP–CC and combined services for nutrition and infection (NUT–HC). Growth patterns and causes of mortality became the key indicators of health problems in children. It was at Narangwal that the term and methodology of 'verbal autopsies' were first developed to get practically useful information by questioning family members according to a standard format and having diagnoses agreed to by a panel of doctors.

A major feature of this research was to involve village people in both planning and implementation. It proved relatively easy to get understanding and co-operation for an experimental design to test alternative packages of services. These packages were adding services to what was available from the government primary health centre (PHC) and villagers were used to the incomprehensible selectivity of governmental programmes. For ethical reasons all control and FP Ed. villages were within intensive areas immediately adjacent to PHCs so that they would not be without acute care. Socio-economic indicators showed that the groups of villages receiving the most project services tended to be deprived and conservative because villages near PHCs were located along roads and in more affluent areas. Community participation was excellent, especially in providing for and protecting the family health workers (FHWs, young women who were retrained ANMs), who were formally adopted as daughters of their villages.

Because of differences in workload, it was not enough to try to measure inputs simply by the number of personnel assigned to a village cluster. Using the functional analysis work-sampling methodology developed earlier, we got detailed data on service inputs, activities, and costs. This also permitted separation of research costs from service input. Each component of input could be linked to the use of services as a measure of output and also to the contribution of each activity to programme impact or outcome. The following measurement methods proved especially useful:

1. Service records analysis required standard procedures for organizing service records maintained by field staff so that data on specific activities could be readily extracted. For inputs, this included type and content of service, problem, intervention, and follow-up. For outputs, there were summary service utilization counts by category of worker and by group in the study population. Outcomes were measured directly. Quality of care was also assessed.

2. Health service utilization surveys were essential to measure the other

sources of care. New interventions never enter a vacuum. One hundred house-holds randomly distributed in each group of villages were interviewed in each quarter of the year to obtain two-week recall of illnesses and all health care received from indigenous and private practitioners, home treatment, and government facilities. The household surveys included: health status, sources of health care and expenditures, types of provider care, and numbers and cost of contacts with providers.

3. Cost analysis was based on expenditure data for specific service components. This relied on work-sampling of staff time, which is the largest input into labour-intensive primary care. Together with expenditures on supplies, facilities, transport, etc., this permitted putting 'price tags' on each package of services which could be used in calculations for possible replication in other settings.

5.6 Reorientation of Staff

Training was essential for all activities at Narangwal. All staff educated themselves and others. Promoting change depended on defining new patterns to simplify work routines and delegate them peripherally to get services as close as possible to village homes. A primary purpose was to empower the people to solve their own problems, recognizing that the most important health workers are not doctors but mothers.

For implementation in national programmes, we simplified the rapid training of village workers. Teaching methods were problem- and competency-based and co-ordinated with self-learning manuals that evolved from practical work. The six weeks' training that evolved started with orientation to help workers appreciate village people and their needs. In the first week practical interventions for household health care were described along with the FHW's responsibilities. Then each new FHW lived for a week with an experienced FHW to observe daily routines. They returned for a week of classes to discuss the scientific basis for each activity and to learn specific skills. This was followed by another week of living with their preceptors to try out what they had learned. Another week in class discussion was specifically to answer remaining questions and give theoretical background. Then they returned again to the field for a final week to take responsibility under supervision.

Continuing in-service training was through a weekly meeting of field staff for discussions and demonstrations. New innovations were introduced, topics important at specific seasons—such as ORT for diarrhoea in the summer or case management for pneumonia in the winter—were reviewed, and opportunity was given to raise questions and share experiences. Most importantly, these meetings maintained morale and mutual support.

Training of supervisors was difficult because a new supportive orientation had to be learned by professionals who were used to authoritarian methods.

Table 5.1. Family-planning entry points for routine services

Service record forms had blocks to be checked when family planning had been discussed at each of the following entry points:

during routine fertility surveys of non-pregnant, menstruating eligible women

at the time of confirmation of pregnancy

at the time of post-abortion care, if a pregnancy ended in abortion

at about the thirty-sixth week of pregnancy, during an antenatal visit

at the fourteenth-day postpartum and neonatal examination visit

at the sixth-week postpartum examination, combined with the well-baby check-up

during the fifth, seventh, and tenth months after delivery, combined with well-baby check-up, immunization, and weighing of the child

at all routine health check-ups, routine weighings, and dietary advice for children under 3 years old

after completion of a child's basic immunizations

after identifying or treating health problems, including malnutrition, prematurity, anaemia, congenital disease, accidents, and severe illness of children.

They had to learn skills in empowerment and how to work through the FHW or village volunteer, rather than taking over. The basic dictum was that, after a supervisory visit, the prestige of the FHW should have increased among villagers, her self-image and confidence should have become greater, and her knowledge and skills should have improved.

Surveillance proved to be essential for all services. To establish routines that were readily monitored for complete coverage it was essential that simple indicators be used to ensure that services reached those that needed them most. Lists were maintained to identify those who required special attention for high risk or because of eligibility for specific services. Entry points were worked out when individuals were most open to particular educational messages. Ten such entry points for family planning from health services were identified (Table 5.1). Activities in each of the services are listed in Table 5.2.

5.7 Findings

5.7.1 Family-planning utilization

(*a*) From two cross-sectional surveys of knowledge and practice of contraception the following conclusions emerged: knowledge about modern contraceptive methods increased in all villages with family-planning services; statements admitting to knowledge of traditional or folk methods declined

Table 5.2. Components, of service packages

Family planning

1. Education and motivation	Intense educational efforts were provided in FP Ed.; education was well integrated with health-care delivery in FP + WS + CC and FP + WS; it was poorly integrated in FP + CC where different doctors supervised the two services.
2. Contraceptive services	Condoms, pills (Ovulen and an Indian-marketed low-dose pill, Primovolar); IUDs (Lippes and Narangwal Tavithi); injectable Depo-Provera; vasectomies and tubectomies were provided under similar conditions in all experimental groups.
3. Follow-up	The same methods and specific patterns of follow-up were established for all groups.

Women's services

1. Monitoring fertility and early diagnosis of pregnancy	Routine in FP + WS + CC, FP + WS and FP + CC; also carried out in simplified form in FP Ed.
2. Prenatal and postnatal care, and supervision of deliveries done by *dais* (indigenous midwives)	Well-developed pattern in FP + WS + CC and FP + WS modified simple prenatal care provided in FP + CC as part of child care.
3. Diagnosis, treatment, and referral of illness	Done only in FP + WS + CC and FP + WS.

Child care

1. Periodic health check-ups to 3 years of age	Weekly and eventually biweekly monitoring of morbidity status in FP + CC and all nutrition and infection villages; much less frequent home visiting in FP + WS + CC, eventually every 2 months.
2. Periodic measurement of weight and height	Routine ranged from every month for infants to every 3 months at 3 years of age for both FP + WS + CC, FP + CC, and all nutrition and infection villages.
3. Immunization	Smallpox and DPT in FP + WS + CC, FP + CC, and all nutrition and infection villages.
4. Nutrition supplementation and education	Selective provision of supplements to malnourished or faltering children, and education of mothers of all children in FP + WS + CC and all nutrition villages but not in infection villages.
5. Diagnosis, treatment, and referral of illness	Early care emphasized in FP + WS + CC, FP + CC, and all infection villages, but not nutrition villages, especially to develop early home care for diarrhoea and pneumonia.

---

sharply; control village use-rates of modern contraceptives remained unchanged as measured in the two cross-sectional surveys, continuing at a level of about 9 per cent of eligible couples.

(*b*) Longitudinal contraceptive practices as a result of project services showed acceptance curves in experimental groups which were essentially parallel and still rising when the project was terminated by Indo-American disagreements following the Bangladesh War. As a result of the premature termination, we were not able to show the plateauing that we had expected in the conceptual models for our research planning. Detailed data are in the World Bank monographs on the Narangwal Project (Kielmann and Associates 1983). Figure 5.2 shows acceptance curves for couples who had ever used family planning. Time relationships varied because the groups of villages had different starting times. The reason was that project funding was obtained incrementally as we were able to show interesting results. The implementation of programmes in the last two groups was helped greatly by learning from the first two groups. The dramatically higher starting-point in FP Ed. is because they were a more developed group of villages with ready access to a government PHC. Current user rates for FP + WS + CC and for FP + WS steadily increased throughout the project (Table 5.3), but the results were mixed for the two groups of villages with shorter periods of observation. The curve for FP Ed. started high and rose in parallel with the other curves.

An effective user rate was calculated by correcting the current user rates according to the varying effectiveness of the mix of contraceptives in each group of villages. This rate comes closest to measuring the probable protection from pregnancy provided by the family-planning programmes in each experimental group. As shown in Figure 5.3, effective user rates showed a steady increase in all experimental groups, with absolute levels being on an average 25 per cent lower than current user rates. Couples were encour-

Table 5.3. Current users of family planning by duration of services in each experimental group (percentages)

Experimental groups	Duration of services and rates at end of:		
	13/4 years	31/4 years	41/2 years
FP + WS + CC	22	26	34
FP + WS	25	34	41
FP + CC	27	28	—
FP Ed.	30	—	—

Note: Unusual time intervals occurred because services were started at different times and project was terminated abruptly for political reasons.

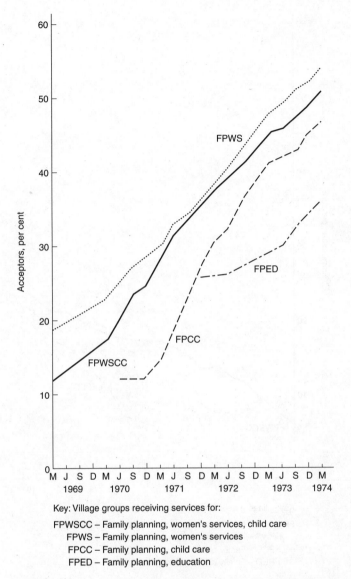

Key: Village groups receiving services for:

FPWSCC – Family planning, women's services, child care
FPWS – Family planning, women's services
FPCC – Family planning, child care
FPED – Family planning, education

Fig. 5.2. Currently married women age 15–49 who had accepted modern family-planning methods at any time, by experimental group, including prior acceptors (control group maintained a rate of less than 9 per cent throughout the study)

aged to shift to more effective methods. There were major differences in the final mix of contraceptives used in various groups of villages (Table 5.4). The FP Ed. group had the most use of the less effective methods (especially condoms).

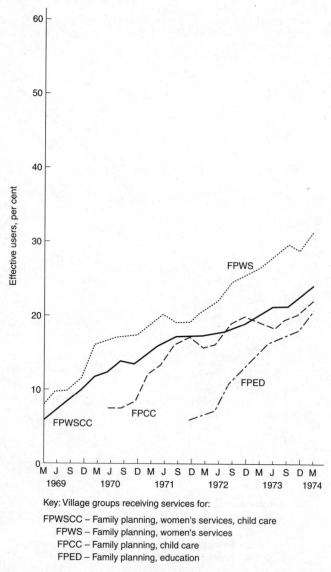

Fig. 5.3. Currently married women age 15–49 who were 'effective users' of family planning at specified times, by experimental group (impossible to calculate in the control group because of lack of precise information on methods used over time)

5.7.2 Changes in fertility

(*a*) The Punjab was experiencing general fertility reduction during the project period as part of general socio-economic development. The numbers of babies born in each group was small and therefore the rates

Table 5.4. Percentages of contraceptive methods currently used at end of project by experimental groups

Contraceptive method	FP + WS + CC	FP + WS	FP + CC	FP Ed.
Condom	35	29	31	48
Pill	5	1	5	0.4
IUD	8	25	3	7
Inj. Depo Provera	30	20	20	19
Vasectomy	7	14	23	13
Tubectomy	15	11	18	13

Table 5.5. Age standardized general fertility rate by calendar year and experimental group

	Year				% change
	1970	1971	1972	1973	1970–3
FP + WS + CC	155.6	152.7	154.8	129.0	−17.1
FP + WS	159.3	146.8	162.3	129.2	−18.9
FP + CC		163.9	140.1	144.0	−12.1
FP Ed. (adj)[a]			177.7	160.2	−9.8
Cont−P (adj)[a]	144.8	156.2	131.6	141.1	−2.6
Other nutrition	148.8	156.3	120.4	141.1	−5.7

[a] Adjustment based on under-reporting of vital statistics because of lack of health workers in these villages, especially in following up babies born at mother's homes due to village exogamy.

fluctuated considerably (Table 5.5). Fertility rates also started from different levels.

(b) In FP + WS + CC and FP + WS general fertility rates dropped by 17 to 19 per cent from 1970 to 1973 (Table 5.5) (Taylor and Singh 1975). In FP + CC the decline was 12.1 per cent and in FP Ed. it was 9.8 per cent. In the control and other nutrition villages that received no project family-planning services the rates of decline were 2.6 per cent and 5.7 per cent respectively. Adjustments were made in the vital statistics calculations for control because there was no health worker in these villages and in FP Ed. there was a retrained village schoolteacher. There was less follow-up of children born while mothers were at their own mother's home owing to village exogamy.

5.7.3 Changes in attitudes and beliefs

A major effort was made to measure attitudes and beliefs through two cross-sectional surveys of women 15–49 years of age.

(*a*) *Attitudes and beliefs about family planning*: the proportion of women who expressed general approval of family planning was much lower than the very high rates reported in earlier surveys in India, with only 54 per cent approving of family planning for a family like theirs and 28 per cent disapproving. This may have been because of backlash against complications from sterilization and IUDs in camps organized in the national programme. During the project the general approval rate increased to 66 per cent. The lowest initial approval rate was in FP + WS + CC, which seemed to be the most conservative group of villages, as indicated by the lowest prior practice of family planning and highest ideal family size (Taylor *et al*. 1983). In contrast to the basis of the government programme, 90 per cent of families were in favour of spacing rather than having the desired number of children and then stopping.

Attitudes about what people considered an ideal number of children for a family like theirs were the same in both surveys. About 55 per cent said they wanted three or less children and this went up to 77 per cent for four or less. The number changed rapidly as more sons were born (Figure 5.4) The highest proportion of respondents in the first survey who considered four or more children ideal was in FP + WS + CC, probably another indication of conservatism.

Attitudes to specific methods of family planning are of special interest in relation to two contraceptives. There was strong public demand for injections, which were requested by 40 per cent of women in the first survey. After injectable Depo-Provera was provided, the proportion favouring injections dropped to 33 per cent, but this became our most effective method. In the first survey there was great anxiety expressed because of reports in the public media about complications of IUDs in national mass campaigns. This declined by the second survey, especially in the FP + WS villages, where use was promoted as part of postpartum care and the ratio eventually rose to 25 per cent (Table 5.4).

Sources of communication showed strong association between approval of family planning and whether woman had talked with their husbands about family planning. The lowest frequency of talking with husbands was in FP + WS + CC, again probably related to conservatism. There were strongly positive associations between talking with husbands and caste, husband's education and occupation, and older age of woman at marriage (Taylor *et al*. 1983).

(*b*) *Attitudes and beliefs relating to child survival*: gathering evidence on the child-survival hypothesis was one of the main research objectives of the project. We postulated that conscious awareness of improved child survival is not a necessary condition for fertility limitation, but subconscious expectations of a high probability of child death may serve as a powerful motivational force to have extra children. Awareness of improved survival of children on the first survey was not high: only one-third of women said that more children survive

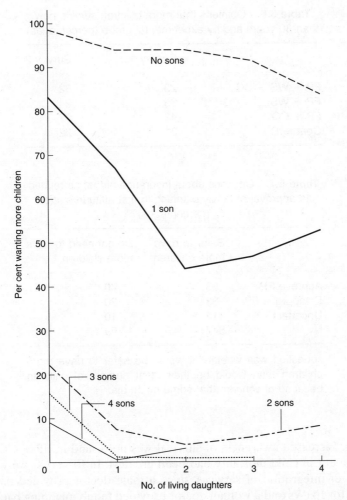

Fig. 5.4. Per cent of wives age 15–39 wanting more children, by number of living daughters and sons

now than thirty years ago, while one-fifth said less survive and almost one-half said the same number survive or were uncertain. Child mortality had, in fact, dropped to about half of what it had been ten years earlier at the time of the Khanna project, probably as a result of general socio-economic development.

In the second survey (Table 5.6), there was about a one-third decline in numbers saying that more children survive than thirty years ago. The one exception was in the FP + WS + CC experimental group, where there was almost a one-third increase in awareness of greater survival. This may be related to deliberate efforts to use child survival as an entry point for family

Table 5.6. Opinions that more children survive now than 30 years ago by experimental group (percentages)

	Survey 1	Survey 2
FP + WS + CC	23	32
FP + WS	35	24
FP + CC	42	27
Cont − P	31	22

Table 5.7. Opinions about insurance births[a] as related to approval of family planning in first attitude survey (percentages)

	Safer to have more children	Do not need to have more children
Approve FP	53	70
Disapprove FP	33	20
Uncertain	14	10
N	547	1,759

[a]question was whether it would be safer to have more children than would be their ideal number of children because of concern that some might die.

planning. Increased awareness of survival was not found in FP + CC, where improvement in child mortality had been greatest. In FP + CC we were not able to get integration of services, since a male doctor provided paediatric back-up for FHWs and a woman doctor provided family-planning back-up, so that FHWs also separated these functional areas in their own work. These findings support the proposition that parental awareness of survival is normally a subconscious expectation but that a deliberate use of family-planning entry points, as in FP + WS + CC, can bring about change.

One question probed attitudes to 'insurance births' by asking whether parents thought it would be safer to have more children than their ideal number because some might die. Cross-tabulation showed clear association with women indicating approval of family planning being much more likely to express the need for insurance births, while ratios were reversed among those who disapproved (Table 5.7). The second survey showed a general shift to less expressed need for insurance births in all groups (Table 5.8). Those who were aware that fewer children die were more likely to respond positively to a question in which they were asked whether they would take this decline into

Table 5.8. Opinion about whether it is safer to have more children than their ideal number, showing changes in attitude between surveys at beginning and end of project by experimental groups (percentages)

	Survey 1	Survey 2
FP + WS + CC	42	62
FP + WS	54	74
FP + CC	54	74
Cont − P	52	75
Other nutrition	48	75

Table 5.9. Responses about whether perceived differences in child mortality influence desired number of children—by experimental group in second survey (row percentage)

Village group	N	Differences influence decision	Does not influence decision	Depends on will of God	Unwilling to think about alternatives
FP + WS + CC	523	50	31	9	10
FP + WS	333	38	43	10	9
FP + CC	359	40	38	12	10
Cont − P	337	36	38	12	14
Other nutrition	878	38	40	7	15
Total	2,430	41	38	9	12

account in thinking about how many children they would have. One-half of women in FP + WS + CC said that they would take improved chances of survival into account in thinking about their own family size, as compared with 36–40 per cent in other groups (Table 5.9), perhaps again because of the use of entry points. Greater awareness of child survival was positively associated with caste, husband's education, occupation, and talking with husbands about family planning.

5.7.4 Health services utilization

(*a*) Maintaining preventive services required careful structuring of functions and supervision to make sure that they were not crowded out by curative services. Time pressure in FP + WS + CC probably explains why a greater percentage of time of FHWs was taken for preventive women's services

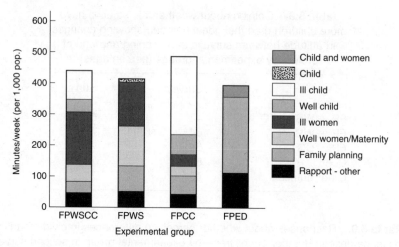

Fig. 5.5. Average time spent providing direct services by family health workers

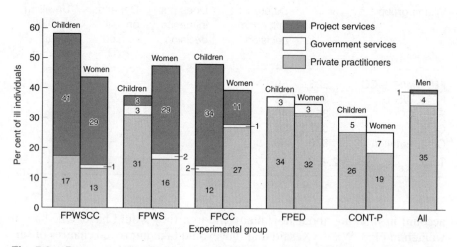

Fig. 5.6. Per cent of ill individuals receiving treatment from different sources of care in each experimental group, 1973–1974

(including maternity care) in FP + WS and preventive children's services in FP + CC (Taylor *et al.* 1983) (Figure 5.5).

(*b*) Services by project personnel only partially replaced other services, mostly indigenous practitioners (Figure 5.6). Use of project services were, therefore, mainly additive and not a replacement for previous patterns of use.

(*c*) A significant finding was that surveillance methods improved equitable distribution so that services could be targeted to the poor and low caste

Table 5.10. Percentages of families using project preventive and curative services for children and women and for family planning by caste

	Caste		
	Low	High	
Women's services			
Curative	68	71	N.S.
Preventive	77	71	p < 0.05
Children's services			
Curative	67	64	N.S.
Preventive	62	44	p < 0.001
Family planning			
Pre-project users	13	20	p < 0.001
Non-users who became users during project	39	33	p < 0.04

(Taylor and Parker 1967) (Table 5.10). Preventive services for both women and children were used significantly more by low-caste families. Use of family planning went from significantly favouring high caste to greater acceptance among low-caste couples. This capacity to improve distribution directly shows that surveillance for equity is feasible and effective.

5.7.5 Health benefits from service programmes

Health benefits were most apparent in the nutrition and infection villages (Kielmann and Associates 1983).

(*a*) Nutrition monitoring with selective supplementation of children who had growth faltering improved both weight and height. This sounds obvious, but as far as we know, this is the first research demonstration in which the growth patterns of total populations of children were shown to have benefited from a nutrition programme in comparison with a control group of villages (Figure 5.7). Nutrition care, caste, and gender each showed an independent differential impact on weight for age of 0.5 kg. and on height of 2 cm., so that a high-caste boy from a nutrition village averaged 1.5 kg. and 6 cm. more than a low-caste girl from a control village.

(*b*) Neonatal mortality was lowered in all villages with intensive home visiting when surveillance at home occurred every two weeks. But in FP + WS + CC, which had less intensive child care with home visits only at two-month intervals, neonatal mortality declined only slightly (Figure 5.8).

Infant mortality also showed the greatest response with two-week home visiting in villages where infection control was provided (Figure 5.9) but only moderate reduction with less frequent surveillance. The greatest impact on infant mortality was with concentrated infection control (HC) and almost an

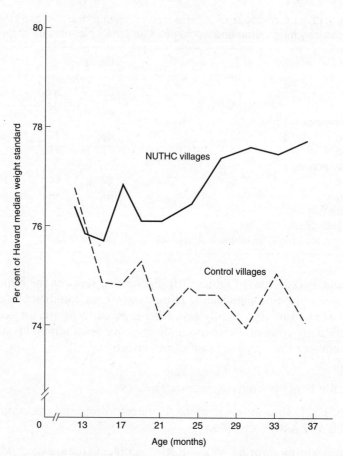

Fig. 5.7. Average weight, adjusted for sex and caste and expressed as a percentage of Harvard median weight standard, in cohorts of children in villages receiving integrated nutrition and health care in comparison with children in control villages, 1970–1973

equal effect from combined services (NUTHC) and moderate change in nutrition care (NUT).

The 12–35-month-old child mortality rates were nineteen in the control group compared with eight in FP + WS + CC and eleven in NUT and HC groups (Figure 5.10).

(*c*) The principal synergistic relationship was not biological but in the way combined services interacted. Integrated services produced as much nutrition benefit as was achieved in nutrition-only services and as much mortality reduction as in the health-care-only villages for essentially the same overall input as was required in each of the separate services. This was mainly because of the greater efficiency of integrated services.

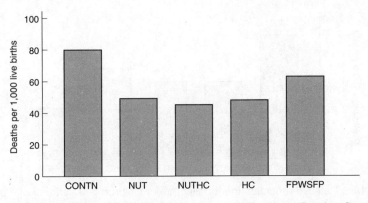

Fig. 5.8. Relative reduction in neonatal mortality rate by Input Service Group after services were well established, 1970–1973

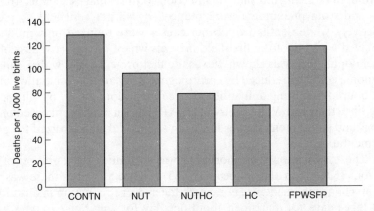

Fig. 5.9. Relative reduction in infant mortality rate by Input Service Group after services were well established, 1970–1973

(*d*) The mortality rates in FP + WS + CC require more explanation. Because of their greater workload these FHWs made home visits only at two-month intervals. In villages with visits every two weeks it became evident that FHWs did surveillance and care themselves with little effort to turn responsibility over to mothers, as time pressures required FHWs to do with bimonthly visits. It was obviously much easier for family members to identify problems and care for older children. It would be of special interest to see whether a more deliberate and longer effort could have produced equivalent impact by improving family surveillance for neonates and infants or whether this role could have been filled by community volunteers.

(*e*) Surveillance leading to early diagnosis and treatment was most

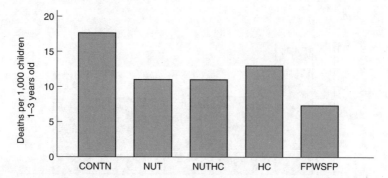

Fig. 5.10. Relative reduction in mortality rate of children 1–3 years of age by Input Service Group after services were well established, 1970–1973

important in reducing mortality in infection control villages. Deaths from diar-rhoea and from pneumonia were reduced by 48 per cent and 45 per cent respectively, while deaths from other causes were reduced only moderately. Narangwal was one of the first field projects where the effectiveness of ORT in total populations was shown. It was the first project to show that childhood pneumonia could be reduced by early diagnosis by careful observation of rapid and laboured breathing and antibiotic treatment done safely by village auxil-iaries. Since then, the WHO protocol for ARI case management based on these findings and subsequent studies has been tested and standardized for general implementation.

(*f*) The major impact on morbidity was to reduce the duration of acute infections (Kielmann and Associates 1983) (Figure 5.11), but there was essen-tially no change in incidence. For cough the average reduction in duration was about three days, for diarrhoea about one day, for vomiting two days, and for fever about one and a half days.

5.7.6 Services and resources required to achieve programme effects

Detailed functional analysis relating input to output to outcome measure-ments permitted specific cost-effectiveness analysis (Kielmann and Associates 1983; Taylor *et al*. 1983).

(*a*) Effective health and family-planning services do not need to be expen-sive. In villages with combined services (FP + WS + CC) the annual per capita costs of total MCH and family-planning care were less than $2. From func-tional analysis data and the staff composition, we calculated that the eventual distribution of effort in the entire project was approximately 30 per cent for service, 50 per cent for research, and 20 per cent for administration and support services.

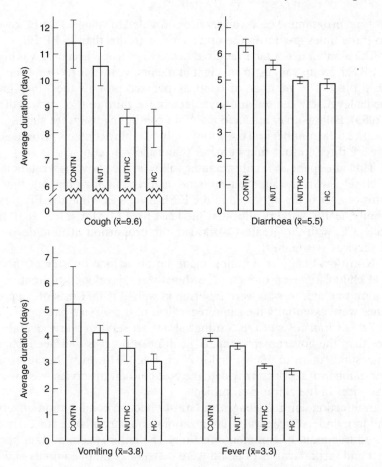

Fig. 5.11. Duration of morbidity episodes by experimental group and type of problem

(*b*) There was close association between use of specific types of health services and acceptance of family planning. Family-planning acceptance was about 35 per cent higher in groups receiving women's preventive services and with both curative and preventive services for children, and about 22 per cent higher among women who used illness care services.

(*c*) Costs for those components of services applied directly to family planning, both for acceptors and for continuing users, were lowest in the FP + WS + CC and three to four times higher in the FP Ed. group. The cost per capita for family planning ranged from 24 cents in FP + WS + CC to $1.08 in FP Ed., the cost per acceptor from $13 in FP + WS + CC to $39 in FP Ed., the cost per couple year of protection from $11 to $32, and the cost for an estimated birth averted from $35 to $107.

(*d*) Total programme costs (all services provided to villages) were, however, two to three times greater in the other service groups than in FP Ed.

(*e*) The number of contacts required to convince a new acceptor was highest in the FP Ed. group, ranging from eight in the first year to forty-six at the close of the project. The number of contacts per acceptor in the other groups reached a level between ten and seventeen in the third year of service (Taylor *et al.* 1983). Follow-up contacts to maintain continuing use were similar in all groups. The total number and costs for family-planning contacts prior to acceptance were three to four times greater than follow-up contacts.

(*f*) The time spent on family planning followed the above cost relationships fairly closely, with the greatest amount of direct family-planning time per acceptor or user being allocated in the FP Ed. villages, while the FP + WS + CC family health workers allocated the least time (Taylor *et al.* 1983). In FP + WS + CC, with the greatest workload, the proportion of time devoted to direct services was highest.

(*g*) Nutritional supplementation made up about one-quarter of the total costs of child care, even though procedures were developed to limit supplementation to children who were faltering in weight gain. Costs of supportive activities were essentially the same regardless of the service package.

(*h*) The overall costs of the Narangwal project services were several times greater than the government primary health centre costs had been when we had measured them in 1968 (Taylor *et al.* 1983). However, because of the greater number of services provided, the cost per unit of service was lower for most services in the Narangwal project.

(*i*) In infection control villages, the most effective combination of services for children under 1 year was immunizations and surveillance for early diagnosis and treatment of common infections. The latter was important because the first and second causes of death were diarrhoea and pneumonia and both were readily diagnosed and safely treated early by auxiliaries (McCord and Kielmann 1978).

(*j*) The overall ratio of services provided by FHWs as compared with doctors was about 10:1. As the project progressed, FHWs were able to take on increasing responsibility, and they consistently provided good-quality services.

5.8 Summary Judgements about the Process of Field Research

5.8.1 Things that we did right

In our judgement, the following items contributed to whatever success we had in the Narangwal projects:

(*a*) Becoming a part of the villages we were studying and involving village communities in the research cannot be stressed too strongly. Equally important was the psychological set that living in the village gave to members of the staff. There was considerable self-selection among those who applied to work on this village project. Both national and international staff tended to be individuals with a natural affinity for simple living and a genuine regard for village people. Recruiting individuals who had been personally involved in field programmes serving poor people ensured a continuing sense of programmatic reality which kept services practical and inexpensive.

(*b*) Involving all staff members in research planning and innovation was important. Many of the best ideas came from family health workers and village volunteers. They told us what would or would not work and their suggestions tended to be more realistic and innovative than those proposed by 'experts'. This involvement of peripheral workers was tremendously important for their morale and sense of worth.

(*c*) Having the research based in both Indian and foreign academic institutions also proved important. There is a growing need for reflective and analytic thinking about basic issues and sharing of comparative experience from around the world. Problems in the field could be referred readily to world experts. This kind of prospective field research must have a time-perspective that permits a careful tooling-up period and then sufficient time in the field to measure complex variables. For the fieldwork to be adequately reported, as much time should be devoted to analysis and write-up as to the original field research.

(*d*) Provision of adequate logistic support was difficult because the research base was set up in a village situation without the usual support and service facilities. The Rural Health Research Centre had to develop its own rather complete administrative organization providing control of finances, logistics, and a special workshop to maintain transportation. For housing, we renovated ordinary village homes to provide safe water supply, sanitation, screening, and ventilation.

(*e*) Careful attention to measurement methods and quality control of statistical information was maintained under rigorous field conditions.

(*f*) Constant involvement and feedback from government officials helped greatly in the field work. One of the greatest contributions of Narangwal was a series of annual three-day conferences in tents in the village. Senior officials from the central and state ministries of health and family planning and representatives of other official agencies and universities participated enthusiastically. In field visits and discussion groups, data from the previous year's research were presented for interpretation by those who would be most involved in implementation. We were frequently surprised by the rapid implementation of findings which became government policy and were incorporated in five-year plans and government reports.

(*g*) Each year the project staff had a week for intensive review of experiences and plans in a Himalayan hill station. These meetings maintained morale and good interpersonal relationships and helped reduce strains associated with being constantly together for work and day-to-day living.

(*h*) A delicate balance between Indian personnel and the Johns Hopkins faculty had to be maintained. When the full range of activities was established, there were at any one time about 165 Indian staff and one to three members of the John Hopkins faculty who came together from six different countries.

(*i*) We provided educational opportunities for staff, so that over fourteen years twelve staff members did graduate work in public health in the USA and England, with three receiving doctorate degrees. In addition, a large number of staff members were provided with financial support for education leading to degrees in India.

5.8.2 Things that we did wrong

In retrospect, some activities should have been done differently.

(*a*) Delays in implementing parts of the experimental design proved to be a major weakness of this research. This was mainly because funding became available only as we demonstrated the feasibility of this kind of longitudinal research. A variety of statistical techniques have helped in drawing inferences, but some causal relationships have been diffused.

(*b*) Continuing changes in services provided as inputs presented difficulties in the analysis. Service inputs evolved after pragmatic evaluation at the annual conferences. In each group we started with a pilot year of testing in one village. Staff were encouraged to experiment constantly with improving service activities. Innovations that proved effective were built into standing orders and training programmes. It should be noted, however, that the evolution of services occurred within strictly defined limits of the contents of service packages.

(*c*) Analytic problems were also caused by delays in evolving a tight information system, but these differences were not as great as in the service components. In the second round, some questions which had emerged as being important were added to questionnaires. We had to set up multiple ways of getting information on births and deaths because of village exogamy, which resulted in many mothers returning to their home villages for the first one or two births.

(*d*) A single Indian institutional linkage would have been more useful than our multiple linkages. The primary liaison with the government of India through the Indian Council of Medical Research functioned well. We also had working relationships with the Ludhiana Christian Medical College, the Chandigarh Post-Graduate Medical Research Institute, and the All India Institute of Medical Sciences in Delhi. As political uncertainties developed, however, it would have been better for programme continuity to have had one strong institutional affiliation.

(*e*) A lack of formal career structure made it difficult to maintain continuity of leadership. Without a single strong institutional base, our Indian staff had no security or long-term career commitment. We had to use government salary scales, which were low, but the Punjab government helped greatly by assigning some health staff on deputation. Even with considerable turnover in staffing, a strong core remained throughout. The turnover meant that Narangwal served as a continuing training centre for fieldworkers, since many of our staff took positions in teaching institutions, in government services, or to obtain further education. The relaxed democratic relationships among staff were confusing to some staff members, who would have been more comfortable with a traditional bureaucratic structure.

(*f*) The political pressures that led to the premature termination of the project meant that the last two years were a period of great uncertainty owing to deteriorating Indo-American relationships following the Bangladesh War. Nevertheless, this project survived for a year longer than any other American project in India at that time.

(*g*) Inability to proceed with a planned implementation of Narangwal findings in other parts of India was a disappointment. For approximately three years there had been intensive discussion with the government and the Indian Council of Medical Research about starting a demonstration project in Bihar. We would have taken what had been learned at Narangwal and implemented the service packages in a whole district within the cost constraints, personnel levels, and administrative structures of the Indian national programme. This has, however, happened spontaneously in projects such as Jamkhed (Arole and Arole 1994).

5.9 Conclusions

In the population project we had hoped to continue fieldwork until each experimental group reached a plateau of family-planning use. The premature termination of the project made it impossible to test our original models, since all curves were still rising at the end of the project. We can make the following judgements on the basis of our findings. In the group of villages receiving family planning alone—FP Ed.—staff were complaining at the end of the first year that they had run out of things to talk about, and therefore a general programme of socio-economic development for women was started. The methods used tended to have little influence on family-planning practice and there were other indications that a plateau would have appeared soon. In villages receiving women's services and family planning there was abundant evidence that a clear synergism had been established with programme linkages that seemed feasible and readily accepted. In accordance with the child-survival hypothesis, we had assumed that about five years would be needed before subconscious changes in awareness of child survival would modify 'insurance motivation' for family planning. The results showed, however, that there was a direct programme synergism with child-care services that was produced by the use of selected entry points just as with women's services. Evidence is also suggestive that targeted education associated with these entry points increased awareness of child survival in FP + WS + CC.

Total MCH and family-planning care was provided at a cost less than $2 per capita per year. Two components of services were particularly effective: (i) 90 per cent of services were provided by village auxiliaries (FHWs), who were rapidly trained auxiliary nurse midwives, and (ii) a major role of the health services was to empower the village people, especially mothers, to solve their own problems and provide the necessary care for their children.

In the project on nutrition and infections mortality of children under 4 was reduced by almost half. Detailed analysis permitted the partialling-out of specific components of impact. First, neonatal mortality was reduced by pre-natal nutritional supplementation, mainly with iron and folic acid, and the elimination of neonatal tetanus. Secondly, infant mortality was lowered mainly by early diagnosis and treatment of diarrhoea and pneumonia and moderately by better nutrition. Thirdly, mortality of 1–3-year-old children was reduced by clear synergism between improvement of nutrition and infection control. In the nutrition-care villages, the average weight of 3-year-olds was increased by 0.5 kg. and height by 2 cm. Lastly, the clearest evidence of synergism was the programme interaction in which integrated-care villages showed nutrition benefits equivalent to those in nutrition-only villages as well as the mortality and morbidity benefits achieved in health-care villages using essentially the same inputs required for each service alone.

References

Arole, M., and Arole, R. (1994), *Jamkhed—A Comprehensive Rural Health Project*, Macmillan, London.

Johns Hopkins University (1976), *Functional Analysis of Health Needs and Services*, Asia Publishing House, New Delhi.

Kielmann, A. A., and Associates (1983), *Child and Maternal Health Services in Rural India: The Narangwal Experiment*, i: *Integrated Nutrition and Health Care*, World Bank Research Publication, Johns Hopkins University Press, Baltimore.

Klein, R. E., Arenalos, P., Delgado, H., Engle, P. L., Guzman, G., Irwin, M., Lasky, R., Lechtig, A., Martorell, R., Mejia Piraral, V., Nussel, P., and Yarbrough, C. (1976), 'Effect of Maternal Nutrition and Fetal Growth and Infant Development', *Pan American Health Organization Bulletin*, 10: 701.

McCord, C., and Kielmann, A. A. (1978), 'A Successful Programme for Medical Auxiliaries Treating Childhood Diarrhea and Pneumonia', *Tropical Doctor*, 8: 220–5.

Mata, L. J., Urrutia, J. J., and Lechtig, A. (1971), 'Infection and Nutrition of Children of a Low Socioeconomic Rural Community', *American Journal of Clinical Nutrition*, 24: 240–9.

Scrimshaw, N. S., Taylor, C. E., and Gordon, J. E. (1968), *Interactions of Nutrition and Infection*, World Health Organization Monograph 57, World Health Organization, Geneva.

——Behar, M., Guzman, M. A., and Gordon, J. E. (1967), 'Nutrition and Infection Field Study in Guatemalan Villages, 1959–1964', *Archives of Environmental Health*, 14: 657–62.

Takulia, H. S., Taylor, C. E., Sangal, S. P., and Alter, J. D. (1967), *The Health Center Doctor in India*, Johns Hopkins University Press, Baltimore.

Taylor, C. E., and Parker, R. P. (1967), 'Integrating PHC Services: Evidence from Narangwal, India', *Health Policy and Planning*, 2(2): 150–61.

——and Singh, R. D. (1975), 'The Narangwal Population Study—Integrated Health and Family Planning Services', Johns Hopkins University, Dept. of International Health, Baltimore, mimeo.

——Kielmann, A. A., and De Sweemer, C. (1978), 'Nutrition and Infection', in M. Rechcigl (ed.), *Nutrition and the World Food Problems*, Karger, Basle.

——Alter, J. D., Grover, P. L., Sangal, S. P., Andrews, S., and Takulia, H. S. (1976), *Doctors for the Villages*, Asia Publishing House, New York and Delhi.

——Sarma, R. S. S., Parker, R. L., Reinke, W. A., and Faruqee, R. (1983), *Child and Maternal Health Services in Rural India: The Narangwal Experiment*, ii: *Integrated Family Planning and Health Care*, World Bank Research Publication, Johns Hopkins University Press, Baltimore.

Wyon, J. B., and Gordon, J. E. (1971), *The Khanna Study: Population Problems in Rural Punjab*, Harvard University Press, Cambridge, Mass.

Part II

Latin America

6 A Comparison of Supplementary Feeding and Medical Care of Preschool Children in Guatemala, 1959–1964

NEVIN S. SCRIMSHAW AND MIGUEL A. GUZMÁN

In the 1950s there was only limited recognition of the fact that malnutrition is often precipitated by episodes of infection and that malnourished children were more susceptible to infection, a synergistic interaction. The Institute of Nutrition of Central America and Panama (INCAP) was established in 1949 and immediately began studying factors responsible for the high prevalence of protein–calorie malnutrition including kwashiorkor. It was observed that almost every case of kwashiorkor was precipitated by antecedent infections (Béhar and Scrimshaw 1960), and that the more malnourished children had infections of greater frequency and severity.

As in most developing countries, the officially reported causes of the high mortality of infants and preschool children were incomplete and inexact. Deaths in which malnutrition is the direct or the underlying cause were almost entirely misinterpreted, and usually did not appear in the official statistics. For example, during 1956 and 1957 the cause of the 222 deaths among children 0–4 years of age in four Guatemalan villages, including one (Santa Catanria Barahona) selected for the current study, was reviewed by visiting the households immediately afterwards (Béhar, Ascoli, and Scrimshaw 1958). Forty of the deaths occurred with clear signs of kwashiorkor, forty-two with respiratory infections, and thirty-seven with diarrhoeal disease. The official records indicated only one death from malnutrition, and the kwashiorkor deaths were all ascribed to ascariasis. However, it was also apparent that, without the impact of infections, there would have been few or no cases of kwashiorkor. Moreover, few children would have died from an episode of infection had they been nourished sufficiently to have had normal resistance to infectious disease (Béhar, Ascoli, and Scrimshaw 1958).

Information on the frequency of infections and of malnutrition is even more unreliable. In general, however, their incidences are high in the preschool years, particularly during the first two years of life. In Guatemala, breast-feeding commonly extends to twenty-four months, but beyond six months it no longer provides the protein and calories needed for proper growth and development. In developing countries such as Guatemala, a weaning child is particularly vulnerable to acute diarrhoea because of exposure to an unsanitary environment, lack of acquired immunity, and decreased resistance because of malnutrition (Gordon 1964). Both malnutrition and diarrhoea peak in the 6–24 month age span, with the process of weaning as a common factor (Scrimshaw, Taylor, and Gordon 1968). Accordingly, excess morbidity and mortality among preschool children result from the synergistic impact of both malnutrition and infection (Scrimshaw 1970).

The national medical service, to the extent that the population was reached by it, provided only limited curative and almost no preventive medicine. The demand from the population and most of the physicians in the health service was for more curative services. Yet clearly, curative medicine could neither correct the malnutrition associated with weaning, nor prevent the occurrence of infectious diseases sufficiently to restore normal growth and development to young children. In this situation, INCAP sought funds for an investigation that would compare the effects of enhanced curative medicine, nutritional improvement, or both, on the health of preschool children as compared with only the usual government health services. Funds were approved in 1958 by a Study Section of the US National Institutes of Health, but it was unwilling to provide funds for testing the hypothesis that the combined effect of control of infection and improvement of nutrition would be greater because they believed that this was obvious.

As approved, the design tested only two basic assumptions:

1. that improved nutritional status of preschool children resulting from daily supplementation would reduce the incidence, severity, and duration of diarrhoeal, respiratory disease and other complications of the common communicable diseases of childhood, and improve growth and development;
2. that good medical care would reduce morbidity and mortality from infectious disease and thereby improve preschool child growth and development.

Malnutrition develops slowly over time by progressive decay of nutritional status. For this reason, cross-sectional surveys for assessing prevalence are not appropriate for answering these questions. Similarly, the significance of infection does not rest on a single acute event but relates to a progression of events. A long-term field investigation of a population in its natural environment, with follow-up of illnesses and periodic appraisals of nutritional status, is appropriate for the study of the interrelationships between malnutrition and infection. Association can be documented, without establishing cause–effect type of interrelations. However, for confirming causation, appropriate intervention trials are necessary.

Ideally, randomly selected individuals should have been assigned to each intervention, but, given the nature and complexity of the interventions for this investigation, such an approach was not practical. The only practical alternative was allocation of interventions to different, but comparable communities. With this design, comparisons of morbidity in the feeding community with that of the control community provided a basis for testing the hypotheses. Similarly, the comparison of nutritional status between the treatment community and the control community was the basis for testing nutritional benefits resulting from no infections. Complementary observations collected during the field study allowed identification and evaluation of contributions from broad ecological factors inherent to the cultural patterns and environment of the study communities.

The original reports of the study were in nine volumes; the volume number is given before the reference in the headings that follow.

6.1 Experimental Design (I: Scrimshaw, Guzmán, and Gordon 1967)

The design called for the selection of three predominately Mayan villages in the highlands of Guatemala, as similar as possible in all major characteristics. One village had good medical care for all. The second village received supplementary food for all preschool children and their mothers during pregnancy. The third was a control village receiving only scant health attention from the government programme. Mortality, disease-specific morbidity, anthropometric measurements, dietary intake of preschool children, clinical evaluation, and examination of faecal samples for parasites were done routinely for five years on all children under 5 years of age as described below.

6.2 Search for Suitable Study Villages (II: Scrimshaw *et al.* 1967*a*)

The first step in any field study is securing authorization and understanding from government agencies at all levels, and the acquiescence of local leaders and the communities. Therefore, the project was presented to health officials at the national and departmental levels and to civil authorities at the departmental and municipal levels for each locality. It was also presented to schoolteachers and religious leaders for approval. Since Guatemala was one of the member countries of INCAP, approval of the national and departmental civil and health authorities was easily obtained, but careful and patient effort was required to assure co-operation of the local leaders. Only then was the project presented to the village with a special effort to ensure the participation and support of both prestige leaders (informal) and clique leaders (heads of religious societies or other local groups). Conflict with other INCAP studies was avoided, and there were no other organizations working in the selected villages.

Eight years of prior fieldwork by INCAP had found the communities in this area of the Guatemalan highlands to be co-operative and willing participants in intervention studies. Moreover, permanent migration was rare, and drop-out rates low for preschool children. Although there was some short-term seasonal migration of adult males to the lowlands for work on sugar, cotton, and coffee plantations, their families usually remained behind in the home communities.

Reasonable proximity to a base of operations was essential for efficient logistics, but relative isolation was also required. In Guatemala, the highland rural population resides in small (200–2,000 persons), compact, and semi-isolated villages, many of them within 50 km. of INCAP. The area is 2,000 metres above sea-level, and experiences a rainy season from about May to September and a dry season from about October to April. Roads are more or less passable even in the rainy season. Annual rainfall averages 120 cm. per year with a yearly mean temperature of 18 °C, with a low of 10 °C in December and a high of 21 °C in May. The incidence of diarrhoea varies with the season. It is lowest during the dry season, in the months of December through February, and highest during the rainy season from May to August.

Prevalence of disease was a consideration of paramount importance in determining the suitability of villages in the area selected, the necessary duration of the study, and the size of the study populations. Previous INCAP work had shown incidences of diarrhoea ranging from 180 to 400 cases per 100 children under age 5, and a death rate of 20.5 per 1,000 children (Scrimshaw *et al.* 1962). Similar specific information was not available for upper respiratory tract infections, measles, and whooping cough, but death records indicated that their frequency was also high, despite government efforts to provide DPT and measles vaccines to every young child. Seven of the ten leading causes of death were listed as infectious diseases including parasites (Béhar, Ascoli, and Scrimshaw 1958).

The high prevalence of nutritional deficits in the area had been well documented by INCAP. Mean weight-for-age for children under 5 years of age in this population fell below the sixteenth percentile, and kwashiorkor was clearly identified as a common and frequently fatal disease in the area (Scrimshaw and Béhar 1965). Although some villages were visited occasionally by physicians of the National Health Service, practitioners of folk medicine generally attended to the health needs of the highland people, and obstetrical services were commonly provided by untrained, usually illiterate, midwives. For clinic or hospital service, travel to provincial capitals or to Guatemala City was the norm.

The time required for the preliminary survey of the area and its people (approximately one month) was unusually short because of extensive previous work by INCAP and experienced field personnel. Usually, this indispensable component in the planning of field studies requires a much longer period of time.

6.3 Basis for Village Selection (II: Scrimshaw *et al.* 1967*a*)

From available estimates of disease incidence and mortality for the selected area, it was determined that villages with a population of about 1,000, assuming that 16 per cent of the total population were children under 5 years of age, should yield reliable data for evaluating changes in nutritional status and incidence of infections resulting from interventions. Twenty predominately Mayan agricultural communities, with minimal contact with each other, were visited. Some of these villages were discarded promptly, while others required repeated visits before final selection could be made.

The mayor was interviewed in each promising village to obtain data on total population, ethnic composition, and predominant economic activity. Civil registries were examined for deaths and their recorded causes. Village cemeteries were visited to verify random sets of death records. Inspection of houses for assignment into appearance categories provided a basis for gross comparisons of living conditions and sanitation among villages. Housewives were interviewed for information on eating patterns with special reference to infants and young children. Finally, the three most comparable villages were selected, taking into account disease frequency, and accessibility to INCAP.

Random selection from a listing of eligible villages within 75 km. of the base of operations could result in technical and logistic complications. Small size of populations, diversity of ethnic stock, and location in diametrically opposite directions from INCAP are examples of some of these complications.

The chosen villages were overwhelmingly Mayan, located in the highland area surrounding Guatemala City, accessible by all-weather roads, and with agriculture as the only source of livelihood. The villages were close enough to each other and INCAP for supervisory visits to all in a single day, yet not close enough to allow significant interchange among them. The villages judged best to satisfy the above criteria were Santa María Cauqué (SMC), Santa Catarina Barahona (SCB), and Santa Cruz Balanya (SCZ).

6.4 Characteristics of the Villages Selected (II: Scrimshaw *et al.* 1967*a*)

Previous INCAP research in Santa María Cauqué (SMC), a village with 923 inhabitants, provided ample information on its health and dietary practices and documented little or no change over the previous ten years. The general environment of SMC was also well within the frame of reference for the area. As support for the previous activities of INCAP in this village, the health authorities of Guatemala had provided a simple clinic building, well suited for delivering rudimentary medical care and services to the community. Accordingly, SMC was selected for the 'treatment' intervention.

With a population of 753, Santa Catarina Barahona (SCB) adjoined a larger community for which INCAP data showed environmental and health conditions similar to those of SMC. Furthermore, INCAP had evaluated physical growth in schoolchildren of both SCB and SMC, finding that these two villages had similar growth patterns and nutritional status. Because of the smaller area of SCB, administration of a feeding programme would be less difficult. Accordingly, SCB was chosen as the 'feeding' village. The community willingly provided two rooms for the feeding programme.

The selected control village, Santa Cruz Balanya (SCZ), had the largest population (1,363 inhabitants), but this was considered desirable. SCZ had not been studied previously and required a longer period of reconnaissance. However, it proved to have broadly comparable characteristics and conditions to SMC and SCB. The population was co-operative and accepted the nature and aims of the programme, and it voluntarily provided a small room as headquarters for the study. Although it was not to receive medical care or food, INCAP agreed to help the village in other ways, including a roof for the assembly hall, arranging for the improvement of the entry road, and contributions to various community activities.

The populations of all three villages were predominately Mayan Indian as judged by dress and language used in the household. The proportion who did not identify themselves as Indian was 2 per cent in SCB, 4 per cent in SMC, and 6 per cent in SCZ. An average of 44 per cent were under age 15 and 17 per cent were under 5 years of age.

The overall nutritional status of preschool children aged 1–4 years was poor (weight deficit of 10 per cent or greater for age) in all three villages (84 per cent in SMC, 88 per cent in SCB, and 82 per cent in SCZ). SCB had a smaller proportion of preschool children with second- and third-degree malnutrition (weight-for-age deficits of 25 per cent or more) than either SCZ or SMC. In all three villages calorie and protein intakes of the children were relatively poor, although children in SMC had a better diet, contradicting findings for weight-for-age deficits. Overt clinical signs of nutritional disease were few or non-existent.

Intestinal parasites were found in 60 per cent of the children and over half of them had more than one parasite. Ascaris was found almost universally, while *Entamoeba coli*, *Giardia lamblia*, and *Trichuris trichiura* were present in 10–20 per cent of the children. Deficiencies in environmental sanitation were universally evident.

Dwelling characteristics were similar in the three villages. Those classified as poor (roof of straw, cornstalk walls, and dirt floors) were predominant. Without exception, chickens and dogs shared dwellings with household members.

Water for these villages, supplied from common sources, was distributed through public spouts dispersed throughout the villages, and individual households had to carry water by hand for varying distances. There was no prior

Table 6.1. Completed weaning in 267 children in the three study villages

Month weaning completed	Total children	Per cent
–0.5	1	0.4
6–11	4	1.5
12–17	25	9.4
18–23	99	37.0
24–35	123	46.1
36–47	15	5.6

information on morbidity, but a survey of deaths over the previous ten years provided estimates of crude death rates of 24, 25, and 31 per 1,000 in SMC, SCB, and SCZ respectively. Infant mortality was high—136, 182, and 186 per 1,000 live births in SMC, SCB, and SCZ respectively.

All children in the three villages were breast-fed, and the weaning process very rarely started before the third month of life. The commonest time for a systematic addition of supplements to the diet of an infant was 8–9 months after birth. Indeed, the majority of children continued to receive some breast milk for a prolonged period of time, often beyond age 24 months. Weaning practices were similar in the three villages, and pooled data for complete weaning in 267 children during the five years of study (Table 6.1) document the prolonged breast-feeding (V: Scrimshaw *et al.* 1968).

A summation of all of the evidence indicated that, despite some minor differences and discrepancies, the three villages were as nearly equivalent and comparable as could be expected when dealing with free-living populations (II: Scrimshaw *et al.* 1967*a*).

6.5 Study Design (III: Scrimshaw *et al.* 1967*b*)

6.5.1 The feeding intervention

The feeding programme implemented in SCB was designed to improve substantially the nutritional status of preschool children, without intentionally altering the sanitary conditions of this village. The programme was planned and supervised by an experienced nutritionist. A high-quality protein food, consisting of 18.5 g. Incaparina, 30 g. dried skimmed milk, and 17.5 g. of sugar, was offered six days a week, as a midmorning snack, to preschool children and pregnant and nursing mothers. Cooked as a gruel, an 8-oz. (227 g.) serving supplied 15 g. of good quality protein, 225 calories, and satisfied daily vitamin requirements. A banana was included with all servings, and provided 125 additional calories.

Table 6.2. Food supplement received by preschool children of Santa Catarina Barahona[a]

Year ending April	Total children	None		1–24		25–49		50–74		75+	
		Children	%	Children	%	Children	%	Children	%	Children	%
1960	127	14	11.0	15	11.8	14	11.0	19	15.0	65	51.2
1961	170	63	37.0	11	6.5	8	4.7	10	5.9	78	45.9
1962	171	41	24.0	20	11.7	21	12.3	21	12.3	68	39.8
1963	179	38	21.2	35	19.6	19	10.7	26	14.5	61	34.1
1964	200	45	22.5	51	25.5	32	16.0	30	18.0	36	18.0

[a] By per cent of prescribed amounts and years of the study, May 1959–April 1964.

Since breast-feeding usually satisfies nutrient requirements up to 6 months of age, the supplement was not encouraged for infants under this age without evidence of growth retardation. The food was prepared and distributed at one of the two rooms provided for the programme. Occasionally, however, in case of incapacitating illness, the supplement was taken to the home of recipients. Individual records were kept in terms of both attendance and approximate amount of supplement consumed (III: Scrimshaw *et al.* 1967*b*).

The food supplement was designed to increase the calorie intake of preschool children by one-third and to double their intake of high-quality protein. In practice, however, this was not the case. As shown in Table 6.2, not only did the amount of supplement received by a child vary greatly, but also the proportion of children that received 75 per cent or more of the prescribed amount of supplement declined progressively from 51 to 18 per cent during the five-year study. Conversely, the proportion of children that did not take part in the feeding programme increased from 11 per cent in the first year to 37 per cent in the second and settled around 20 per cent for the remainder of the time.

In an attempt further to improve the nutritional status of the preschool children in this village, nutrition education activities were carried out during the first eighteen months of the study by a resident home economist who talked with the mothers collectively and individually. Visual aids and demonstration techniques were used extensively to assure correct delivery and reception of intended messages. As follow-up, the leaders organized community meetings to inform all housewives in the village. New couples received special attention by home visits from a health educator. In all instances, focus was on proper use and handling of local food resources for maximum nutrition benefits for the family and, more specifically, for children under 5 years of age. Unfortunately, the sequential dietary surveys provided no evidence that this programme was effective.

6.5.2 The medical intervention

The full-time services of the same physician and nurse, both with graduate public-health training, were provided five days per week with all necessary medicines dispensed without charge. The clinic had offices, a waiting-room, simple laboratory, and living-quarters for the nurse and the fieldworkers who recorded morbidity by household visits. The more sophisticated laboratories of INCAP were available for back-up services, including diagnostic microbiology. A part-time sanitarian promoted latrine construction and personal hygiene. A safe water supply was assured at all times, although households still had to carry water from a central fountain. Immunizations were left to the routine of the public-health service, and this proved to be a serious deficiency in the programme. The services were provided to the entire community but with special attention to children under 5 years of age. Detailed individual charts were kept within standardized family files.

6.5.3 The control community

As a control community, SCZ was to remain without change in medical, sanitary, or nutritional practices. A physician visited this village at weekly intervals to supervise field operations, but did not offer medical care. A medical and laboratory team visited SCZ at quarterly intervals to carry out the routine surveys required by the study. This personnel was seldom involved in medical problems of the village, and resident fieldworkers refrained from giving medical or nutritional advice. A variety of social and educational activities—evening movies, puppet shows, athletic events—were provided for this village. Schoolrooms were improved and the access road to the village rebuilt and graded as token exchange of benefits to ensure continued co-operation (III: Scrimshaw *et al.* 1967*b*).

In both SCB and SCZ there were rare occasions when it was humanely and ethically imperative to provide emergency medical services to seriously ill persons. Most often this resulted only in providing transportation to a hospital and such incidents seldom involved preschool children.

6.5.4 Activities common to all three villages

In addition to village-specific activities and the keeping of a detailed diary of significant events and progress in the continuing programme, the study plan required basic data collection by common procedures in the three study villages as follows (III: Scrimshaw *et al.* 1967*b*):

Population censuses taken at the start of the study and repeated at yearly intervals thereafter recorded changes in family structure and available facilities. This information was used for stratification of families by social and economic conditions. The censuses also documented changes in village characteristics for evaluating possible association with study interventions.

Disease morbidity and information on injuries for children under 5 years of age was obtained through biweekly home visits. Occurrence, duration, treatment, and symptoms such as fever, coughing, respiratory distress, anorexia, nausea, vomiting, convulsions, skin rash, oedema, and diarrhoea, were recorded. When diarrhoea was present, the number of stools, their consistency, and the presence of blood were recorded. The nature and circumstances of injuries and of events in the life of a child with likely health significance were also noted. Programmed home visits were the responsibility of two full-time fieldworkers in residence at each village.

Deaths were documented by the fieldworkers who learned of such occurrences soon after the event, as can be expected in a small community. The date and place of death, age, birth certificate number, and cause of death according to the civil registry were recorded for each event. In the course of weekly supervisory visits, the study epidemiologist asked the fieldworkers to provide details of circumstances for each death as needed to diagnose a probable cause and its assignment to one of the broad classification groups used in this study.

Nutritional status was evaluated primarily by anthropometric measurements. Weight-for-age and tricipital skinfold thickness were considered measures of caloric intake adequacy for growth. Height-for-age was used as an index of development and adequacy of protein intakes. All measurements were made quarterly in blind duplicates by experienced INCAP personnel, using standardized procedures and equipment with routinely programmed checks of reliability. Periodic physical examinations were discarded in the first year because they were not useful. This was due to the scarcity of clinical signs, their lack of specificity, and poor reproducibility.

Roentgenograms of both wrists of preschool children were also made at the start of the study and at yearly intervals thereafter. Evaluation of ossification status in these roentgenograms provided an index of maturation.

Dietary adequacy was measured by direct home inquiry at the start of the study, and at yearly intervals thereafter. All dietary surveys were executed by experienced INCAP nutritionists. A combination of observation, weighing, and history-taking through daily visits, programmed over consecutively staggered three-day periods, was the method of procedure. All days of the week were represented equally. In each village, ten to fourteen families were randomly selected for these surveys. Seasonal food production and availability, with particular reference to the foods added or withdrawn from the diets of infants at the beginning or end of weaning, were also noted in the course of the diet surveys.

Prevalence of enteric infectious agents was determined at quarterly intervals for comparison with the frequency of acute diarrhoeal disease and the incidence of kwashiorkor. Rectal swabs were collected, promptly inoculated in the field to appropriate culture media, and incubated on the same day at the central INCAP laboratory. Fecal samples were examined for intestinal parasites and used in isolating enteroviruses. Routine procedures of INCAP were used for these investigations.

Epidemiology of acute diarrhoeal diseases was a special investigation conducted in the treatment village. Cases were evaluated epidemiologically and examined bacteriologically for enteric pathogens during the five years of study. These examinations were generally based on a single stool or rectal swab, but, during a trial period of eighteen months, fecal samples were collected on successive days until either a positive result or five successive negatives were obtained.

6.6 Data Management

Data management was the responsibility of the INCAP Division of Statistics and included the coding of data, production of interim reports, and eventual statistical analysis. All data collected on a daily basis was reviewed by the field supervisors. At this time, discrepancies and omissions were rectified, either by the fieldworkers or by personal inquiry by the supervisor. On a weekly basis the data were submitted to the project epidemiologist for review, reassurance of completeness, and classification.

In this study, the infectious-diseases category was predominant and included: diseases of the digestive tract, respiratory diseases, common communicable diseases, parasitic diseases, and other infectious diseases. Other broad categories considered in this classification scheme were: accidents, poisoning, and violence; congenital malformations, neoplasms, nutritional diseases, metabolic and degenerative diseases; skin diseases and other ill-defined diseases.

All diagnoses and classifications were made by a physician with reference only to clinical information collected by non-medical fieldworkers. Most of the methodology required for collecting data as outlined above had been developed and used in earlier INCAP field studies in the region (III: Scrimshaw *et al*. 1967*b*).

6.7 Stages of the Study

Most of the technical and professional personnel needed for the project were already in residence at INCAP, had participated in previous studies, and were familiar with the proposed methodology. Accordingly, the tasks required for assembling staff, selecting methods, and defining field organization were completed in the unusually short period of two months, and a pilot study for testing personnel and procedures started in March 1959. Late in April 1959, the staff reviewed the protocol of standard operations and modified it in accord with the pilot experience. Data collection for the definitive study began 1 May 1959 and continued for five years, through April 1964.

In interpreting the data, there needs to be a distinction between the first three and the final two years of the project. During the first three years, the project was closely controlled by the original investigators. However, in the final two years, responsibility for the project was assigned to an individual whose priority was his own study of the cognitive performance of children who had been receiving the supplement in the feeding village. The consequences of this are considered both in describing and in discussing the results.

6.8 Results

The main results were presented in six papers that can be summarized as follows:

6.8.1 Mortality (IV: Ascoli *et al.* 1968)

(*a*) In the treatment village, deaths among children between 1 and 4 showed a 50 per cent greater decline than expected from rates of the preceding nine years. The decline for the control village was also greater than expected, exceeding that of the treatment village. The best result was in the feeding village, with a 300 per cent improvement over the expected rate (see Table 6.3).

(*b*) Infant mortality in the feeding village improved 19 per cent during the study after having remained the same during the preceding nine years. Infant mortality in the control village was unchanged. Although the decrease was greatest in the treatment village (36 per cent), it followed the trend of the previous nine years.

Table 6.3. Deaths 0–4 years of age in three rural villages of Guatemala (*SMC*: 'treatment village', *SCB*: 'feeding village', and *SCZ*: 'control village')

	Neonatal	Postnatal	First year	1–4 years
SMC				
1950–8				
Total	26	30	56	46
IM[a]	63	73	136	50
1959–64				
Total	7	16	23	25
IM	27	61	88	35
SCB				
1950–8				
Total	22	34	56	40
IM	71	110	182	56
1959–64				
Total	11	13	24	11
IM	67	79	146	24
SCZ				
1950–8				
Total	59	61	115	101
IM	88	99	186	81
1959–64				
Total	33	37	70	42
IM	90	101	191	50

[a] IM: deaths per 1,000 live births.

(*c*) Deaths among males and females of preschool age were essentially equal.

(*d*) There were three epidemics of measles in the feeding village during the five years, probably because it was so near to a market town. The relatively high case fatality rates from measles, 6.8 per cent in one outbreak, remained so in the surrounding villages over the five years of the intervention. However, the only death from measles in the feeding village was in a child who did not participate in the study.

6.8.2 Total infectious disease morbidity (V: Scrimshaw *et al.* 1968)

(*a*) In all three villages infectious illnesses were high in infancy and peaked in the second year of life, dropping rapidly thereafter. At all ages they were highest in SMC, the treatment village.

(*b*) The total illnesses observed in each village are given in Table 6.4. During the first three years, the amounts of disease in the feeding village were markedly less when compared to the treatment village and only slightly less than that recorded in the control village.

(*c*) Children participating in the programme 75 per cent or more of the time had the lowest total number of days of illness and the shortest average duration of illness episodes. These results were significantly less than for children participating less than 25 per cent of the time. Illnesses per child were less in those who participated 25 per cent of the time or more compared with those receiving the supplement less frequently than this.

6.8.3 Diarrhoeal disease mortality (VI: Gordon *et al.* 1968)

(*a*) As shown in Table 6.5, the lower diarrhoeal disease prevalent in the feeding village during the first three years compared with the other two was very pronounced, and diarrhoea prevalence was highest in the treatment village. In the fourth year, with the change in management of the programme, there was a sharp increase in diarrhoea morbidity in the feeding village to a level similar to that of the control village though less than that of the treatment village. By the fifth year, the feeding village morbidity from diarrhoea equalled that of the treatment village, and exceeded that of the control village.

(*b*) In the feeding village, 34 per cent of diarrhoeal attacks lasted less than four days, while corresponding percentages were 25 per cent for the treatment village and 21 per cent for the control village.

(*c*) Overall, about 11 per cent of children in a given quarter had moderate diarrhoea, about 8 per cent mild diarrhoea, and only 1 per cent of the children had a severe episode. In the second year of life, about 73 per cent were without diarrhoea in a given quarter and in the fourth year this increased to 86 per cent.

Table 6.4. Illnesses of children, ages 0 through 59 months, in three Guatemalan villages[a]

Year ending April	No. of children[b]	Annual days of illness per child	Average days duration	Illnesses per child per year
Santa María Cauqué (Treatment village)				
1960	189	71.1	20.9	3.4
1961	207	59.8	12.7	4.7
1962	212	57.7	11.6	5.0
1963	211	41.8	10.8	3.9
1964	224	48.2	10.2	4.7
1960–4	1043	55.3	12.7	4.4
Santa Catarina Barahona (Feeding village)				
1960	118	10.0	7.6	1.3
1961	138	11.4	8.7	1.3
1962	151	9.6	6.8	1.4
1963	146	16.7	6.5	2.6
1964	150	46.6	9.5	4.9
1960–4	703	19.4	8.2	2.4
Santa Cruz Balanyá (Control village)				
1960	199	13.3	7.2	1.9
1961	230	12.0	8.0	1.5
1962	231	12.9	7.6	1.7
1963	241	17.5	8.5	2.1
1964	240	22.3	7.7	2.9
1960–4	1141	15.8	7.8	2.0

[a] By years, May 1959–April 1964.
[b] Based on actual count of children with disease instead of mid-year census figures used in previous mortality rate calculations.

(*d*) The incidence of diarrhoea was lowest in the dry season months of December to February and highest in the rainy season from May to August.

6.8.4 Respiratory disease morbidity (VI: Gordon *et al.* 1968)

(*a*) Respiratory disease was consistently and significantly less in the feeding village than in the treatment village. However, it was lowest in the control village, presumably because of its greater isolation.

(*b*) Respiratory diseases decreased with increasing participation in the supplementary feeding programme. Those who received food less than 25 per cent of the time had 107 respiratory episodes per year compared with sixty-five for those participating 25–74 per cent of the time and fifty-four for those whose participation was 75 per cent or greater.

Table 6.5.   Incidence of acute diarrhoeal disease by year for children 0–4
years old

Year ending April	Santa María Cauqué (Treatment village)		Santa Catarina Barahona (Feeding village)		Santa Cruz Balanyá (Control village)	
	No. of cases	Cases/100 children/year	No. of cases	Cases/100 children/year	No. of cases	Cases/100 children/year
1960	380	200.0	59	48.0	245	122.5
1961	547	264.2	112	80.0	230	99.6
1962	636	299.1	144	94.7	254	109.5
1963	480	227.5	239	164.8	349	143.6
1964	481	214.7	326	218.8	398	165.1

(*c*) About one-third of all respiratory illnesses in the three villages had a duration of less than one week. Approximately another half ended in the second week, and a further sixth within the third week.

(*d*) Respiratory illnesses of a month or more were most frequent in the treatment village, approximating 6 per cent of the total; in the other two villages the proportion was about 2 per cent.

(*e*) Both the availability of treatment and the feeding saved lives from respiratory disease. Case fatalities due to respiratory disease were more than 50 per cent less in the treatment (1.2 per cent) and feeding villages (1.7 per cent) than in the control (4 per cent). This difference also held for mortality, which was 15.5 per 1,000 preschool children at risk in the treatment village and 12.8 in the feeding village, in contrast to 23 in the control.

6.8.5 Parasitic infections (VI: Gordon *et al*. 1968)

(*a*) By the age of 6 months, 21 per cent of children harboured at least one intestinal parasite. The rate increased progressively with age to reach 89 per cent in children between 4 and 5 years of age. *Ascaris* and *Trichuris* were the most common, but only rarely produced identifiable symptoms.

(*b*) Despite the sanitary measures attempted in the treatment village, there was no evidence of success either in controlling general disease incidence or in improving parasite rates in children. The parasite rate was unchanged after three years in all three villages.

6.8.6 Physical growth (VII: Guzmán *et al*. 1968)

(*a*) There were no differences in mean height and weight observed between boys and girls. Boys and girls in the feeding village tended to grow faster in both height and weight than those of either the treatment or the control village. There were no differences between the treatment and control villages in these measurements. The differences in growth between the feeding and the other two villages resulted in a net difference of approximately 3 cm. in height and 1 kg. in weight by the end of the fifth year of life.

(*b*) Although equal at the start of the study, the head circumference of boys increased faster than that of girls in the three villages. In both sexes the head circumference at birth was about 70 per cent of the measurement at 5 years of age, and at 12 months about 90 per cent. Preschool children of both sexes in the feeding village had greater head circumferences than their counterparts from either the treatment or control villages. For all three villages, these measurements were significantly smaller than US children of comparable ages.

(*c*) Wrist ossification *T*-scores were low in all three villages compared with reference standards for well-nourished children. The feeding village had a slightly higher score than the other two at the start, and the difference increased significantly during the study. It showed no improvement in either the treatment or the control villages.

6.9 Collateral Studies

The series of nine papers summarized above covered the specifically defined objectives of the study. They are rich in details and insights that cannot be presented in this relatively brief summary. In addition, even more reports by study investigators were generated by collateral findings, or were stimulated by the initial results. These included additional observations on diarrhoeal disease (Gordon 1964, 1965; Gordon *et al.* 1965; Gordon and Scrimshaw 1965*a,b*; Mata 1964, 1967; Mata *et al.* 1965; Mata, Catalán, and Gordon 1966; Catalán, Mata, and Fernández 1965; Ascoli and Mata 1965), bone maturation (Garn *et al.* 1964*a,b*, 1967; Rohmann *et al.* 1964; Béhar *et al.* 1964), chicken pox (Gordon *et al.* 1965), measles (Salomon, Gordon, and Scrimshaw 1966; Scrimshaw *et al.* 1966), and child growth and development (Behar 1968; Guzmán 1968; Guzmán *et al.* 1968; Viteri, Arroyave, and Behar 1966). The populations were also used by other investigators for 'piggy-back' studies of oral conditions (Sweeney and Guzmán 1966), and breast-feeding and weaning practices (de Gonzalez 1963; de Gonzalez and Béhar 1966). SMC subsequently became the site for an eight-year study of children from birth to 5 years of age, summarized by Leonardo Mata in *The Children of Santa María Cauqué* (Mata 1978).

6.10 Discussion of Results

The results of this study have been available for more than twenty years and they have been commented upon and interpreted in a variety of ways. The penultimate paper (VIII: Béhar *et al.* 1968) was perhaps too frank in pointing out confounding factors, including the inevitable variations among apparently well-matched villages. The result was that too often reviews of this study, emphasized the confounding factors, instead of stressing the important policy significance of the results.

In our summary of results in this chapter we have described the significant beneficial effects of the nutrition supplement especially during the first three years when the project was the responsibility of the original principal investigator. This occurred even though participation was far short of programme goals. What was equally striking, and much less anticipated, was the almost total lack of demonstrable benefits for preschool children from the costly and high-quality medical care offered in the treatment village. The only significant benefit associated with the medical care was that the lives of several severely ill children were saved, but not any more than were saved by the food supplement.

In order to avoid accepting this unexpected conclusion, confounding factors have been overemphasized by some reviewers who have mistakenly cited the results as minimal or inconclusive. Some have sought to discount the results by suggesting that the medical treatment must have been inadequate. This was certainly not the case. The clinic building was attractive, well equipped, and had laboratory back-up provided by INCAP. No household was more than about five minutes from the clinic. Both the physician and the nurse had advanced training and, with occasional rare exceptions, were in the village five days a week throughout the study. Moreover, there was virtually no limit on free availability of medicines. No industrialized country, much less any developing country, could possibly afford to provide this level of care to a community of less than 1,000 persons, except on an experimental basis. The only reasonable conclusion is that a programme of medical care alone, no matter how sophisticated, cannot prevent the malnutrition and infectious disease morbidity that so greatly affect populations of this type in developing countries.

The main problems in the health of preschool children in the village were diarrhoea, respiratory infections, and the communicable diseases of childhood. Immunization against the latter is a preventive, not a curative measure. In this case it was the responsibility of the government, and only erratically provided, despite repeated requests. Similarly, the availability of treatment did not prevent the spread of respiratory disease.

As to diarrhoeal disease, nothing in the clinic programme had any influence on the contact spread of diarrhoeal infection from contaminated hands and a dirty physical environment. For an experimental period of three years, every child coming to the clinic with diarrhoea received either antibiotic or sulphonamide, but, in comparison with prior diarrhoeal prevalence or with rates in the other two villages, the high prevalence rates remained high. The mere presence of the clinic did not lead to the improvement in personal hygiene needed to reduce contact spread of diarrhoeal infection.

If providing curative medicine of this quantity does so little for the health of young children, the sporadic and poor-quality government curative services certainly could not help reduce the high morbidity and mortality among the preschool children in Guatemala. The only potentially effective preventive measure by the government health service at the time of the study was immunization, but the visits by mobile teams to the villages was erratic and poorly planned. There were also occasional breaks in the cold-chain that rendered the results unreliable. As a result, outbreaks of measles occurred shortly after a visit by an immunization team.

The policy significance of the results in the feeding village was often discounted because their magnitude seemed small. However, despite the fact that nothing was introduced in the feeding village that would directly affect exposure to the infectious diseases that caused most of the ill-health in Guatemalan villages, their prevalence, severity, and consequences were reduced, even when only one-half of the children received 50 per cent or more of the prescribed supplement.

There are several different ways of looking at the feeding-village results. The commonest has been that the differences were small, but so was the average degree of participation. The remarkable finding was the result of any significant responses for this single intervention in such adverse circumstances. The results lend credence to the value of nutritional improvement. Equally, they confirm that nutritional improvement alone is not sufficient to overcome the lack of other health measures.

There was an attempt to include preventive services in the treatment village and, in fact, in the summary of the final paper IX (Scrimshaw *et al.* 1969), reference is made to a 'program of preventive medicine and medical care'. However, the actions taken were either irrelevant, or failures of execution.

Potable water was assured, but the infections harming young children were not water-borne. Young children were becoming infected by contact spread of diarrhoea. Since the villagers still had to carry the water considerable distances to their homes, they could not use it liberally for personal hygiene. Additional pit latrines were built, but there was little evidence either of their use by young children, or of an association between diarrhoea and availability of latrines. Promotion of breast-feeding would have been meaningless in these populations in which prologed breast-feeding is universal and the health statistics would have been immeasurably worse if this had not been the case.

In retrospect, it is clear that for the programme in the treatment village to have been a success it would have needed to incorporate effective primary health care that stressed prevention. An effective programme of immunization would have eliminated the effects of chicken pox, whooping cough, and measles that are periodic problems in all three villages. Improved availability of water and emphasis on its use for personal hygiene would have reduced the contact spread of diarrhoeal disease. Periodic weighing of all children until incorporated into the family diet could have prevented most moderate-to-severe malnutrition *if* properly used to monitor nutritional status and to stimulate remedial efforts by the mother. Both *preventive* medicine and *supplementary* feeding together would probably have been required effectively to reduce both morbidity and mortality of preschool children to levels characteristic of industrialized countries.

There remains the paradox that diarrhoeal and respiratory disease in the treatment village and ultimately also in the feeding village actually increased instead of decreasing because of interventions. The only way that we were able to account for this was the increased number of persons leaving and entering the village as a direct result of the programme. Not only did the doctor, nurse, and community workers come each weekday, but visitors to the programme were very frequent. Bringing mothers and children together, either for clinic visits or the feeding programme, facilitated the contact spread of both diarrhoeal and respiratory disease. Credence to this interpretation is given by a sharp increase in morbidity in the feeding village during the last two years of the programme, when many additional people entered the village on a daily basis for cognitive studies of the children.

By contrast, because of a lack of interesting activities and a deliberate desire to keep the control village undisturbed, additional visitors to it were infrequent, as were activities that brought mothers and children into a confined area. As already indicated, the control village was more distant from Guatemala City, other townships, and a main highway than either of the other two villages. Moreover, it had its own market, whereas, in the other two villages, families frequently travelled to larger markets in nearby towns.

Much was learned about the problems of conducting studies of this sort. It was noted that a field study as long as this one inevitably must experience errors as well as changes of personnel that will affect its operations. Moreover, administrative difficulties and unexpected events are likely to occur and disturb what was conceived as a sound plan. When multiple villages are involved, differences eventually emerge, no matter how carefully they were originally matched. Additionally, there is always the risk that a chance event in one village—flood, earthquake, or epidemic—may weaken or completely invalidate the experimental design. We were aware of these hazards and attempted to minimize them.

In addition to the incomplete participation in the feeding programme, mention must be made that children from 4 to 24 months of age, who needed the supplement most, were fewest in number, while those less in need, the 3- and 4-year-old children, were in the majority among participants in the feeding programme. The latter could attend alone, while someone needed to spend valuable time (already scarce) to bring in the younger ones. Moreover, only a few of the children attended regularly throughout the entire study. The number present on a given day was fairly uniform, but the composition of the group varied from day to day. When an effect shows through such strong confounding factors, it is either a strong effect or else an artefact; it is incumbent on the investigators to try to distinguish between the two. In these studies, comparisons between the treatment and feeding villages are reliable and significant. However, comparisons involving the control village are less reliable and suspect because of the ways in which it differed from the other two.

6.11 Medical, Social, and Public Health Benefits of the Study

In addition to the comparisons between medical care and feeding, discussed at length above, the study contributed to a better definition and understanding of the general health of young children in the area. It confirmed not only the high incidence of acute diarrhoeal disease and upper respiratory infections, but also documented the prominence of the communicable diseases of childhood. The results showed that these diseases are of longer duration, more severe, and more likely to be fatal in this underprivileged population than in well-nourished populations.

At the time of planning this study, undernutrition and malnutrition were recognized as endemic among children of underprivileged populations although they remained largely hidden until exacerbated by an infection. We postulated then that the differences in child morbidity and mortality observed between these populations and those more privileged arose from the synergism between malnutrition and infection, which produces an effect beyond the simple addition of their respective independent negative contributions to health. The passage of time and additional studies have strengthened our early conclusion.

This basic ecologic interaction between a host and its environment should be the focus of preventive efforts instead of the traditional disease-specific approach still commonly used by narrow specialists. Two outstanding facts emerge, both strongly supported by evidence from other less privileged populations so as to characterize them as general principles. One is that, in all regions, the highest death rates after infancy occur in the second year, being comparable in magnitude to the postneonatal infant mortality rate. It follows that preventive measures focused on this period are more likely to be effective than those that take the conventional 1–4-years-of-age approach. It is always easier to get compliance from the older preschool children at the expense of efforts to increase coverage of the children most in need.

Public health statistics tend to focus on mortality rates. Expressing the size of the problem by the number of persons ill, instead of by the number who die, was of considerable practical value. The demonstration of a multifactorial causality also brought recognition that a programme for control must include measures against a variety of factors. Singling out individual elements, whether in succession or indiscriminately, will not be as effective as a common approach to diseases having an interlocking and interacting effect. Perhaps the most important reminder provided by this study is that an approach based on concerted action against the major factors, social as well as biological, can be expected to give better results than measures against any one singly or in succession, even those as important as malnutrition or infectious disease (IX: Scrimshaw *et al.* 1969).

References

Ascoli, W., and Mata, L. J. (1965), 'Studies of Diarrheal Disease in Central America: VII. Treatment of Preschool Children with Paramomycin and Sulfamethoxypridazine under field Conditions in a Guatemalan Highland Village', *American Journal of Tropical Medicine and Hygiene*, 14: 1057–61.

—— Guzmán, M. A., Scrimshaw N. S., and Gordon, J. E. (1968), 'Nutrition and Infection Field Study in Guatemalan Villages, 1959–1964: IV. Deaths of Infants and Preschool Children', *Archives Environmental Health*, 15: 439–45.

Béhar, M. (1968), 'Prevalence of Malnutrition among Preschool Children', in N. S. Scrimshaw and J. E. Gordon (eds.), *Malnutrition, Learning, and Behavior,* MIT Press, Cambridge, Mass.

—— and Scrimshaw, N. S. (1960), 'Epidemiology of Protein Malnutrition', in I. Galdston (ed.), *Human Nutrition Historic and Scientific*, International Universities Press, New York.

—— Ascoli, W., and Scrimshaw, N. S. (1958), 'An Investigation into the Causes of Death in Children in Four Rural Communities in Guatemala', *Bulletin of the World Health Organization*, 19: 1093–102.

—— Rohmann, C. G., Wilson, D., Viteri, F., and Garn, S. M. (1964), 'Osseous Development in Children with Kwashiorkor', *Federation Proceedings*, 23: 338.

—— Scrimshaw, N. S., Guzmán, M. A., and Gordon, J. E. (1968), 'Nutrition and Infection Field Study in Guatemalan Villages, 1959–1964: VIII. An Epidemiological Appraisal of its Wisdoms and Errors', *Archives Environmental Health*, 17: 814–27.

Catalán, M. A., Mata, L. J., and Fernández, R. (1965), 'Estudio sobre portadores de *Shigella*', *Guatemala Pediátrica*, 5: 55–66.

Cochran, W. G., and Cox, G. M. (1950), *Experimental Design*, John Wiley & Sons, New York.

De González, N. I. S. (1963), 'Breast-Feeding, Weaning, and Acculturation', *Journal of Pediatrics*, 62: 557–81.

—— and Béhar, M. (1966), 'Child-Rearing Practices, Nutrition and Health Status', *Milbank Memorial Fund Quarterly*, 44: 77–96.

Garn, S. M., Béhar, M., Rohmann, C. G., Viteri, F., and Wilson, D. (1964*a*), 'Catch-Up Bone Development during Treatment of Kwashiorkor', *Federal Proceedings*, 23: 338.

—— Rohmann, C. G., Béhar, M., Viteri, F., and Guzmán, M. A. (1964*b*), 'Compact Bone Deficiency in Protein-Calorie Malnutrition', *Science*, 145: 1444–5.

—— Rohmann, C. G., Wagner, S., and Ascoli, W. (1967), 'Continuing Bone Growth throughout Life: A General Phenomenon', *American Journal of Physical Anthropology*, 26: 313–17.

Gordon, J. E. (1964), 'Weanling Diarrhea: A Synergism of Nutrition and Infection', *Nutrition Reviews*, 22: 161–3.

—— (1965), 'Weanling Diarrhea: Synergism of Nutrition and Infection', *Pediatrics Digest*, 7: 146.
—— and Scrimshaw, N. S. (1965*a*), 'Nutrition and the Diarrheas of Early Childhood', in R. M. Acheson (ed.), *Comparability in International Epidemiology, Milbank Memorial Fund Quarterly*, New York.
—— —— (1965*b*), 'Nutrition and the Diarrheas of Early Childhood in the Tropics', *Milbank Memorial Fund Quarterly*, 43: 233–9.
—— Béhar, M., and Scrimshaw, N. S. (1964), 'Acute Diarrhoeal Disease in Less Developed Countries: I. An Epidemiological Basis for Control', *Bulletin of World Health Organization*, 31: 1–7.
—— Jansen, A. A. J., and Ascoli, W. (1965), 'Measles in Rural Guatemala', *Journal of Pediatrics*, 66: 779–86.
—— Guzmán, M. A., Ascoli, W., and Scrimshaw, N. S. (1964), 'Acute Diarrheal Disease in Less Developed Countries: II. Patterns of Epidemiological Behaviour in Rural Guatemalan villages', *Bulletin of World Health Organization*, 31: 9–20.
—— Ascoli, W., Pierce, J., Guzmán, M. A., and Mata, L. J. (1965), 'Studies of Diarrheal Disease in Central America; VI. An Epidemic of Diarrhea in a Guatemalan Highland Village, with a Component due to *Shigella dysenteriae* Type I', *American Journal of Tropical Medicine and Hygiene*, 14: 404–11.
—— Ascoli, W., Mata, L. J., Guzmán, M. A., and Scrimshaw, N. S. (1968), 'Nutrition and Infection Field Study in Guatemalan Villages, 1959–1964: VI. Acute Diarrheal Disease and Nutritional Disorders in General Disease Incidence', *Archives Environmental Health*, 16: 424–37.
Guzmán, M. A. (1968), 'Impaired Physical Growth and Maturation in Malnourished Population', in N. S. Scrimshaw and J. E. Gordon (eds.), *Malnutrition, Learning and Behavior*, MIT Press, Cambridge, Mass.
—— Béhar, M., and Scrimshaw, N. S. (1966), 'The Conditioning Effect of Illnesses on the Rates of Gain in Height and Weight in Chronically Malnourished Children', *Proceedings of the Seventh International Congress of Nutrition* (abstracts) 49–50.
—— Rohmann, C., Flores, M., Garn, S. M., and Scrimshaw, N. S. (1964), 'Osseous Growth of Guatemalan Children Fed a Protein-Calorie Supplement', *Fed Proc*, 23: 338.
—— Scrimshaw, N. S., Guzmán, M. A., and Gordon, J. E. (1968), 'Nutrition and Infection Field Study in Guatemalan Villages, 1959–1964: VII. Physical Growth and Development of Preschool Children', *Archives Environmental Health*, 17: 107–27.
Mata, L. J. (1964), 'Agentes causales de las diarreas', *Revista Colegio Médico Guatemala*, 15: 64–71.
—— (1967), 'Importancia Biológica de la biota (flora) normal', *Revista Colegio Médico Guatemala*, 18: 95–100.
—— (1978), *The Children of Santa María Cauqué*, MIT Press, Cambridge, Mass.
—— Catalán, M. A., and Gordon, J. E. (1966), 'Studies of Diarrheal Disease in Central America: XI. *Shigella* Carriers among Young Children of a Heavily Seeded Guatemalan Convalescent Home', *American Journal Tropical Medicine and Hygiene*, 15: 632–38.
—— Lüttman, R., and Sanchez, L. (1964), 'Microoganismos enterpatógenos en ninos con diarrhea severa', *Revista Colegio Médico Guatemala*, 15: 176–84.
—— Alberfazzi, C., Negreros, A., and Fernandez, R. (1965), 'Prevalence of *Shigella, Salmonella* and Enteropathogenic *Escherichia coli* in Six Mayan Villages', *American Journal of Public Health*, 55: 1396–402.

Rohmann, C. G., Garn, S. M., Guzmán, M. A., Flores, M., Béhar, M., and Pao, E. (1964), 'Osseous Development of Guatemalan Children on Low-Protein Diets', *Federation Proceedings*, 23: 338.

Salomon, J. B., Gordon, J. E., and Scrimshaw, N. S. (1966), 'Studies of Diarrheal Disease in Central America: X. Associated Chickenpox, Diarrhea, and Kwashiorkor in a Highland Guatemalan Village', *American Journal of Tropical Medicine and Hygiene*, 15: 997–1002.

Scrimshaw, N. S. (1959), 'Protein Malnutrition and Infection', *Federal Proceedings*, 18: 1207–11.

—— (1970), 'Synergism of Malnutrition and Infection. Evidence from Field Studies in Guatemala', *Journal of the American Medical Association*, 212: 1685–92.

—— and Béhar, M. (1965), 'Malnutrition in Underdeveloped Countries', *New England Journal of Medicine*, 272: 134–7.

—— Guzmán, M. A., and Gordon J. E. (1967), 'Nutrition and Infection Field Study in Guatemalan Villages, 1959–1964: I. Study Plan and Experimental Design', *Archives Environmental Health*, 14: 657–62.

—— Taylor, E. E., and Gordon, J. E. (1959), 'Interactions of Nutrition and Infection', *American Journal of Medicine Science*, 237: 367–403.

—— —— —— (1968), 'Interactions of Nutrition and Infection', *World Health Organization Monograph Series*, 57, World Health Organization, Geneva.

—— Bruch, H. A., Ascoli, W., and Gordon, J. E. (1962), 'Studies of Diarrheal Disease in Central America: IV. Demographic Distributions of Acute Diarrheal Disease in Two Rural Populations of the Guatemalan Highlands', *American Journal of Tropical Medicine and Hygiene*, 11: 401–9.

—— Salomon, J. B., Bruch, H. A., and Gordon, J. E. (1966), 'Studies of Diarrheal Disease in Central America: VIII. Measles, Diarrhea and Nutritional Deficiency in Rural Guatemala', *American Journal of Tropical Medicine and Hygiene*, 15: 625–31.

—— Guzmán, M. A., Kevany, J. J., Ascoli, W., Bruch H. A., and Gordon, J. E. (1967*a*), 'Nutrition and Infection Field Study in Guatemalan Villages, 1959–1964: II, Field Reconnaissance, Administrative and Technical; Study Area; Population Characteritics; and Organization of Field Activities', *Archives Environmental Health*, 14: 787–801.

—— Ascoli, W., Kevany, J. J., flores, M., Icaza, S., and Gordon, J. E. (1967*b*), 'Nutrition and Infection Field Study in Guatemalan Villages, 1959–1964: III. Field Procedure, Collection of Data and Methods of Measurement', *Archives Environmental Health*, 15: 6–15.

—— Béhar, M., Guzmán, M. A., and Gordon, J. E. (1969), 'Nutrition and Infection Field Study in Guatemalan Villages, 1959–1964: IX. An Evaluation of Medical, Social and Public Health Benefits, with Suggestions for Future field Studies', *Archives Environmental Health*, 18: 51–62.

—— Guzmán, M. A., Flores, M., and Gordon, J. E. (1968), 'Nutrition and Infection Field Study in Guatemalan Villages, 1959–1964: V. Disease Incidence among Preschool Children under Natural Village Conditions, with Improved Diet and Medical and Public Health Services', *Archives Environmental Health*, 16: 223–34.

Sweeney, E. A., and Guzmán, M. A. (1966), 'Oral Conditions in Children from Three Highland Villages in Guatemala', *Archives of Oral Biology*, 11: 687–98.

Viteri, F., Arroyave, G., and Béhar, M. (1966), 'Estimation of Protein Depletion in Malnourished Children by Creatinine Height Index', *Proceedings of the Seventh International Congress of Nutrition* (abstracts) 46–7.

7 Longitudinal Community Health Research for Equity and Accountability in Primary Health Care in Haiti

GRETCHEN BERGGREN, WARREN BERGGREN,
HENRI MENAGER, AND EDDY GENECE

Man is not a machine that one can reconstruct as occasion demands, upon other lines for quite other ends, in the hope that it will then proceed to function in a totally different way, just as normally as before. Man bears his age-long history with him; in his very structure is written the history of mankind.

Carl G. Jung

7.1 Introduction to Two Longitudinal Community Health Research (LCHR) Studies in Rural Haiti

The investigators undertook two longitudinal community health research (LCHR) studies to assess primary health-care activities in rural Haiti. The work was motivated by the need to demonstrate that selected interventions can reduce the impact on the community of the most frequent preventable, fatal and crippling diseases. Methods developed for surveillance also brought equity and accountability to primary health care at the community level.

The impetus for these studies originally came from the late Dr William Larimer Mellon, Jr., founder of the rural Hôpital Albert Schweitzer (HAS), Haiti, who increasingly advocated preventive medicine within a community development context. In 1968 public-health practitioners joined hospital staff members to develop outreach projects which could bring equity and coverage in preventive medicine to the district of 100,000 served by the hospital. A small LCHR project began at the same time in a defined population near the hospital in order to inform decision-makers about the most frequent preventable fatal and disabling diseases. Data gathered by the project could help officials who set priorities for community health from a limited budget. Initial methods

The studies were supported by the Grant Foundation of the Albert Schweitzer Hospital of Haiti, the Rockefeller Foundation, the Division of Family Hygiene of the Government of Haiti, the Batelle Memorial Institute, Bread for the World of Germany, IDRC/Canada, and the UNFPA through its funding of Haiti's Division of Family Hygiene.

used in the project were those developed in the Khanna Study (Wyon and Gordon 1971). A second LCHR study, undertaken by the same investigators, was carried out under the supervision of the Haitian government's Division d'Hygiène Familiale (DHF), known as the Projet Intégré de Santé et de Population (PISP) near Petit Goave. Both studies followed specific communities prospectively for births, deaths, and selected causes of morbidity (see figure 7.1). The community health practitioners wished to test the hypothesis that trained volunteer resident home-visitors (RHVs)—chosen because they were

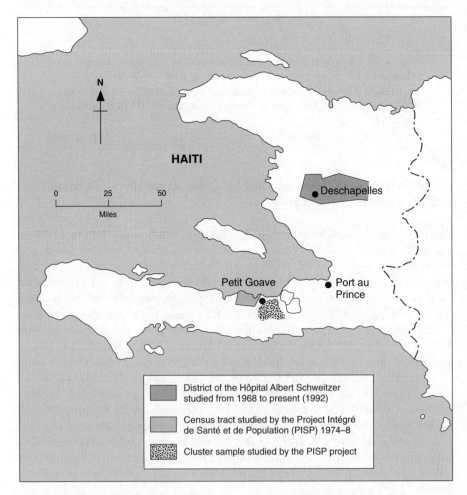

Fig. 7.1. Map of Haiti showing the Hôpital Albert Schweitzer district near Deschapelles and the three census tracts near Petit Goave studied by the Project Intégré de Santé et de Population of the Department of Public Health and Population of the Government of Haiti

young leaders acceptable to their communities—would effectively work with medical personnel towards reducing the most common preventable diseases affecting women and children. The RHVs, known as *collaborateurs volontaires*, would train neighbourhood families to adopt behaviour that would eliminate tetanus of the newborn, and reduce the number of deaths from other diseases such as diarrhoea, measles, malnutrition, and tuberculosis.

A second hypothesis was that the activities of both the curative and the preventive medical systems would be more appropriate if informed by community-based information gleaned through RHVs and their supervisor-trainers. Third, the investigators wished to prove that appropriate preventive measures, taken at the grass-roots level, would not only prove cost-effective but also bring down the high fertility and child-mortality rates. A fourth hypothesis was that the families initially trained in behaviour crucial to mother and child survival would continue such behaviour, and that death rates would remain low. This last hypothesis was investigated in 1992 in a twenty-year follow-up study at HAS.

The community-based information system which emerged from the studies became a key to coverage and health surveillance. It also provided feedback to communities for practitioners in making decisions in primary health care. A more equitable distribution of life-saving interventions included immunization, growth monitoring/promotion, periodic deworming of children, the provision of trained birth attendants and early referral for illness, antenatal care, and family planning. Voluntary resident home-visitors (RHVs) were supervised by paid, locally recruited, part-time community health workers (CHWs) and itinerant primary health-care teams who reached 90 per cent of children under 5, and women in the reproductive age-groups. Key elements of the information system have now been adopted by Save the Children, USA, in child-survival projects worldwide.

An important lesson learned was that *reporting vital events was essential for health surveillance and education, and contributed to appropriate primary health care.* By the end of the first year, RHVs reported all vital events, had a lively interest in helping interpret their meaning, and were eager to prevent unnecessary deaths in their communities.

7.1.1 Similarities and differences in the two LCHR studies

The two studies differed in the following respects:

1. *Private vs. government affiliation.* The Hôpital Albert Schweitzer (HAS) study was carried out under private auspices in 1967–72 near Deschapelles, Haiti, and funded by the Grant Foundation and partly by funds procured by the Harvard School of Public Health. A retrospective follow-up of the HAS study was carried out in 1992. The second study, Projet Intégré de Santé et de Population (PISP) 1974–8, replicated some of the techniques developed

in the first, utilizing only government personnel under Haiti's Division of Family Hygiene, which worked to enhance and expand community primary health-care services into rural Haiti. Funding included the usual government sources with some limited research funds through the Harvard School of Public Health. Demographic consultants from the latter and from the Haitian Insititute of Statistics assisted in project design and evaluation.

2. *Size of the population studied and comparison area.* The HAS study utilized a twenty-three-village census tract of about 9,000 people as a training area and to develop new methods in community-oriented primary health care (COPHC), spreading selected interventions to the greater population of 100,000 served by HAS; the PISP study developed three census tracts to reach a total population of 33,000 as well as a cluster sample comparison area. Each of the PISP census tracts differed somewhat in the ecologic setting and in accessibility to referral services; different nutrition intervention approaches were tried in each of the three census tracts.

Both studies occurred in specific geographic communities where all resident families were registered and followed longitudinally by volunteer RHVs (1:100 families), and their CHW supervisors (1:400 families) chosen in collaboration with local village development committees and their superior authorities.

7.1.2 The investigators and the team structure

The investigators included Haitian and American professionals trained in public health, sociology, anthropology, or demography. Haitian practitioners were a part of the Department of Community Health of HAS or working under the direction of Haiti's Division of Family Hygiene. In both projects the Haitian and American team trained and supervised RHVs and rural auxiliaries known as *Agents de Santé*, or CHWs recruited from their own communities. Each CHW helped recruit and train one voluntary RHV for every 100 families served.

7.2 Goals of the Haiti LCHR Studies

The project's goal was to improve the health and survival of rural Haitian families. Goals common to both studies included:

(a) identification of key determinants and consequences of high mortality, fertility, and migration rates in rural Haiti;

(b) documentation of the impact of a set of primary health-care interventions based on ongoing 'community diagnosis' from the above;

(c) demonstration of the usefulness of community-based health surveillance to identify mothers and children at risk, and provide early intervention (such as temporary targeted food supplements to help children whose growth is faltering regain their appetites);

(*d*) enhancement of knowledge about rural mobility and family structure in rural Haiti, with related implications for health and nutrition planning; and

(*e*) a test of the hypothesis that family behaviour necessary to save the lives of mothers and children, once adopted, would continue in communities where there had been a 'buy-in' on the part of the citizenry.

7.3 Background on Rural Haiti

7.3.1 Relevant history

Haiti occupies the western third of the island of Hispaniola and was considered a valuable colony of France during the eighteenth century. The total land area is 27,700 sq. km., much of which is low mountains, heavily forested when first discovered. African slaves were brought to Haiti as early as 1510; slave ships continued to arrive from Africa over the next two centuries, bringing the agricultural labour necessary for large plantations of rice, tobacco, and sugar cane. The first slave uprising recorded by French historians was in 1522, followed by others in 1679 and 1691. Runaway slaves and their descendants were declared free in 1784; they played a key role in the final revolution which ended with Haitian independence in 1804 (Herskovits 1937).

Haitians formed the first black republic; the land, with its burned and pillaged plantations became theirs. Planting hillside crops of corn, millet, and cassava enabled rural farmers to survive on small parcels of land they claimed as their own; a few large plantations belonged to Haitian military leaders. Irrigated crops included rice and beans, which remain the staple of the Haitian diet.

7.3.2 Rural Haiti since 1960

In the 1960s the *Institut Haitien de Statistique* (IHS) estimated that there were 618 people per sq. km. of arable land. By 1990 this figure was estimated to have nearly doubled, Haiti having lost much arable land to erosion while the population grew. Haiti's civil registration system is such that vital events go unregistered much of the time. The IHS supplied the following survey information in 1970 (all are annual rates given per 1,000 unless otherwise indicated):

Crude birth rate:	44
Crude death rate:	21
Infant mortality rate:	147/1,000 births
Child death rate (1–4-year-olds):	33
Life expectancy:	47.5 years
Rate of population growth:	20.3 per 1,000 person-year

Source: Institut Haitien de Statistiques (1970)

Today Haiti has few large and many small plantations of coffee, cocoa, and tobacco; it does not produce enough cereals to meet its own needs. Once-forested hillsides have been denuded as trees are cut for fuel; eroded, Haiti's rich soil washes into the sea.

Haitian farmers have survived many political regimes, remaining dignified and independent despite their extreme poverty. They live on scattered hillside plots of land which become smaller as they are divided for sons and daughters to inherit. Dwellings are small one- or two-room, mud or cement-floored huts on tiny land parcels owned by the family. Men and women inherit the land equally; and it is not unusual for a peasant farmer to own scattered bits of property whose legal title is in dispute.

In 1970 less than 20 per cent of unions in rural Haiti were recognized as legal. The common Haitian conjugal union is the *plaçage*, or common-law marriage, recognized as an institution by Haitian ethnologists, and documented as being very unstable. Historically, conjugal unions were destroyed by slave-owners who sold slaves with little consideration for their union status. Rural Haitian men may be polygamous, with more than one *plaçage* wife, each living in a different *localité* (village) where the male farmer has land that must be tended (Williams, Berggren, and Murthy 1975). The unstable union pattern is intertwined with rural mobility and with the relocation of children (Rawson and Berggren 1974). When unions split, children are divided between parents, or may be sent to live with relatives.

Farm women (80 per cent illiterate) supply at least half the agricultural labour and market most of the excess produce. The majority attend at least one local market per week, displaying and selling their produce in the midst of a carnival atmosphere of bargaining, selling, and buying.

Traditionally a farm family lives in a small group of houses known as a *lacour*, or courtyard of an extended family. As few as ten or as many as several dozen such *lacours* compose the smallest named unit, known as a *localité* but dubbed a village by outsiders.

Poor families have one large meal a day, often shared by extended family members. Breakfast is hardly more than a snack (coffee and bread); the evening meal is often sparse. Haitian mothers breast-feed, but usually not exclusively, since custom dictates that they leave their infants behind when they go to market or work in the fields. Most families can afford animal protein once a week at best; some have meat only once a month. The average daily calorie intake has been estimated as between 1,200 and 1,700 calories per day, with carbohydrates forming 72 per cent of the daily intake (Bureau of Nutrition of the Department of Public Health and Population of Haiti 1978). Children suffer most, especially toddlers, who cannot be expected to consume their daily calorie requirement at one sitting. Once weaned from the breast, however, uneducated mothers tend to expect a child to do so.

Modern Haitian families are very mobile; the effect of this is seen especially in the USA and Canada. Of 336,394 Haitians legally entering the USA between 1956 and 1972, about 230,000 were known to have remained. It was estimated that equally as many may have entered illegally. The migration rate increased over the following ten years, peaking with the arrival of hundreds of Haitian 'boat people' on Florida shores who staked their lives on the chance to get out of Haiti, even at the risk of losing their own lives and the life savings they gave to unscrupulous boat captains. During the 1970s, an estimated 12 per cent of natives lived outside Haiti (Allman 1979).

The two LCHR studies reviewed here provide insights into the determinants and consequences of high mobility and its effect on family structure in rural Haiti. In these studies, the authors documented facts about Haitian conjugal unions dissolving at the time of migration, and the consequent separation of children from their biological mothers. The risk of child displacement and some of the consequences to the child are explored.

7.4 Strategies

7.4.1 Strategy and interventions of the community health department of the Hôpital Albert Schweitzer (HAS)

The strategy adopted by the Community Health Department of HAS was 'to deliver appropriate health and nutrition services at the village level'. Accomplishing this 'required identification of the health problems, identification of the persons at risk for each problem, and planning and provision of appropriate services for the persons at risk. The Department's plan of action entailed performing all three functions simultaneously and gathering data to evaluate services' in twenty-three villages, a census tract near the hospital (Berggren, Ewben, and Berggren 1981).

The HAS community health team implemented market-place immunizations against tetanus and then began enrolling families in census-based community-oriented primary health care (COPHC), beginning with an original 'census tract' in 1968. Longitudinal community health studies depended on the reports received by voluntary resident home-visitors (RHVs) from their own villages (*collaborateurs volontaires*). Prior to this, hospital workers had erratic information on the outcome of their curative and health-education efforts.

Each month an HAS itinerant technical support team brought supplies such as vaccines and weighing-scales, in order to help local RHVs carry out appropriate preventive health clinics at the neighbourhood-level health rallies. Each RHV invited mothers and children from his or her neighbourhood of about 100 families, and reported on all pregnancies, births, deaths, and in- or out-migrants on a monthly basis. Attendance at rallies was 80 per cent or higher, owing in part to the fact that the itinerant technical support team arrived at dawn, the best time to get hold of people in rural Haiti.

Some of the locally recruited and trained RHVs became part-time paid community health workers (CHWs) (later called *Agents de Santé*) who would participate in the mapping, house-numbering, door-to-door family registration, and initial community diagnosis exercises, including enumeration of the population. They would identify, help recruit, and train new RHVs (preferably female) as liaison workers.

Although the above strategy applied initially to only twenty-three villages (population 10,000), services were gradually expanded to include a population of 60,000 by 1972. Today (1992) nearly 180,000 people are registered and followed in a similar way. The mostly male RHVs, however, were gradually dropped over the next fifteen years, and are now being replaced by trained women workers called *animatrices* (each serves ten to fifteen families on a voluntary basis). As interventions proved appropriate in the census tract, they were spread to other sectors of the catchment area and included: immunization against tetanus of all women of reproductive age in the hospital catchment area through market place immunizations (W. Berggren 1974), and creation of 'rally posts' or assembly points in villages so that technical assistance could be brought to enrolled populations, beginning in the census tract and gradually moving throughout the valley to enrolled communities so that the following could be accomplished (Berggren, Ewbank, and Berggren):

- immunization of all pre-school children and their mothers;
- teaching of oral rehydration therapy to all caretakers;
- nutrition training for child caretakers through growth monitoring/counselling and the use of a home-based record;
- *temporary* nutrition supplementation targeted at the growth-faltering child;
- quarterly deworming with piperazine;
- identification, through case-finding and sputum collection, of persons with tuberculosis for referral and assistance in ongoing treatment;
- demonstration education in nutrition through the use of itinerant nutrition rehabilitation and education centres (CERNS), where mothers could participate in a three-month rehabilitation of their malnourished children while learning to use the least expensive local foods in a 'typical' village kitchen (King *et al.* 1978; G. Berggren *et al.* 1984);
- continued identification, recruitment and training of traditional birth attendants (TBAs) (G. Berggren *et al.* 1983);
- identification and referral for antenatal care of pregnant women found in the census tract or in market-place immunizations;
- active education of all women in the reproductive age-group about family-planning methods.

During the 1980s, HAS built outlying dispensaries with trained auxiliaries who supervised CHWs in carrying out their own small 'rally-posts' without the technical support team. This brought HAS activities more in line with an operating government norm, but adequate maternal and child health coverage diminished until HAS workers created *animatrices* to act as liaison for an even smaller neighbourhood of about fifteen families.

7.4.2 Strategy transfer from a private project into a government setting: The Project Intégré de Santé et de Population (PISP)

The PISP project under the Division of Family Hygiene (DFH) was in many ways a replication, this time under government auspices, of the HAS project. The same senior investigators advised the PISP project; however, the Haitian staff were a part of the normal government health services.

A set of interventions chosen by the DFH and the PISP team on the basis of their combined experience included the use of an itinerant technical support team to back up the community-based team in door-to-door interventions which included distribution of contraceptives and oral rehydration therapy (ORT) packets. The PISP project chose not to use market-place immunizations as a first line of action. Rather, there would be widespread use of quarterly neighbourhood rally-posts and a greater reliance on RHVs. To the interventions described for HAS were added:

- promotion of multiple methods of family planning with door-to-door distribution of condoms, pills, and contraceptive foam, with referral to government centres for the IUD;
- promotion of oral rehydration therapy and the trial of packet distribution;
- active referral of all patients with fever to the village volunteer, who was supplied with antimalarials for free distribution;
- a mini 'antenatal' clinic where pregnant women were examined, immunized (if necessary), and counselled in the rally-post.

Because the neighbourhood health rallies could occur only quarterly, interim monthly weigh-in and supplement distribution rallies were targeted to the children suffering growth-faltering. Growth-monitoring and promotion through the periodic health rallies introduced for the first time in rural government services the use of the home-based weight-for-age growth chart and record for children.

CERNS were used to rehabilitate malnourished children in one census tract but modified to become a two-week 'Nutrition Demonstration and Education Foyer' in another. This was an itinerant two-week workshop to teach families how to begin the rehabilitation process for their malnourished children under the supervision of the *monitrices* trained to work in CERNS (G. Berggren *et al.* 1984).

7.5 Longitudinal Community Health Research Objectives

Objectives at the Hôpital Albert Schweitzer were:

(*a*) to perform community diagnosis and interpret the findings for decision-makers;

(*b*) to involve the community in interpretation of findings into action against common preventable killing and crippling diseases;

(*c*) to document impact of interventions brought to neighbourhood level; for example:

   (i) analysis and interpretation of ongoing age-specific fertility rates, age/cause-specific mortality rates, and key morbidity rates; and

   (ii) analysis and interpretation of increased 'user rates' of family planning, under-5's clinics, and the like, once they were available at the neighbourhood level;

(*d*) to document enhanced coverage and equity in primary health care with the methods adopted;

(*e*) to identify children and families at high risk for malnutrition and to provide targeted temporary nutrition supplements as well as village-level nutrition rehabilitation and education services;

(*f*) to interpret findings into action such as counselling about breast-feeding, child-spacing, and family planning;

(*g*) to develop the instruments necessary to meet the above objectives and document the impact of the activities.

In meeting the above objectives, the investigators expected that the data analysed could inform decision-makers about primary health-care priorities. Unexpected findings in the areas of child displacement and 'fostering' in both projects precipitated special investigations into the behavioural patterns behind family building or dissolution in rural Haitian families.

7.6 Study Design

7.6.1 Study design in the HAS project

The study design for the HAS project was a simple 'before and after' documentation of changing vital rates and nutritional status over time. The study was aided by a retrospective fertility history survey of 100 per cent of women in the census tract (Berggren, Ewbank, and Berggren 1981). It was hampered by lack of a comparison area, which would have been politically unacceptable to the Haitian government at the time. National data for rural areas became available for comparison purposes through the Institut Haitien de Statistiques only at the end of the study period.

A follow-up retrospective survey carried out in 1992 was applied to a sample of women in the original census tract and in two other, more remote census tracts.

7.6.2 Objectives and study design in the PISP project

The PISP project shared the same objectives as the HAS project; in addition, it needed to demonstrate that a grass-roots community health approach could work under the government system, using existing personnel but with the addition of a technical support team. Three census tracts, of approximately 10,000 population each, were served on the northern half of the southern peninsula near the town of Petit Goave (see Figure 7.1). Differing levels of primary health care and nutrition intervention were implemented in each of the three census tracts. A fourth cluster-sample area was chosen through random sample methods for a multi-round demographic survey. Findings for the three census tracts could then be compared to those from the random sample area.

The three census tracts, their differing nutritional interventions, and differing primary referral facilities were as follows:

Trou Chouchou, an area without any health infrastructure and limited access; the nutrition intervention would be growth monitoring/counselling (as prescribed by the Haitian government's DFH), with the addition of temporary food supplements targeted to the growth-faltering child.

Meilleur, a mountainous tobacco, coffee, and bean-growing area with a government dispensary; the nutrition intervention would include an itinerant two-week nutrition education and rehabilitation exercise carried out in a local, borrowed kitchen (G. Berggren *et al.* 1984).

Grand Goave, an area boasting a small town, a government health post, and maternity unit with beds attended by a physician; the nutrition intervention would be a full-fledged nutrition rehabilitation and educational CERN.

The cluster-sample comparison area with thirty clusters of approximately 300 persons each in villages located outside the census tracts. These villages had only those treatment facilities available to rural Haitians in general; there were no grass-roots health workers.

Indicators followed in three intervention areas over a three-year period included age-specific, cause-specific death rates, age-specific fertility rates, migration rates, and childhood malnutrition rates using the Gomez (weight-for-age) classification. Later selected indicators were documented in the cluster-sample area through a multi-round demographic survey.

7.7 Demographic Methods

7.7.1 Steps to the utilization of the demographic method

The method included the following steps:

    (*a*) choice of villages with consensus of local community leaders;
    (*b*) procurement or creation of detailed village maps and house-numbering;

(c) field-testing and application of a census form, for use as a family enrolment instrument to be updated quarterly and reapplied annually;

(d) training of farmers from local communities as health worker/reporters (CHWs, or *Agents de Santé*, one per 400 families);

(e) identification, recruitment, and training of local volunteers (resident home-visitors, or RHVs, preferably women) as liaisons to their communities (one per 100 families);

(f) identification, recruitment, and training of traditional birth attendants (TBAs) in safe delivery and birth-reporting;

(g) derivation of CHW rosters of under-5's and of women in the reproductive age-group to be carried door-to-for for update;

(h) installation of a vital-events reporting system with the local RHVs. Forms were tested and a protocol developed for home-visit and vital-event reporting. RHVs assisted the paid community health workers to complete the vital-events report forms.

The roster replaced the 'home visitor's diary' and permitted the CHW to follow the family planning status of each woman (aged 15–49) and the nutrition and immunization status of each child under the age of 5. Vital events were recorded monthly on colour-coded forms. These were posted to the original family enrolment and to separate birth, death, and migration registers for each census tract. The colour-coded forms were then filed separately for completion purposes. All deaths were certified by physicians as to cause (see below).

Deaths were recorded at the household by the RHV, cross-checked with other records by the CHW, and recorded by cause of death as reported by (i) the family, (ii) the health workers (after a brief non-formal 'verbal autopsy'), and (iii) a physician who reviewed the report. At HAS autopsies were performed on some cases.

Birth investigations were carried out in such a way as to compute age-specific fertility rates, contribute to the understanding of birthing practices, and to record the birth by name of the birth attendant, most of whom were traditional birth attendants (TBAs). This method contributed to the HAS staff's ability to recruit and train those most active as opposed to those who might have been chosen by the community for political reasons.

Migration information was recorded in such a way as to contribute to an understanding of the propensity to migrate. Reports included geographic origin and destination as well as reasons for migration.

Finally, a twenty-year retrospective fertility history survey, undertaken at HAS, informed the investigators on the sustainability of their results.

7.8 Human Resources, Service, and Research Activities

Differentiation of the research activities from the ongoing service activities is important for replicability and for cost-reporting purposes. Only the latter will be replicated in most instances; research personnel can be subtracted.

Resources for referral services were in place for primary health-care back-up; in the case of HAS, secondary and even some tertiary facilities were available. In the HAS service area, during the 1980s, each CHW was assigned 500 families or more, without community volunteers, to the detriment of adequate coverage. The PISP project respected the government norm but insisted that all CHWs identify, recruit, and help train volunteers RHVs to serve their own neighbourhoods. By 1988 the HAS project returned to the use of volunteers, this time in the form of women *animatrices* to get coverage. Given the scattered nature of Haitian homes on rural hillsides, one CHW could not be expected to achieve coverage without community participation in the form of volunteers to serve as 'extra arms' and liaisons for health education and reporting purposes. Professional community-health practitioners included a nurse-supervisor or physician-supervisor for the itinerant technical support team and locally recruited nutrition demonstration educators or *monitrices* (about 4:30,000 population in the PISP project). The latter were itinerant workers, rotating around the impact areas to set up temporary nutrition demonstration/rehabilitation units.

Resources for the demographic/research component common to both projects included:

- part of the time of a physician community health director;
- a physician-assistant community health director with responsibility for the demographic/research component;
- locally trained clerical assistants for the above who also supervised reporting services from the RHVs and CHWs;
- part of the time of the members of the itinerant technical support team. For the PISP project, covering a population of 32,000, there were fifteen CHWs and sixty locally recruited RHVs (four voluntary RHVs for each full-time CHW);
- part of the time of the two or three community development workers with specialized training in health education and/or community leadership.

7.9 Source of Data

Several major sources of data existed by the end of the each project:

1. annual census data from the family registration form;
2. birth, death and migration reports;
3. the following nutritional parameters on children under 5 in the HAS project: height, weight, head circumference, breast-feeding status, and whether or not receiving a dietary or medical supplement to counter growth-faltering; longitudinal weight for age data in the PISP project;
4. data from HAS on clients' clinic record, including classification of all major diagnoses, according to ICDA standards;

5. use of out-patient and in-patient hospital facilities, as determined by address; people from outside the study area were separately recorded;
6. data from CERNs and nutrition demonstration foyers.

Complementary sources of data came from special studies—for example, from tuberculosis surveys, from fertility histories, and from behavioural studies.

7.9.1 Treatment of data

(*a*) *Data from the HAS project*. Data from HAS were hand-tabulated locally for interpretation and sharing. Later they were coded on 'Visi-scan sheets' and transferred to computer facilities under the supervision of specially trained university research assistants.

Nutrition data on each child including monthly weights, heights, and head circumference were coded into separate files.

Analysis and interpretation of the data were carried out with the assistance of institutions in Haiti as well as the Harvard School of Public Health (USA).

(*b*) *Data from the PISP project*. All data from the PISP project were hand-tabulated or were processed after having been coded by either the Haitian Institute of Statistics or the Department of Population Sciences at the Harvard School of Public Health under the supervision of faculty members who served as consultants.

Life-table analyses were used to determine changes in life expectancy rates. World Fertility Survey (WFS) techniques were used for a sample of women interviewed to corroborate the fertility findings and to allow WFS to pilot their instrument. A similar instrument was applied in 1992 to a sample of 3,000 women aged 15–49 in the HAS study area. A special study of local traditional healers by a Haitian sociologist was added to the data of the PISP project (Clerisme 1979).

7.10 Results

Preliminary field analyses from the LCHR data revealed age/cause-specific death rates that became a kind of compass to guide decision-makers in the two projects described. Based on information from these studies, the practitioners involved could give feedback to communities and could make appropriate choices for programmes to improve health and survival. Application of the methods described brought a more equitable distribution of services (90 per cent coverage) and documented the feasibility of surveillance methods in rural Haiti (Berggren, Ewbank, and Berggren 1981; Projet Intégré 1982).

7.10.1 An output result: increased coverage with surveillance

The use of volunteers for door-to-door follow-up enhanced coverage and provided an equitable distribution of services, two keys to improved primary health care (Taylor 1992).

Door-to-door family enrolment was followed by a personal prompt from RHVs to get children to services. This resulted in far more equity in the health system and an 85–90 per cent coverage rate. In villages less than one mile from HAS, fewer than 30 per cent of children were fully immunized when the project began, even though immunization was free. This figure jumped to 90 per cent within two years. A census-based system appears to be a *sine qua non* in Haiti. Local community development teams enhance this process; leaders followed discussions about causes of death and took steps to encourage compliance.

Community participants bought in the idea that 'no child should be left out'. However, an HAS twenty-year follow-up study revealed that coverage dropped when RHVs were no longer recruited and trained. Health rallies would be poorly attended and would not achieve coverage without a local 'personal prompt'. Therefore HAS currently trains a new level of RHV, a volunteer female *animatrice* (one per twenty families) who helps with local 'under-5's clinics' created bimonthly with an itinerant technical support team. Health workers depend on use of the census-form and the home-based personal health records derived from it. Even though reporting of vital events could not be maintained for financial reasons in all parts of the hospital district, coverage has been maintained through insistence on door-to-door enrolment and follow-up. This principal finding fed into those of the Narangwal Study and others that community-based registration is essential to coverage (Taylor 1992).

7.10.2 Documentation of disappearance of tetanus of the newborn as a major cause of infant mortality

A combination of population-based data from the census tract and records of hospital admissions proved that tetanus of the newborn was eliminated in the HAS hospital district (see Figure 7.2) with interventions including immunizations of all women in the reproductive age-group, whether at market-places or at health rallies. Education of traditional birth attendants to prompt clients to be immunized played a role, as did case investigation with education of local villagers.

Deaths from tetanus of the newborn disappeared in the PISP project by the end of the first year, with 80 per cent coverage through the immunization of all women with three doses of alum-precipitated tetanus toxoid administered one month or more apart (Paisible and Berggren 1984).

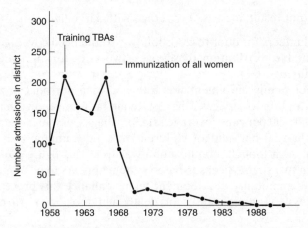

Fig. 7.2. Total admission for tetanus of the newborn from within Schweitzer Hôpital district, near Deschapelles (population 100,000), Haiti, 1958–1991

7.10.3 Reduction in mortality rates

Infant mortality rates in the HAS census tract were cut by nearly two-thirds and 1–4 year mortality rates were cut in half at a cost of $1.60 per capita (see Table 7.1) (Berggren, Ewbank, and Berggren 1981; Taylor 1992).

A retrospective survey of fertility histories showed that infant mortality rates dropped from 110 per 1,000 live births in the five-year period immediately preceding the project to thirty-four in 1972, with no difference between retrospective and prospectively recorded rates. By contrast, prospective studies in three other defined populations studied in 1974 showed infant mortality rates three times higher (see PISP study). The project had affected the largest single component of infant mortality in Haiti, that of tetanus of the newborn.

At HAS, at the beginning of the project one could demonstrate that 1–4-year mortality rates were already reduced to 11 per 1,000 per year, compared to the national estimate of twenty-three. This rate continued a steady decline over the study period to half that level. By contrast, the PISP study found that rate to be 26 per 1,000 or higher in their comparison area in 1977 (see Table 7.2).

The PISP project also saw a decline in infant morality. Over a period of three years, rates fell from 240 to 101 in Trou Chouchou; from 133 to 99 in Grand Goave; from 122 to 108 in Meilleur (Paisible and Berggren 1984).

Reduction of 1–4-year age-specific death rates from 26.5 per 1,000 per year to 14.6 and 11.3 for Trou Chouchou and Grand Goave, respectively, and to 22.6 per 1,000 per year for Meilleur compared to the comparison area finding of twenty-six per thousand (Paisible and Berggren 1984).

Table 7.1. Programme impact as indicated by childhood mortality rates from longitudinal studies before and after intervention through population-based community health out-reach programmes in Haiti, 1968–82

	Infant mortality		1–4 Year mortality (Deaths/1,000 population)	
	Before	After	Before	After
Albert Schweitzer Hospital census tract (rural) (population 10, 132)	75/1,000* (1967–72)	30/1,000 (1974)	16/1,000 (1967–72)	4/1,000 (1974)
Integrated Project of Health and Population, Petit Goave area (rural) (population 33,054)	133/1,000 (1974)	105/1,000 (1978)	26/1,000[a] (1970–4)	16.6/1,000 (1978)
Cité Simone (depressed urban area) (population 30,000)	185/1,000[a] (1980)	116/1,000 (1982)	57/1,000 (1980)	Pending
Comparison area (rural) (cluster sample from non-intervened population) (population 9,989)	118/1,000 (1977)		26.7/1,000 (1977)	
Republic of Haiti (Haiti Inst. Statistics) (population 5,000,000)	140/1,000 (Pop. Studies Vol. 33, No. 3, p. 517, 1979)		26/1,000 (Haiti Inst. Statistics 1975)	

[a] Retrospective study of fertility histories of all women in the 15–49-year-old age-group in the designated area.

Reminiscent of the 'village effect' in the Narangwal Study (Kielman, Taylor, *et al.* 1983), the Meilleur census tract seemed to present a much greater challenge in the reduction of early childhood (1–4 year) mortality rates. Rates remained high (three times higher than those in the HAS area) despite immunization coverage of 85 per cent, training of mothers in oral rehydration therapy, and demonstration education in nutrition.

7.10.4 Life expectancy increases and years of life saved

In the HAS study, life expectancy was 57.1 years in 1968 compared to the national estimate of 47. By 1972 life expectancy in the census tract increased to 66.4. Analysis of years of life saved, based on expected numbers, revealed

Table 7.2. Hôpital Albert Schweitzer (HAS) census tract study and integrated project of health and population (PISP) study deaths/1,000 children aged 1–4 in rural Haitian census tracts of 10,000 each

	Year of intervention				
	0	1	2	3	9
HAS study (1968–76)	16	12.1	9.2	9.4	8.4
Trou Chouchou (1974–8)	26	13.7	16.1	14.6	—
Grand Goave (1974–8)	26	13.0	13.5	11.3	—
Meilleur (1974–8)	—	26.8	22.9	22.6	—
Non-intervened area	—	—	26.7	—	—
Haiti National Institute Statistics (1970)	—	—	—	—	26.6

111 years of life saved per 1,000 person-years of follow-up, or 1,064 years of life saved at $1.60 per capita (Berggren, Ewbank, and Berggren 1981).

Life expectancy increased by more than three years in all three census tracts in the PISP study. By the end of the PISP observation, the life expectancy in the study area was 66 years, as compared to the national estimate of 49 years (Paisible and Berggren 1984).

7.10.5 Determinants of fertility reduction

In the PISP project there was a consistent steady downward trend in birth rates during the active door-to-door distribution of contraceptives:

Annual crude birth rates (per 1,000 population) in the PISP project for the period studied declined from 47.8 to 40.4 in Trou Chouchou; from 45.5 to 37.8 in Grand Goave; and from 33.1 to 30.6 in Meilleur. Findings were statistically significant for Trou Chouchou and Grand Goave but not for Meilleur, a more traditional and highly Roman Catholic area with very stable families and a later age at first child-bearing.

Despite the HAS policy of offering IUD (Lippes loop) insertion as a method of family planning over the study period, the crude birth rate remained at about 36.5 per 1,000 and did not decline over the study period. The general fertility rate over the period fluctuated around 174 (Berggren, Murthy, and Williams 1974). Mothers in other areas in Haiti, however, were experiencing higher birth rates (see the above) (Paisible and Berggren 1984).

Age-specific fertility rates (ASFR) for each area were also documented annually, highlighting a trend in reduction in the ASFR in the peak fertility years. In the PISP project, this was in part due to family planning (mainly pills and condoms).

At HAS, only one method was offered during the early years: the IUD. The cumulative net continuation rate for IUD use compared well with studies in Puerto Rico and elsewhere. Nurse-midwives performed the insertions and carried out follow-up examinations with results equal to or better than physicians performing the same task (Berggren, Vaillant, and Garnier 1974). However, the overall data seemed to point to an unlikely receptivity to the IUD as a family-planning method. In focus-group interviews, women asked for other methods such as an injection to prevent pregnancy. Acceptance in the peak fertility years was offset by an increase in the fertility rate among teenagers. Here, age/parity-specific fertility rates over the period revealed increases as parity increased, at least until parity six. Controlled for parity, the rates declined rapidly with age; however, if controlled for age they rose with parity and declined only moderately after parity six (Berggren, Murthy, and Williams 1974).

Age at first union, stability of unions, and their relation to fertility were the subject of special documentation. Late age at first birth was reflected in the finding that 49 per cent of women were single at age 19 with a rapid drop to 29 per cent single at age 20. For both men and women, about half the first unions last less than two years. For women, an interim period between unions of two years or more contributes to prolonged interpregnancy intervals (Berggren, Murthy, and Williams 1974).

The above was closely related to migration patterns. Migrations often involved dissolving *plaçage* unions with prolonged interpregnancy intervals. The total fertility rate (TFR) of migrants versus non-migrants showed that migrants had a much lower fertility than those who never migrated (an overall TFR 3.2 as compared to 5.5 for non-migrants). This finding was significant at the 99 per cent level with an F value of 25.3. Migrants tended to move from village to village more often after conjugal unions split.

Documented socio-cultural determinants reducing fertility included prolonged breast-feeding (18 months was the mode) and broken unions (one-third of women, at any point in time, were not cohabiting owing to the absence of the male consort) (Williams, Berggren, and Murthy 1975). In addition, the projects found that women rely on the practice of traditional methods of birth control, especially withdrawal. The age at first child-bearing averaged 21 years of age over the study period; 83 per cent of women between 15 and 19 years of age had not yet entered into union in 1970.

7.10.6 Nutrition intervention and results

In 1967 HAS serial weighing of 95 per cent or more of children under 6 revealed that 3–6 per cent were oedematous with kwashiorkor, or were in third-degree malnutrition (Gomez classification), weighing less than 60 per cent of the Harvard standard median (Gomez *et al.* 1956). Subsequently, the project introduced growth monitoring/counselling for children under 5 in the census tract with monthly measures of length, weight, and head circumference; breast-feeding practices were also noted. Precocious diagnosis of malnutrition allowed team members to initiate early and appropriate action, with the result that kwashiorkor disappeared. A temporary (two-week supply) dry-food supplement was distributed as 'medicine' for the growth-faltering child, and village-level demonstration education in nutrition through the CERN proved crucial to the documented reduction in admissions for malnutrition (W. Berggren 1971).

The Haitian diet of pureed beans enriched with oil and served with traditional Haitian staple cereals proved adequate to recuperate malnourished children in Haiti and was also cost-effective (King *et al.* 1966). Admissions for severe malnutrition from within the hospital district of 100,000 fell from nearly 800 in 1968 to 398 in 1971. The investigators reported on the cost-effectiveness of itinerant nutritional rehabilitation and education centres (CERNS) compared to hospital treatment (King *et al.* 1978).

Results of the PISP nutrition intervention focused on results of the *Foyers de Demonstration en Nutrition* (FDNs), a modification of the CERN. The death rates in children who had been malnourished, and in their younger siblings, was significantly decreased if the mother had participated in FDN nutrition demonstration-rehabilitation in her own village (G. Berggren *et al.* 1984). This study of the mother's ability to prevent malnutrition and death in younger siblings of malnourished children despite their poverty gave new validity to the practice of educating mothers to rehabilitate their children using locally available, inexpensive foods.

7.10.7 Population mobility and characteristics of migrants and migrations

Documentation of rural Haitian mobility was a harbinger of the future emigration of Haiti's 'boat people' to the USA during the 1980s. The HAS census data on migration rates shifted from a small net immigration rate to a substantial net emigration rate (−20.9 per 1,000) in 1971. In the PISP project, the natural rate of growth was around 2 per cent per year; but the population did not increase because of substantial emigration (Paisible and Berggren 1984). In Grand Goave (population 10,884, with a health centre, and situated on a major road) the project documented a negative growth rate for all three years, as high as −2.5 per cent in 1977. Meilleur (population 12,675), a census tract in a coffee-growing area with only a dispensary, experienced a negative growth rate of −0.8 per cent in 1977 and a positive rate of +0.3 per cent in 1978.

At HAS, migration rates were also studied for highland (hillside) vs. lowland villages, with highland villages being more stable and tending to experience in-migration during a 'food-shortage' year when the price of cereals rose precipitously. In a twenty-year follow-up study, the highland villages had doubled in size where the lowland villages had increased by only 30 per cent (Menager and Berggren 1992).

Economic factors were the main cause of migration. With family plots as small as a few acres, children had no reasonable possibility of inheriting enough land to become successful farmers on their own. Young men emigrated to towns and cities, seeking work. Young girls worked as domestic servants in the homes of wealthier relatives or town-dwellers. Focus-group interviews with parents whose daughters had emigrated in this way between the ages of 8 and 12 revealed that they had hoped that their daughters would be 'taken care of' and even sent to school by the sponsoring families.

7.10.8 Family mobility, child displacement, and fostering

Overall, about one-fifth of the child migrations were related to a dissolving union. It was possible to demonstrate that, in the cases of dissolving unions, children were often found 'migrating alone' to the home of a relative. They accounted for 34 per cent of immigrant male children and 26 per cent of immigrant female children. The HAS study showed high age-specific migration rates for toddlers. Males up to 4 years of age had an immigration rate of 64 and an out-migration rate of 56 per thousand in 1968. But under-5 females were even more mobile, with rates of 80 and 53 per thousand. The surprise was how often such children were found 'migrating alone', being separated from one or both biological parents. Children born to polygamous *plaçage* unions may have been passed from one wife to another or left behind with relatives when the couple separated or moved on. In the PISP study, 38 per cent of women in the reproductive age-group stated that their male consort had fathered children elsewhere, often in what appeared to be a pattern of serial unions. One woman proudly pointed to the four stepchildren she had raised, each from a different *plaçage* union of her consort.

At HAS, emigration rates for 10–14-year-old girls exceeded that of boys, and in 1971, the rate was double: 158 per /1,000 for girls, to 86 per 1,000 for boys. Many of these young girls were recorded as 'migrating alone', with the reason for migration being that they would be 'taken care of' by someone. Investigation revealed that girls of this age are needed to carry wood and water and to babysit. They are usually unpaid and unschooled. The project personnel documented cases where a person from the capital city, not necessarily a relative, came to collect the child, promising to 'take care of her' but in fact inducting her into long hours of arduous labour. In at least three instances, such children returned home in poor physical condition; one died in Port au Prince, apparently from tuberculosis. Interviews with families revealed that they had held false hopes about their daughters.

An understanding of the nature of conjugal unions is relevant to family mobility and child displacement. The HAS study documented that 15 per cent of conjugal unions are polygamous; in the PISP study 20 per cent were admittedly so. Female partners consider themselves to be in *plaçage* unions. The number of unions a woman has had increases with age and time. The PISP study found that, by five years after her initial union, the average woman would have had a second; by fifteen years she would have had a third (Paisible and Berggren 1984). Each new union usually required a migration and led to the displacement of biological children.

At HAS, during the four-year observation period, about one-third of the 15–24-year-old population emigrated from their villages. Another 10 per cent moved within the census tract to another village. Their offspring were often subsequently 'passed around' from family to family with dire nutritional consequences. So, an in-depth study of the determinants and consequences of child-transfer was done.

7.10.9 'Fostering' and gender-related child relocation in rural Haiti

An anthropological documentation of determinants and consequences of child relocation in one village near HAS after a preliminary analysis of residence patterns showed that 17.5 per cent of children under 10 years of age did not live with both natural parents. Of 165 such children born to couples in that community, twenty-six were found to have had residency established outside the community at the time of the study. However, another group of twenty-six children had migrated into the community. The most significant finding of the study of these children was the adverse consequence in terms of their nutritional status. Of children under the age of 6 in this community, more than one-half had already been screened into nutrition rehabilitation centres, when the HAS nutrition surveillance programme discovered their growth faltering. Half of them were living with only one parent or with another relative. Further analysis revealed a statistically significant association between malnutrition and child–parent separation (Rawson and Berggren 1973).

The PISP study used a multiple decrement life-table to study the risk of a child being 'orphaned' by being separated from his or her biological mother (see Table 7.3). In the first year of the study, by the time a child had survived to 24 months of age, he or she had a 20 per cent risk of being separated from the biological mother either by being orphaned or by being left behind in a move or a dissolving union. Such children fared poorly; for under-1s, 13.5 per cent died within the first six months of separation from the mother (Paisible and Berggren 1984: 113).

Table 7.3. Per cent of rural Haitian children separated from their biological mothers in first 24 months of life

Month of life	Trou Chouchou	Grand Goave	Meilleur
6	10	9	5
12	14	16	8
18	19	17	11
24	20	19	13
Per cent dying within 6 months of separation	7.1	16.7	18.2

Source: Projet Intégré de Santé et de Population, prospective longitudinal studies in three defined populations near Petit Goave Haiti, 1974–8.

7.10.10 Special substantive results of the studies

For reasons of brevity, some results of the studies are not reported here. These include:

- documentation of delayed age-at-first-menses (age 15.5);
- documentation of relationship of length of postpartum amenorrhoea to prolonged breast-feeding (an average of eighteen months in Haiti, with concomitant postpartum amenorrhoea of about twelve months on average);
- documentation and interpretation of the risk of infant separation from the mother in the first year of life, with its consequences;
- documentation of age-specific, cause-specific death rates with significant findings such as: more women age 15–49 die of tuberculosis than of maternity-related causes; gastroenteritis remained a leading cause of death even in the face of an active oral rehydration therapy programme;
- documentation that babies are born into five different types of conjugal union, each with different stability and each with different consequences for child survival;
- documentation of the epidemiology of hookworm disease, with some of its determinants and consequences;
- documentation of the role of traditional healers, their ratio to population, propensity to co-operate with medical practitioners, and usefulness to the community.
- documentation of the effect of Nutritional Demonstration and Rehabilitation Foyers in terms of the mother's subsequent ability to prevent malnutrition among siblings younger than those rehabilitated.

7.11 Discussion

7.11.1 Can research and service be combined?

Research and services were combined in these studies. Both the HAS and the PISP projects showed that, in their initial home visits, CHWs could confirm the census quickly, go immediately to the task of educating the family about the health rallies, and, in each neighbourhood of about 100 families, they could seek one person who had demonstrated willingness and capability to help as a voluntary liaison worker. This person would be trained in the task of identifying vital events and making initial reports on them so that the birth, death, or migration could be investigated and the report completed by the CHW. The projects succeeded in demonstrating that simply reporting on vital events provided a valuable service to a family, because it put health workers in position to give counselling at times of family crisis. Recording a birth, for example, provided the opportunity to prompt a mother to get her child immunized, to avail herself of family-planning services, or to initiate her participation in growth-monitoring.

Given the scattered housing pattern of rural Haitians, it is better to think of them as living in neighbourhoods within a village. Each neighbourhood has a potential volunteer who can help the CHW. The ratio of volunteer workers to population appears to be about 1:100 families or less; HAS now uses one volunteer *animatrice* (usually a young, literate woman) for every fifteen families. A lesson learned is that volunteers need motivation, and that a 'mother's group' can pass the responsibility around from year to year.

7.11.2 Family behavioural change and tetanus immunization

Family behavioural change has been a crucial factor in the disappearance of tetanus. Whereas in 1967 the convulsions of tetanus were thought to be caused by an evil spirit, with no hope of recovery, from 1972 onwards, with the disappearance of tetanus, there has been a change in popular beliefs. Rural families in the Artibonite Valley now appear to believe that it is unacceptable to give birth without the mother having been immunized to protect the newborn from tetanus. Complete immunization against tetanus reaches nearly 100 per cent of women aged 15–49, with no prompting needed.

7.11.3 Underlying determinants of in-migrations to the HAS census tract in the Artibonite Valley

The general instability of the Haitian population, in terms of both conjugal unions and high migration rates, was, to some degree, a reflection of economic circumstances. Nearly 20 per cent of in-migrant males aged 15–44 gave as their reason for migrating 'non-agricultural employment' and another 18 per cent gave as a reason simply 'unemployed, unsettled'. Only fifteen per cent of the male immigrations were related to the formation of a new conjugal union.

7.11.4 Cultural insights

This neo-African culture reflects in its family-building structure much of its historical background and the influence of economic problems on an already impoverished people. Haitians are descendants of African slaves who brought with them many traditions about raising children, including the 'sharing' of a child by the extended family. Males often report that their uncles, more than their fathers, and their aunts as much as their mothers' participated in raising them and providing role models. Ethnologists have pointed out that the nuclear family as Western society sees it is not necessarily the same crucial element for the African child. The tendency for the extended family to take responsibility for all children born into it, and to provide temporary or long-term housing for displaced adults' is seen as a strength of African culture.

In both the HAS and the PISP studies, one sees a reflection of the above, and at the same time adverse consequences (at least in nutritional terms) for relocating children. Child relocation can be seen as a strength carried over from the African cultural setting, or as a detrimental consequence of highly unstable conjugal unions and family mobility, occurring in Haiti under adverse economic conditions. In dealing with these families, the authors found that a child once displaced was also apt to be displaced again, and that malnutrition is a common result (Rawson and Berggren 1973). The PISP longitudinal studies found that up to 20 per cent of under-2s are separated from their bio-logical mothers, and that 13 per cent die in the first six months thereafter. Therefore, as protective as 'child-sharing' might be in the African cultural setting, in Haiti its effects seem adverse for the child.

Not well documented in the PISP study is the plight of rural Haitian girls who may be displaced as early as 8 years of age to bear heavy work burdens in families other than their own, usually relatives or better-off urban families. The HAS study at least documented the high mobility rates for pre-pubertal girls; a follow-up study is needed.

Rapid assessment procedures such as the use of focus groups are beginning to bring understanding to the situation of women who head single-parent fam-ilies and whose common complaint is 'My mister abandoned me.' These insights are important for those who set targets for family planning: women outside unions do not wish to give up the 'fertility card' they feel may be nec-essary to gain a new male consort.

Union status was a confusing subject and one of special interest, since it was crucial to the understanding of household structure and child relocation in rural Haiti. At the time of family registration, interviewers found that up to one-third of 15–49-year-old women who had already been in a conjugal union were without a male consort. An early classification utilized five major categories of union; children are born to all five types. Armed with these definitions, census-takers often categorized unions in an even more complicated way, using more than one symbol to explain a woman's union status. For example, 'P/S,P/S,M' meant a person had been in *plaçage* twice and then separated, and was now in a legal marriage.

7.12 Practical Implications for Health Programme

(*a*) These studies indicate the desirability of home-based health records for every age-group, since rural Haitians are highly mobile and are unlikely to continue to attend the same health centre for long. Haitian mothers in both studies proved that they do not lost home-based personal health records if health providers are faithful in their insistence on their being presented and interpreted, and will use them as educational tools.

(*b*) Resistance to family planning can be expected from women whose union status is in fluctuation. More educated Haitian women may feel that between unions it is in their own interest to continue the use of contraception, or to have contraceptives always available. However, until this philosophy or belief is shared by their less-well-off sisters, up to one-third of women are not likely to be using family-planning methods.

(*c*) The adverse consequences of child relocation are not understood by Haitian families, who think relocation will provide a better life for the child. Education about keeping a family intact, and the importance of bonding in child development could be included in the outreach programmes of many institutions in Haiti. Nutrition education, for example, need not dwell exclusively on scientific facts about what a child needs to eat and how often. Haitian families care for their children and deserve a better chance to understand the value of family stability for both mothers and children.

(*d*) Rawson's conclusions from his anthropological study of child relocation are relevant for health programmes since they indicate that: (i) child relocation is an important underlying cause of malnutrition; if recognized early enough, simple preventive measures can be taken; (ii) child-spacing and smaller family size would reduce the risk of relocating a child; hence family planning could contribute positively; (iii) in addition, the health staff should identify relocated children promptly and then institute nutrition education of the child's new guardian; more frequent monitoring of the child's height, weight, and health status. Practical methods of record-keeping and follow-up are essential at the neighbourhood level.

References

Allman, James (1979), 'Fertility, Mortality, Migration and Family Planning in Haiti', *Population Studies*, 3: 505–21.

Beghin, I., Forgere, W., and King, K. (1970), *L'Alimentation et la nutrition en Haiti*, Presses Universitaires de France, Paris.

Berggren G., and Favin, M. (1992), 'Social Mobilization for the Elimination of Tetanus of the Newborn', *Working Paper of the Mothercare Project*, John Snow, Boston, Mass.

——and Garenne, M. (1993), Preliminary Report on a 1992 Follow-up of the Hôpital Albert Schweitzer Census Tract (unpublished), Harvard Center for Population and Development Studies, Cambridge, MA.

——Berggren, W., and Ewbank, D. (1980), 'Haiti's Artibonite Valley Migration and Instability', *Migration Today*, 8(1): 3–23.

——Hebert, J., and Waternaux, C. (1985), 'Comparison of Haitian Children in a Nutrition Intervention Program with Children in the Haitian National Nutrition Survey', *Bulletin of the World Health Organization*, 63(6): 1141–50.

——Murthy, N., and Williams, S. (1974), 'Rural Haitian Women: An Analysis of Fertility Rates', *Social Biology*, 21: 368–78.

——Vaillant, H., and Garnier, N. (1974), 'Lippes Loop Insertion by Midwives in Healthy and Chronically Ill Women in Rural Haiti', *American Journal Public Health*, 64(7): 719–22.

——Berggren, W., Verly, A., Garnier, N., and Peterson, W. (1983), 'Traditional Midwives, Tetanus Immunization, and Infant Mortality in Rural Haiti', *Tropical Doctor*, 13: 79–87.

——Alvarez, M., Genece, E., Amadee-Gedeon, P. M., Henry, Mirielle (1984), *The Nutrition Demonstration Foyer: A Model for Combating Malnutrition in Haiti*, Hoviprep Monograph Series 2, International Food and Nutrition Program of MIT, MIT Press, Cambridge, Mass.

Berggren, W. L. (1971), 'Evaluation of the Effectiveness of Nutrition Rehabilitation and Education Centers', in P. L. White (ed.), *Proceedings of the Western Hemisphere Congress on Nutrition III*, Dept. of Food and Nutrition, Division of Scientific Activities, American Medical Assn. Press, Chicago.

——(1974), 'Administration and Evaluation of Rural Health Services: I. A Tetanus Control Program in Haiti', *American Journal of Tropical Medicine and Hygiene*, 23(5): 936–49.

——and Berggren, G. (1971), 'The Changing Incidence of Fatal Tetanus of the Newborn', *American Journal Tropical Medicine and Hygiene*, 20: 491–4.

——Ewbank, D., and Berggren, G. (1981), 'Reduction of Mortality in Rural Haiti through a Primary Health Care Program', *New England Journal of Medicine*, 304: 1324–30.

————Genece, E., Henry, M. (1983), *Enquête sur la nutrition et la santé*, Projet Intégré de Santé et de Population, Division d'Hygiène Familiale, Fardin Press, Port au Prince.

Bordes, A. (1982), 'The Impact of Breastfeeding and Pregnancy Status of Household Contraceptive Distribution in Rural Haiti', *American Journal of Public Health*, 72(8): 835–8.

Bureau of Nutrition of the Dept. of Public Health and Population of Haiti (1978), *Haitian Nutrition Status Survey*, Dept. of Health Education and Welfare Press, Washington.

Clerisme, Calixte (1979), *Recherches sur la medecine traditionelle*, Projet Intégré de Santé et de Population de Petit Goave, Dept. of Public Health and Population of the Govt. of Haiti, Fardin Press, Port au Prince.

Commission on Health Research for Development (1990), *Essential Links: Harnessing Research for Health and Development*, vi, Oxford University Press, Oxford, pp. 971–7.

Finlay, S. (1990), 'Report on Neonatal Tetanus in Haiti', special report to the Immunization Office of Pan American Health Organization in Washington.

Gomez, F., Ramos-Galvan, R., Frank, S., *et al.* (1956), 'Mortality in Second and Third Degree Malnutrition', *Journal of Tropical Pediatrics*, 2: 77–83.

Herskovitz, M. J. (1937), *Life in a Haitian Valley*, Knopf Press, New York.

Institut Haitien de Statistiques (1970) *Statistical Report on Haiti*.

Jelliffe, D., and Jelliffe, P. (1961), 'The Nutritional Status of Haitian Children', *Acta Tropica*, 18: 1–45.

Kielmann, A., Taylor, C. E., DeSweemer, C., Parker, R. L., Chernichovsky, D., Reinke, W. A., Uberoi, I. S., Kakar, D. N., Masih, N., Sarma, R. S. S. (1983), *Child and Maternal Health Services in Rural India: The Narangwal Experiment*, World Bank Research Publication, John Hopkins University Press, Baltimore.

King, K. W. (1964), 'Development of All-Plant Mixtures Using Crops Indigenous to Haiti: Amino-Acid Composition and Protein Quality', *Economic Botany*, 18: 311–22.

——(1968), 'Food Patterns in Dietary Surveys in Rural Haiti', *Journal of the American Dietetic Association*, 53: 114–18.

——Fougere, W., Foucauld, J., Dominique, G., and Beghin, I. (1966), 'Response of preschool children to high intakes of Haitian cereal-bean mixtures', *Archivos Latinoamericanos de Nutricion*, 16: 54–64.

—— —— Hilaire, A., Webb, R. E., Berggren, W., and Berggren, G. (1978), 'Preventive and Therapeutic Benefits in Relation to Cost: Performance over Ten Years of Mothercraft Centers in Haiti, *American Journal Clinical Nutrition*, 31: 679–90.

Management Sciences for Health (MSH) (1992), 'Using Maps to Improve Services in Family Planning', *Family Planning Manager*, 1(5).

Menager, H., and Berggren, G. (1992), 'Preliminary Report to the Hôpital Albert Schweitzer Alumnae Reunion', (unpublished).

Morley, D., and Woodland, M. (1979), *See How They Grow*, Oxford University Press, New York.

National Institute of Nutrition, Bogotá (1969), *A Practical Guide to Combating Malnutrition in the Preschool Child: Report of a Working Conference on Nutrition Rehabilitation and Mothercraft Centers*, Appleton-Century Croft, New York.

Paisible, P., and Berggren, G. (1984), *Démographie et fécondite dans le Projet Intégré de Santé et de Population*, Projet Intégré de Santé et de Population, Dept. of Public Health and Population of the Govt. of Haiti, Fardin Press, Port au Prince.

Projet Intégré de Santé et de Population (PISP) (1982), *Administration et organisation d'un programme communautaire de santé et de population en milieu rural*, Dept. of Public Health and Population of the Govt. of Haiti, Fardin Press, Port au Prince.

Rawson, I., and Berggren, G. (1973), 'Family Structure, Child Location and Nutritional Disease in Rural Haiti', *Environmental Child Health*, 19(4): 288–98.

Scrimshaw, S., and Hurtado, E. (1987), *Rapid Assessment Procedures for Primary Health Care*, Latin America Studies Center, UCLA, Los Angeles, Calif.

Sebrell, W. H., *et al.* (1959), 'Appraisal of Nutrition in Haiti', *American Journal Clinical Nutrition*, 7: 1–48.

Sirinit, K., Soliman, A., Van Loo, A. (1965), 'Nutritional Value of Haitian Cereal-Legume Blends', *Journal of Nutrition*, 86: 415–23.

Tamari, Mary Ellen (1985), Personal communication from doctoral thesis research, unpublished.

Taylor, Carl, E. (1984), 'The Uses of Health Systems Research', *WHO Public Health Papers 78*, World Health Organization, Geneva.

—— (1992), 'Surveillance for Equity in Primary Health Care: Policy Implications from International Experience', *International Journal of Epidemiology*, 21(6): 1043–9.

Williams, S., Berggren, G., and Murthy, N. (1975), 'Conjugal Unions in 425 Rural Haitian Women', *Journal of Marriage and the Family*, Nov., 1022–7.

Wyon, J. D., and Gordon, J. F. (1971), *The Khanna Study: Population Problems in the Rural Punjab*, Harvard University Press, Cambridge, Mass.

Part III

Africa

8 Design, Results, and Comments on the Machakos Project in Kenya

JEROEN K. VAN GINNEKEN, ALEX S. MULLER,
AND OMONDI-ODHIAMBO

8.1 Study Design and Methodology

8.1.1 Objectives

In 1971 a longitudinal population-based project was initiated in a part of the Machakos district of Kenya with a view to developing means of improving mother and child health in a rural area. The objectives were as follows:

1. to obtain accurate data on morbidity and mortality from measles, whooping cough, other acute respiratory infections, and acute diarrhoeal disease in children 0–4 years of age;
2. to obtain data on nutritional status, social behaviour and attitudes, socio-economic status, and biological and physical environment, and to study the influence these may have on observed disease patterns;
3. to obtain accurate data on maternal and perinatal morbidity and mortality in relation to antenatal and delivery care received;
4. to develop a system for registration of births, deaths, and causes of death for all age-groups and for the diseases mentioned above (1) among children 0–4 years of age, capable of producing data useful for the planning, operation, and evaluation of health services and suitable for use in a typical district in Kenya with limited resources; and
5. to study and measure the influence, if any, of the presence of a medical research team on mortality.

In the course of the project two more objectives were added:

6. to test the impact of several health interventions under field conditions and to determine in particular the clinical efficacy of two rather than three pertussis vaccine immunizations during infancy; and
7. to study the relationship between nutritional status during pregnancy and birth weight, lactation performance and growth during infancy.

During the implementation of the project it was decided, in view of methodological problems and staff constraints not to pursue objectives (4) and (5).

8.1.2 Study area

Originally, two areas approximately 80 km. east of Nairobi were selected for the study. All research activities took place in one area (B), while in a nearby control area (A) only an annual census to obtain information on vital events was carried out. However, the results of the demographic studies in the control area A have never been fully analysed and the results reported in the various publications refer nearly everywhere to studies undertaken in experimental area B. The area selected is part of the northern division of Machakos district. Table 8.1 shows the sublocations involved, the *de facto* number of inhabitants, and the population density according to the baseline survey in November 1973.

The area is divided into two by the Kanzalu range of hills. The sublocations of Kambusu and Kingoti belong to the western part, which is relatively fertile. Katheka, Ulaani, and Katitu are on the flat, semi-arid eastern side of the Kanzalu range. Coffee is an important cash crop in the western part, while sub-sistence farming (cowpeas, maize, cattle) predominates in the eastern part. The altitude ranges from approximately 1,300 to 1,700 metres. Mean annual rain-fall is 900 mm.

The population belongs to a Bantu tribe, the Kamba. Most people live in compounds consisting of two to four huts and a food store; the compounds are scattered throughout the area. There are no villages in the sense of con-centrations of a large number of homesteads, except to a certain degree around trading centres. Though the sublocations are subdivided into six to eight *utui* (villages), these often do not form geographically well-defined units. But for the purposes of the project they have been used to number the households. There are also a number of market-places in the area. The largest—Kinyui—consists of thirty to fifty shops on both sides of the main road, but very few shop-owners actually live in the market area.

Table 8.1. Study area, total population, and population density according to 1973 survey

Location and sublocation	De facto population	Surface area sq. km.	Population density per sq. km.
Mantungulu			
Kambusu (West)	4,258	8	532
Kingoti (West)	6,497	17	382
Katheka (East)	1,847	15	123
Mbiuni			
Ulaani (East)	3,413	29	118
Katitu (East)	2,568	18	143
Total	18,583	87	214

The average number of household members is six. As in many parts of Kenya, there is considerable migration. About a quarter of all heads of households have a job in one of the larger towns in Kenya—most of them in Nairobi—and come home for the weekend, or once a month. Because of shortage of land, a considerable number of families migrate from the study area or maintain one farm within and one outside the area, moving back and forth several times a year.

8.1.3 Demographic surveillance

Four phases can be distinguished in the implementation of the demographic surveillance system.

The first phase consisted of establishment of close links with the chiefs, subchiefs, and other local leaders of the area. The chiefs organized open-air meetings (*baraza*) with the people in various parts of the study area during which the project staff introduced themselves and explained the aims of the project.

The second phase consisted of carrying out the demographic baseline survey of the entire population, including the preparation of detailed maps of every village and the numbering of every household. Initially these maps consisted of crude sketches made by the fieldworker on the spot. At a later stage, the quality of the maps was improved by use of fairly recent aerial photographs of the area obtained from the Office of Lands and Surveys. A form was used to gather the following information on every member of a household: name, relationship to the head of the household, sex, age, whether present or absent, whether father and mother were alive, and fertility information on females aged 12 years and over.

A household was defined as a group of people habitually eating and sleeping together on the same compound, and one demographic survey form was used for each household. It became clear that not all fieldworkers applied the same criteria when entering a person on the form as a member of the household; therefore it was decided to register only the *de facto* population, i.e. only those who had slept in the household during the night immediately preceding the interview. Every person considered to be a member of the household by its head, whether present or not (*registered* population), was later added to these rolls in order to provide the denominator for vital events and incidence rates.

After two months of initial training and testing of questionnaires, the actual demographic survey was started. This included mapping of all the *utui* in one of the five sublocations comprising the study area. All households were given a card marked with a number, which was also painted on the door after permission had been obtained from the chief and the people at a *baraza*. Lists were made of the household numbers in the various sublocations. With these lists and the maps drawn by the field staff, fieldworkers were assigned twelve to fifteen households per day for which they had to complete demographic survey forms. After finishing with all the *utui* in one sublocation, the entire staff moved on to the next.

It was found that many people did not know their age in calendar years and use was made of a 'calendar of events' that listed all important events that had taken place in the area since approximately 1880 that were known or remembered from hearsay. For children 0–4 years of age, it was usually possible to obtain a birth date accurate to a month from a birth certificate or a record of baptism kept by the parents.

As a rule, the informant was the head of the household or his wife. If necessary, fieldworkers were allowed to obtain information from any other member of the household over 15 years of age who happened to be available for interview.

The demographic baseline survey, including recruitment and training of field staff, took ten months; at the end of this all demographic information was completely updated (Sept.–Oct. 1973).

The third phase started with the introduction of fortnightly demographic data collection in November 1973. At first all households in one sublocation were visited every two weeks by three fieldworkers to obtain information on births, deaths, and migration. After three months, demographic surveillance was done in the entire study area, which had been divided into twelve clusters of approximately 300 households. Each fieldworker was assigned to one cluster, whenever possible to that in which he himself lived. Fortnightly demographic surveillance was continued from November 1973 to September 1978.

The fourth phase consisted of introduction of four-weekly demographic surveillance in September 1978. This phase continued until April 1981, during which time fieldworkers visited each household every four weeks. Demographic surveillance lasted altogether for a period of seven and a half years from November 1973 to April 1981.

8.1.4 Disease surveillance

The disease surveillance system was established after completion of installation of the demographic surveillance system in November 1973. Training field staff to recognize specific signs and symptoms of disease in infancy and childhood began in November 1973, and continued until April 1974. A disease surveillance form was designed that included two screening questions: 'Has the child been ill since the previous visit?' and 'Does the child look ill?' If the answer to both questions was no, the fieldworker was required only to observe and record whether a child had a running nose and cough. If the answer to either question was 'Yes', the mother was asked about vomiting and diarrhoea during the past two weeks, the temperature was taken, and observations relating to measles, respiratory distress, and dehydration were recorded. Every suspected case of measles or whooping cough was reported by the fieldworker to the doctor during his regular clinic visit. If the mother allowed, nose swabs for culture and finger-prick blood for the determination of serum antibody levels were taken as well. During these clinics any other children accompanying the mother were also examined and treated.

Because an increasing number of measles and pertussis cases were being seen at nearby health facilities, disease surveillance was started one month ahead of schedule. As a result, the documentation of epidemics of these diseases was begun in their early stages. No doubt this was at the expense of training, but this was compensated for by the considerable amount of on-the-job training provided by the medical project staff. Therefore case-identification is assumed to have been fairly accurate even during the early days of the measles and whooping cough outbreaks. Owing to the work involved in covering epidemics of measles and whooping cough at the same time, surveillance of acute diarrhoea and acute respiratory illness was not considered sufficiently standardized to be included in the system until 1976. Disease surveillance was simplified in August 1979, thereafter being restricted to measles and whooping cough. Disease surveillance was in operation for seven years from April 1974 to April 1981.

In addition to the disease and demographic surveillance, a number of other studies have taken place. Many of these have been longitudinal studies, such as the DPT vaccine trial, the study on the outcome of pregnancy, and the nutrition studies of pregnant and lactating women and children under five. Implementation of these studies was possible owing to the presence of well-organized demographic and disease surveillance systems.

8.1.5 Project staff

Initially, the responsibility for the project rested with an epidemiologist, a biologist, a sociologist, and a demographer. All of them were based at the Medical Research Centre in Nairobi. In addition, a statistician was available, joined later by a part-time computer programmer and three statistical clerks. A few months before the beginning of disease surveillance, a paediatrician and a public-health specialist joined the project team. The team expanded with the intensification of research in nutrition, sociology, and agriculture, while the original project members were replaced by others. Throughout the project, nearly all the Kenyan project members pursued higher studies at the University of Nairobi or at other universities, sponsored by the Medical Research Centre. In addition, a number of scientists from the Department of Tropical Hygiene of the Royal Tropical Institute in Amsterdam participated in specific studies. The Royal Tropical Institute was until 1982 the parent institute of the Medical Research Centre. Other participating scientists came from universities in Kenya, Great Britain, and the USA. Each member of the academic staff had to spend on average one or two days a week with the field staff.

The local field staff comprised five interviewers and one field supervisor, all with one to four years of secondary schooling. Later, the field staff was increased to twelve interviewers and three field supervisors. With the expansion of research in nutrition, the field staff was further increased to nineteen interviewers and four field supervisors. Both male and female fieldworkers were recruited. All of them were permanent residents of the study area. For the major activities—demographic baseline survey, demographic surveillance, and disease surveillance—extensive instruction manuals were written and periodically revised (Omondi-Odhiambo 1979). Meetings were held about once a month with the field staff at which the written instructions were discussed and new procedures explained.

A problem encountered in the later stages of the project was maintaining the fieldworkers' motivation. Their work was mainly routine and not all of them were able to keep up a high standard; as a result, several had to be replaced. One method of maintaining motivation was to provide them with the results of the studies they were involved in, and ask for their views and comments on the findings.

8.1.6 Range of studies and publications

With the help of the demographic and disease surveillance, a number of studies were carried out on the epidemiology of a number of diseases, especially measles, whooping cough, diarrhoea, and schistosomiasis. Another major longitudinal study took place on determinants of perinatal and neonatal mortality. The study led to the identification of major risk factors and to development of criteria for antenatal screening.

Several longitudinal studies were also conducted on nutritional problems during pregnancy and after childbirth and in children under 5. These focused on the relationships between nutritional status during pregnancy, birth weight, lactation performance and growth during infancy, and childhood. Other longitudinal studies dealt with the impact of various health interventions. A major study in this category is the pertussis vaccine trial on the effect of two doses given six months apart during infancy, in comparison with the conventional schedule of three doses every three months. Another study dealt with the most suitable way of administering measles vaccine by comparing the efficacy of five different routes of administration. Other health intervention studies dealt with the impact on schistosomiasis of treatment with a new drug, the impact of a training programme of traditional birth attendants, and the impact of a nutrition rehabilitation programme.

Several anthropological studies were carried out in the framework of the Machakos Project. These included studies on the traditional medical care system, on traditional antenatal and delivery care, and on beliefs and practices related to major childhood diseases in particular. In addition, several cross-sectional surveys were done on agricultural, socio-economic, and hygienic conditions prevailing in the study area and on use of modern and traditional health care.

Many of the results of the various projects were initially published in a number of articles in *Tropical and Geographical Medicine* and the *East African Medical Journal* between 1977 and 1983. Major results were later published in *Maternal and Child Health in Rural Kenya: An Epidemiological Study* (van Ginneken and Muller 1984).

Finally, several projects were carried out on the analysis of data of the demographic surveillance system. These studies dealt with levels of child and adult mortality, causes of death of children and adults, determinants of infant and child mortality, and mobility patterns (in- and out-migration and circulation). The results of these analyses were published in the above-mentioned volume and in a series of articles (van Ginneken *et al.* 1984; van Vianen and van Ginneken 1984; Boerma and van Vianen 1984; Omondi-Odhiambo 1985; van Ginneken, Omondi-Odhiambo, and Muller 1986; and Omondi-Odhiambo, van Ginneken, and Voorhoeve 1990).

8.2 Demographic Concepts and Definitions

The demographic data collection method used in the Machakos Project is a population registration system, which makes it necessary to specify operational definitions of certain concepts such as population size, and birth, death, and migration rates. The definitions of such terms, as commonly used in regard to African countries, are those which have been developed in connection with censuses and single-round surveys. Those definitions may not be optimal when working with population registers. Another reason why adjustments in definitions of such concepts are necessary is that in the case of the Mackakos Project we are dealing with sub-national populations, unlike censuses and single-round surveys which often refer to national populations. Concepts and operational definitions used in Machakos which need further discussion are: the *de facto* population, the registered population, birth rates, death rates, and migration rates.

8.2.1 Definition of *de facto* and registered population

The *de facto* population of a household consisted of those persons who slept in that household on the night preceding the visit by a fieldworker. Visitors were not included if they were found in the household by a fieldworker for the first time, but if still there during a subsequent visit they were counted as being present.

The registered population consisted of present and absent household members. Persons were defined as absent when they belonged to a household according to the opinion of the head of that household and when they visited their residence more or less regularly throughout the year, in particular during weekends and holidays. Visitors became members of the registered population when they were found to be present in the study area during a second visit by a fieldworker.

There were several reasons why this broad population definition was employed. It is necessary for several epidemiological and other studies to include absentees. Absent male members of households make important economic and social contributions to the study area and it is unrealistic to deny their existence. Our definition corresponds to the opinion of the inhabitants of the area themselves concerning who does and who does not belong to a household.

The concept of the registered population is broader than that of the *de jure* population frequently used (e.g. Marks, Seltzer, and Krotki 1974; Shryock and Siegel 1971, United Nations Economic Commission for Africa 1974). According to normal demographic practice, only those absent members who have their usual place of residence in a particular area (Shryock and Siegel 1971) are included in the *de jure* population, and for Africa this is proposed to be 'the place he/she has lived in most during the last 12 months' (United Nations Economic Commission for Africa 1974). We did not follow this recommendation, but included in the registered population heads of households and other household members who work in Nairobi or other places and who return to their residence in the study area during weekends, holidays, etc.

Instead of introducing a new term 'registered population', we could also have used the term '*de jure* population', saying that, for our type of demographic data collection method, it was necessary to modify the existing operational definition of this term. We prefer, however, to adopt the term 'registered population' to distinguish it from the normally used definition of '*de jure* population'.

8.2.2 Definition of two types of birth and death rates

These rates were calculated using the *de facto* as well as the registered-population approach, because sometimes they differ. Birth and death rates for the registered population were calculated in the normal way.

A number of deliveries occurred in hospitals located outside the area and the deaths during the period preceding the survey are not accurately known (United Nations Economic Commission for Africa 1974: 34). So a strict calculation of the *de facto* rates was not possible. Instead, they were calculated on a 'generally present' basis. The demographic surveillance is both a registration system and a multi-round survey, which means that information on present/absent status is available twenty-four times per year (until September 1978). The generally present rates are based on the principle that vital events are enumerated for that part of the population which was generally present in the year preceding these events. A birth was defined as *de facto* birth when the mother was present half of the time or more (that is twelve or more times out of the twenty-four) in the twelve months preceding delivery. Likewise, a death was classified as a *de facto* death when the person who died was present half of the time or more in the twelve months prior to the occurrence of the death. Similar rules were applied to the denominators of the *de facto* rates. The denominator consists of persons who were generally present in the twelve months prior to the middle of the year. Special rules were adopted to deal with in-migrants and infants who died when less than 1 year old.

8.2.3 Definition of migration rates

Another adjustment that needed to be made in the definition of in- and out-migrants dealt with the length of time required for visitors to become in-migrants and for absent members of the study population to become out-migrants.

The UN recommendation for African censuses is that a minimum of six months of continuous presence in a particular area is required for a visitor to be classified as an in-migrant and to become a member of the *de jure* population; anyone who has been there for less than six months remains classified as a visitor or temporary resident. Likewise, six months of continuous absence are required for a person to become an out-migrant and to be removed from the *de jure* population. The dates of migration are taken as those of their arrival and departure (United Nations Economic Commission for Africa 1974).

We, however, classified visitors as in-migrants when they were encountered on a second visit by a fieldworker, and absentees were removed from the registered population when they were found to be absent on two successive visits. This removal of absentees could only be decided several months after their actual departure, because they could have returned to the study area after having been absent during two successive visits by a fieldworker. After continuous absence for a period varying from three to six months, the date of out-migration was the date of the first of the two successive visits by a fieldworker when absence was noted.

With population registration systems covering a limited area within a country, it is also desirable to consider permanent changes of residence within the area in which this system has been established. We have called such moves '*intra-area migration*'. It is desirable to take this into account in order to prevent migration rates from becoming dependent on the population size in the area under study. If this is not done, a relationship appears between the area and its migration rate: the smaller the area, the larger the in- and out-migration rates. We have, therefore, presented data on both intra-area migration and on in- and out-migration, and we have called the combined rates '*total in-*' and '*total out-migration rates*'.

8.3 Results of Demographic Studies

8.3.1 Population growth, crude birth and death rates

The distribution of the study population by age and sex resembled that of the district as a whole. Comparing the survey results with the 1979 census of the Machakos District shows, however, that the age-groups between 15 and 44 years were somewhat underrepresented in the study population, while several of the older age-groups were overrepresented. These differences are probably due largely to overestimation of ages by adults, particularly women.

The *de facto* population increased from about 18,600 at the end of 1973 to 23,700 at the end of 1980, and the registered population from about 22,100 to 34,700 during the same period. Information on demographic rates is given in Table 8.2. The annual natural increase was 37.4 per 1,000, while net loss from outmigration was 3.5 per 1,000 between 1974 and 1980. The rate of natural increase was fairly constant between 1974 and 1980, but the balance between migration in and out fluctuated widely during the same period. The population grew rapidly between 1974 and 1978 and only slightly in 1979 and 1980.

Crude birth and death rates in 1974–80 calculated with *de facto* and registered approaches as defined in the previous section, are given in Table 8.3. The *de facto* crude birth and death rates and the rate of natural increase averaged 45.7, 6.7, and 39.0, respectively, per 1,000 each year from 1975 to 1978. It can be seen that the *de facto* rates are somewhat higher than the registered rates, which implies that fertility and mortality of the absentees are somewhat lower than those of the present (*de facto*) population.

The total fertility rates calculated in 1975–8 with the *de facto* population approach are likewise somewhat higher than calculated with the registered-population approach. Various reasons have been mentioned elsewhere as to

Table 8.2.   Rate of natural increase, net migration rate and population growth rate per 1,000 registered population in 1974–80

Year	Midyear population	Rate of natural increase per 1,000	Net migration rate per 1,000	Population growth rate per 1,000
1974	23,484	33.7	9.2	42.8
1975	24,407	37.3	0.2	37.5
1976	25,521	36.1	15.1	51.2
1977	26,729	36.5	5.2	41.7
1978	27,946	38.6	8.7	47.3
1979	28,679	38.6	−33.6	5.1
1980	28,993	39.8	−23.1	16.7
Average 1974–80		37.4	−3.5	33.9

Table 8.3. Crude birth and death rates and rate of natural increase per 1,000 *de facto* and registered population 1974–80

Year	Crude birth rate		Crude death rate		Rate of natural increase	
	De facto	Registered	*De facto*	Registered	*De facto*	Registered
1974		42.1		8.4		33.7
1975	45.8	43.3	6.5	6.1	39.3	37.3
1976	44.4	42.7	7.0	6.6	37.4	36.1
1977	45.4	43.3	6.7	6.7	38.7	36.5
1978	47.0	45.1	6.7	6.5	40.3	38.0
1979		44.6		6.0		38.6
1980		44.5		4.8		39.8
Average						
1975–8	45.7	43.6	6.7	6.5	39.0	37.1

why we think that these lower fertility and mortality rates of absentees are genuine and not due to underreporting of vital events (van Ginneken *et al.* 1984).

8.3.2 Infant and child mortality

Mortality rates during the first year after birth show the probability of dying to be highest within twenty-four hours after birth and to decline gradually until the fourth month. Death rates rose again between six and nine months after birth. Male mortality was considerably higher than that of females in the first week after birth; in later months, the differences were small. The overall infant mortality rate was 49.7 per 1,000 births.

Four apparent reasons for infant mortality can be identified in Machakos District: a dry season from the middle of January to the middle of March; a wet season marked by long rains from the middle of March to the end of June; a dry season between July and the middle of October; and a wet season marked by short rains from the middle of October to the middle of January. Unlike many African countries, where death rates change profoundly with season, Machakos's mortality, based on infant and child mortality data, did not vary significantly by season.

The study area's infant mortality of about 50 per 1,000 live births was also lower than reported in two recent national sample surveys. One mentioned the infant mortality rate for Kenya as 83 per 1,000 live births; the other, 87 per 1,000 live births (Mott 1982). The difference between the study area and Kenya as a whole appears to be genuine and not due to underreporting of infant deaths as has been argued by van Ginneken *et al.* (1984). One of the reasons mentioned was, for example, that use was made of data derived from the longitudinal outcome of pregnancy study in addition to the regular data from the demographic surveillance system. The relatively low infant and child mortality rates in the study area are a reflection of the more favourable economic, social, and hygienic conditions in the study area than in many other parts of Kenya (van Vianen and van Ginneken 1984).

8.3.3 Causes of child and adult deaths

The Machakos Project derived information on causes of death from several sources. These sources of data as well as the results are described in more detail in Omondi-Odhiambo, van Ginneken, and Voorhoeve (1990). Table 8.4 presents the 678 deaths recorded by the Machakos Project between 1975 and 1978 and the cause of death, listed by the three-digit level of classification in the ninth revision of the International Classification of Diseases, or ICD (World Health Organization 1977). Cause-specific death rates per 100,000 persons are

Table 8.4. Causes of death, all age-groups, 1975–8

Cause of death and ICD code[a]	No. of deaths	% of all deaths	Death rate per 100,000
Diseases of the respiratory system (460–519)	107	15.8	102
Congenital anomalies and perinatal conditions (740–779)	87	12.8	83
Intestinal infectious diseases (001–009)	73	10.8	70
Measles (055)	55	8.1	53
Diseases of the circulatory system (390–459)	49	7.2	47
Tuberculosis (010–018)	48	7.1	46
Other infectious and parasitic diseases (rest of 001–139)	45	6.6	43
External causes of injury and poisoning (800–999)	42	6.2	40
Nutritional and metabolic diseases (240–279)	30	4.4	29
Neoplasms (140–239)	25	3.7	24
Diseases of the digestive system (520–579)	24	3.5	23
Malaria (084)	21	3.1	20
All other	27	4.0	26
Unknown	45	6.6	43
All causes	678	100.0	648

[a] Ninth revision of the International Classification of Diseases.

also shown. Because the number of reported deaths is limited, only the major groups of causes of death are represented.

This table also summarizes the relative contribution of each cause of death to the total number of deaths from all causes. The leading cause of death was respiratory illness, particularly pneumonia, which accounted for 15.8 per cent of all deaths (or 102 deaths for every 100,000 persons). Respiratory illness is a disease of the very young and the very old. Second in rank were congenital anomalies and conditions originating in the perinatal period (hereafter abbreviated as congenital anomalies and perinatal conditions). Such conditions caused 12.8 per cent of all deaths (or 83 per 100,000). Intestinal infectious diseases (particularly diarrhoea) and measles ranked third and fourth, respectively, with 10.8 and 8.1 per cent of all deaths. Malaria caused relatively few (3.1 per cent), probably because of the area's high altitude.

There is a clear division between the causes of death among children less than 5 years old and those more than 5. Congenital anomalies and perinatal conditions (12.8 per cent), respiratory diseases (such as pneumonia and influenza) and intestinal infectious diseases, especially diarrhoea (9.7 per cent each), and measles (7.1 per cent) were the leading causes of death among infants and children under 5 years of age.

Diseases of the circulatory system (7.2 per cent), tuberculosis (6.2 per cent), diseases of the respiratory system (7.0 per cent), external causes of injury and poisoning (5.6 per cent), and other infectious and parasitic diseases (5.6 per cent) were important causes of death for children 5 years or older. Causes related to neoplasms and diseases of the circulatory and digestive systems were reported only for children at least 5 years of age (3.7, 7.2, and 3.5 per cent of all deaths, respectively).

About 62 per cent of all deaths occurred at home and 38 per cent in a hospital. Deaths due to diseases of the circulatory system and malaria occurred more frequently at home than elsewhere, and those due to congenital anomalies and perinatal problems, measles, and neoplasms took place more often in a hospital.

The present study confirmed that the cause-of-death structure in the Machakos area resembled that in a number of developing countries. The main difference between Machakos and many developing countries is that the death rates from these major causes are relatively low in Machakos. A number of reasons for this were already mentioned above (see also van Ginneken *et al.* 1984; van Vianen and van Ginneken, 1984).

8.3.4 Permanent and temporary migration

Migration rates as defined above in 1974–7 are shown in Table 8.5. Total in-migration rates—that is, intra-area plus in-migration rates—were somewhat higher than out-migration rates. Intra-area migration rates made a substantial contribution to the total migration rates. Gross migration rates, calculated here

Table 8.5. Migration rates per 1,000 registered population, 1974–7

Year	Intra-area[a] and in-migration rate			Intra-area[b] and out-migration rate			Gross migration rate	Net migration rate
	Intra-area	In-migration	Total	Intra-area	Out-migration	Total		
1974	54.8	68.1	122.9	54.4	60.6	115.0	183.3	7.9
1975	53.6	57.4	111.0	49.4	56.5	106.0	165.4	5.0
1976	42.2	64.1	106.3	36.0	54.9	90.9	158.1	15.4
1977	40.0	52.1	92.1	45.6	43.0	88.6	137.9	3.4

[a] To residence in study area from another residence within this area.
[b] From residence in study area to another residence within this area.

by averaging the two intra-area rates and adding the in- and out-migration rates, declined from 183 per 1,000 in 1974 to 138 per 1,000 in 1977. This decline is probably due to some extent to changes in procedures of measuring migration. Net migration rates correspond generally very well with similar rates shown in Table 8.2 (van Ginneken, Omondi-Odhiambo, and Muller 1986).

A further characteristic of the study area is that temporary or circulatory migration is widespread. On weekdays 19 per cent of the registered population is on average absent. Absence is more common among men, especially in the ages between 20 and 50 (45 per cent of registered population) than among women (20 per cent) (van Ginneken, Omondi-Odhiambo, and Muller 1986).

8.4 Results of Studies on Maternal and Child Health

In a previous section an overview was given of the range of studies which have been undertaken in the framework of the Machakos Project. In this section results will be presented of four major epidemiological studies focusing on maternal and child health.

8.4.1 Determinants of perinatal mortality

After diagnosing a woman as pregnant, fieldworkers would fill out a questionnaire covering previous pregnancies and deliveries, where she intended to deliver, and any complaints related to the pregnancy. Height was measured with a headboard and tape measure.

After the woman gave birth, fieldworkers filled out another form with questions about the recent delivery and the care received. If a pregnancy was undetected, fieldworkers filled out both questionnaires after the delivery. During the last two years of the study, the fieldworkers weighed babies born at home as soon after birth as possible. When a pregnancy ended in stillbirth or a child died within its first week of life, the project physician interviewed and examined the mother in order to establish the most likely cause of perinatal death.

The Machakos Study included all women who delivered between 1 January 1975 and 31 December 1978 after a gestation of at least twenty-eight weeks. All belonged to the study population at the time of delivery, regardless of whether delivery took place inside or outside the study area.

Before presenting the main results of the study, a brief description of obstetric care in the study area will be given. Most women who gave birth at home were assisted by one of the thirty or so traditional midwives in the area. These were usually elderly women known for their skills and experience. Some were also herbalists. None had any medical training. Other women were assisted by a relative, usually the mother or mother-in-law, and sometimes by the husband or a neighbour. Some gave birth completely on their own. Formally trained midwives and doctors were only found in health centres and hospitals, where midwives attended uncomplicated deliveries, and physicians or medical assistants attended difficult deliveries. For more detail on sources of data and results, see Nordbeck, Voorhoeve, and van Ginneken (1984) and Voorhoeve, Muller, and W'Oigo (1984).

The total number of children born was 4,768 including fifty-two pairs of twins (one for every ninety-one deliveries). The rates for perinatal and other mortality in early infancy are provided in Table 8.6. In the study area, perinatal mortality was 46 per 1,000 births. The perinatal rate was 39 per 1,000 total births for home deliveries, and 65 per 1,000 for total births for hospital deliveries. Of all deliveries, 73 per cent took place at home and 27 per cent in

Table 8.6. Outcome of pregnancy, 1975–8

Outcome	No.	Type of rate	Annual rates
Total children born	4,768	n.a.	n.a.
Live births	4,627	Crude birth	43.6 per 1,000 persons
Late foetal deaths (stillbirths)	141	Stillbirth	29.6 per 1,000 total births
Perinatal deaths[a]	221	Perinatal mortality	46.4 per 1,000 total births
Neonatal deaths[b]	107	Neonatal mortality	23.1 per 1,000 live births
Infant deaths[c]	230	Infant mortality	49.7 per 1,000 live births
Maternal deaths	4	Maternal mortality	0.8 per 1,000 deliveries

n.a. Not applicable.
[a] First-week deaths and stillbirths.
[b] First-month deaths.
[c] First-year deaths.

the hospital. Age and parity related to perinatal mortality in the usual manner: rates were highest for the children of the youngest and oldest women, of women without a previous delivery, and of women with seven or more children. Marital status was also related to perinatal mortality: the rate was higher among the babies born to unmarried than to married women. Birth interval was related to mortality as follows: a short interval between the previous and the present live birth or stillbirth was not associated with increased perinatal mortality, but after intervals of six years or more mortality increased steeply. The mother's height was another risk factor: the children of short women (less than 150 cm) experienced on average a higher perinatal mortality than those of taller women. The number of previous perinatal deaths was also related to subsequent mortality: mothers who had not lost a child had lower rates than mothers who had. Among fifty-eight breech deliveries, twenty-nine babies were stillborn, and four died during the first week of life. The resulting perinatal death rate of 569 per 1,000 births was fourteen times the rate of 40 per 1,000 for vertex deliveries. Twinning also strongly influenced mortality: the perinatal death rate was 183 per 1,000 among pairs of twins compared with 43 among single births.

Two other factors strongly influenced mortality: length of gestation and birth weight. Gestational age was known for a biased sample of 1,049 pregnancies. The sample was biased because women who gave birth to a low-birth-weight infant or lost their baby at birth had a higher chance of being questioned. Perinatal mortality was much higher than average for the twenty-seven children with a gestational age of less than 34 weeks and also higher than average for the ninety-three children with a gestation of 42 weeks or more. Birth weights measured within the first 48 hours were available for 1,091 live-born single babies. Neonatal mortality rates were much higher among children with a low birth weight (less than 2,500 g.) than among those with a high one (2,500 g. or more).

Using this information, the project identified four groups of pregnant women who had a significantly higher risk than other women of losing their baby at birth (see Table 8.7). These four groups of pregnant women, totalling 13 per cent of all pregnant women, were associated with 41 per cent of all perinatal deaths. More than half of the perinatal deaths of the babies of these four high-risk groups could probably have been avoided if appropriate obstetric care and antenatal screening had been available.

8.4.2 Measles

During the surveillance visits, children whom the mother or fieldworker suspected of having measles were sent to a project physician who verified the diagnosis using carefully designed diagnostic criteria. Cases were classified as possible, probable, or definite, based on these criteria (Voorhoeve *et al.* 1977).

Table 8.7. Births and perinatal deaths, by risk group

Risk group	Births		Perinatal deaths	
	No.	Per cent	No.	Per cent
Breech (single birth)	46	1	31	14
Twins	104	2	19	9
Primigravidae				
At risk	160	3	16	7
Not at risk	774	16	33	15
Multigravidae				
At risk	372	8	24	11
Not at risk	3,312	70	98	44
Total	4,768	100	221	100

In 1974–81 three epidemic waves of measles occurred, and measles was also present between epidemics. At the height of the epidemics, between eighty and 170 cases were reported for each two-month period. In the first epidemic (April 1974 to April 1976), 422 cases of measles were reported, and twenty-six deaths attributed to measles occurred within four weeks of the onset of the measles rash; the case-fatality rate was 6.3 per cent. The second epidemic (April 1976 to April 1989) produced 978 cases and fourteen deaths, a case-fatality rate of 1.4 per cent. In the third epidemic, up to April 1981, 734 measles cases were reported, with eight deaths, a case-fatality rate of 1.1 per cent. Of all measles cases, 27 per cent were children at least 5 years old: half were between 5 and 7, and half between 7 and 15. Only four cases were older persons, who were 17, 19, 23, and 35 years of age. Very few cases occurred in infants below the age of 6 months. In the second half of the first year of life the incidence rose considerably, to peak at 9 and 10 months of age. More cases occurred between 6 and 12 months of age than in any other six-months age-group. This may occur because, apart from waning maternal antibodies, the secondary-attack rate is high (54 per cent) in households where an older sibling acts as an index case or because children contract the infection while visiting a health facility for an unrelated complaint. See Table 8.8 for the incidence rates by age between 1974 and 1981. Most deaths from measles occurred before the second birthday.

In children under 5, the case-fatality rate observed over the total seven-year period was 2.4 per cent (thirty-seven out of 1,545); in persons over 5, it was 1.9 per cent (eleven out of 589). For the first two epidemics the project compared data from the population-based surveillance study with data from the Kangundo Hospital, the referral hospital for the study area (Muller *et al.* 1977).

Table 8.8. Average annual incidence of measles, April 1974–April 1981

Age (years)	Estimated number of cases at risk[a]	Average population at risk[a]	Average annual incidence[b]
Less than 1	352	1,097	46 (41–51)[c]
1	455	1,081	60 (55–65)
2	295	1,030	41 (36–46)
3	255	964	38 (33–43)
4	188	928	29 (25–33)
5	150	928	23 (19–27)
6	143	896	23 (19–27)
7–14	292	5,974	7 (6–8)
15 and above	4	14,387	0.04
Total	2,134	27,285	11 (11–11)

[a] At the end of 1977.
[b] Per 1,000 persons.
[c] 95% confidence limits.

The case-fatality rate of persons admitted to the hospital with measles was 22 per cent in both periods. This contrasts sharply with the case-fatality rates of the entire population, which were 6.2 and 1.4 per cent, respectively. In 1974–8, the median age of persons hospitalized and of all persons with measles was 18 and 31 months, respectively.

The Machakos Project investigated the impact of nutritional status on the outcome of measles, using the data collected on the mid-upper-arm circumference in children before they contracted measles. The surveillance system measured this circumference routinely every three months and more frequently in cases of illness. No statistically significant difference in nutritional status, as measured by arm circumference, was found between the children who died of measles and those who survived. Only children whose arm circumference had been measured within three months of the onset were included in the analysis. The survivors were selected from the definite measles cases and matched for age, date of onset of the disease, and sublocation. When the data were broken down by sex and age (those above and below the median age for contracting measles), the measurements were no different for the deceased than for the survivors (Leeuwenburg *et al.* 1984*b*).

Combining the age-specific incidence of measles with data from a 1975 collaborative study on seroconversion after vaccination (Kenya Ministry of Health, and World Health Organization 1977) resulted in a recommendation of the optimal age for measles immunization. In a population with the same age distribution of measles cases as Machakos, 9 months is the optimal age for administering the measles vaccine (World Health Organization 1982).

In an Attenuvax II vaccine trial, only the vaccine administered by syringe and needle or dermojet evoked a significant antibody response. The other three methods (nose drops, needle-bearing cylinder, and bifurcated needle) produced titres not significantly different from those of the control group (Kok, Kenya, and Ensering 1983).

8.4.3 Pertussis

Pertussis is much more difficult than measles to diagnose in a brief household visit. Typical paroxysms may not occur during the visit, or mothers may consider any frequent cough to be whooping cough. Laboratory support is not particularly helpful: isolating *Bordetella pertussis* is only possible in the early stages of the disease.

In the pertussis vaccine trial the effect of two doses given six months apart was compared with the conventional schedule of three doses every three months during infancy (Muller, Leeuwenburg, and Voorhoeve 1984).

Two epidemic waves occurred between April 1974 and April 1981; the small number of cases among children in the vaccine trial coincided with the second epidemic. The largest number of cases occurred in children less than 1 year old, and children 6 years of age or younger accounted for 84 per cent of all cases. The median age was 3.5 years. Out of 1,465 cases, 758 were in females, giving a sex ratio of 0.93. Pertussis incidence rates are presented in Table 8.9.

Between April 1974 and April 1981, a case-fatality rate of 1 per cent was attributed to pertussis. Half occurred in children below the age of 1 (a

Table 8.9. Average annual incidence of pertussis, April 1974–April 1981

Age (years)	Estimated number of cases	Average population at risk[a]	Incidence[b]
Less than 1	270	1,097	35 (31–39)[c]
1	150	1,081	20 (17–23)
2	171	1,030	24 (20–27)
3	189	964	28 (24–32)
4	183	928	28 (24–32)
5	168	928	26 (22–29)
6	106	896	17 (14–20)
7–14	228	5,974	6 (5–6)
Total less than 15	1,465	12,898	16 (15–17)
Total population		27,285	8 (7–8)

[a] At the end of 1977.
[b] Per 1,000 persons.
[c] 95% confidence limits.

case-fatality rate of 2.6 per cent); the rest were evenly distributed among children 1 to 4 years of age. None of the children in the vaccine trial died from pertussis (Muller, Leeuwenburg, and Voorhoeve 1984).

The case-fatality rate of 1 per cent, although lower than that in most developing countries, is still formidable compared with that in the developed countries. It is much higher than the incidence of serious adverse reactions to the vaccine reported from, for example, the Netherlands (Hannik and Cohen 1979) and England (Miller *et al.* 1981). The project tested the titre distributions of the two- and three-dose groups. One month after the last (the second or the third) dose of DPT vaccine was administered, no difference existed in the titres. At longer postvaccination intervals, antibodies waned more rapidly in the two-dose group than in the three-dose group. Differences between the groups were statistically significant after an interval of two years ($p < 0.001$). The proportion with no demonstrable titre rose in the two-dose group from 10 per cent after one month to 38 per cent after two years or more. The corresponding percentages for the three-dose group were 6 and 23 per cent, respectively. The rate of pertussis cases was the same, 8.15 in the two-dose and 8.55 in the three-dose group. Compared with the 1,281 children of the same birth cohort who were not in the trial, the rate of pertussis cases in the vaccinated children was reduced by 54 per cent. The unvaccinated children were not a random control group, because some had probably received DPT immunizations elsewhere. Therefore these percentages do not express actual vaccine efficacy.

The vaccine trial suggests that mass immunization campaigns using two DPT doses given six months apart may be suitable for protecting children living in remote areas that lack access to continuous mother and child health services. There are, of course, many parts of the world where DPT is available, either on a continuous basis in regular mother and child health clinics or at intervals considerably shorter than six months. A three-DPT schedule is preferable in such situations because it obviates the problem of children contracting whooping cough during the six-month interval between the first, non-protecting DPT dose and the second one (administered before the age of 9 months). Children are vulnerable to incidence and mortality during this interval period.

8.4.4 Diarrhoea

Two-week surveillance data are available from April 1974 to the middle of 1977 (Leeuwenburg *et al.* 1984*a*). The age-specific incidence rates of diarrhoea in children who were reported or observed to be ill are given in Table 8.8. The differences between age-groups are striking: children 0–5 months of age had virtually the same incidence as children 12–23 months of age, while those 6–11 months old had a consistently and significantly ($p < 0.001$) higher percentage of diarrhoea than the younger or older children.

Table 8.10. Average-two-week incidence of diarrhoea in children under 5 years of age (percentages)

Item	Age (months)					
	0–5	6–11	12–23	24–35	36–59	Total
Incidence in						
Ill children, June 1974–June 1977	3.4	5.6	3.4	1.3	0.5	2.2
All children, April 1976–June 1977	15.8	24.5	15.9	7.4	3.7	10.5
Average number of children per two-week period, June 1974–June 1977	394	422	832	797	1,454	3,899

From April 1976 to June 1977, diarrhoea information was obtained on all children whether the mothers considered them ill or not. During that time, the incidence of diarrhoea, by age-group, was four to seven times higher in all children than in children who were reported ill (see Table 8.10).

From April 1974 to December 1977, out of 306 deaths of children under 5, forty-six children (twenty-two males and twenty-four females) were reported to have died of diarrhoea and vomiting. Of these children, thirty-three were under 1 year of age; thirteen were 0–5 months. The median age of death was 7 months, the mode was 6 months, and the mean was 13; the age at death ranged from 2 to 57 months.

8.5 Conclusions

The Machakos Project produced high-quality information relevant to health care. It produced age-specific figures on the incidence of measles, which yielded a recommendation of the optimal age to immunize children for measles; it studied the adequacy of two pertussis immunizations during infancy; and it analysed the impact of a pregnant woman's nutritional status and of the delivery care received on the outcome of pregnancy. All of these contributions were made possible by the epidemiological and demographic surveillance system, which provided regular follow-up for a number of years.

Information on the incidence of disease and the outcome of pregnancy could have been collected in a cross-sectional study using the mother's recall, but the reliability of such a study would never be known. In addition, the project's solid infrastructure, which included collecting complete demographic information on the total population rather than on the target groups alone, allowed the addition of investigations that had not been considered at the onset, but appeared useful later.

The design of the project called for long-term, continuous commitment of a relatively large number of scientific staff, adequate administrative and logistic support throughout, and, most of all, a patient and hospitable study population. Some of these requirements can be translated into financial terms, others are a matter of motivation or purely good fortune. All of these requirements were met most of the time. Particular mention needs to be made of the fact that for more than eight years (including one year of preparations and the baseline survey) the relationship with the population and its leaders has been warm and unblemished. The response rate has been virtually 100 per cent for all studies. Hospitality and co-operation were extended to fieldworkers, supervisors, and researchers alike, as a matter of course.

It is important to realize that longitudinal, population-based studies are laborious and expensive, lacking in glamour, and they do not provide the reward of immediate results. Such studies are, however, essential when the health of the community rather than of the individual is our concern. In this respect we believe that the Machakos Project has produced valuable information that could not have been obtained by simpler, cheaper methods, and that the results are relevant to policy-makers in both health and the scientific communities.

References

Boerma, J. T., and van Vianen, H. A. W. (1984), 'Birth Intervals, Mortality and Growth of Children in a Rural Area of Kenya', *Journal of Biosocial Science*, 16: 475–86.

Hannik, C. A., and Cohen, H. (1979), 'Pertussis Vaccine Experience in the Netherlands', *Third International Symposium on Pertussis*, DHEW Publication, NIH 79-1830, National Institutes of Health, Bethesda, Md.

Kenya Ministry of Health and World Health Organization (1977), 'Measles Immunity in the First Year after Birth and the Optimum Age for Vaccination in Kenyan Children', *Bulletin of the World Health Organization*, 55: 21–32.

Kok, P. W., Kenya, P. R., and Ensering, H. (1983), 'Measles Immunization with Further Attenuated Heat Stable Vaccine Using Five Different Methods of Administration', *Transactions of the Royal Society of Tropical Medicine and Hygiene*, 77: 171–6.

Leeuwenburg, J., Gemert, W., Muller, A. S., and Patel, S. C. (1984*a*), 'The Incidence of Diarrhoeal Disease', in J. K. van Ginneken and A. S. Muller (eds.), *Maternal and Child Health in Rural Kenya: An Epidemiological Study*, Croom Helm, London.

——Muller, A. S., Voorhoeve, A. M., Gemert, W., and Kok, P. (1984*b*), 'The Epidemiology of Measles', in J. K. van Ginneken and A. S. Muller (eds.), *Maternal and Child Health in Rural Kenya: An Epidemiological Study*, Croom Helm, London.

Marks, E. S., Seltzer, W., and Krotki, K. J. (1974), *Population Growth Estimation: A Handbook of Vital Statistics Measurement*, Population Council, New York.

Miller, D. L., Ross, E. M., Alderslade, R., Belleman, M. H., and Rawson, N. S. (1981), 'Pertussis Immunisation and Serious Acute Neurological Illness in Children', *British Medical Journal*, 282: 1595–9.

Mott, F. L. (1982), *Infant Mortality in Kenya: Evidence from the Kenya Fertility Survey*, Scientific Report Series, 32. International Statistical Institute, Voorburg, The Netherlands.

Muller, A. S., Leeuwenburg, J., and Voorhoeve, A. M. (1984), 'Pertussis in a Rural Area of Kenya: Epidemiology and Results of a Vaccine Trial', *Bulletin of the World Health Organization*, 62: 899–908.

——Voorhoeve, A. M., 't Mannetje, W., and Schulpen, T.-W. (1977), 'The Impact of Measles in a Rural Area of Kenya', *East African Medical Journal*, 54: 364–72.

——Ouma, J. H., Mburu, F. M., Blok, P. G., and Kleevens, J. W. L. (1984), 'Study Design and Methodology', in J. K. van Ginneken and A. S. Muller (eds.), *Maternal and Child Health in Rural Kenya: An Epidemiological Study*, Croom Helm, London.

Nordbeck, H. J., Voorhoeve, A. M., and van Ginneken, J. K. (1984), 'Use of Perinatal Mortality Data in Antenatal Screening', in J. K. van Ginneken and A. S. Muller (eds.), *Maternal and Child Health in Rural Kenya: An Epidemiological Study*, Croom Helm, London.

Omondi-Odhiambo (1979) (ed.), *Manual of Instructions to Fieldworkers*, Medical Research Centre, KEMRI, Nairobi.

——(1985), 'Age Estimation in Clinical and Public Health Research', *East African Medical Journal*, 62(12): 861–76.

——van Ginneken, J. K., and Voorhoeve, A. S. (1990), 'Mortality by Cause of Death in a Rural Area of Machakos District in 1975–78', *Journal of Biosocial Science*, 22: 63–75.

Shryock, H. S., and Siegel, J. S. (1971), *The Methods and Materials of Demography*, US Dept. of Commerce, Washington.

United Nations Economic Commission for Africa (1974), *Manual of Demographic Sample Surveys in Africa*, UNECA, Addis Ababa.

Van Ginneken, J. K., and Muller, A. S. (1984) (eds.), *Maternal and Child Health in Rural Kenya: An Epidemiological Study*, Croom Helm, London (repr. by AMREF, Nairobi, 1987).

——Omondi-Odhiambo, and Muller, A. S. (1986), 'Mobility Patterns in a Rural Area of Machakos District, Kenya in 1974–1980', *Tijd schrift voor Economische en Sociale Geografie*, 77(2): 82–91.

——Muller, A. S., Voorhoeve, A. M., and Omondi-Odhiambo (1984), 'Demographic Characteristics of a Rural Area in Kenya in 1974–1980', *Journal of Biosocial Science*, 16: 411–23.

Van Vianen, H. A. W., and van Ginneken, J. K. (1984), 'Analysis of Demographic Data Collected in a Rural Area of Kenya', *Journal of Biosocial Science*, 16: 463–73.

Voorhoeve, A. M., Muller, A. S., and W'Oigo, H. (1984), 'The Outcome of Pregnancy', in J. K. van Ginneken and A. S. Muller (eds.), *Maternal and Child Health in Rural Kenya: An Epidemiological Study*, Croom Helm, London.

——Schulpen, T. W. J., Gemert, W., Valkenburg, H. A., and Ensering, H. E. (1977), 'Agents Affecting Health of Mother and Child in a Rural Area of Kenya. 3: The Epidemiology of Measles', *Tropical and Geographical Medicine*, 29: 428–40.

——'t Mannetje, W., and van Rens, M. (1978), 'Agents Affecting Health of Mother and Child in a Rural Area of Kenya. 4: The Epidemiology of Pertussis', *Tropical and Geographical Medicine*, 30: 125–39.

World Health Organization (1977), *International Statistical Classification of Diseases, Injuries, and Causes of Death*, i, WHO, Geneva.

——(1982), 'The Optimal Age for Measles Immunization', *Weekly Epidemiological Record*, 57: 89–91.

9 The Pholela Health Centre:
Understanding Health and Disease in South Africa through Community-Oriented Primary Care (COPC)

STEPHEN M. TOLLMAN, SIDNEY L. KARK,
AND EMILY KARK

9.1 The Pholela Health Centre: Origins

The Pholela Health Centre, located in rural Natal, South Africa, was established in April 1940. To grasp its significance, even then, the socio-political circumstances prevailing in the country must be appreciated.

Following passage of the 1913 Land Act, South Africa's African peoples,
comprising some 85 per cent of the total population, were relegated to 13 per
cent of the country's land area (Thompson 1990). This precursor of the racially
exploitative apartheid system was reinforced by the Land Act of 1936. These
'homelands', largely rural and inhospitable, were distant from the major urban
centres and unable to sustain a growing agricultural population or develop a
solid industrial base.

From 1939 to 1948 the Smuts–Hofmeyr government pursued a policy that
was liberal for those times. This had a considerable influence on health policy
in South Africa. Dr Henry Gluckman was appointed Minister of Health in
1946, having previously served as chair of the 1942 National Health Service
Commission, and a subsequent Health Centre Advisory Committee. The
Gluckman report recommended a National Health Service available 'to all
sections of the people of this country according to their needs and not according to their means' (Gluckman 1947). Under the leadership of Dr Gluckman
and Dr George Gale, Chief Health Officer of the Department of Health until
the accession of the whites-only National Party in 1948, major steps were taken
to lay the basis for a comprehensive health service in South Africa that would
be founded on a network of health centres throughout the country. The first
of these, the Pholela Health Centre, was to be a model and a forerunner for
the network.

In 1938 Sidney Kark, having completed several years of graduate intern-
ships, was appointed Medical Officer to head the field team for a 'National
Bantu Schoolchildren Nutrition Survey', planned for 1938/9 under the direction of Dr H. S. Gear, Deputy Chief Health Officer of the Department of

Health of the then Union of South Africa. The final report of the survey (Kark and Le Riche 1944) concluded:

Diet deficiency diseases, syphilis, malaria, bilharzia, tuberculosis, scabies and impetigo, preventable crippling, and many other less severe or less common diseases, form no small array of factors which are contrary to the maintenance of good health and nutrition. No amount of juggling can succeed in separating the influence of one as opposed to the others where they so commonly occur together. The outstanding fact is that they are all preventable. . . . The problem is thus not only one of providing this or that particular food factor, but rather a need for a general increase of all foodstuffs which will tend to build up a healthy Bantu population, averting starvation as well as the many more specific deficiency diseases.

During the course of the survey Kark was offered an appointment as Medical Officer in charge of the first of three proposed state health units to be located in the black rural 'reserves'.

9.1.1 Establishing the Pholela Health Centre

In April 1940 Sidney and Emily Kark, both medical doctors, initiated the Pholela Health Unit.[1] They were soon followed by another couple: Edward Jali, a medical aid graduate from Fort Hare University, and Amelia Jali, a graduate nurse of the McCord Zulu Hospital, Durban. This team of four were the founders of the Pholela Health Centre, the task of which was defined as follows:

It should combine curative and preventive services, including the following essential functions: (i) prevention and treatment of disease; (ii) health education, with particular reference to the organisation of maternal and child welfare services; (iii) local cooperation and community responsibility. . . . The activities of the health centre were to be coordinated with those of other local agencies such as the authorities responsible for agriculture and education. (Kark 1951)

Several months later, the Department of Health posted four experienced male malaria assistants, from other parts of Natal, to be retrained as members of the Health Centre staff (although Pholela was not a malaria area.)

Training of the health assistants focused on basic subject-matter and supervised field experience. Subjects included: elements of physiology; diseases, especially infectious disease; nutrition and nutritional disorders; family health, including maternal and child health; personal hygiene and health promotion. The importance of understanding local concepts of health and disease was stressed, along with methods of health education.

The health assistants' field-training programme emphasized:

---

[1] The Pholela Health Unit was set up by the Ministry of Health to function independently of any government health service. In rural areas, this was virtually non-existent. The Pholela model was expected to be the basis for it. As the first centre of its kind, it had considerable freedom of operation, with little need to defer to any district or regional health authority.

1. practical nutrition, including a demonstration vegetable garden at the health centre, encouragement of home and school gardens, and initiation of school meals;
2. demography in health work, e.g. home health census, community health education through home visits, group discussions at schools (children and students, teachers, parents), village meetings, and church gatherings;
3. encouragement of self-help by families and community groups in promoting their own health and well-being.

Initial activities of the Centre included:

1. meetings with chiefs, elders, teachers, and other community leaders to explain the purpose of the proposed work;
2. establishing a general curative clinic, open to all, in a disused farm building;
3. public health control of local infectious disease outbreaks, notified by the local magistrate and district surgeon—diseases included smallpox, typhoid and typhus fevers, and family diseases such as tuberculosis and leprosy;
4. health and nutrition surveys of schoolchildren, in consultation with their teachers;
5. immunization programmes;
6. a maternal and child health programme;
7. development of sub-centres elsewhere in the Pholela district;
8. community surveys of health relevant behaviour and activities, with careful recording and reporting back to the health team.

9.1.2 Initial obstacles

Although inadvertently, the Centre's activities provoked suspicion and resentment among chiefs, indunas (headmen), and the local people. They objected to the government purchasing land for a clinic about which they were not consulted; to the appointment of outsiders rather than local people as community workers; and to the health assistants' approach of visiting homes 'like spies', rather than allowing people the choice of using the clinic when they pleased.

9.1.3 Recruiting local staff

In response, the Health Centre staff was soon modified by the appointment of people from the local community. Among these were women as well as men health assistants (community health workers), an admissions clerk and health recorder, and several nurse-aides. Furthermore, representatives of teachers, women's groups, and community elders, both church and secular, met frequently with staff of the Health Centre.

9.2 Health Centre Practice: Introducing a Methodology

The first group of five community health workers (CHWs) were allocated specific work areas, each being responsible for a population of some 4,000 to 5,000 people. Their main tasks were communicable disease control and community health education. Weekly Health Unit staff meetings were held with the CHWs to review their work. From this, clinic-based staff learned that they knew little about the family life and social circumstances of their patients. A need to identify the home circumstances of community members emerged. Family files, combining patients' clinic records with the home-based field records of the health assistants, were thus initiated.

After about a year, two key innovations were introduced in Pholela: first, an *initial defined area* (IDA) of some 130 households (900 individuals) was designated for intensive study and service. Apart from their overall responsibilities, each CHW was allocated twenty-five to thirty homes in the IDA. An address for each home was assigned, after careful mapping of its position and its relation to available water supplies. Second, a *household health census*, administered by the CHWs, was instituted. This was updated by routine reports of all births, deaths, and the movements of each household in the IDA.

A year later, a review of findings clearly demonstrated improved health status in the IDA. The need to expand this approach became evident. Annually thereafter, the defined area was extended until it covered about a third of the total population of 30,000. This process of annual extensions allowed regular assessment of changes in health status through comparison of the intensively serviced area with that most recently incorporated. Appropriately indexed cards—health records of each family—were designed and arranged so as readily to correlate clinical findings with field data from home visits, school health services, etc.

The intensive activities developed with the families and community of the defined area led to an approach that was formulated in the following terms:

1. to co-ordinate medical care of individuals with interventions directed towards changing the health-related behaviour of families and the community;
2. to carry out social, behavioural, and epidemiologic investigations for community diagnosis, as the foundation for intervention programmes;
3. to organize an ongoing system of surveillance and evaluation of the various programmes, by measurement of changes in community behaviour and health status (Kark and Kark 1981: ch. 8).

This could only be achieved by a record system readily able to provide information on the community's health, determining factors, and the activities of the Health Centre. Health data included.

1. Demographic information providing basic denominator and numerator data on:

    (*a*) population, according to age, sex, education, occupation, marital
        status, kinship networks;
    (*b*) pregnancies and births;
    (*c*) deaths;
    (*d*) migrations.
2. Information on determinants of health, largely accumulated through
   special surveys that addressed:
    (*a*) social structure, especially kinship and family responsibilities in
        health care;
    (*b*) work and social activities, including seasonal variations;
    (*c*) seasonal dietary surveys of vulnerable groups such as infants,
        schoolchildren, and pregnant women; food-production surveys
        including crop yields, seasonal milk and home-garden production,
        and ownership of livestock and poultry;
    (*d*) housing and the environment, including a detailed survey of each
        homestead; purity of water sources and potential for protection;
        and disposal of refuse and excreta;
    (*e*) utilization of health-centre services, and the effect on this of tra-
        ditional concepts of health and disease.
3. Health and morbidity information, acquired largely from the team's clinical and survey records. Acute diseases were noted on special forms, thus
   permitting surveillance of infectious disease and acute nutritional failure.
   Clinical and field records were periodically summarized for each family,
   and abstracted for analyses of morbidity and mortality indices, immunization rates, and growth and nutrition status. This was all related to measurements of health-related behaviour, and the environment of families
   and community as a whole[2] (Kark and Kark 1981: ch. 8).

By careful analysis, it was possible to measure change over time in the
various activities listed. The 'longitudinal' picture that resulted was among
the outstanding features of community-oriented primary care (COPC). A
weekly team conference (or 'epidemiology-in-practice' session) to discuss
these findings was attended by the whole Health Centre staff. These were
intense and rewarding sessions, and participants accepted the need for
confidentiality.

Outstanding features of the community diagnoses were:

- high rates of mortality, especially in infancy, due mainly to acute upper
  and lower respiratory tract infections and gastroenteritis;
- high rates of malnutrition and growth failure, including pellagra and
  kwashiorkor;

---

[2] The extent of integration between the clinical and community aspects of the Pholela practice
is striking. Absence of the traditional separation between curative and preventive/promotive services, and the unifying objective of *community* health status, as opposed to individual status alone,
enabled this integration to take place.

- high incidence of infectious disease, particularly tuberculosis and sexually transmitted diseases, especially syphilis;
- endemic skin disease, largely scabies and impetigo;
- frequent epidemics of smallpox, typhoid and typhus fevers, measles, whooping cough and epidemic conjunctivitis, with serious complications due to malnutrition;
- depression and hysteria, together with various syndromes of bewitchment and 'possession'.

Based on the Pholela example, a number of other health centres were established as training sites for COPC practice. These later combined to form an Institute for Family and Community Health (IFCH), founded in 1945 in Durban, South Africa (Kark, Kark, and Tollman 1991). Over a fifteen-year period, 1945–1960, these eight health centres generated an extraordinary wealth of information, allowing detailed comparative studies of mortality and morbidity in culturally, ethnically, and geographically diverse communities. Their closure, in 1960, was a tragedy for South African health care.[3]

A comparative study of infant mortality among Zulu and Hindu communities (located in five of the Institute's COPC practice sites) is the subject of the next part of this chapter, and demonstrates the profound role of culture and family behaviour when differences in infant mortality rate are assessed. The final section, addressing the transmission of syphilis among rural Africans at Pholela, analyses the impact that socio-economic imperatives can impose on a segment of the community.

9.3 A Comparative Study of Infant Mortality in Five Communities

9.3.1 Demographic and socio-economic profiles

1. *Demographic profile.* To compare infant mortality and its possible determinants among different communities, records from five areas served by the Institute were investigated. Three of the communities were African, predominantly Zulu: two from Durban, and one from the rural community of Pholela; the other two, both urban, were Indian and largely Hindu. The communities were residentially distributed as follows (see details in Table 9.1).

---

[3] In 1948 the right-wing, ideologically driven National Party came to power. Soon after, state support for the Institute and all Health Centres was drastically reduced. By 1960 the Institute, and its associated Dept. of Social, Preventative and Family Medicine at Natal University, had closed. Many senior staff left South Africa, while others were transferred to government services at local hospitals and clinics. With the closure of Pholela, rural health services in South Africa remained underdeveloped and continued essentially as missionary-initiated hospital-based services.

Table 9.1. Basic data of the study: population studied, number of births, stillbirths, and deaths in infancy of the five communities

	Year	Size of population	Total births	Live births	Still-births	Neonatal deaths	Deaths of infants 1–12 months	Total infant deaths
Zulu								
1. Rural 'Native Reserve'	1943	2,937	113	110	3	10	17	27
	1944	5,184	207	194	13	10	27	37
	1945	5,926	236	232	4	13	36	49
	1946	5,919	273	258	15	15	25	40
	1947	6,524	285	275	10	13	23	36
	1948	6,622	296	272	24	11	27	38
	1949	7,481	284	269	15	11	20	31
	1950–51	8,549	385	373	12	15	22	37
2. Urban Slum	1947	2,556	185	175	10	8	18	26
	1948–9	3,264	173	165	8	7	10	17
3. Urban Municipal Housing Project	1948	1,040	43	41	2	1	1	2
	1949	3,974	207	200	7	5	8	13
	1950	4,047	222	215	7	6	12	18
	1951–2	7,120	244	237	7	12	7	19
Hindu								
1. Urban Slum	1950	4,005	135	130	5	2	6	8
	1951–2	4,772	150	146	4	0	7	7
2. Urban Municipal Sub-Economic Housing Project	1947	2,186	106	104	2	2	2	4
	1948	2,603	111	108	3	0	8	8
	1949	4,604	127	127	0	2	4	6
	1950	5,169	150	146	4	2	6	8
	1951–2	5,435	226	220	6	3	5	8

Source: Kark and Chesler 1956.

> *Zulu*:   urban municipal housing project
>   urban slum
>   rural (Pholela)
> *Hindu*:   urban municipal housing project
>   urban slum

The communities were investigated at different times, coinciding with the phasing-in of a neighbourhood family health service. In each service accurate records of live births, stillbirths, and infant deaths were maintained. The information presented here is for the earlier years of these services to limit the influence of health interventions on the mortality rates being compared. Note that the figures refer to *all* families living in the defined areas; they do not reflect any selection bias that could result from differential usage of the services provided.

2. *Socio-economic profile* (see Table 9.2). Key features include:
  (i) the larger average family size of both Hindu communities;
  (ii) the greater monthly income per head of the urban Zulu and, particularly, the low income of the Hindu in the urban housing project;
  (iii) the markedly better educational experience of Zulu women in contrast with the highly restricted level of the Hindu.

9.3.2 Infant mortality in five communities

A detailed presentation of infant mortality rates, disaggregated into stillbirths, neonatal deaths (0 to 4 weeks), and post-neonatal deaths (4 weeks to 12 months) is provided in Table 9.3.

1. *Infant mortality rate (IMR)*. Ranking the rates shows the overall IMR in both Hindu communities to be much lower than that of the Zulu communities (except for the urban housing group). This diverges from the pattern which might be expected if socio-economic factors were the major explanatory variables. As indicated in Table 9.2, the urban Zulu communities score far better on income and educational variables.

A careful look at components of the IMR offers clues to this pattern, further explained by examination of maternal reproductive patterns (discussed below) in the different communities.

2. *Stillbirths*. Although the Hindu rates are lower than the Zulu, the only significant difference is between the Hindu urban housing project and the Zulu urban slum and the Zulu rural communities (Kark and Chesler 1956).

3. *Neonatal deaths*. The outstanding feature is the exceptionally low neonatal death rate among the Hindu communities: 12.8 and 7.2 per 1,000 births respectively. These rates are significantly lower than any of the Zulu communities and, indeed, compare favourably with advanced communities elsewhere at that time (Kark and Chesler 1962: ch. 5).

Table 9.2. A comparative statement of important social and environmental factors in the five communities studied

	Zulu			Hindu	
	Rural Pholela	Urban Slum	Urban Municipal Housing Project—'Hilltops'	Urban Slum—'Marshlands'	Urban Municipal Housing Project
Size of family and income					
Families studied	943	696	387	363	632
Average size of family	7.3	4.1	6.8	8.9	7.9
Average monthly income per head (in shillings)	Comparable figure not available	45	41	42	29
Crowding index					
Homes studied	943	790	658	Comparable figures not available	939
Average no. of persons per room	2.0 (per hut)	3.4	2.0		3.1
Educational standard of women	No. %	No. %	No. %	No. %	No. %
Women aged 20–40 years	1,185 —	669 —	601 —	520 —	627 —
Never attended school	451 38.1	91 13.6	27 4.5	396 76.2	459 73.2
Passed std. VI or higher class	73 6.1	188 28.1	301 50.1	8 1.5	15 2.4

Source: Kark and Chesler 1962.

Table 9.3.   Stillbirth and infant mortality rates in three Zulu and two Hindu communities

	No. of live births recorded	Still-births[a]		Neonatal deaths (0–4 weeks)[b]		Post-neonatal deaths (4 weeks to 1 year)[b]		Total infant mortality (under 1 year)[b]	
Zulu		No.	Rate	No.	Rate	No.	Rate	No.	Rate
1. Rural Pholela—									
first 4 years	794	35	42.2	48	60.5	105	132.2	153	192.7
next 4 years	1,189	61	48.8	50	42.1	92	77.4	142	119.4
2. Urban Slum—									
first 2 years	340	18	50.3	15	44.1	28	82.4	43	126.5
3. Urban Municipal Housing Project— 'Hilltops'—									
first 4 years	693	23	32.1	24	34.6	28	40.4	52	75.0
Hindu									
1. Urban Slum— 'Marshlands'—									
first 2 years	276	9	31.6	2	7.2	13	47.1	15	54.4
2. Urban Municipal Housing Project—									
first 4 years	705	15	20.8	9	12.8	25	35.5	34	48.2

[a] Number of stillbirths per 1,000 total births (stillbirths and live births combined).
[b] These rates are expressed as the number of deaths per 1,000 live births.
Source: Kark and Chesler 1962.

4. *Post-neonatal mortality*. This picture is more mixed, with both urban housing projects showing rates below those of the urban slums. The Hindu urban housing group shows a significant difference relative to all Zulu communities except the urban housing project; there is no significant difference between the Zulu urban housing group and the Hindu slum community (Kark and Chesler 1956).

In brief, then the most remarkable comparative result is the very low neonatal mortality rate among the two Hindu communities. This is reflected in the overall infant mortality rates, notwithstanding the less favourable income and maternal education levels among the Hindus.

Table 9.4. Birth rates in five Zulu and Hindu communities

	Average live birth rate[a] during period of study
Zulu	
1. Rural Pholela—	
Early period	40.6
Later period	40.3
2. Urban Slum	59.6
3. Urban Municipal Housing Project— 'Hilltops'	47.6
Hindu	
1. Urban Slum— 'Marshlands'	32.8
2. Urban Municipal Housing Project	37.8

[a] birth rate = no. of live birth, per 1,000 population.

Source: Kark and Chesler 1962.

9.3.3 Maternal reproductive patterns among five communities

Careful examination shows major differences in reproductive patterns when the three Zulu and two Hindu communities are compared. The analysis focuses on birth and motherhood rates, maternal age at time of birth, and childbearing by unmarried mothers.

1. *Birth rate.*[4] All the communities have high birth rates (see Table 9.4). Those of the Zulu, however, are somewhat higher than the Hindu. The Zulu urban slum has a much higher rate than that for the Zulu housing project. This is probably explained by the different age structures of these two populations. Whereas families lived in the housing project, the slum tended to be a much younger population of young adults from rural areas and male migrant workers.

2. *Motherhood rate.*[5] Reviewing Table 9.5, from the year 1950/1, it is convenient to review first the age-groups from 15 to 24 years, and then the category 25 to 34 years. In the age-group 15 to 24 years, Zulu women demonstrate a far higher motherhood rate than Hindu women. The comparison between

[4] Defined as number of live births per 1,000 population.
[5] Defined as percentage of women in a particular age-group with a live or stillborn child during specified year.

Table 9.5. Motherhood rates in five Zulu and Hindu communities 1950–1 (motherhood rate = % of women in a particular age-group with a live or stillborn child in one year)

Age-group of mothers	10–	15–	20–	25–	30–	35–	40–49
Number in age-group							
Zulu:							
Rural Pholela	453	417	394	316	266	214	369
Urban Municipal Housing	—	204	223	178	149	184	218
Project—'Hilltops'							
Hindu:							
Urban Municipal Housing	—	253	194	161	123	116	137
Project							
Women delivered during the year							
as percentage of total women							
Zulu:							
Rural Pholela	0.7	11.0	19.0	23.4	18.8	12.6	2.1
Urban Municipal Housing	0	14.2	28.7	24.2	18.8	13.6	4.1
Project—'Hilltops'							
Hindu:							
Urban Municipal Housing	0	7.9	15.5	24.9	17.1	9.5	2.9
Project							

The difference between the Zulu and Hindu women of the two municipal housing projects is significant at these ages. The difference in the age-group 15–19 being 2.1 times as great as the standard error of the difference, and that of the 20–24 age-group being 3.3.

Source: Kark and Chesler 1962.

the Zulu and Hindu housing projects is especially pronounced, with the Zulu rate almost double that of the Hindu. The Hindu motherhood rates are highest in the 25 to 29-year group, and fall to lower levels thereafter.

It thus appears that the 'reproduction rates of Zulu women, especially the urban group, are higher than those of the Hindu and that this difference is mainly due to the more common occurrence of births among younger Zulu women' (Kark and Chesler 1962: ch. 5).

3. *Maternal age at childbirth*. This reflects the differences in motherhood rates. In the urban housing projects 32 per cent of births among the Zulu are to mothers 20 to 24 years, in contrast to 24 per cent among Hindu women. In the age-group 25 to 29 years the reverse holds true, with 32 per cent of Hindu births occurring then and 22 per cent among the Zulu (Kark and Chesler 1962: ch. 5).

4. *Childbearing among unmarried mothers*. Social structure and cultural and community values differ markedly among the five communities. This picture is further complicated by socio-economic and political factors such as migrant labour patterns and group areas legislation. It is, therefore, difficult adequately to interpret the differences. Overall, the striking trend is for a far higher rate of childbearing among unmarried Zulu women from both urban and rural areas. Kark and Chesler remark that 'urban Zulu women commonly continue to have several children while unmarried, whereas in the rural community the unmarried mother with more than one child is less common' (Kark and Chesler 1962: ch. 5).

Two further details are relevant. First, that while syphilis affected up to a quarter (30 to 24 per cent) of expectant urban Zulu mothers investigated, the corresponding figure for Hindus was 0.9 to 1.1 per cent (Kark and Chesler 1962: ch. 5). Second, that the Hindu mothers are recorded as suffering from 'obvious and very gross malnutrition' (Abramson 1962: ch. 24). Both factors would also have an effect on stillbirth and neonatal mortality rates.

9.3.4 Social factors

The central feature of this analysis is that the well-established social and environmental determinants of infant mortality are insufficient, in themselves, to account for the disparity between the Hindu and Zulu communities studied.... If poverty is [the] major adverse factor in survival of the foetus and newborn, we would expect different results from those found in the Hindu communities (Kark and Chesler 1962: ch. 5).

This applies most markedly to the unexpectedly low neonatal mortality rate of the Hindu. Major influences accounting for this low rate must include the age of mothers at childbirth, along with their parity distribution. Comparing the motherhood rates of the two groups in urban municipal housing, a significantly higher percentage of Zulu women aged 20 to 24 had babies compared with Hindu women of the same age.

These are also striking differences between Hindu and Zulu in the areas of women and the home, antenatal and postnatal care of mother and child, and their patterns of urbanization. According to Kuper, an anthropologist who worked closely with these communities, much of this is connected to their respective and differing worldviews. Religion is dominant among the Hindu, and, although there is belief in witchcraft, the overriding belief is that health and well-being come through personal harmony. Thus the health of the individual can be profoundly affected by his or her own actions. The Zulu, in contrast, have a theory of causality of illness that is attributed to evil-doers—persons outside of the self. Ancestors are also important and, if antagonized, seen as liable to provoke illness or misfortune. Serious illness, therefore, cannot be cured by treating the patient alone (Kuper 1962: ch. 4).

1. *Women and the home*. Hindu and Zulu societies are both male domin- ated. Nevertheless they show major differences in family organization. In the Zulu family, men have control over central aspects of home life, forcing women into domestically subservient positions. Among the Hindu, women exert domestic control in both religious and social spheres, including illness. In both societies domestic antagonisms may arise, particularly among co-wives, sisters- in-law, and their mothers (Kuper 1962: ch. 4).

2. *Care of mother and child*. Different perspectives characterize the Zulu and Hindu expectations of pregnant and post-delivery women. Although the Zulu woman is regarded as vulnerable, her condition is considered natural and normal and 'she is expected to do her usual work and keep up her strength by eating and drinking well.... [following birth] she is expected to resume routine activities after the cleansing ceremony—generally after the third day' (Kuper 1962: ch. 4).

Among the Hindu, 'pregnancy is treated as a psychological as well as physi- cal condition ... [following birth] mother and baby remain in the room of birth for the first six to sixteen days and receive considerable attention ... [in total] they are confined to the home for approximately forty days' (Kuper 1962: ch. 4).

3. *Urbanization*. The Indian community in South Africa has never experi- enced the degree of social disruption that Africans have suffered. Thus, fol- lowing the removal of the indentured laws in 1911, Indians drifted steadily towards the towns, and were able to set up stable family homes. For Africans, the system of migrant labour profoundly and irreversibly disturbed their social equilibrium (see discussion in 9.4.1 and 9.4.2 below). Rural families were split, and to this day stable family life has still to be achieved for great numbers of adults living in towns.

The studies described shed light on the many factors that together combine to produce a community's infant mortality rate. At the same time, the complexity of this phenomenon is indicated, particularly the difficulty of relatively weighing different social, cultural, behavioural, and political components.

It seems justified to argue that the more secure and prominent position of the Hindu woman at home (including her key role in family decisions around sickness and health, and the expectations of her following childbirth), together with the far more stable and protected Hindu family, contribute significantly to the improved child survival experienced by these communities.

In contrast, the Zulu family (in keeping with other African groups) is exposed to prolonged and major stress through the brutal and strictly enforced migrant labour system. Frequent family break-ups interact with the more sub-servient domestic position of Zulu women, and together combine to produce a domestic situation of extreme stress, with consequent negative implications for the health of newborns.

Thus, neonatal mortality among Hindu communities residing in Durban during the 1940s and 1950s is considerably lower than Zulu families in both urban and rural settings.

9.4 The Social Pathology of Communicable Disease: The Case of Syphilis

9.4.1 Introduction: migrant labour in South Africa

The discovery of diamonds near Kimberley in 1867, the creation of a massive gold-mining industry on the Witwatersrand soon after, and the ensuing indus-trialization of South Africa led to the rapid emergence of a predominantly male migrant labour system unlike anything previously experienced in South-ern Africa.

The gold-mining industry, and the wealth it generated, has played a major role in the economic development of South Africa and its neighbours. From its earliest years the industry attracted able-bodied males from throughout Southern Africa, including Basutoland (Lesotho), Swaziland, Rhodesia (Zim-babwe), and Portuguese East Africa (Moçambique) (van der Horst 1942). However, in South Africa itself, a body of legislation was passed to expand forcibly the pool of migrant workers in order to meet the rapidly growing needs of the mines and industry. This development irretrievably undermined traditional subsistence farming, and shifted the African economy from an agri-cultural to a cash base.

In consequence, the extended African family has been split. Migrant males go from their ancestral homes to the towns, where, living in overcrowded quarters and with severely limited recreation opportunities, they establish loose liaisons and, sometimes, an urban family. The rural 'homelands' have developed a skewed profile of predominantly the young, the old, and the sick, with women being responsible for the major part of agricultural and domestic work.

9.4.2 Migrant labour in Pholela

The extent to which migrant labour disrupted normal social relations in Pholela can be gauged from the results of a small but detailed study. This documented all arrivals and departures, during the year 1942, from households in the first 130 families comprising the 'initial defined area' (Kark 1962: ch. 14).

In the age-groups 20–9 and 30–9, the proportion of men working elsewhere was 87 per cent and 71 per cent respectively. Taking both groups together, i.e. men 20 to 39 years, nearly 80 per cent ($n = 90$) were away for between six months and a year, with 35 per cent absent for the entire year.

Thus the community was severely depleted of its able-bodied men, and the ratio of women to men varied from three to five, depending on the time of year.

9.4.3 Syphilis transmission in rural Pholela

The presence of large numbers of young men in the towns, without their families, with restricted social outlets, and with ready access to unattached women, provided a fertile environment for promiscuity, prostitution, and the spread of syphilis. The periodic movement of these menfolk back to their homes was a ready vehicle for the transmission of syphilis into some rural areas. By mid-1944 ninety-four people per 1,000 in the Pholela community were infected with syphilis.

The transmission process can be appreciated by an analysis of seventy-six cases of syphilis and gonorrhoea seen at the Pholela Health Centre between 1943 and mid-1944 (see Table 9.6). Of thirty-two infected married women, twenty-nine (91 per cent) had acquired this from their recently returned husbands. Twenty-three (72 per cent) of the men propagating the infection had acquired it in town.

This contrasts with the picture for married men. Only two out of twenty were infected by their wives, the majority being infected through an extra-marital union. Among single men, most were infected while in town (six out of ten cases). Single women appeared to contract the infection primarily in their local district (thirteen out of fourteen) from men who acquired the infection in a range of locations.

Although small, the study demonstrates that the returning migrant was the main propagator of syphilis in rural communities. This was recognized by local people, who referred to syphilis as *isifo sedolopi* ('town disease').

The system of migrant labour made it impossible to eradicate syphilis. Nevertheless, the Health Centre's attention to case-management, coupled with an active community awareness and education programme, did produce noteworthy results. These are shown in Table 9.7, where, over a fifteen-year period, a major decline in syphilis incidence is demonstrated.

9.4.4 Other infections

Clearly syphilis is but one, though powerful, example of infectious-disease transmission from urban to rural areas. Gonorrhoea, other sexually transmitted diseases, typhoid, and tuberculosis were also commonly conveyed by this

Table 9.6. Epidemiological study of 76 cases of primary and secondary syphilis and acute gonorrhoea attending the Pholela Health Centre

Marital status of the patients	No. of patients	Contact from whom the patient contracted the infection				Place where the patient contracted the infection				Place where contact contracted the infection			
		Married partner	Engaged to be married	Temporary 'love affair'	?	Local	Town	Other	?	Local	Town	Other	?
Married women	32	29	—	2	1	27	4	—	1	6	23	1	2
Married men	20	2	—	17 (plus 1 by his mistress)	—	10	8	2	—	4	10	4	2
Single women and girls	14	—	4	10	—	13	1	—	—	4	4	2	4
Single men	10	—	—	10	—	3	6	1	—	—	7	2	1

Source: Kark 1962.

Table 9.7.   Incidence of new cases of syphilis in the
Pholela defined area

Year	No. of new cases	Mid-Year population	Incidence per 1,000 population
1943	12	887	13.52
1945	347	5,184	6.69
1947	287	6,524	4.40
1949	228	6,622	3.44
1951	128	8,549	1.50
1957	83	10,496	0.79

Source: Slome 1962.

route. Over time, growing numbers of women and their families turned to the Health Centre for help in controlling the potential complications borne home by their returning husbands (Kark and Kark 1991).

Over the period 1949 to 1953, tuberculosis caused 90 out of 419 deaths where the cause was known in the initial defined area (total deaths being 696). There emerged a pattern of infected men, too sick to maintain employment, returning to rest or die in their place of birth (Slome 1962: ch. 21).

Although the laws restricting freedom of movement for Africans have recently been abolished, migrant labour remains an established and dominant aspect of rural and economic life. Tragically, this will contribute directly to the growing epidemic of HIV/AIDS in South Africa today.

9.5 Conclusion

The essence of COPC is to wed the clinical observations of daily primary care with a community-wide epidemiologic approach that rests on careful enu-meration of the members of a defined community. Illness in individuals cannot be isolated from their social and cultural environment; community-wide health problems are reflected in the health of individuals. Carefully conceived, lon-gitudinal research can make a major contribution to the information neces-sary to set local health priorities, plan interventions, monitor their progress, and evaluate their impact.

Descriptive and analytic studies, using information that is regularly and systematically derived from ongoing record systems, and special surveys where necessary, can provide the insights needed to address major public-health problems at individual, family, and community level. It is these principles that the studies on infant mortality and syphilis endeavour to demonstrate.

References

Abramson, J. H. (1962), 'The "Marshlands" Health Service', in S. L. Kark and G. W. Steuart (ed.), *A Practice of Social Medicine*, E. & S. Livingstone, Edinburgh.

Bennet, F. J. (1960), 'Mortality in a Rural Zulu Community', *British Journal of Preventive and Social Medicine*, 14: p. i.

Gluckman, H. (1947), 'The National Health Council', *South African Medical Journal*, 21 (13 Sept.), 643–8.

Kark, S. L. (1949), 'The Social Pathology of Syphilis in Africans', *South African Medical Journal*, 23 (29 Jan.), 77–84.

——(1951), 'Health Centre Service', in E. H. Cluver (ed.), *Social Medicine*, Central News Agency, South Africa.

——(1962), 'Migrant Labour and Family Health', in S. L. Kark and G. W. Steuart (eds.), *A Practice of Social Medicine*, E. & S. Livingstone, Edinburgh.

——(1974), *Epidemiology and Community Medicine*, Appleton-Century-Crofts, New York.

——and Cassel, J. C. (1952), 'The Pholela Health Centre', *South African Medical Journal*, 26: 101–4, 131–6.

——and Chesler, J. (1956), 'Survival in Infancy: A Comparative Study of Stillbirths and Infant Mortality in Certain Zulu and Hindu Communities in Natal', *South African Journal of Laboratory and Clinical Medicine*, 2(2): 134–59.

——   ——(1962), 'A Comparative Study of Infant Mortality in Five Communities', in S. L. Kark and G. W. Steuart (eds.), *A Practice of Social Medicine*, E. & S. Livingstone, Edinburgh.

——and Kark, E. (1981), 'Community Health Care in a Rural African Population', in S. L. Kark, *The Practice of Community-Oriented Primary Health Care*, Appleton-Century-Crofts, New York.

——   ——(1991), 'Social Networks in Traditional (Folk) Medicine', unpublished manuscript.

——and Le Riche, H. (1944), 'A Health Study of South African Bantu School-Children. Report on a Somatometric and Clinical Study Conducted during 1938–1939', *Manpower. Scientific Journal devoted to Manpower Research in South Africa*, 3: 2–141.

——Kark, E., and Tollman, S. M. (1991), 'Pholela: The Origins of Community Oriented Primary Care (COPC)', Paper presented to the seminar 'Socio-cultural Determinants of Morbidity and Mortality in Developing Countries: The Role of Longitudinal Studies', Oct. 1991, Senegal.

Kuper, H. (1962), 'Infant Rearing in Different Culture Groups', in S. L. Kark and G. W. Steuart (eds.), *A Practice of Social Medicine*, E. & S. Livingstone, Edinburgh.

Slome, C. (1962), 'Community Health in Rural Pholela', in S. L. Kark and G. W. Steuart (ed.), *A Practice of Social Medicine*, E. & S. Livingstone, Edinburgh.

232 *Tollman, Kark, and Kark*

Thompson, L. (1990), *A History of South Africa*, Yale University Press, New Haven and London.

Tollman, S. (1991), 'Community-Oriented Primary Care: Origins, Evolution, Applications', *Social Science in Medicine*, 32(6): 633–42.

Van der Horst, S. T. (1942), *Native Labour in South Africa*, Oxford University Press, London.

10 Three Decades of Research on Population and Health:

The ORSTOM Experience in Rural Senegal, 1962–1991

MICHEL GARENNE AND PIERRE CANTRELLE

10.1 Background

When African countries became independent in the late 1950s and early 1960s, research on population was virtually non-existent in tropical Africa. At this time, modern demography was emerging as a new science. Until then, demography had focused mostly on population genetics and on mathematical models aiming at describing population dynamics. Modern epidemiological and statistical methods, now widely used throughout the world, were largely ignored in the field of population studies. Anthropologists paid little attention to demographic and health processes. Their focus was on local myths, religions, and social structure. Little attention was devoted to the cultural factors of population and health in tropical Africa. The concept of multidisciplinary research was not yet fashionable, and most researchers were working isolated in their own field.

Before 1954 most of the little available demographic data were based on censuses and vital registration of European populations living in Africa. There were only a handful of scattered bodies of reliable data based on African populations. These were usually localized and based on a small sample: for instance, local vital registration systems in cities and parish registers in rural areas. Other large-scale demographic data were considered unreliable: for instance, the administrative enumerations consistently showed a strong undercount of the total population, especially of young children.

The first systematic studies of African populations started in the early 1960s. A team of researchers working at Princeton University published one of the first comprehensive accounts of African demography (Brass *et al.* 1968). At about the same time, a group of French demographers published a summary of their experiences and findings on tropical Africa, with emphasis on the sample surveys conducted by the *Institut National de la Statistique et des Etudes Economiques* (INSEE) since 1954 (Cantrelle 1967). The first seminar on African demography was organized by Franck Lorimer and held in Paris in

1959. It was followed by two other seminars, in Ibadan in 1966 (Caldwell and Okonjo 1968) and in Nairobi in 1969 (Ominde and Ejiogu 1972). The first IUSSP conference on African Demography was held in Accra, Ghana in 1971 (Cantrelle 1974*c*).

Likewise, public-health research in tropical Africa was strongly biased towards the needs of adults and of expatriates. Health research was restricted to tropical diseases, especially those diseases whose germs recently became identified or for which a vaccine or a treatment recently became available. According to Becker and Collignon (1989), most of the scientific publications prior to 1960 dealt with the following diseases: yellow fever, malaria, trypanosomiasis, plague, tuberculosis, schistosomiasis, filariasis, leptospirosis, and dysenteries. Other diseases, now recognized as major causes of death or major sources of morbidity such as watery diarrhoea, acute respiratory infections (ARI), measles, pertussis, tetanus, meningitis, and poliomyelitis, were virtually ignored. There was little research done on maternal and child health, on maternal mortality, on health systems, on family planning, on the impact of vaccination, and on other topics which are now seen as the most challenging health problems that face the region.

10.2 Initial Impetus

10.2.1 The 1962–6 project

Prospective community studies in rural Senegal started being conducted within the context of the reorganization of the country after it declared independence on 4 April 1960. The first Economic and Social Plan, 1961–4 called for the implementation of a project designed to improve knowledge of demographic rates. More specifically, the plan estimated that it would be important to have a series of demographic data based on vital registration. This series would test the validity of the 1960 sample survey—the first national demographic survey conducted in Senegal. In addition, new legislation for universal vital registration was passed in 1961. There was a need to evaluate the completeness of vital registration and to assess the functioning of the new vital registration system.

To facilitate demographic data collection, the UNTAB (the United Nations Technical Assistance Bureau, now UNFPA) created a one-year position from July 1962 to June 1963. Pierre Cantrelle was chosen as the project director, under the supervision of Louis Verrière, who was a statistician from INSEE. Cantrelle met Louis Verrière for the first time in September 1961 in New York at the IUSSP conference. After the conference, they went to visit F. Lorimer, A. Coale, and W. Brass at Princeton University and discussed the project with them. They agreed that the priority was to conduct a feasibility study of the recording of births, deaths, and marriages for at least three years. The UNTAB position, initially created for one year, was extended for one more year, to June 1964. In 1964 the *Office de la Recherche Scientifique et Technique Outre-Mer*

(ORSTOM), a French research organization founded in 1943, created a position for a demographer. Cantrelle was recruited and the demographic project in Senegal was later managed and supported by ORSTOM.

The field work was originally supported by the French *Fond d'Aide et de Coopération* (FAC). A budget was set up for one year and extended for two more years (1963–5). The Population Council of New York participated in the financing of the data analysis. Later, the overall project expenses were primarily funded by ORSTOM, and the marginal cost of specific projects was supported by other institutions.

10.2.2 P. Cantrelle's itinerary

Pierre Cantrelle was a physician who had been initially recruited in 1954 at *l'Institut Fondamental d'Afrique Noire* (IFAN) in Dakar, for a position in physical anthropology. He soon became interested in public-health issues and demography. He participated in the 1954 National Demographic Survey in Guinée, the first demographic sample survey conducted in tropical Africa. He conducted a micro-demographic and anthropological study in a village in Fouta Jallon (Dantari). In 1957–8 Cantrelle conducted the demographic, consumption, and clinical components of a major multidisciplinary study in the Senegal River Valley (Boutillier *et al.* 1961) called *the Mission Socio-economique du Fleuve Sénégal* (MISOES). During this study, the high frequency of measles as a cause of death in the African population was first documented. The MISOES study also highlighted specific features of the level and age pattern of mortality in infancy and childhood, and the prevalence of malnutrition in the population. The survey also made an early attempt to use non-medical personnel for community-based studies of morbidity and mortality and to have a local vital registration system organized by village volunteers. Cantrelle also participated in other pioneer demographic sample surveys conducted by INSEE in tropical Africa: Upper Volta (now Burkina-Faso) in 1960, Dahomey (now Benin) in 1961. During the Dahomey survey, an attempt to organize vital registration was also conducted.

10.2.3 Measles vaccines

The early 1960s witnessed the production of the first measles vaccines, after the isolation of the measles virus by Enders in 1954. In 1963 two Edmonston-B vaccines became available, one inactivated, the other a live vaccine. The live vaccine was tested in a rural community in 1963 in Tattaguine and in Niakhar, Senegal, a study in which Cantrelle played a major role (Rey *et al.* 1964, 1965). However, the vaccine was found to produce many adverse reactions. Later, a further attenuated vaccine was studied in 1966 in three rural communities: Khombole, Niakhar, and Paos-Koto. The new vaccine was found safe and efficient.

10.2.4 The 1961 vital registration act

The newly independent nation of Senegal felt that monitoring the dynamics of the national population was a priority. In 1960 vital registration had a low coverage nationwide, with marked differences in data about different population groups that could be explained by its complex history. Initially, vital registration was compulsory for French citizens only. In 1916 the registration of births, deaths, and marriages became compulsory for the residents of the four communes (Dakar, Saint-Louis, Rufisque, and Gorée), who became *de facto* French citizens. In 1933 vital registration was extended to certain categories of the African population: military personnel, government employees, and other taxpayers. In 1950, vital registration was extended to all those residing within 10 km. of a vital registration centre. The vital registration act of 23 June 1961 made the registration of births and deaths compulsory for all Senegalese citizens.

It is within this context of research on vital registration, population dynamics, and measles prevention that the prospective community studies began in rural Senegal.

10.3 Evolution of Objectives

The studies had three main phases: 1963–6, 1967–82, 1983–ongoing. These are summarized in Table 10.1.

10.3.1 Phase I: Sine-Saloum, 1963–6

The Phase I studies focused on demographic data collection. The main question the project sought to address was: could reliable demographic data be collected in rural areas of tropical Africa? A decision was made to collect precise prospective vital data within a small sample, rather than conduct large-scale retrospective surveys of more doubtful quality. In addition, data on measles morbidity and mortality were systematically recorded. An evaluation of the cost of data collection was built into the project. The study was directed by Cantrelle and had two Senegalese supervisors: Mamadou Diagne and Boubacar Fall. A Sereer sociologist was recruited to help with the definitions of age, marriages, and deaths, but he stayed for only a few months and had to leave for personal reasons. Fieldworkers were chosen from the staff of the statistics division (*Direction de la Statistique*).

10.3.2 Phase II: Ndemene-Ngayokheme, 1967–82

In 1966, when the demographic data collection project was taken over by ORSTOM and external financing ceased, Cantrelle urged the Senegalese

Table 10.1. ORSTOM Prospective community studies in senegal

Fatick (North-West)	Nioro du Rip (South-East)
Phase I: Sine-Saloum: December 1962–February 1966	
All Niakhar *arrondissement*	1/2 Paos-Koto *arrondissement*
65 villages	135 villages
35,187 people in 1966	18,988 people in 1966
Phase II: Ndemene-Ngayokheme: December 1962–February 1983	
All Ngayokheme *secco*	All Ndemene *secco*
8 villages	30 villages
about 5,000 people	about 6,000 people
sub-sample of previous area	sub-sample of previous area
Phase III: Niakhar: March 1983–ongoing	
CR Ngayokheme + 1/2 CR Diarere	(terminated)
30 villages	
about 25,000 people	
extension of previous area	
18 villages from phase I	
8 villages from phase II	

Note: In phase I, birth cohorts were followed up until April 1968.

authorities to carry out a long-term demographic study in several sample villages. The purpose would be to observe long-term trends in mortality, fertility, and nuptiality, to study social structure, to monitor the implementation of the recent Vital Registration Act, and to evaluate in rural areas the effects of the 1966 crisis which resulted from low yields of the two main crops: millet and peanuts. The budget of the study was constrained by the standard annual allocation of researchers at ORSTOM. Two small sub-samples of about 5,000 people each were selected. The longitudinal observation of eight villages in the north-western area and of thirty villages in the south-eastern area lasted until March 1983. Since it included villages from the previous project, the Phase II data consist of the twenty years of observation between December 1962 and January 1983.

The fieldwork was conducted, under the supervision of Cantrelle, by a team of three to four professional fieldworkers who were tenured employees of ORSTOM. All of them are still working for ORSTOM, though Cantrelle left Senegal in 1969. Many young demographers participated in the study and were trained to do fieldwork during this period: Bernard Lacombe, Jacques Vaugelade, Francis Gendreau, Benoit Ferry, Dominique Waltisperger, Christine Guiton, Gilles Pison, and Michel Garenne. Several of them undertook similar studies later in various parts of Africa. A comprehensive assessment of the demographic situation was done in 1981, with funding from the Ford foundation.

10.3.3 Phase III: Niakhar, 1983–ongoing

When Michel Garenne arrived in Senegal, in December 1982, he gathered a multidisciplinary research team to do further studies based on micro-demographic data. The focus was on the interactions between demography, epidemiology, and anthropology in the study of mortality determinants. The first major study that helped to reshape the project was on the relationship between nutritional status and mortality. A study of the causes of death estimated by verbal autopsies was built into the project. A sample size of about 5,000 children age 0–4 was needed as well as a study site. Niakhar was chosen to be the first study area. Ndemene was dropped as a study area primarily because of the difficulty of working in several different languages. The Niakhar area was predominantly Sereer, whereas the Paos-Koto area, which had been recently settled, included five significant ethnic groups and languages (Wolof, Poular, Mandikas, Sereer, Tukuler) as well as other minorities. A final census was taken in Ndemene in January and February of 1983. The Ndemene area was closed afterwards and the Ngayokheme area was included in the new Niakhar area, which now encompassed twenty-two new villages, many of them belonging to the Phase I Niakhar area.

Michel Garenne's professional background was in mathematics and statistics. He had a Master's degree in demography from Paris University and a Ph.D. in demography from the University of Pennsylvania, Philadelphia. His main interest was the integration of epidemiological and anthropological information to promote better understanding of demographic phenomena. He gathered a multidisciplinary team of nutritional epidemiologists and anthropologists (Bernard Maire, Olivier Fontaine, Jean Pierre Beau, André Briend, Khady Dieng, René Collignon, and Charles Becker). The team conducted several studies: on the relationship between nutritional status and mortality, funded by the European Economic Community (EEC), and on verbal autopsies, measles transmission, and maternal mortality, funded by Family Health International (FHI). Later, specific morbidity and mortality studies on diarrhoea, cholera, and malaria were also conducted. In 1983 Garenne also founded the Research Unit *Population et Santé* at ORSTOM. It was first chaired by Cantrelle and gathered people interested in multidisciplinary research in the fields of population and health: demographers, nutritionists, sociologists, and geographers. A new team of twelve fieldworkers was recruited and trained to meet the needs of this new research area.

After the 1983–6 projects were completed, the research unit felt the need to participate more actively in the worldwide effort on child survival and to contribute directly to the control of mortality in a population. In 1986 a new Expanded Programme for Immunization (EPI) was started in Senegal. The research unit decided to contribute directly by doing a study of high-titre measles vaccines and their potential for reducing early mortality from measles and by evaluating the impacts of pertussis and tetanus immunization. A separate study of risk factors of neonatal tetanus was also conducted during the same period by Odile Leroy. The study of high-titre measles vaccines became a randomized vaccine trial monitored by the Task Force for Child Survival, with funds from the Rockefeller Foundation, the World Health Organization (WHO), the World Bank, the United Nations Programme for Development (UNDP), and the United Nations Children's Fund (UNICEF).

During the 1983–9 period, many young researchers, African, European, and American, were welcomed into the team and allowed to gather data for MA or Ph.D. dissertations. An interesting dynamic was thus created, which was very favourable for multidisciplinary research. The field station attracted other researchers from different backgrounds, in particular economists, agriculture specialists, and ecologists who studied other aspects of the society. Notable among them was a group gathered by André Lericollais and Pierre Milleville, which spent several years in Niakhar (Lericollais 1995).

10.4 Study Populations

10.4.1 Phase I

Phase I studies were conducted in two separate areas of Sine-Saloum: Niakhar and Paos-Koto (see Figures 10.1 and 10.2). Sine-Saloum was at that time the most populated region of Senegal, located in the heart of the peanut-growing region. Initially the target was to follow up two areas totalling about 70,000 persons. This target was later reduced to 50,000 persons because of budget constraints and the unexpected length of time taken to complete the first census. Initially, only a sample of villages in the Sine-Saloum region was thought to be preferable. But contiguity between villages meant reduced transportation costs. It was decided that studying two different contiguous areas simultaneously would permit at the same time a more detailed knowledge of the population, would facilitate in-depth research, and still give an idea of the variety of situations. The two areas were chosen for comparing two different demographic situations. The Niakhar area was located in the Sine, a dry part of the orchard savannah, an area of high population pressure leading to emigration trends. The Paos-Koto area was located in the Saloum, an area of heavier rainfall, with a lot of available land and strong immigration flows. The Niakhar area was ethnically, economically, and culturally homogeneous, with 96 per cent of the population belonging to the Sereer group, whereas the Paos-Koto area was ethnically heterogeneous and was more of a settlement of pioneers who were on the average richer than their counterparts in the Sine.

The limits of the study area were defined by administrative boundaries. The Sine area included the whole *arrondissement* of Niakhar. The Saloum part included half of the Paos-Koto *arrondissement*. The choice of the *arrondissements* of Niakhar and Paos-Koto from among the other *arrondissements* of Sine-Saloum were made in consultation with the local authorities (*préfet*).

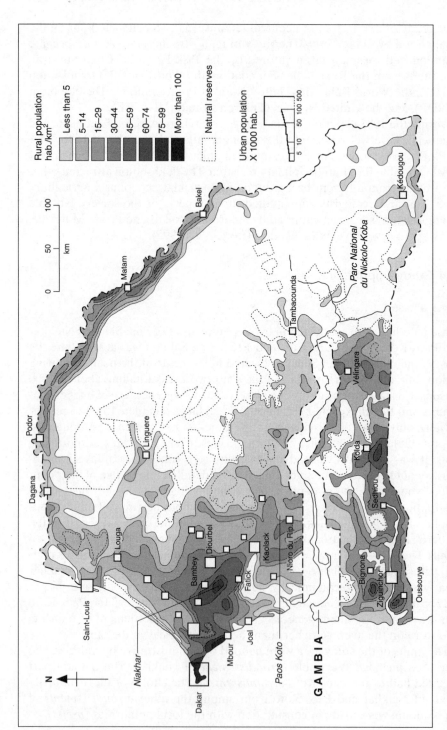

Fig. 10.1. Population density in Senegal, 1971, and location of study areas

Source: ORSTOM, 1992

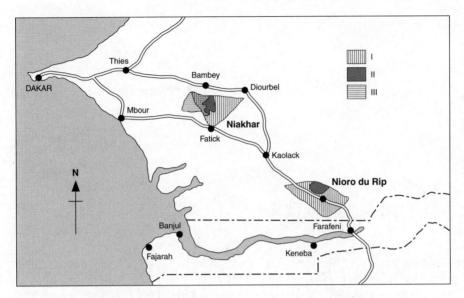

Fig. 10.2. Situation of research areas in rural Senegal, 1963–1991

10.4.2 Phase II

The villages of Phase II areas were chosen as a sub-sample of Phase I villages. The administrative unit was the *secco*, an administrative unit organized around the collection of peanuts, a practice that was nationalized at that time. The sample size was fixed by budget constraints to about 5,000 people. The *secco* of Ngayokheme was selected because it was included by the Senegalese government as a pilot area for the future rural communities (*Communautés Rurales*). The choice of Ndemene was made because it was the only *secco* of approximately 5,000 persons.

10.4.3 Phase III

The Phase III area was chosen as an extension of the Phase II area of Ngayokheme because the homogeneity of the population was considered a priority for in-depth multidisciplinary research (see Figure 10.3). Rural communities (CR) were created in 1974 and the Ngayokheme CR included nine new villages in addition to the eight villages included in the former *secco*. However, these seventeen villages did not have enough children for the project on malnutrition. There were two possibilities of extension: towards the east (Patar) and towards the west (Diohine). Diohine was chosen mainly because of its local private dispensary, which provided the opportunity to

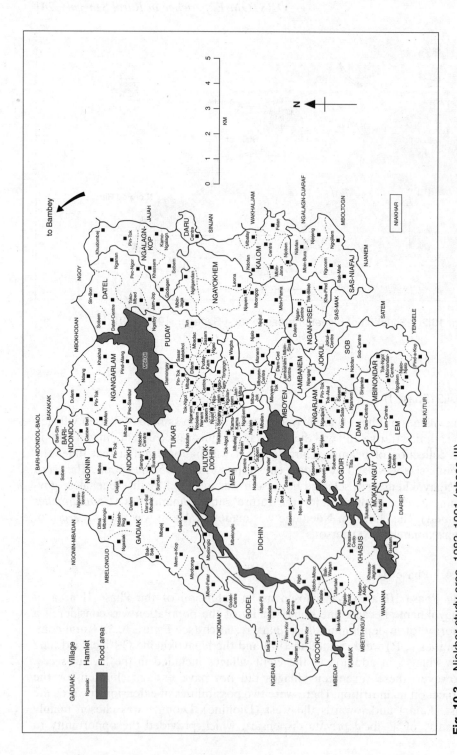

Fig. 10.3. Niakhar study area, 1983–1991 (phase III)

Source: ORSTOM, 1991, adapted from A. Lericollais, C. Becker, and T. Sene

compare two local systems of health care. Besides, Diohine had already been studied by the team when evaluating a food supplementation programme (PPNS).

10.5 Methodological Issues

10.5.1 Earlier experiences

When the first study began in 1962, there was very little experience in longitudinal demographic data collection in rural areas of less developed countries. Only two studies were available to P. Cantrelle when he started: the Yangtze River Valley Study in China (Chiao, Thompson, and Chen 1938) and the Guanabara Study in Brazil (Nations Unies et Gouvernement Brésilien 1964). The Khanna Study had just finished and had not yet been published; the Keneba Study and the Pakistan Growth Experiment were under way.

At that time, demographic data collection was hampered by the idea that recall biases were dominant. It was thought that people in tropical Africa were unable to report births and deaths properly when asked more than a few months after the event occurred. Nowadays, a better relationship exists between fieldworkers and the population, people understand better the purpose of demographic surveys, and are less likely to lie systematically. Also, methods of posing questions have improved. We now realize that the idea that gathering reliable demographic information was impossible in Africa was largely a misconception. It is now common to have good retrospective surveys on events going back twenty to thirty years before the interview.

10.5.2 Annual census

The Phase I studies began with a vital registration based on an annual census and continuous recording of vital events in the villages. For the annual census, the list of compounds was updated with the help of the head of the village and completed in the field. Compounds are locally defined with the word *mbind*. Each compound is visited and each individual resident mentioned in the previous census is called by name. This method provides information on deaths and emigrants. New residents are detected by recording births, incoming wives, and other immigrants. Changes in marital status and in other variables of interest are also recorded during the roll call. The annual census was maintained from 1964 to 1987 as the sole means of recording demographic events with a few exceptions—years without a census (1967, 1975, 1976, 1979), and years recording demographic events during morbidity and nutrition surveys in 1983–4.

10.5.3 Continuous recording of events

During the first twenty years, continuous recording of events by fieldworkers was done only in 1963, and that too every three months: that is three visits in addition to the annual census. To reduce the cost of going to each household too often, the recording was based on the local vital registration, on independent records made by village headmen, and on verifications made in the field by the supervisors. This procedure lasted during all of Phase I. It was dropped later because it was found to be too costly and not as accurate as the records obtained by the annual census. Compared to the annual census, the dual record evaluation showed that the official vital registration covered only 32 per cent of births, the village registers about 50 per cent, and the visits by supervisors about 90 per cent (Cantrelle 1969*a*).

The systematic continuous recording of events was resumed in January 1987 for the vaccine trial and has been maintained since. This time it was based on weekly visits to each household within the study area. Despite these very frequent visits, each year some births and deaths were found to be missing at the annual census. Missing births were mostly births to migrant women who had not yet been entered in the file. Missing deaths were deaths at any age which were not reported, most likely because the fieldworker simply did not ask the correct questions.

10.5.4 Registration and questioning method

The organization of the questionnaire and the way families were questioned seem to be a major determinant of data quality. In the first project (1963–6), the basic questionnaire was the annual census which was recorded on a household sheet. During subsequent rounds, the colour of the ink was changed (blue in 1963, red in 1964, green in 1965) and new information on household composition were noted on the same sheet. Obviously, this procedure, used during the three years of the first project, was not adequate for a surveillance of long duration.

In 1968, an individual card was introduced. The individual card system was tested first in Khombole and was used in Ndemene and Ngayokheme until 1983. It contained all the necessary information on residence, socio-economic status, marital status, and other relevant information (pregnancies, stillbirths, measles, vaccination, weaning, causes of death). The individual card system was very flexible. First, it documented all information about an individual in one place. Second, it enabled the fieldworkers to recompose households by just binding individual cards with a rubber band, therefore adjusting the structure of the population at any time by just moving the cards within the household (deceased members and emigrants were put at the end) or among households when individuals moved from one household to another. Third, the card system was suitable to the manual counting of events every year.

In 1983 computer printouts were introduced to provide uniformity in data entry every year. Each sheet, however, displayed only current information about an individual, which was sometimes a handicap when compared to the card system. But the computer could determine the precise questions to be asked at the next census based on the changing age of the person and his or her previous status. This had major advantages: it simplified and standardized the task of the fieldworkers; it provided all the information on a household at the same place; it ensured that proper questions were asked every year (Garenne 1985); it allowed for permanent checks in the computer files and for the permanent correction of errors; and it made it easy to add new questions when needed. In addition to the printed household file, separate question-naires were devised for specific events, which not only allowed for greater detail and specificity, but also enabled the researchers to group annual events serially.

10.5.5 Definition of residence

The definition of residence is crucial for a follow-up study and for the definition of births and deaths. It raises difficult questions in areas where there is a large amount of in- and out-migration, and imposes choices in the func-tion of the objectives of the demographic surveillance. The definition of residence was always based on *de jure* criteria and on long durations of stay, the idea being not to lose demographic information that was available and relevant for the study, and not to introduce events connected with short-term visitors. In Phase I, migrants were defined by either the intention to move per-manently or an absence of at least four years. In Phase II, the intention criteria were retained but the four-year rule was reduced to one year—that is, an absence at two successive censuses with no return in between. This allows one to distinguish the case of temporary workers who are absent during a few months in the dry season. The definition was refined in 1981 for special categories of migrants—in particular, schoolchildren, teachers, and visiting husbands—to fit the local situation. The fact that censuses were conducted in the dry season never allowed the proper recording of presence of the *navetanes*, the temporary workers who came only for the harvest in the rainy season. On the contrary, it was the *noranes*, the temporary workers who moved out during the dry season when there is no agricultural work, who were systematically recorded. Note that the definition of residence for birth (birth to a resident mother) differs from a regular administrative definition that would apply in a vital registration system, where place of birth is the basis for counting the event. In the demographic surveillance, a birth in Dakar to a resident mother was counted and a birth in the study villages to a non-resident mother was not counted. The opposite was true for the vital registration.

10.5.6 Mapping

Large-scale maps (1/50,000) were available when the study started in 1962. In addition, rough drawings of compounds in each village, numbered according to location, were done at that time. The maps were not used after the team of fieldworkers became permanent and was acquainted with the population. Locations of compounds in villages were redrawn in 1983 and in 1985 to match the extended study area, using air photographs; a complete mapping of all compounds was completed in 1992 from a new set of air photographs by Lericollais and Becker.

10.5.7 Computerization

The series of demographic events were put on computers recording all data as far back as the first project. In the 1960s, for the Phase I project, mechanography was used for sorting and counting punched cards, but this system was slow. Computers of the third generation were used to enter data of Phase II in 1974 and in 1981. From 1981 to 1986 events were entered every year after the census. In January 1987 data were transferred to an IBM-compatible network of microcomputers and were entered continuously in a relational database system, which will be described in a forthcoming paper.

10.5.8 Discussion

The work within a traditional society, where nothing is fixed by law and almost everything is negotiable, including name and age, raises numerous questions for scientists. Sereer people have several first names that they can use. Sometimes, they even change names and/or age class. Moreover, mothers may give the same first name to more than one child. This is particularly common for a newborn when an older sibling has recently died. It has happened that a man had two wives with the same first and last names. Although these questions can be resolved, they take time, skill, knowledge, and attention. There are many ways to estimate age with reasonable accuracy in this context, which are explained in the instructions for fieldworkers. The strategy used in Senegal has always been to use all of the available information appropriately (traditional counting, seasons, historical events) and not to rely on a single standard method.

The demographic surveillance system produces a population register in which names have to be recorded. This raises the important issue of confidentiality. The community study is midway between a demographic survey, which maintains confidentiality by not recording names and provides wide access, and a health register, in which information is complete but access restricted.

10.5.9 Interventions

The study area was the site of several specific health interventions. The first intervention was vaccination with the further attenuated live measles vaccine of 1966. Mortality and morbidity after vaccination were monitored. A more formal vaccine trial of two high-titre measles vaccines (Edmonston-Zagreb and Schwarz) was conducted in 1987–90. This study was followed up by another trial of an acellular vaccine against pertussis in 1991–6. The efficacy of the tetanus vaccination during pregnancy was also monitored. Other interventions organized by other institutions were also monitored: the Basic Health Services project and the more recent Primary Health Care system, a food supplementation programme (PPNS), and a programme to detect and refer high-risk pregnancies. A system to screen and refer malnourished children was set up and a small centre to treat malnutrition was opened in one of the local dispensaries (Toucar). The use of essential drugs was promoted and the research team participated at various points in the organization and management of the drug supply, in particular for the prevention and treatment of malaria. Cases of poliomyelitis and other physical handicaps were recorded, and twice a year handicapped people received the necessary assistance and prostheses. Cases of epilepsy were also recorded and treated when possible.

The main issue confronted by personnel conducting major interventions such as vaccine trials was the issue of informed consent. We found it extremely difficult to explain this and randomized trials to people who had spent all of their lives in a traditional remote society such as the Sereer.

10.5.10 Legacy

Almost three decades of observation, intervention, and research represent a major achievement. This continuity of work was possible only because of the determination of Pierre Cantrelle throughout this entire period. The series of demographic data obtained in Niakhar is almost unique in tropical Africa, with the exception of the three villages of Keneba, Manduar, and Jali which were followed up by the British Medical Research Council (B-MRC) in The Gambia. The prospective community studies in Senegal have served as a training centre for researchers from Senegal and many other countries. Niakhar was also a demonstration area for visitors, who came from all over the world. The site has been the focus of numerous multidisciplinary research projects and has led to further research that would never have occurred at first to the founders of the study. The large body of data obtained has already been used by various researchers with different backgrounds and will be the source of future research projects.

Perhaps the first significant scientific contribution of the Niakhar Study was to show that detailed reliable demographic data could be obtained through the labour-intensive process of the follow-up survey. The various advantages and pitfalls of the follow-up survey were extensively documented in the early years (Cantrelle 1964, 1967, 1969a, 1974a), and continued being studied in the later years, especially when personal computers were introduced and utilized to improve the data collection (Garenne 1982, 1985, 1993; Garenne and Cantrelle 1989).

The second important contribution of the study was to the knowledge of mortality patterns in a rural area of Africa (Cantrelle 1971, 1975). The age pattern and seasonality of deaths remain a source of interesting controversy in the literature (Cantrelle 1974b). The pioneering study of the relationship between birth intervals, breastfeeding, and child survival is one of the most quoted pieces of work in the field (Cantrelle and Leridon 1971). The study on the relationship between malnutrition and child survival is the largest ever conducted in tropical Africa (Garenne et al. 1987a). It has not only led to better knowledge of malnutrition as a process, but has also pinpointed the value of using arm circumference as a basic tool for screening children at risk (Briend et al. 1989). In addition, it has given us an intrinsic measure of the prevalence of malnutrition (Garenne et al. 1987b), and has led to an analysis of the causes of death related to poor nutritional status. A programme of nutritional supplementation was evaluated (Garenne and Cantrelle 1986a) as well as other health interventions (Garenne, Cantrelle, and Diop 1985; Cantrelle et al. 1986; Beau, Fontaine, and Garenne 1989). Extensive studies on causes of death were conducted, first using empirical methods (Cantrelle 1986), and later using the so-called 'verbal autopsy' technique (Garenne and Fontaine 1986). This technique, pioneered on a large scale in Niakhar, was later utilized in many countries, and the Niakhar verbal autopsy questionnaire was translated into several languages.

The third major contribution was made in the field of measles research, one of the major causes of death among infants and children, by studying the effects of measles vaccines. A series of infectious diseases which were also important causes of death were also studied. Cantrelle was the first to note the excessive measles mortality of African children (Cantrelle 1968, 1969b). The studies on the incidence and transmission of measles (Garenne and Aaby 1990), cholera (forthcoming), other diarrhoeal diseases (Fontaine et al. 1984), and neonatal tetanus (Leroy and Garenne 1987, 1990) produced new insights on the relationship between factors of exposure to infectious diseases and child survival. The detailed studies of the impact of measles vaccination on disease transmission and mortality are virtually unique in the world (Garenne and Cantrelle 1986b). The results of a vaccine trial of high-titre measles vaccines have been the focus of a controversy and have had major research and policy implications (Garenne et al. 1991a, 1991b, 1993a, 1993b). AIDS has appeared recently in the study area; the first notified death occurred in June 1989, which led to new studies on this disease (Garenne, Becker, and Cardenas 1991).

Other key aspects of demography have also been addressed. The natural fertility regime was studied with its biological and social components (Cantrelle and Ferry 1979; Cantrelle, Leridon, and Livenais 1980). The nuptiality regime based on widespread polygamy and its relationship with diminishing fertility as the husband's age increases is a classic study (Garenne and van de Walle 1989).

Other interesting outcomes have included the focus upon the relationship between population and the environment and its impact on migration (Cantrelle 1971; Garenne and Lombard 1988; Garenne, Cantrelle, and Sarr 1995). Anthropological aspects of demography led to works of general interest (Garenne and van de Walle 1985; Cantrelle and Locoh 1989; Becker and Collignon 1989). Little has been done on the socio-economic determinants of mortality. One reason for this was the overwhelming homogeneity of the population and the low level of modern education (Cantrelle and Lericollais 1968). Risk factors associated with socio-economic characteristics explained merely a 20 per cent difference in mortality and virtually no difference in fertility, when biological and epidemiological risk factors could account for risk ratios of $1:10$ or $1:50$. Among the socio-economic determinants investigated, the rapid urbanization in the country appeared to be the most significant by generating massive migration flows towards the city. Instead of investing in endogenous rural development, the population of Niakhar relies more and more on Dakar for its survival.

References

Beau, J. P., Fontaine, O., and Garenne, M. (1989), 'Management of Malnourished Children with Acute Diarrhea and Sugar Intolerance', *Journal of Tropical Pediatrics*, 35: 281–4.

Becker, C., and Collignon, R. (1989), *Santé et population en Sénégambie des origines à 1960*, INED, Paris.

Boutillier, J. L., Cantrelle, P., Causse, J., Laurent, C., and Ndoye, T. (1961), *La Moyenne Vallée du Sénégal*, PUF, Paris.

Brass, W., Coale, A. J., Demeny, P., Heisel, don F., Lorimer, F., Romaniuk, A., and van de Walle, E. (1968), *The Demography of Tropical Africa*, Princeton University Press, Princeton.

Briend, A., Garenne, M., Maire, B., Fontaine, O., and Dieng, K. (1989), 'Nutritional Status, Age and Survival: The Muscle Mass Hypothesis', *European Journal of Clinical Nutrition*, 43: 715–26.

Caldwell, J. C., and Okonjo, C. (1968), *La Population de l'Afrique tropicale*, Population Council, New York.

Cantrelle, P. (1964), 'L'État-civil et les autres sources de renseignements sur l'évolution démographique au Sénégal', *Rapport de fin de mission* ONU, Dakar.

——(1967), 'Mortalité: facteurs', ch. 6 in *Manuel de démographie comparée: Afrique Noire, Madagascar, Comores*, Délégation Générale à la Recherche Scientifique et Technique, Paris.

Cantrelle, P. (1968), 'Mortalité par rougeole dans la région du Sine-Saloum (Sénégal) 1963–1965', in *Conditions de vie de l'enfant en milieu rural en Afrique*, pp. 156–8, Centre International de l'Enfance, Paris.

—— (1969*a*), 'Étude démographique dans la région du Sine-Saloum (Sénégal). État civil et observation démographique', *Travaux et documents de l'ORSTOM*, 1, ORSTOM, Paris.

—— (1969*b*), 'Connaissance de la rougeole parmi les populations africaines' (pp. 13–14) and 'Mortalité par rougeole au Sénégal', (pp. 17–19), in *Conditions de vie de l'enfant en milieu rural en Afrique*, Centre International de l'Enfance, Paris.

—— (1971), 'Etude de cas: Population et ressources dans une zone rurale du Sénégal. Ducument CEA Population Conference, Accra; repr. in *Afrique médicale*, 105: 1029–36, and 106: 47–52.

—— (1971), 'Mortalité périnatale et infantile au Sénégal', in *Proceedings of the IUSSP Congress, London, 1969*, IUSSP, Liège, pp. 1032–42.

—— (1974*a*), 'La Méthode d'observation suivie par enquête à passages répétés, OS/EPR', Laboratories for Population Statistics, University of North Carolina at Chapel Hill, *Scientific Report*, 14.

—— (1974*b*), 'Is there a Standard Pattern of Tropical Mortality?' in P. Cantrelle (ed.), *Population in African Development*, Ordina, Liège, i. 33–42; repr. in *Afrique Médicale*, 104: 933–40.

—— (1974*c*), *Population in African Development*, Ordina, Liège.

—— (1975), 'Mortality, Levels, Patterns and Trends', in J. C. Caldwell (ed.), *Population Growth and Socio-Economic Change in Africa*, Population Council, New York, pp. 98–118.

—— (1980), 'Mortalité infanto-juvénile d'hivernage dans le Sine-Saloum', *Environnement Africain*, 4(14–16): 413–28.

—— (1986), 'Problèmes posés par l'étude des causes de décès', in 'Estimation de la mortalité du jeune enfant (0–5 ans) pour guider les actions de santé dans les pays en développement', *Séminaire INSERM*, 145: 241–54.

—— and Ferry, B. (1979), 'Approche de la fécondité naturelle dans les populations contemporaines', in H. Leridon and J. Menken (eds.), *Natural Fertility*, Ordina, Liége, pp. 317–70.

—— and Lericollais, A. (1968), 'Évolution de la scolarisation dans une zone rurale du Sénégal (Arrondissement de Niakhar, 1949–1956)', in *Conditions de vie de l'enfant en milieu rural en Afrique*, pp. 226–32, Centre International de l'Enfance, Paris.

—— and Leridon, H. (1971), 'Breastfeeding, Mortality in Childhood and Fertility in a Rural Zone of Senegal', *Population Studies*, 25(3): 505–33.

—— and Locoh, T. (1989), *Social and Cultural Factors affecting Health in West Africa*, Rockfeller Foundation Exploratory Health Transition Program Workshop 1, Canberra.

—— Leridon, H., and Livenais, P. (1980), 'Fécondité, allaitement et mortalité infantile: Différences inter-ethniques dans une même région (Saloum, Sénégal)', *Population*, 3: 623–48.

—— Diop, I. L., Garenne, M., Gueye, M., and Sadio, A. (1986), 'The Profile of Mortality and its Determinants in Senegal, 1960–1980', in *Determinants of Mortality Change and Differentials in Developing Countries. The Five-Country Case Study Project*, UN Population Studies, 94, United Nations, NY, pp. 86–116.

Chiao, C. M., Thompson, W. S., and Chen, D. T. (1938), *An Experiment in the Registration of Vital Statistics in China*, Scripps Foundation for Research in Population Problems, Oxford, Ohio.

Fontaine, O., Garenne, M., Beau, J. P., and Faye, E. (1984), 'La Morbidité par diarrhée aigüe en milieu rural au Sénégal', *Colloque INSERM: La Diarrhée du jeune*, 121: 295–300.

Garenne, M. (1982), 'Problems in Applying the Brass Method in Tropical Africa: A Case Study in Rural Senegal', *Genus*, 38(1–2): 119–34.

——(1985), 'Le Concept de l'étude longitudinale et ses implications pour la collecte des données: Example d'un questionnaire informatisé pour améliorer l'enregistrement des décès précoces au Sénégal', *Actes du Séminaire de l'Institut du Sahel*, Bamako.

——(1994), 'Do Women Forget their Births? A Study of Birth Histories in Rural Senegal', *United Nations Population Bulletin*, 36: 43–54.

——and Aaby, P. (1990), 'Pattern of Exposure and Measles Mortality in Senegal', *Journal of Infectious Diseases*, 161: 1088–94.

——and Cantrelle, P. (1986a), 'Mortalité des enfants ayant participé à un programme de protection nutritionnelle (Diohine, Sénégal)', in 'Estimation de la mortalité du jeune enfant (0–5 ans) pour guider les actions de santé dans les pays en développement', *Séminaire INSERM*, 145: 541–4.

————(1986b), 'Rougeole et mortalité au Sénégal. Étude de l'impact de la vaccination effectuée à Khombole 1965–1968 sur la survie des enfants', in 'Estimation de la mortalité du jeune enfant (0–5 ans) pour guider les actions de santé dans les pays en développement', *Séminaire INSERM*, 145: 515–32.

————(1989), 'Prospective Studies of Communities: Their Unique Potential for Studying the Health Transition: Reflections from the ORSTOM Experience in Senegal', in John Cleland and Allan Hill (eds.), *The Health Transition: Methods and Measures*, Proceedings of an International Workshop, London, 7–9 June 1989, pp. 251–88.

——and Fontaine, O. (1986), 'Assessing Probable Causes of Deaths Using a Standardized Questionnaire. A Study in Rural Senegal', *Proceedings of the IUSSP Seminar on Morbidity and Mortality*, Sienna, 7–10 July 1986, pp. 123–42.

——and Lombard, J. (1988), 'La Migration dirigée des Sereer vers les Terres Neuves', *Actes des Troisièmes Journées démographiques de l'ORSTOM*, Paris.

——and van de Walle, F. (1985), 'Knowledge, Attitudes and Practices Related to Child Health and Mortality in Sine-Saloum, Senegal', *Proceeding of the IUSSP Conference*, Florence, 4: 267–78; repr. in J. C. Caldwell and G. Santow (eds.), *Selected Readings in the Cultural, Social and Behavioural Determinants of Health*, Health Transition Series, no. 1, Highland Press, Canberra, pp. 164–73.

————(1989), 'Polygyny and Fertility among the Sereer of Senegal', *Population Studies*, 43(2): 267–83.

——Becker, C., and Cardenas, R. (1992), 'Heterogeneity, Life Cycle and the Potential Impact of Aids in a Rural Area of Africa', in Tim Dyson (ed.), *Sexual Behaviour and Networking: Anthropological and Socio-cultural Studies on the Transmission of HIV*, Ordina, Liège, 269–82.

————and Diop, O. L. (1985), 'The Case of Senegal', in J. Vallin and A. Lopez (eds.), *Health Policy, Social Policy and Mortality Prospects*, Ordina, Liège, pp. 315–40.

Garenne, M., Becker, C., and Sarr, I. (1995), 'La Dynamique d'une population Sereer: Niakhar 1963–1989', in A. Lericollais (1995).

——Maire, B., Fontaine, O., Dieng, K., and Briend, A. (1987*a*), 'Risques de décès associés à différents états nutritionnels chez l'enfant d'âge préscolaire', ORSTOM, Dakar; 2nd edn. in *Série études et thèses*, ORSTOM, Paris.

————————(1987*b*), 'Un critère de prévalence de la malnutrition: La Survie de l'enfant. Actes des 3° Journées Scientifiques Internationales du GERM, Saly, 6–10 Octobre 1987', in D. Lemmonier and Y. Ingenbleek (eds.), *Les Carences nutritionnelles dans les pays en voie de développement*, Karthala, Paris, pp. 12–19.

——Leroy, O., Beau, J. P., Whittle, H., Sene, I., and Sow, A. R. (1991*a*), 'Efficacy, Immunogenicity and Safety of Two High Titer Measles Vaccines', Final Report, ORSTOM, Dakar.

————and Sene, I. (1991*b*), 'Child Mortality after High Titer Measles Vaccination: Prospective Study in Senegal', *Lancet*, 338(2): 903–7.

——————(1993*a*), 'Clinical Efficacy of Measles Vaccines after Controlling for Exposure', *American Journal of Epidemiology*, 138(3): 182–95.

——————(1993*b*), 'High-Titer Measles Vaccines: Protection Evaluation', *Archives of Virology*, special issue edited by E. Kurstak, 'Measles and Poliomyelitis': 119–31.

Lericollais, A. (1995) (ed.), *Les Paysans Sereer (Séñegal): Permanences et changements*, ORSTOM, Paris.

Leroy, O., and Garenne, M. (1987), 'La Mortalité par tétanos néonatal: La Situation à Niakhar au Sénégal', in G. Pison, E. van de Walle, and M. Sala Diakanda (eds.), *Mortalité et Société en Afrique*, PUF, Paris, pp. 153–67.

——(1990), 'Risk Factors of Neonatal Tetanus in Senegal', *International Journal of Epidemiology*, 20(2): 521–6.

Nations Unies et Gouvernement Brésilien (1964), *Enquête démographique experimentale de Guanabara*, Etude démographique, no. 3; Nations Unies, New York.

Ominde, S. H., and Ejiogu, C. N. (1972), *Population Gronth and Economic Development in Africa*, Heinemann, London, and Population Council, New York.

Rey, M., Diop Mar, I., Baylet, R., Cantrelle, P., and Ancelle, J. P. (1964), 'Réaction clinique au vaccin rougeoleux vivant atténué (Edmonston B) en milieu coutumier Sénégalais', *Bulletin de la Société de Médecine d'Afrique Noire en Langue Française*, 9: 255–71.

——Baylet, R., Cantrelle, P., Diop Mar, I., and Dauchy, S. (1965), 'La Vaccination contre la rougeole par vaccin vivant. Deux expériences en Afrique tropicale (Sénégal)', *La Presse médicale*, 73: 2729–34.

11 Bandafassi: *A 25-Year Prospective Community Study in Rural Senegal, 1970–1995*

GILLES PISON, ANNABEL DESGRÉES DU LOÛ,
AND ANDRÉ LANGANEY

11.1 Objectives and History of the Bandafassi Study

The Bandafassi Study was initiated in 1970 as a research project on population genetics. Its objectives were to describe the genetic structure of an
African population, to measure the genetic micro-differentiation between
subgroups of this population (e.g. villages, lineages), and to examine which
mechanisms were the more important ones: genetic selection, genetic drift,
founder effects, marriage patterns, or past history of migrations. Information
would be gathered from census, genealogies, and blood types. The population
chosen for the study was the Mandenka Niokholonko, a small population of
about 1,000 in the *département* of Kedougou in Eastern Senegal. The existence
of a larger multidisciplinary project of the Musée de l'Homme of Paris for
studying the entire populations of this department made the choice easy.

   A further objective (both genetic and demographic) of the project was
to measure directly the selective effects of particular genes, such as that
responsible for drepanocytosis (gene S). Survival rates had to be estimated
and differences according to the phenotypes of the persons examined. Such
measures needed the follow-up of persons with known phenotypes over a
period of several years. It was decided to follow the whole population and
regularly to collect demographic information on births, deaths, marriages, and
migrations.

   The demographic surveillance initiated in 1970 in the Mandenka
Niokholonko population was extended to the rest of the population of the
Bandafassi area in two stages: in 1975, twenty-four villages, about 4,000
persons, were added, increasing the population under study to about 5,000;
and in 1980, eight more villages, about 2,000 persons, were added, increasing
the population to about 7,000. In 1984 the use of verbal autopsies (questionnaires) was also introduced to improve information on causes of deaths.
Obtaining accurate demographic data, and studying levels, trends, and factors
of child mortality, rapidly became a major objective along with genetic data
collections.

The demographic surveillance is still going on. As explained later, methods of data collection, though they have been adapted to the demographic objectives, are derived from methods of genetic studies.

11.2 Study Area and Population

11.2.1 Study area

The Bandafassi study area is located in the Department of Kedougou, in the Region of Tambacounda, in Eastern Senegal, near the border between Senegal, Mali, and Guinea-Bissau (Figure 11.1). It corresponds to about half the *arrondissement* of Bandafassi. The climate is characterized by two seasons, a rainy season, from June to October, and a dry season, from November to May, with average rainfall of 1,300 mm. per year. The area is rural, the main economic activities being cultivation of cereals (sorghum, maize, rice), peanuts and cotton, and cattle-breeding. Some money is also earned by a part of the young male population through annual seasonal migrations to cities or other rural areas of the country in search of work.

The area is one of the most remote in Senegal: distances from the main centres of the country are large (700 km. from the capital of the country, Dakar, 250 km. from the capital of the region, Tambacounda); local roads are often unusable during the rainy season, which lasts half the year. The region of Tambacounda has the lowest levels of public equipment, services, and health facilities among all the regions of the country. Vaccination coverage rate is also the lowest: only 27 per cent of children of the region were vaccinated against measles in 1990, as opposed to 48 per cent in the whole country (Sénégal 1990; Pison *et al.* 1995).

11.2.2 Population

The Bandafassi area had forty-two villages and a total population of 8,612 on 1 March 1995. The villages are small—200 inhabitants on average—and are divided in hamlets. Population density is low: about ten inhabitants per sq. km.

The population of the area comprises three ethnic groups which live in separate villages. In order of settlement in the area, these are:

1. The Bedik (28 per cent of the population). This ethnic group, which was probably larger in the past, has its own language, related to the Mande linguistic group.
2. The Mankenka Niokholonko (16 per cent of the population), mentioned above, are part of the Mandenka people found widely in the western part of West Africa.
3. The Fula Bande (57 per cent of the population). They are part of the Fula of West Africa and culturally very close to the subgroup in Guinea.

Fig. 11.1. Localization of the Bandafassi study area in Senegal

The Fula are Muslims, while the other two groups are mainly animists with a few Christians among the Bedik. The Bedik are the oldest occupants of the region and their villages are scattered all over it. The other two groups, more recent, occupy only one area each: the Mandenka in the North and the Fula in the South.

The typical residential unit is a compound in which the members of an extended patrilineal family live; on average, there are fifteen persons in a compound. Bedik and Mandenka compounds are more populated (respectively eighteen and twenty-two persons on average) than the Fula one (Pison and Desgrées du Loû 1993). A compound contains one hut for each ever-married woman and sometimes additional huts for unmarried adult sons and/or for the head of the compound. Polygyny is frequent: there are 180 married women for 100 married men. When a man has several wives, each one has her own hut close to the others. Children sleep in their mother's hut until about age 15. Teenage girls leave the compound to marry, and boys build small huts to sleep in, often with others of their age. Sleeping arrangements sometimes vary. Other children may sleep in the huts of old or childless women, even if their mother lives in her own hut in the compound.

11.3 Data Collection

11.3.1 The baseline survey

The baseline survey was conducted at different dates in the different sub-populations of the area: in 1970 for the Mandenka, in 1975 for the Fula, and in 1980 for the Bedik. In 1975 and 1980, as mentioned above, a new sub-population was added to the population already being studied. The baseline survey was the same for different sub-populations. It consists of a census, and of several surveys that followed.

(A) The census

For each ethnic group, the study started with a census. A list of local villages that contained populations of the group was provided by the local authorities. For each village, a provisional list of compounds was copied from the administrative documents used mainly to collect taxes. Independently, a map of the village was drawn and compounds located, numbered, and identified by the name of the chief of the compound and the name of its lineage. There were differences between the two compound lists—the administrative one and the one from the map. Often two compounds that appeared distinct and separate on the map had been considered as one joint compound in the administrative list. The reason was that the compound had split more or less recently—a change not registered by the administration, which still recognized only one chief for both compounds.

Each compound identified on the map was visited and its chief or an adult member interviewed on its composition. The list of the persons living in the compound was established in the following order:

chief of the compound:
  first wife of the chief of the compound,
  first child born to the first wife,
  second child born to the first wife,
  etc.
  last child born to the first wife.

second wife of the chief of the compound:
  first child born to the second wife,
  etc.
last wife of the chief of the compound.

If a son was married and living in the compound—a common situation—his wives and their children were included in the list just after him.

When all the wives of the chief of the compound and their children (and, eventually, the wives and children of the sons) had been listed, we checked whether other adult males, related or not to the chief of the compound, were living with him, and asked the same questions about his wives and their children. Finally, questions were asked about the presence of other persons not yet listed, either adult women or children.

Each person on the list was asked to provide his/her surname, clan and lineage names, sex, age, marital status, name of present spouse(s) if married, and village of birth for adult women. There was no question on the relationship with the head of the compound, but information was collected on filiations: names and identities of the father and mother of each person. Links between parents and children were identified. This information, combined with the genealogical information collected after the census, was used to derive relationships between members of the compound.

(B) Surveys accompanying the census

To improve the information of the census and collect other data necessary for ethnographic and genetic studies, specific surveys were organized just after the census.

Age survey. The Bandafassi area has a low level of schooling, and civil registration was very inefficiently done at the time of the first census. As a consequence, declarations of age were often erroneous. In preliminary surveys, errors on age of the adults appeared so large that the question on age was omitted. Only the children's age was noted. A separate age survey was conducted after the census to estimate the ages of the adults, and corroborate the ages declared for children without direct questioning. This indirect method was based on two kinds of information: the classification of the population of a village by order of birth and the calendar of the circumcision groups. The ordering of population of a village by order of birth provides relative ages. To obtain absolute ages, we turned to classifications based on circumcision groups. Circumcision, which is performed roughly at around 15 years of age, with variations according to ethnic group and period, is an important festival. It usually takes place in February or March, every three or four years. Circumcision groups, identified by members' names, were listed in chronological order for each village. The dates of the circumcision festivals were estimated from both the chronological order of the festivals of all the villages in the area, and a historical calendar. These data, together with various assumptions concerning mean age at circumcision, form the basis of our computations of ages. Our estimation centres on the age at which each male was circumcised. Once we computed the age of these males, we could derive, by interpolation, the ages of the non-circumcised population, women in particular (Pison 1980a,b, 1985a).

Genealogical survey. After the census, each compound was revisited, and genealogies starting from known ancestors and going down to living collateral relatives were collected by interviewing the chief of a compound and any of the resident adult females (Pison 1985c). For each of them, called 'Ego', a marriage and birth history of the father was taken. It resulted in a list of her paternal siblings (full or half siblings). Questions were asked about the names, status (alive or dead), address of each of them, and also about their own marriage and birth. Similar information was collected about the next generations, the children and grandchildren of each sibling or of each Ego, down to the youngest generation. After the collection of information on marriages, births, and descendants of the father, each Ego was questioned about the marriages, births, and descendants of the mother. It is necessary to question polygynous populations separately about the father's and the mother's side because of frequent remarriages producing half siblings of one or the other side, paternal or maternal. The questions about the maternal side of Ego were fewer because the information on those siblings who were both maternal and paternal, i.e. full siblings, had already been collected.

Once information about the siblings of Ego—identity, spouses, and descendants—had been collected, similar information was collected on the immediately preceding generation, i.e. the father and the mother of the Ego: questions were asked about siblings, spouses, and descendants of each one. The whole operation was then repeated several times going up the genealogy to the oldest known ancestors of the Ego.

These genealogies were collected first for anthropological and genetic purposes. They were also useful for demographic purposes. Matched with the census, they permitted the detection and correction of errors. For example, checking systematically whether each relative mentioned as living at an address in the study area had been registered in the census showed that at least 4 per cent of the population was missing in the census (Pison 1982b). Errors on the identity of the parents of some individuals were also detected and corrected.

Genealogies are also used in the project to derive information about relationships between the members of the compound, and, in particular, the relationship of each one with the head of the compound.

Marriage and birth histories. During the census, we also collected marriage and birth histories of adult women. These data were collected not for retrospective analysis but as a means of lowering the risks of omission of residents. However, the census data were incomplete and inaccurate, especially for births, since we interviewed the heads of the compounds and not the women themselves. Several years after the census, marriage and birth histories were collected again, but accurately, by interviewing the women.

11.3.2 Annual survey

The annual survey is a multi-round demographic survey. Once each year, usually in February or March, all villages or hamlets are visited and information on events which occurred since the last visit is collected. This is done in two steps.

Collection of demographic information

In the first step, the list of people present in each compound at the preceding visit is checked and information is obtained on new births, marriages, migrations, deaths, and current pregnancies. Information is provided by the heads of the compound or key informants in the village. Not every compound is visited systematically. Experience shows that the villages or hamlets are so small and there is so little privacy that vital events are known to almost everyone. A well-chosen informant is able to provide much basic information with errors not being more frequent, and probably less than if each head of compound was interviewed.

   The persons belonging to a compound are enumerated using a nominative list. A new list is printed each year. For each person, the list provides personal information: identification number, sex, age, personal names, family and lineage names, village of birth, and similar information on his/her parents (his/her father and his/her mother). For each married woman the list also provides information on her current spouse and her birth history (list of her children, dead or alive). Printing such detailed information on the list lowers the risks of error in identification. It also facilitates the matching of information when the same event concerns several persons within the study population who do not live in the same compound. When, for example, a man gets married to a woman who was previously living in the study area but in a different compound, the information on the marriage is collected twice, in the compound of the man and that of the woman. In our study, the matching is done immediately: when the event is first notified, the new spouse is looked for in the list of her compound. This is possible because the survey is done by only one team that has all the nominative lists of the different villages. The immediate matching makes the work easier. Doing it after the fieldwork would make it more difficult to clear up confusion arising from names or addresses not corresponding. Questions are printed on the nominative list itself and information is transcribed directly on the list.

Collection of information on causes of death

For each death identified in the first stage of the annual survey, information on cause is obtained from a close relative of the dead person, usually the mother in case of a child death. Before 1984 we asked a simple question, such as: 'Why did the person die? Of what disease?' Since 1984 we have been using a verbal autopsy questionnaire designed for the Miakhar Study, also in Senegal (Garenne and Fontaine 1990; Desgrées du Loû *et al.* 1996).

Duration of the demographic surveillance

The surveillance started at different dates in the different sub-populations of the area. As a consequence, the periods and durations of the follow-up are different: 1970–95 (twenty-five years) for the Mandenka, 1975–95 (twenty years) for the Fula, and 1980–95 (fifteen years) for the Bedik.

The Bedik have been studied previously by Jacques Gomila, who had conducted a census and had collected genealogies in 1963–4 (Gomila 1971). He updated his 1964 census in 1970. So in 1980 we could do a follow-up on this baseline survey for this sub-population more easily than in the two other ones. Instead of taking a new census, we simply updated the 1970 one.

Information needed in different disciplines has also been collected: for example, blood samples were taken in the years 1970–7 and in 1990 for genetic and medical studies, while researchers in ethnology, linguistic and medical anthropology have been working in the area for several years.

11.4 Definition of the Study Population

In the census, a person has been considered as a member of the compound if he/she was declared as such by the head of the compound. The definition included even those who were not physically present and had not slept in the compound during the night preceding the census. Some members of the compound were absent for months, even years. However, people who had been absent for a very long time, four years or more, were excluded from the study population.

11.4.1 Exit

In 1975 we adopted a definition of an emigrant, the objective being to exclude people who were no longer living in the area, and to make a distinction between 'definite migrants', who were to be excluded, and 'seasonal migrants', who were to be kept in. As seasonal emigrants sometimes remain two to three years outside the home area before returning, we decided that a person who was absent at four successive yearly rounds without coming back in between had emigrated and was no longer part of the study population. He/she was no longer on the nominative list, and no question was asked about him/her at the fifth round following the first one where he/she was first declared absent. We chose as date of exit from the study population the date of the fourth round and not the exact date of departure. Such a definition results in the inclusion of some vital events occurring outside the study area. For example, we registered births from women belonging to the study population but who were physically absent at the time of delivery. These births are included in the numerators for the calculation of rates. Information on them are, however, less accurate than the information on the births which took place in the study area. For the former category of newborn babies, special criteria of exit were adopted: they are considered emigrants at the same date as their mother.

11.4.2 Entry

Entry in the study populations is either by birth to a woman of the study population or by immigration. Information on immigrants is collected from questions asked when the list of compounds of a village is checked: are there new compounds or new families since the last visit? When the list of people in a compound has been checked, they are asked if new persons have come to live in the compound since the last visit. These questions do not provide totally satisfactory information: new compounds or new persons are frequently declared one or several years after their actual arrival or formation. They may still be registered by the administration in their former location and pay taxes there. Most migrants who settle in the area are Fula coming from Guinea. Often they return to their country after a few years. When they first arrive in the study area and build huts, their neighbours consider them nomads who do not intend to stay long. The population of the village waits for several years before considering them as new villagers.

Some of the immigrants are ancient villagers who had left the area several years before and were thus excluded from the study population. We tried to find out which compound they were registered in and then match the new information with the old.

11.4.3 Movements inside the area

Movements from one compound to another inside the area are routinely noted. Some categories of the population, such as older widows or orphans who frequently come and go for short periods of time and live in several compounds, may be considered as members of several compounds or none. As a result, their movements are not always declared.

The omissions and the delays on the registration of some migrations (entry or exit) or movements inside the area result in some discrepancies between the true composition of compounds and that recorded by the surveillance system, and these differences tend to increase with time. Periodically, an independent census should be taken to correct this drift. This has not yet been done, however, in the Bandafassi Study.

11.5 Information Organization

11.5.1 Coding

Immediately after the census, each person was given an identification number. It is unique in the whole population, and is not to change during the study period. It has no meaning in itself, having been attributed sequentially from 1 to n. Identification numbers have been given to every person, dead or alive, present or emigrated, mentioned in the census or in any of the surveys conducted afterwards.

All information collected during the census and the accompanying surveys has been coded with the exception of personal names. Villages (and any locality in general) were given codes from 1 to n, and the compounds of the village were given numbers from 1 to n. The combination of the village code and the compound code is the identification number of the compound which is unique and never changes, like identification numbers for persons.

11.5.2 Database structure

Information is stored in a database whose structure is presented here.

First census information. Information collected during the baseline survey (census, genealogies, etc.) is stored in baseline files and that collected during the follow-up in follow-up files. The baseline files whose information describes the population at one time, i.e. the beginning of the study, are never modified. Errors detected after the census have, however, been corrected. The main baseline files are RECENS, which provide information on the persons registered during the census and the accompanying surveys, and the RECENSCAR, which provide information on the compounds at the first census. To keep the size of records small in RECENS, marriage information has been stored in a separate file, HISTMAT, which contains one record per marriage, past or present, of a person in RECENS.

Follow-up information. Information on events registered during the follow-up is stored in several files, one for each category of events: deliveries (ACCOUCH), deaths (DECES), marriages (UNIONS), migrations (MIGRATIONS), and pregnancies (GROSSESSE).

Information on new persons entering the population is provided by ACCOUCH for newborn children and NOUVIND for immigrants.

The compounds are treated as live units which, like persons, are affected by events—in particular, birth (creation of a new compound), death (dispersion or splitting of the compound), or changing the head of the compound. When a new compound is created, it derives from another one (its 'mother'). All such information on events affecting compounds are in the file MODIFCAR.

Link in data files. Different data concerning the same person may be kept in different files. They can be matched using identification numbers. One frequent question that arises is: what is the status of X at the last visit, or at one particular date? It is answered by reading the information on the status of the person at the census (in RECENS) or, if not present at the census, when he/she entered the population either as a newborn child (in ACCOUCH), or as an immigrant (in NOUVIND) and then going through events files to check if this status was modified afterwards.

11.5.3 Information on family structure

As mentioned above, information on the relationship of each person with the head of the compound is not coded and stored in the database. It is derived from other data, especially genealogical information which consists of the links between each person and his/her father and mother. Family trees are built starting with the current head of each compound and going on to identify his first wife, the first child of this wife, and so on to relatives, and then unrelated persons staying in the compound in a logical order. The persons who belong to the compound are ranked according to the following rules: children follow their mother and are listed by birth order, women married to the same man follow him in marriage order, and adult males related to the head of the compound are listed after him in a predefined order: full siblings, half-maternal siblings, half-paternal siblings, first full cousins, etc. Information on each person's relationship with the head of the compound and his/her rank in the compound is updated automatically by the computer program.

The pulling-together of these genealogies was a heavy task. Such information is useless for most longitudinal studies with demographic or biomedical objectives. Data collection is usually restricted in such studies to kinship links between living people and possibly with the previous generation. Applying our method of genealogical data collection may, however, simplify the handling of information on family relationships in studies planned to last a long time in places where household composition may change frequently. This is particularly true of populations with large households and complex relationships between members, as is often the case in Africa.

11.6 Manpower, Collaborations, and Costs

11.6.1 Manpower

Most of the data have been collected and processed by the authors. They are biologists, specializing in population genetics or epidemiology, with additional training in demography. We were assisted in the field by local people who helped us in establishing good links with the population and translated the questions and answers.

11.6.2 Collaborations

Collaboration with national and expatriate researchers working in Senegal has been limited until now. One reason is that the project has no institutional base in the country. A second reason is the long distance of the study area from Dakar, and the difficulties of the field work. The region is considered one of the most remote areas of the country. Most civil servants who are posted there had no choice and consider their assignment a punishment. When Senegalese students or young researchers have been asked to collaborate, most of them have refused because of the unwelcome prospect of spending time in the field in such a remote place. Even expatriate biomedical researchers working in Dakar who have been invited to participate have often declined. In the early 1990s, however, we started collaborating with a local medical doctor to study the causes of deaths.

11.6.3 Relations with the health-care system in the study area

In villages that are covered by the primary health-care system and have a hygienist, the annual data collection is usually done in the presence of the latter and with his help. One hygienist has understood the relevance of such data as a measure of the impact of his activity. Taking models from the surveillance system, he spontaneously started registering the births in his village to show the villagers that the babies born to women who delivered without his help died more frequently of neonatal tetanus than those who were born in his presence. Though his registration data are incomplete, because of lack of information and control, his high motivation would make him a good fieldworker if the project was to develop in the future.

11.6.4 Cost and funding

The cost of the study is low. Data collection and processing require about three person-months of a research-assistant and one person-month of a local assistant per year. There are also some travel expenses (one plane ticket and the cost of a car for one month per year). This very low cost is related to the fact that there are no permanent fieldworkers to be paid and no field station to be maintained.

The project has received funds throughout from French institutions: Centre National de la Recherche Scientifique (CNRS-UMR 152) and Museum National d'Histoire Naturelle. Funding was also provided by the Institut National d'Etudes Démographiques (INED) during the period 1978–93, the Institut National de la Santé et de la Recherche Médicale during the period 1987–90, and the Institut Français de Recherche Scientifique pour le Développement en Coopération (ORSTOM) during the period 1976–8.

11.7 Utilization of the Data and Resulting Publications

11.7.1 Overview of results

Methods. Several of our publications have focused on methodological aspects of population studies in illiterate populations. We have paid particular attention to the collection of information on age and discussed the relevance of collecting genealogies in demographic studies. We have tried out specific methods for demographic surveillance and database management for longitudinal studies over long periods of time (Pison 1979, 1980*a*,*b*, 1982*a*,*b*, 1985*a*,*c*, 1986*b*, 1987*a*; Langaney, Dallier, and Pison 1979).

Population structure and demographic patterns. Demographic information has been analysed to determine the age and sex composition of the population, population movement (birth, death, and growth rates), and the characteristics of nuptiality, fertility, and mortality (Pison and Langaney 1985; Pison and Desgrées du Loû 1993). A summary of results for the period 1981–91 is given in Table 11.1. The total population increased from 6,921 to 8,155 during the period, i.e. an annual growth rate of 16 per 1,000. The demographic patterns are typical of a rural West African population: high birth rate (47 per 1,000), rather high death rate (25 per 1,000), and a low emigration rate (6 per 1,000).

Nuptiality and fertility. The total fertility rate of the period 1981–91, 6.2 children per woman, is close to the national level for Senegal, 6.6 during the period 1981–6 and 6.0 during the period 1989–92 (Ndiaye, Sarr, and Ayad 1988; Ndiaye, Diouf, and Ayad 1994; Pison *et al.* 1995). There are large ethnic differences in fertility in Bandafassi, which are correlated with differences in nuptiality (Table 11.2).

There is in particular a relationship between age at first marriage and age at first birth, though it is quite complex. Age at first marriage and age at first birth differ among the groups, but the correlation between the two is weaker than one would have expected. Women in the Fula ethnic group marry, on average, at age 16.6 and have their first child at age 17.9, or thirteen months later. On average, Mandenka women marry at age 19.4, but often they have already had their first child; their average age at first birth is four months earlier that their age at first marriage. Finally, among the Bedik, premarital births are even more common for the women: the average age at first marriage is 20.6 years, composed with an average age at first birth of 19.2 years, or fourteen months earlier.

Infertility, which is higher among the Bedik (10 per cent of women aged 40–59 years never had a live birth) than the two other groups, the Fula (6 per

Table 11.1. Demographic indicators in Bandafassi (Senegal), period 1981–91

Population size and age and sex structure
size of the population on 1 March 1981	6,921
size of the population on 1 March 1991	8,155
sex ratio (number of men for 100 women)	93
% of the population aged less than 15 years in 1991	42

Annual demographic rates (per 1,000)
annual birth rate	47
annual death rate	25
annual natural growth rate	22
annual net migration rate	−6
annual growth rate	16

Nuptiality
proportion of 15–19-year-old women single (%) in 1991	57
proportion of 20–24-year-old women single (%) in 1991	9
singulate mean age at marriage for women in 1991 (years)	18.5

Fertility
total fertility rate (mean number of children per women)	6.2
mean age of mother at birth (all births of the period 1981–91) (years)	27.8
mean age at first birth (derived from proportions of women unfertile per age in 1991) (years)	18.5
proportion of women of age-group 40–59 years unfertile (no live birth) (%)	7
mean duration of closed birth interval (all birth intervals) (months)	33.8
mean duration of closed birth interval (only birth intervals with the first child surviving age 2 years) (months)	36.3

Mortality
infant mortality rate (per 1,000)	176
risk of death from birth to age 5 years (5q0) (per 1,000)	325
life-expectancy at birth (years)	40
life-expectancy at age 20 years old (years)	40

cent) and the Mandenka (4 per cent), also partly explains the fertility differences among the ethnic groups.

Mortality. Life expectancy at birth was 40 years during the period 1981–91 (Pison and Desgrées du Loû 1993). Between the periods 1981–6 and 1986–91, it increased from 34 to 47 years. This tremendous increase is due to a large drop in infant and child mortality: the probability of dying between birth and age 5, 5q0, went down from 407 per 1,000 in the first period to 244 in the second. Measles used to be a major cause of child mortality until 1987. Factors of measles mortality have been analysed extensively; the results are summarized in a following section on measles mortality.

Table 11.2. Ethnic differentials in nuptiality and fertility in Bandafassi (Senegal), period 1981–91

	Ethnic group		
	Bedik	Mandenka	Fula
Proportion of 15–19-year-old women single in 1991	91%	74%	35%
Proportion of 20–24-year-old women single in 1991 (%)	21%	7%	4%
Singulate mean age at marriage of women in 1991 (years)	20.6	19.4	16.6
Total fertility rate (number of children)	5.4	5.8	6.7
Mean age at first birth in 1991 (computed from proportions of women infertile) (years)	19.2	19.0	17.9
Mean duration of closed birth interval (all birth intervals) (months)	34.5	34.0	33.4
Mean duration of closed birth interval (only birth intervals with the first child surviving up to age 2 years) (months)	36.5	37.7	35.9
Proportion of women of age-group 40–59 years infertile (%)	10%	4%	6%

Adult mortality also decreased, but more slowly. Life expectancy at age 20 increased from 43 to 45 years between the periods 1981–6 and 1986–91.

Polygyny and mating patterns. Polygyny is common: there are 180 married women for 100 married men. This situation has provided us with an opportunity to describe in detail the polygynous marriage system and its influence on fertility, family, and household composition and kinship (Pison 1982a, 1985b, 1986b, 1988). Mating patterns have been analysed to examine the influence of different factors on the choice of the spouse. Though ethnic groups and castes are highly endogamous, factors such as village division or kinship have less influence than previously thought. The prevalence of endogamy among village members or preference for some category of kins—the frequent choice by a man of a spouse who is a matrilineal cross-cousin—are both explained by geographical distances and the demographic structure of the population (Pison 1982a; Lathrop and Pison 1982).

Population genetics and human evolution. Anthropometric and genetic data have been used to study the genetic micro-differentiation of the populations of the area, and the genetic diversity of human beings today (Gomila 1971; Langaney and Le Bras 1972; Bouloux, Gomila, and Langaney 1972; Langaney, Gomila, and Bouloux 1972; Langaney and Gomila 1973; Mauran-Sendrail et al. 1975; Lalouel and Langaney 1976; Constans et al. 1978; Tiercy et al. 1992).

11.7.2 Factors of child mortality, particularly mortality from measles

The vaccination programme, which started in 1987, has had a major impact on child mortality (Desgrées du Loû and Pison 1992, 1994; Desgrées du Loû, Pison, and Aaby 1995).

The evolution of 5q0 over the period 1970–94 is shown on Figure 11.2. During the first part of the period child mortality was high, with great fluctuations from year to year; the trend was that of a slow decrease of mortality. In the mid-1980s child mortality decreased rapidly and yearly fluctuations were much less afterwards. This change results mostly from the introduction of immunizations.

The role of immunization. In early 1987, immunizations were introduced in the area. As there had previously been no regular immunizations before and as immunizations were the only change introduced in the area during this period, this allowed us to study the impact of immunizations on mortality in different age-groups. We compared mortality rates in the six years before and six years after the introduction of immunization and observed a much lower mortality after (Desgrées du Loû and Pison 1995; Desgrées du Loû, Pison, and Aaby 1995; Desgrées du Loû, forthcoming). Neonatal mortality declined 31 per cent, between 1 and 8 months of age the reduction was 20 per cent, and between 9 and 59 months of age mortality declined 48 per cent. Excluding acute measles deaths, the reduction was 16 per cent between 1 and 8 months of age and 32 per cent between 9 and 59 months of age. The decline was stronger in villages which maintained high coverage after the initial national campaign, whereas mortality increased again in the villages where the coverage declined. Since the reduction in mortality was most marked after 9 months of age, measles immunization is likely to have been the most important vaccination.

Barriers to immunization. In order to identify obstacles to the Expanded Programme on Immunization (EPI) in such rural areas, we carried out an immunization survey in Bandafassi in 1992, five years after the starting of EPI (Desgrées du Loû and Pison 1992, 1994). Only 41 per cent of children aged 1–10 years were completely vaccinated, with considerable variations in coverage from one village to another, according to their geographical location: 71 per cent of children were completely vaccinated in villages less than 10 km. from the health centre, whereas in remote villages only 10 per cent of children had been completely vaccinated. There was no variation according to ethnic group. From 1987 to 1992, the gap in immunization coverage between the remote villages and those located close to the health centre steadily increased. The study pointed out the need to improve the performance of the mobile teams in the remote villages and to increase awareness about the importance of immunization.

Causes of child death. Information on causes of death is available only for the most recent period. Over the period 1984–93, the two major causes of

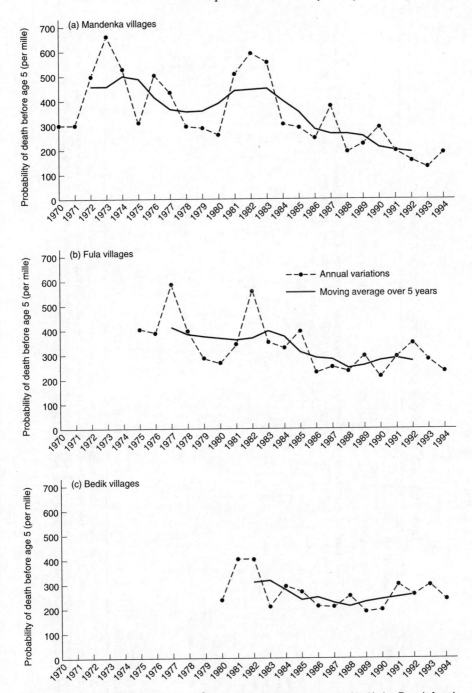

Fig. 11.2. Evolution of child mortality from birth to age 5 (5q0) in Bandafassi, 1970–1994

Table 11.3. Causes of child death by age, Bandafassi, 1984–93

Cause of death	Age-group							
	0–28 days		1–20 months		21–59 months		Total	
	Percentage of deaths	mortality rate (per 1,000)	Percentage of deaths	mortality rate (per 1,000)	Percentage of deaths	mortality rate (per 1,000)	Percentage of deaths	mortality rate (per 1,000)
Gastroenteritis	3	2.6	21	17.0	30	11.9	18	11.4
Measles		0.3	5	3.9	9	3.5	5	2.9
Malaria		0.3	10	7.9	8	3.2	6	4.0
Other infections	3	2.6	20	16.1	9	3.5	12	7.3
Malnutrition			7	5.7	23	8.9	9	5.8
Pneumonia	9	7.4	26	21.4	9	3.5	16	10.0
Prematurity	25	20.1	1	0.8			8	4.9
Neonatal tetanus	38	31.7					12	7.3
Complications of labour	9	7.9					3	1.8
Fever and convulsions	3	2.2	7	5.9	5	2.1	5	3.3
Other	10	8.4	4	3.7	6	2.5	7	4.2
Total	100	83.5	100	82.4	100	39.1	100	63.0
Total no. of deaths	301		405		278		984	
No. of live births or Person-years at risk	3,604.0		4,919.0		7,100.3		15,623.3	

Notes: Mortality rate at 0–28 days: number of deaths attributable to the cause divided by the number of live births.
Mortality rate at 1–20 months or 21–59 months: number of deaths attributable to the cause divided by the number of person-years at risk.
The deaths whose cause is undetermined (138, 158, and 93 deaths respectively for the three age-groups) have been distributed proportionaly to the well-defined causes after excluding measles, malaria, fever, and convulsions.

death during the neonatal period are neonatal tetanus, which accounts for 38 per cent of death, and prematurity/low birth weight, 25 per cent (Table 11.3). For older children aged between 1 month and 20 months, respiratory infections and diarrhoea are the leading causes of death, each being responsible for one death out of four; malaria, also an important cause of death at this age, is responsible for 10 per cent of deaths. For children aged between 21 months and 59 months, the major causes of death are diarrhoea and malnutrition, which are both responsible for one death out of two (Desgrées du Loû *et al.* 1996). Recently, during the period 1993–5, mortality attributable to malaria has strongly increased (it has doubled) with the emergence of chloroquine resistance.

Measles mortality. During the study period, a large number (264) of measles deaths were reported. Before the vaccination programme began in 1987, measles accounted for as many as 28 per cent of the deaths between 1 month and 5 years of age, making measles one of the most important causes of child mortality (Pison 1987*b*; Pison and Bonneuil 1988; Pison, Aaby, and Knudsen 1992; Pison and Desgrées du Loû 1993). As found elsewhere in West Africa (MacGregor 1964), there were more older girls among the fatal cases; 25 per cent of the girls who died were 5 years or older, compared to only 14 per cent among the males. The median age at death was 2.7 years, somewhat higher for females (2.9 years) than for males (2.5 years) (Pison, Aaby, and Knudsen 1992).

Most of the measles deaths (256) occurred during epidemics. Measles outbreaks take place during the dry season, from October to April. Among the Fula, measles epidemics occurred in 1976–7, 1982, and 1985; among the Mandenka, in 1973 and 1981–2; and among the Bedik, in 1982. Epidemics affected only some of the villages. The interval between epidemics was greater than nine years for villages with more than 100 inhabitants. In smaller villages, the median interval was more than thirteen years.

Two important risk factors for mortality in measles infection, which were described first in Guinea-Bissau, have been examined in Bandafassi: (*a*) intensity of exposure—fatality ratios higher for secondary cases infected by someone in their own household than for index cases infected outside the house (Aaby *et al.* 1984), and (*b*) cross-sex transmission of infection—secondary cases of measles in subjects infected from someone in their own household have a higher mortality when the infection is contracted from a subject of the opposite sex rather than of the same sex (ibid. 1986).

It was not part of the original surveillance project in Bandafassi to register infections; only the deaths were recorded. Even though we do not have information on who had measles and how the disease was transmitted, we have indirectly tested the effect of intensive exposure: having a maternal sibling under 10 years of age was found to be an important risk factor for dying of measles during epidemics (Pison and Bonneuil 1988). If cross-sex transmission increases the fatality ratio, we should expect that children whose siblings are of the opposite sex have a higher risk of dying of measles than children with siblings of the same sex. We have, therefore, investigated the risk of dying of measles during an epidemic in families with only two maternal siblings, two boys, two girls, or a boy and a girl. The analysis shows that children in families with a boy and a girl had a significantly higher mortality than children in families with two boys or two girls (Pison, Aaby, and Knudsen 1992). We have also examined the mortality of twins, showing a lower neonatal and post-neonatal mortality for female–female twins than male–male and mixed-sex twins (Aaby *et al.* 1995).

The importance of cross-sex transmission should be examined further because it offers an alternative explanation of variation in mortality by sex. In European–American societies it is usually assumed that somewhat higher mortality is 'natural' or 'biological' for boys (Babbott and Gordon 1954). If there are instances of higher mortality among girls, they are interpreted as a result of preferential treatment of boys (Bhuiya *et al.* 1987). Such variations, however, could be due to differences in the transmission patterns.

The Bandafassi data have also being analysed to examine whether the recent introduction of vaccination in 1987 and the suppression of high-risk transmissions of infection have changed sex differentials in mortality.

Both female and male mortality declined after the introduction of immunization but not equally quickly. The reduction in mortality in the neonatal period was significantly greater in males than in females, resulting in an increase in the female-to-male mortality ratio (from 0.64 to 0.96. After 9 months of age, the reduction in mortality was somewhat greater in females than in males, resulting in a decrease in the female-to-male mortality ratio (from 1.04 to 0.79).

11.8 Conclusion

The methods of data collection used in the Bandafassi Study were influenced by the objectives at the beginning of the project, which were mostly genetic. The data have, however, provided accurate demographic information on a population with very high mortality levels over a long period. Based on this study, it was possible to generate important insights on factors of child mortality in rural Africa, especially relating to the effects of measles infection and immunization.

References

Aaby, P., Bukh, J., Lisse, I. M., and Smits, A. J. (1984), 'Overcrowding and Intensive Exposure as Determinants of Measles Mortality', *American Journal of Epidemiology*, 120: 49–63.

—————————(1986), 'Cross-Sex Transmission of Infection and Increased Mortality due to Measles', *Review of Infectious Diseases*, 8: 138–43.

——Pison, G., Desgrées du Lou, A., and Andersen, M. (1995), 'Lower Neonatal and Postneonatal Mortality of Female–Female Twins than Male–Male and Mixed-Sex Twins in Rural Senegal', *Epidemiology*, 6: 419–22.

Babbott, F. L., and Gordon, J. E. (1954), 'Modern Measles', *American Journal of Medical Sciences*, 228: 334–61.

Bhuiya, A., Wojtyniak, B., D'Souza, S., Nahar, L., and Shaikh, K., (1987), 'Measles Case-Fatality among Under-Fives: A Multivariate Analysis of Risk Factors in a Rural Area of Bangladesh', *Social Science and Medicine*, 24: 439–43.

Blanc, M., Sanchez-Mazas, A., Hubert van Blyenburgh, N., Sevin, A., Pison, G., and Langaney, A. (1990), 'Interethnic Genetic Differentiation: GM Polymorphism in Eastern Senegal', *American Journal of Human Genetics*, 46: 383–92.

Bouloux, C., Gomila, J., and Langaney, A. (1972), 'Hemotypology of the Bedik', *Human Biology*, 44(3): 289–302.

Constans, J., Viau, M., Pison, G., and Langaney, A. (1978), 'Gc Subtypes Demonstrated by Isoelectric Focusing: Further Data and Description of New Variants among an African Sample (Fula from Senegal)', *Japanese Journal of Human Genetics*.

Desgrées du Loû, A. (1996), 'Sauver les enfants: le rôle des vaccinations. Une enquète longitudinale en milieu rural à Bandafassi au Senegal', *Les Etudes du CEPED* 12, Centre français sur la population et le développement, Paris.

——and Pison, G. (1992), 'Les Obstacles à la vaccination universelle des enfants des pays en développement: Une étude de cas en zone rurale au Sénégal', *Dossier et recherches, 36*, Institut National d'Études Démographiques, Paris.

—————(1994), 'Barriers to Universal Child Immunisation in Rural Senegal, Five Years after the Accelerated Expanded Program for Immunisation', *Bulletin of the World Health Organization*, 72(5): 751–9.

—————(1995), 'Le Rôle des vaccinations dans la baisse de la mortalité des enfants au Sénégal', *Population*, 3: 591–620.

—————and Aaby, P. (1995), 'Role of Immunizations in the Recent Decline in Childhood Mortality and the Changes in the Female/Male Mortality Ratio in Rural Senegal', *American Journal of Epidemiology*, 142(6): 643–52.

—————Samb, B., and Trape, J. F. (1996), 'Les Causcs de décès d'enfants en Afrique: Étude de cas au Sénégal avec la méthode d'autopsie verbale', *Population*, 4–5: 845–82.

Garenne, M., and Fontaine, O. (1990), 'Assessing Probable Causes of Death Using a Standardized Questionnaire: A Study in Rural Senegal', in J. Vallin, S. D'Souza, and A. Palloni (eds.), *Measurement and Analysis of Mortality: New Approaches*, Oxford University Press, Oxford, pp. 123–42.

Gomila, J. (1971), *Les Bedik (Sénégal oriental). Barrières culturelles et hétérogénénéité biologique*, Les Presses de l'Université de Montréal.

Lalouel, J. M., and Langaney, A. (1976), 'Bedik-Niokholonko: Inter-Villages Relationship Inferred from Migration Data', *American Journal of Physical Anthropology*, 45(3): 453–66.

Langaney, A., and Le Bras, H. (1972), 'Structure génétique transversale d'une population', *Population*, 1: 83–116.

——and Gomila, J. (1973), 'Bedik and Niokholonko: intra- and inter-ethnic migration', *Human Biology*, 45(2): 137–50.

Langaney, A., and Pison, G. (1979), 'Rougeole et augmentation temporaire de la masculinité des naissances: Coïncidence ou causalité?', *Compte Rendu de l'Académie des Sciences*, Paris, series D, 289: 1255–8.

——Dallier, S., and Pison, G. (1979), 'Démographie sans état civil: structure par âge des Mandenka du Niokholo', *Population*, 4–5: 909–15.

——Gomila, J., and Bouloux, C. (1972), 'Bedik: Bioassay of Kinship', *Human Biology*, 44(3): 475–88.

Lathrop, M., and Pison, G. (1982), 'Méthode statistique d'étude de l'endogamie. Application à l'étude du choix du conjoint chez les Peul Bandé', *Population*, 3: 513–42.

McGregor, I. A. (1964), 'Measles and Child Mortality in the Gambia', *West African Medical Journal*, 13: 251–7.

Mauran-Sendrail, A., Bouloux, C., Gomila, J., and Langaney, A. (1975), 'Comparative Study of Haemoglobin Types of Two Populations of Oriental Senegal: Bedik and Niokholonko', *Annals of Human Biology*, 2(2): 129–36.

Ndiaye, S., Sarr, I., and Ayad, M. (1988), *Enquête démographique et de santé au Sénégal, 1986*, Ministère de l'Économie et des Finances, Dakar, p. 173.

——Diouf, P. D., and Ayad, M. (1994), *Enquête démographique et de santé au Sénégal, 1992–93*, Ministère de l'Economie et des Finances, Dakar, p. 283.

Pison, G. (1979), 'Age déclaré et âge réel: Une mesure des erreurs sur l'âge en l'absence d'état civil', *Population*, 3: 637–48.

——(1980*a*), 'Calculer l'âge sans le demander. Méthode d'estimation de l'âge et structure par âge des Peul Bandé (Sénégal Oriental)', *Population*, 4–5: 861–92.

——(1980*b*), 'La Pluviométrie et l'estimation des âges', *Archives suisses d'anthropologie générale*, 44(2): 187–95.

——(1982*a*), *Dynamique d'une population traditionnelle: Les Peul Bandé (Sénégal Oriental)*, Cahier de l'INED, 99, PUF, Paris.

——(1982*b*), 'Sous-enregistrement, sexe et âge: Exemple d'une mesure directe dans une enquête africaine', *Population*, 3: 648–54.

——(1985*a*), 'Calculating Age without Asking for it. Method of Estimating the Age and Age-Structure of the Fula Bande (Eastern Senegal), *Selected Papers on Population*, 9, INED-INSEE-ORSTOM, Ministère de la Coopération.

——(1985*b*), 'La Démographie de la polygamie', *La Recherche*, 168 (July–Aug.): 894–901.

——(1985*c*), 'Nouvelles méthodes de collecte dans les enquêtes à petite échelle', *Actes du congrès international de la population*, Florence, 5–12 June, 4: 23–38.

——(1986*a*), 'L'Intérêt des observatoires de population pour mesurer la mortalité aux jeunes âges', in *Estimation de la mortalité du jeune enfant (0–5 ans) pour guider les actions de santé dans les pays en développement*, INSERM, 145: 37–48.

——(1986*b*), 'La Démographie de la polygamie', *Population*, 1: 93–122.

——(1986*c*), 'Les Coniagui, les Bassari et la démographie', in *Documents du CRA* (Centre de recherches anthropologiques), special number, Musée de l'Homme, Paris, pp. 65–80.

——(1987*a*), 'Le Recueil de généalogies orales: Intérêt et limites pour l'histoire démographique de l'Afrique', *Annales de Démographie Historique*: 67–83.

——(1987*b*), 'Pourquoi la rougeole tue-t-elle en Afrique? Démographie, structure des familles et létalité de la rougeole, *Actes du colloque national du CNRS 'Biologie des Populations'*, Lyons, pp. 73–9.

—— (1987c), 'Polygyny, fertility and kinship in Sub-Saharan Africa', in E. van de Walle (ed.), *The Cultural Roots of African Fertility Regimes*, Proceedings of the Ife Conference, Population Studies Center, University of Pennsylvania, Philadelphia.

—— (1988), 'Polygamie, fécondité et structures familiales', in D. Tabutin (ed.), *Population et sociétés en Afrique au sud du Sahara*, l'Harmattan, Paris, pp. 249–78.

—— and Bonneuil, N. (1988), 'The Impact of Crowding on Measles Mortality. Evidence from the Bandafassi Data (Senegal)', *Reviews of Infectious Diseases*, 10(2): 468–70.

—— and Desgrées du Loû, A. (1993), 'Bandafassi (Sénégal). Niveaux et tendances démographiques 1971–1991', *Dossier et recherches*, 40, Institut National d'Études Démographiques, Paris.

—— and Langaney, A. (1980), 'Rougeole et anomalies du rapport de masculinité à la naissance', *Population*, 2: 437–41.

—— —— (1985), 'The Level and Age Pattern of Mortality in Bandafassi (Eastern Senegal): Results from a Small-Scale and Intensive Multi-Round Survey', *Population Studies*, 39(3): 387–405.

—— —— (1988), 'Age Patterns of Mortality in Eastern Senegal: Comparison of Micro and Survey Approaches', in J. C. Caldwell, A. G. Hill, and V. Hull (eds.), *Micro-Approaches to Demographic Research*, Kegan Paul International, London, pp. 297–317.

—— Aaby, P., and Knudsen, K. (1992), 'Increased Risk of Death from Measles in Children with a Sibling of Opposite Sex in Senegal', *British Medical Journal*, 304: 284–7.

—— Hill, K. H., Cohen, B., and Foote, K. A. (1995), *Population Dynamics of Senegal*, National Academy Press, Washington.

Sénégal (1990), 'Évaluation du programme élargi de vaccination au Sénégal', Ministère de la Santé Publique, Dakar.

Tiercy, J., Sanchez-Mazas, A., Excoffier, L., Shi-Isaac, X., Jeannet, M., Mach, B., and Langaney, A. (1992), 'HLA-DR Polymorphism in a Senegalese Mandenka Population: DNA Oligotyping and Population Genetics of DRB1 Specificities', *American Journal of Human Genetics*, 51: 591–608.

12 Bandim: *An Unplanned Longitudinal Study*

PETER AABY

12.1 Introduction

The title of the chapter may be a contradiction in terms. However, the project was initially planned to last one or two years. Interaction with the first observations forced us to go on collecting more data, which again produced observations which needed to be explained, etc. This process is essential in research. However, funding of the process may be difficult to obtain these days, with research tending to become routinized as rigorous testing of specific hypotheses. The range of possible answers to the research question needs to be predefined to be funded. This makes much research trivial, at least to an anthropologist whose concept of research is exploring and making sense of the unknown (Aaby 1988).

12.2 History of Project

The present chapter is the history of why and how the project in Bissau became an ongoing inquiry. The emphasis is on the relation between interventions, research, and how observations were made. More detailed information on routine data collected, census, personnel, affiliated researcher, and institutional arrangements are provided in Table 12.1.

12.3 Nutritional Studies, 1978–83

Guinea-Bissau became independent in 1974 after a long and violent war of liberation. Survey data on age distribution of children conducted in the first two years after independence indicated that under-5 mortality in Bissau was likely to be in the order of 500/1,000. The Ministry of Public Health (MINSAP) therefore asked SAREC—Swedish Agency for Research Co-operation with Developing Countries—to organize a study to help MINSAP define the nutritional priorities in preventive health care. The project was to determine the problems in order for the population to be mobilized to change their own nutritional and health-related practices, thus reducing mortality.

The project was explicitly interdisciplinary with an emphasis on social science. The team funded by SAREC consisted of three full-time members, an

Table 12.1. Baseline data for longitudinal studies in Guinea-Bissau, 1978–93

	First phase: 1978–9	Present situation: 1992–3
Locations (Period)	Urban: Bandim (1978–) Rural: Quinhamel (1979–), Oio (1979–), Cacheu (1979–), Tombali (1979–)	Urban: Bandim 1, Bandim 2 (1984–), Belem (1984–) Rural: Quinhamel, Oio, Cacheu, Tombali Gabu (1984–) Caio (1990–) (HIV-2 study site) National cluster sample: 100 × 100 women of fertile age (1990–) (Neonatal and childhood mortality)
Population size	Urban: 6,300 Rural: 13,000	Urban: 37,000 Rural: 20,000 Survey of women + children: 19,000
Census	Bandim 1(1978), Tombali (1979), Oio (1979)	Urban: 1984, 1986, 1993, 1995 Quinhamel: 1983, 1988, 1993, 1995; Oio: 1979, 1983, 1995
Routine data	Pregnancies, births, deaths Growth (weight, height) Breast-feeding Infections (measles, whooping cough, polio) Immunizations (tetanus, measles)	Pregnancies, births, deaths SES risk factors at birth Growth (weight, height, arm-circumference) Breast-feeding, supplementary feeding Infections (measles, whooping cough, polio, chickenpox) Immunizations (tetanus, measles, BCG, DTP, polio)
Intervals for data collection	Urban: 3 months Rural: 6 months	Urban: Pregnancies each month, rest 3 months Rural: 6 months
Morbidity surveys		Urban area: Weekly diarrhoea survey, consultations, hospitalizations
Mortality levels	Urban: IMR: 190/1,000; <5: 450/1,000 Rural: IMR: 200–250/1,000; <5: 500/1,000	Urban: IMR: 100–120/1,000; <5: 200–250/1,000 Rural: IMR: 150–180/1,000; <5: 300–350/1,000
Main studies	Malnutrition and child mortality	Child mortality, measles control, diarrhoea control, neonatal mortality, HIV-2 control, crowding

Table 12.1.   *Continued*

	First phase: 1978–9	Present situation: 1992–3
Interventions	Growth monitoring, tetanus vaccine, measles vaccine,	Growth monitoring, tetanus vaccine, two-dose measles vaccine strategy, immunization at exposure, preventing premature weaning, improved case management of diarrhoea, AIDS control
Assistants	10 fieldworkers	60 field workers and laboratory technicians, 5 supervisors
Researchers	4 expatriates (2 anthropologists, 1 nutritionist, 1 physician)	14 local (physicians, biologist, statistician), 14 expatriates (7 physicians and medical students, 2 epidemiologists, 2 anthropologists, 3 volunteers)
Institution	SAREC, Sweden	Statens Seruminstitut, Denmark
Funding	SAREC	Core: DANIDA; Specialized studies: Danish Research Councils (measles, diarrhoea, HIV-2, statistician), British MRC (HIV-2), EEC (measles, diarrhoea, HIV-2)

anthropologist (the late Jette Bukh, project co-ordinator), a nutritionist (Medea Benjamin, and later Arjon Smits), and a paediatrician (Lars Smedman), and myself as a short-term assistant anthropologist. The team was to undertake anthropometric surveys in different parts of the country. The anthropologists were to live in the villages to determine bottlenecks in production and distribution of food, as well as defining the feasibility of popular mobilization for changing practices. We were to carry out experiments in initiating popular mobilization—a 'health-generation process'. This emphasis was an important factor in our decision to work with total communities rather than using samples, as suggested by statistical consultants.

12.3.1 Urban studies

The project focused on rural areas and it was also envisioned that experiments in popular mobilization should take place in rural areas. However, when team members arrived in October 1978, project vehicles had been delayed by several months. Therefore, it was decided to conduct a nutritional study in Bandim 1, an urban district in the city of Bissau, In collaboration with the political committee and the youth organization, all houses were mapped. In the subsequent census, we obtained information on names, ages, family relations, current pregnancy, schooling, profession, and housing quality for a population of 6,278 persons. In December 1978, after the census, all children under 6 years of age were called for a general examination during which 81.3 per cent of the 1,462 children under 6 years of age were examined for obvious signs of nutritional deficiencies, weighed, and measured for height and arm-circumference. The mother or guardian was questioned about nutritional practices and morbidity.

After the census and the anthropometric survey, antenatal consultations were organized for the women identified as pregnant in the census, and we initiated a registration of all new pregnancies, births, and deaths in Bandim 1. This became the basis for the ongoing registration of the population in Bandim.

12.3.2 Rural surveys

When the work in Bandim had begun, team members started in one of the rural areas (Tombali) inhabited by the Balantas, the major ethnic group in Guinea-Bissau. The plan was to carry out surveys with all the major ethnic groups, all inhabiting distinct ecological zones, to find out whether there were major differences in nutritional status. In Tombali, we conducted first a census of ten villages, and then carried out a general examination of the children under 6 years of age, as had been done in Bandim. However, this procedure was too time-consuming, and it delayed the first surveys in the other regions. The procedure was changed in the other four regions (Biombo, Oio, Bijagos, Cacheu). Following discussions between team members and the local political committee, mothers were called to bring their children under 6 years of age for a general examination. Later on, when time permitted, we carried out household censuses in some of these villages. We managed to register 400 to 500 children under 5 years of age in each of the five regions.

The anthropologists lived among the different ethnic groups for short periods to obtain more detailed socio-cultural background data, as well as information on food production, control over resources, food security, food preparation and distribution, breastfeeding and weaning patterns. Some information was also sought on morbidity and disease perception. Neonatal tetanus was assumed to be a major cause of high mortality rates during the first month of life, and interviews therefore focused on hygiene during delivery. Subsequent studies in the different rural areas indicated neonatal mortality of the order of 100–140/1,000 live births.

12.3.3 Nutritional assumptions and the measles epidemic

In spite of the expected high childhood mortality, which was confirmed by project data, the nutritional status of the children was not really bad; the mean weight-for-age (w/a) being 92 per cent (of the international standard) in Bandim and 88 per cent in Tombali. In Bandim, we had only encountered two marasmic children out of 1,187 examined and no case of kwashiorkor. This apparent contradiction was further reinforced during a measles epidemic which started in the beginning of 1979, shortly after the anthropometric survey. The case–fatality rate (CFR) during this epidemic was as high as 22 per cent for children under 5 years of age, one of the highest CFRs ever registered in an African community. Since the project was to be a mobilization project, we organized community meetings in the eight sub-districts of Bandim, emphasizing the importance of nutrition for severity of measles. During a certain part of the epidemic, measles cases were examined and treated at home by a medical doctor, but mortality was equally high for those children treated at home (only penicillin and chloroquin available). A preliminary analysis of the medically examined children who died of measles also showed that they were not different in nutritional status from other children in the community (Aaby *et al*. 1983). However, we took no immediate consequences from these impressions in terms of reorganizing the data collection.

12.3.4 Re-examination

After one year, we started re-examinations of all children in Bandim and three regions in order to obtain data on growth and mortality in the intervening period. Owing to the epidemic in Bandim, guardians were asked whether the child had had measles in order to obtain an assessment of the full impact of the epidemic.

Susceptible children (no history of measles) attending the re-examination in December 1979 were offered a vaccine. Earlier, no general measles vaccination campaigns had taken place in the country owing to fear of poor storage of vaccines. Vaccinations had not been considered when the project started. The measles vaccines given in December 1979 were a service to the community and not a research project; for example, we did not register the persons receiving the vaccine.

12.3.5 Continued data collection and preventive activities

After the measles epidemic, we felt uneasy about the correct message for health mobilization, and we did not venture into organizing more ambitious community-health programmes. Furthermore, in 1979 MINSAP had started a primary health-care project with focus on essential drugs and the education of village health workers and traditional midwives. In this context, we emphasized the need for more data on determinants of nutritional status and mortality in order to prioritize preventive activities. Before leaving Guinea-Bissau in the spring of 1980, we wrote manuals for routine data collection in Bandim and in the villages in the interior. Both systems were based on the registration of pregnancies in order to obtain adequate data on the very high peri- and neonatal mortality. In Bandim, houses were visited every month and pregnant women were called in to antenatal care at the local health centre. In the villages in the interior, pregnant women were registered at the six-monthly visits, and information meetings were organized for them after the examination of the children. After birth, children were included in the general examinations carried out with an interval of three months in Bandim and six months in the rural areas. Children were weighed in order to identify the malnourished children. More intensive follow-up of families with high-risk children were to be carried out by the nurses in Bandim and by the committee in the villages in the interior. Vaccinations were to be provided at these general examinations as well. Initially only measles vaccine was given, but from 1981 the full set of EPI vaccines became available. All children who did not attend the examination were visited to determine their whereabouts. Thus, it was hoped to obtain reliable information on mortality.

12.3.6 Analysis of data

After eighteen months of work in Guinea-Bissau, the team returned to Sweden in April 1980 to analyse the data and to write the report to be presented to the MOH in Bissau. The data confirmed the initial assumptions about a high mortality level, under-5 mortality being 454/1,000 in Bandim. However, the data on nutrition made little sense, since the state of nutrition was relatively good and the mortality was high. It was only when the analysis of all measles deaths which had occurred in the community during 1979 showed no relation between state of nutrition and the risk of dying that we started looking for a different interpretation. What triggered a new line of inquiry was the observation that mortality tended to cluster in houses with several cases of measles (see below). Furthermore, other deaths as well clustered in the houses with many cases of measles.

These observations, however, made it evident that essential data had not been collected during the epidemic. For example, we missed information on measles infection for children who had been absent, who had moved, or had died. Furthermore, in many cases it was not the mother who had provided the information. We had not recorded the information on the person who had received the measles vaccine. A reinvestigation to recuperate data in Bandim was therefore warranted (Aaby *et al.* 1984*a*).

When preliminary results were presented at an internal meeting in SAREC, we were told not to pursue these questions; the study had not been planned and our hypotheses contradicted fundamental beliefs in medicine. This led to a split in the research team. The exciting moments of questioning common beliefs and trying to provide alternative interpretations had become 'an administrative problem'; we should write only what the whole team could agree upon. However, enforced consensus is not a recipe for analysis. In the end (June 1981), SAREC got two reports and decided that they could not be presented to the MOH in Bissau. SAREC decided to discontinue the funding of the non-medical members of the team and wanted to close the project as soon as possible. However, since a report had not been delivered to the MOH, the assistants in Bissau were financed to continue data collection (until June 1983). Thus work continued in spite of the non-funding of the expatriates.

12.3.7 Follow-up studies of measles

We had to find alternative funding (DANIDA) for making a restudy of the measles epidemic (Aaby *et al*. 1984*a*). In the end of 1981, a recensus was carried out and information on measles infection was collected from all children under 15 years of age. Interviews were conducted in all houses which reported cases of measles during the epidemic. Despite the delay, it was possible to recover most of the missing information, because we had a census of all the persons registered in the community prior to the epidemic. Out of these interviews grew the tradition of interviewing about the transmission history for all cases of measles. Similar studies were started in 1983 in Senegal (Garenne and Aaby 1990; Aaby 1992).

12.4 Monitoring Preventive Health Interventions, 1983–88

Several observations made it essential to continue data collection in Bissau. Prospective data on the transmission of measles and the severity of infection were necessary to control the generality of the first information on the role of intensive exposure. It was also considered important to study the long-term impact of measles infection. Furthermore, preliminary data from Bissau had indicated that measles vaccine had a major impact on child survival.

12.4.1 New organization

To continue the project, we established collaboration with the Danish section of IMCC (International Medical Co-operation Committee) and succeeded in obtaining money from DANIDA (Danish International Development Agency) for sending medical students on a project which emphasized monitoring of preventive activities. Each year, IMCC was to send two last-year medical students to supervise the continued data collection in Bissau and to organize preventive activities. Data collection and routine preventive activities continued in much the same way in Bandim 1. However, when the students started in Bissau, we initiated two new activities: primary health-care work was extended to neighbouring districts in Bissau and we tried to improve measles control through vaccination at 4–6 months of age with higher-titre Edmonston-Zagreb (EZ) measles vaccine.

12.4.2 Routine registration as a way of organizing primary health care (PHC)

National plans in Bissau assumed that nurses should do extension work outside the health centre in order to mobilize the population for the PHC priorities, antenatal consultations, growth monitoring, immunizations, diarrhoea and malaria control, and dealth information. However, little was done, since routines were not sufficiently defined and supervised. In this situation, the experience from Bandim with integrating registration and health-centre activities was considered a model, and it was suggested by the MOH that we should use the experience from Bandim to create a system for other districts. The system managed by the students was built on a simplified version of the Bandim system. However, we did not employ assistants to carry out the registration work. The nurses at the neighbouring health centre (Belem) were given responsibility for certain subdistricts, where they were to find pregnant women and have them attend antenatal consultations, give birth at the hospital, assure that the infants were immunized and grew well, and teach the mothers nutrition, hygiene, and diarrhoea treatment. If carried out properly, the system would also provide important data on health and service delivery.

This project did not work for a number of reasons. The students as supervisors probably had insufficient authority; the nurses had little schooling and lacked motivation. The work done by the students and the nurses undoubtedly increased service delivery in the district, but the data collected by the nurses were useless and data collection was stopped after one year. Concurrently with this more ambitious programme, we had also tried in a different neighbouring district (Bandim 2) to raise vaccination coverage through collaboration between health-centre staff and the local political committee, who made home visits to call in the mothers for vaccination at certain gathering-places in the area once a week. This programme was very effective in raising the vaccination coverage but did not involve the other priorities of PHC in Bissau. Given local conditions, we opted for trying to extend the vaccination coverage in the other districts of Bissau city. Through the years 1985–8, the students succeeded in extending this vaccination work to most of the districts of Bissau. During the initial phase registration of pregnancies, births, child deaths, vaccination, and infections was also initiated in the two neighbouring districts to Bandim 1, i.e. Bandim 2 and Belem. Though the frequency of contact was less than in Bandim 1, the system was maintained by project assistants to monitor measles epidemics and measles immunization when the other activities were abandoned. Thus, at the moment (1994), the project registration in the city of Bissau covers a population of approximately 37,000 people.

12.4.3 EZ measles vaccination

The other major activities during these years were two trials with EZ measles vaccine. The first studies from Bandim had shown that measles vaccine had an enormous impact on mortality. In 1980–3 children had been vaccinated from 6 months of age, but this was subsequently changed to 9 months following the standardization introduced by WHO's Expanded Programme on Immunization (EPI). However, many children developed measles before 9 months of age. When reports appeared of successful immunization with EZ measles vaccine in the presence of maternal antibodies, it was decided, in collaboration with Dr Whittle at MRC Laboratories in The Gambia, to test the clinical efficacy of this vaccine. The reduction in mortality following Schwarz measles vaccination had been so large that I hoped to show that mortality was reduced by use of the EZ vaccine. Two trials were carried out in Bandim 1 between 1985 and 1988. The first trial showed that measles morbidity was reduced by the EZ vaccine when the children had been vaccinated at 4–5 months of age. Though this was promising, experience from the second trial suggested that female recipients of EZ vaccine had reduced survival compared with children in the control group, most of whom were vaccinated with Schwarz standard vaccine (low titre) at 9 months (Aaby *et al.* 1993*a*).

12.5 Research and Monitoring of Primary Health Care, 1989–93

The IMCC project ended in 1988. However, there was still an interest in continued work in Bandim and the other areas of Bissau. When the continuation was planned, the priorities were, among others, more research into the mechanisms of the long-term consequences of measles, the best vaccination strategy, better control of measles, diarrhoea, and neonatal mortality, and studies into HIV-2. At this time DANIDA extended its assistance to Guinea-Bissau by financing a PHC project including construction of health centres and technical assistance for the training and supervision of PHC workers in two regions of the country. As part of this larger project, the Bandim project was funded as a research and monitoring unit, with one physician (Henning Andersen) and myself as a part-time anthropologist and project coordinator.

12.5.1 Handling of data and introduction of microcomputers

During the first year and a half of the project (1978–80), data had been entered at a mainframe computer in Stockholm. When funding stopped, money was not available for routine handling of data in Denmark, nor was it possible to organize handling of data in Bissau. Thus, until 1989, routine data were handled only manually, which naturally reduced the accessibility of the data. With the appearance of transportable computers more resistant to the extreme conditions of humidity and dust in Bissau, it was decided to introduce microcomputers and a database system (DBaseIV) for the handling of routine data. A system has now been constructed in which the routine data on children are entered in separate databases for different types of data, in particular census information, birth-related data, infection and vaccination information, anthropometry data, morbidity data, weaning data, information on movements within study area, and death registration. Data entry in the different databases is organized through the census-registration to assure that information is always linked to the correct ID number. Since much of the information is collected in connection with the three-monthly and six-monthly examinations during which all children in a certain age-group are controlled, the system is constructed in such a way that follow-up will be reviewed and updated on the examination day for all children in a specific village or subdistrict and in a special age-group. The assistant needs only to enter the new weights, arm-circumference, or information on vaccination and infection.

Throughout the project period, the emphasis has been on following the pregnancies and the children under 3 years of age, i.e. the target group for the PHC activities. However, a number of censuses have also been made in all three urban areas, where we have tried to recreate the family relationships of the children identified through the child-related activities.

12.5.2 Continued work on measles

Since children exposed to measles at home have been found to be the high-risk group for severe disease (Aaby *et al*. 1984*a*), we had planned to test whether vaccination with EZ vaccine at the time of exposure was protective against disease and/or mortality. However, the fact that trials of EZ vaccine suggested higher mortality for female recipients of EZ than for the children who had received standard vaccine meant that new studies with EZ vaccine were difficult to carry out (Aaby *et al*. 1991, 1993*a*; Garenne, Leroy, and Sene 1991). During another major measles epidemic in Bandim in 1991, we carried out the experiment with vaccination at the time of exposure using standard Schwarz measles vaccine (not yet analysed, as the physician responsible drowned in a boat accident).

12.5.3 Other studies

Two more specialized longitudinal studies on diarrhoea (Aaby and Mølbak 1990; Mølbak *et al*. 1990, 1992, 1993, 1994*a,b,c*) and HIV-2 infection (Poulsen *et al*. 1989, 1992, 1993, Høgsborg and Aaby 1992, Lisse *et al*. 1990*a*) were initiated in 1987. It was obvious that diarrhoea was the major symptom associated with childhood mortality once measles was controlled by immunization. An epidemiological study of diarrhoea and different pathogens was therefore initiated in 1987. This study has involved the children living in 300 randomly selected houses in Bandim 2. The work has implied an upgrading of the laboratory work at the national public health laboratory where many of the examinations had to be carried out. One of the most important observations from this study is probably that cryptosporidium seems to be an important cause of both acute and delayed mortality. At the moment, this data collection is being used as the basis for an experiment to reduce diarrhoea incidence through improved case-management and reduction in the frequency of premature weaning.

In the beginning of 1986, the first reports were published of a second AIDS virus, subsequently to be named HIV-2. The virus was initially isolated from patients from Bissau and Capo Verde and the epicentre of this virus seems to be Bissau. In 1987, we started a longitudinal study of a random selection of 100 houses from the three urban districts in Bissau city to obtain more information on the natural history, clinical development, and epidemiology of this disease. The cohort of people in these houses has been followed with bi-annual surveys to obtain information on the incidence, and, in alternating years, immunological and case-control studies were carried out to determine the risk factors for the disease. In connection with the studies of the long-term immunological consequences of measles and HIV-2, we succeeded in adapting a method for detection of subsets of T-cell lymphocyte to conditions of field work in tropical countries (Lisse *et al.* 1990*b*).

12.6 Collaboration in Research and Continued Epidemiological Studies, 1993–96

From 1993, the project has changed institutional affiliation again, and is now funded by DANIDA and hosted by the Statens Seruminstitut, Copenhagen. Since there have previously been few Guinean researchers, it has now been defined as an objective to assist Guinea-Bissau with the training of younger professionals in epidemiology.

In view of the disappointing results with the EZ vaccine, there is a need for a new measles vaccination strategy, and a two-dose schedule with the standard vaccine may improve measles control. The long-term consequences of measles as well as the effect of cross-sex transmissions (see below) should also be further studied. Since the measles studies have shown that measles is a disease with both high acute and delayed mortality and this is not a mere expression of underlying weaknesses in the children who die, specific interventions against measles are indicated.

There are good reasons to examine whether other infections behave similarly, or whether their severe forms are results of environmental or host conditions. Other longitudinal epidemiological studies on diarrhoea and HIV-2 are also to continue.

12.7 Observations

The essence of research is new observations. One could, therefore, imagine that methodology would deal with how to make new observations. Rather, it seems that professionalization of epidemiology has entailed that methodology essentially deals with the rules for how to observe something already seen. Reality is 'collected' and analysed in terms of predetermined categories. This type of research may be highly reproducible, but also highly predictable. There may be reason to explore how new observations are made. One of the advantages of longitudinal studies may be that they can generate unplanned observations, and that they allow for verification of new hypotheses with old data without the need for a collection of new information.

In this perspective, some of the major observations from the Bandim project are reviewed. Though important observations have been made in several areas, the following description is limited to research on measles. The most important observations on measles have probably been:

1. Pre-morbid state of nutrition did not determine outcome of infection (Aaby *et al.* 1983).
2. The case–fatality ratio (CFR) of measles was increased when several children were infected in the same social unit (household, house, or compound) (Aaby *et al.* 1984*a*).
3. Secondary cases (infected at home) have an increased case–fatality ratio relative to index cases who contract measles from neighbours (Aaby *et al.* 1984*a*).
4. Deaths cluster in the same houses over time. This has been found to contain at least three mechanisms: previous measles cases may have delayed mortality; children exposed to measles before 6 months of age have excess mortality later in life; and children of mothers exposed to measles during pregnancy have higher peri- and post-perinatal mortality.
5. The delayed consequences of measles are also connected with intensity of exposure (Garenne and Aaby 1990).
6. Infection from the opposite sex increases severity of infection (Aaby *et al.* 1986*a*).
7. There is amplification of severity or mildness, i.e. severe cases generate more severe cases and a mild case generates a mild case.
8. Measles vaccination has a much larger impact on mortality than predicted from the proportion of all deaths ascribed to acute measles deaths, suggesting that measles infection may have long-term negative consequences for survival which are also prevented by measles vaccination (Aaby *et al.* 1984*b*).
9. Children who have measles after vaccination have milder infection and lower CFR (Aaby *et al.* 1986*b*).
10. For girls, early vaccination with high doses of EZ measles vaccine is connected with reduced survival compared with children who have received the standard schedule of Schwarz measles vaccine at 9 months of age (Aaby *et al.* 1993*a*).
11. Though this is still unclarified, it seems likely that the reduction in

mortality after measles immunization is due to a non-specific beneficial effect (presumably immunostimulation) and not mainly to the prevention of the acute and long-term consequences of measles (Aaby *et al.* 1995).

12. The beneficial impact of measles immunization is apparently much more pronounced for girls than for boys (Aaby *et al.* 1993*b*).

13. Treatment with immunoglobulin can reduce the case–fatality ratio in measles (Aaby *et al.* 1987).

14. The hospital is one of the major sources of measles transmission in an environment where the vaccination coverage is good.

It is beyond the limits of this chapter to present all of these observations, but the process leading to some of them will be discussed.

Pre-morbid state of nutrition did not determine outcome of measles infection. This observation was certainly not planned. It was facilitated by the fact that we did a follow-up study trying to reidentify all the children. With hindsight, it is most surprising that it took so long before the observation was made. We disregarded several hints before finally realizing that our assumptions were wrong. The initial anthropometric survey had shown a good state of nutrition in the community. When we made in-depth interviews on maternity history and disease perception, it became evident that measles was the disease feared most by the mothers. The epidemic taught us that they were right: the CFR was as high as 25 per cent for children under 3 years of age. The state of nutrition of the treated children who died was also tested and found to be no different from those who survived. Yet we continued to entertain the possibility that the children examined and treated at home could constitute a particular group. Only minor changes in the data collection were introduced in order to obtain more precise information on the epidemiology of measles, e.g. we asked at the re-examination whether the child had had measles. It was not until a year and a half after the epidemic, when the team had returned to Sweden and we had all the data in the computer, that it became definitely clear that state of nutrition could not be the major determinant of the level of measles mortality (Aaby *et al.* 1983). At the same time it became evident that essential information was missing (Aaby *et al.* 1984*a*).

The case–fatality ratio (CFR) in measles was increased when several children were infected in the same social unit (household, house, or compound). When common assumptions have failed, there is a strong inducement to formulate alternative hypotheses. We found no relation between CFR and breast-feeding, housing conditions, age, education, work situation of the mother, or adoption of the child. The only tendency was a slightly higher CFR in the polygynous families. We imagined that an explanation of the high CFR in Bissau had to be sought in a multitude of different factors, including higher rates of complications and improper treatment of the ill, e.g. withholding of water. While in Sweden we receivd a list with follow-up data from a re-examination done by our assistants in one of the rural areas (Quinhamel). On the lists for each village, there were groupings of two or three measles deaths suggesting that deaths often belonged to the same family. Hence, disease somehow became more severe when several children were ill at the same time. This hypothesis could be verified with the data from the outbreak of measles in Bandim (Aaby *et al.* 1984*a*). The 'observation' of clustering was very much a visual affair; the clustering on the list produced a new categorization which has turned out to be very important, since all subsequent studies have confirmed the tendency (Aaby 1995).

Secondary cases (infected at home) have an increased case–fatality ratio relative to index cases who contract measles from neighbours. This observation was essentially a deduction from the previous observations. The observation of clustering of deaths in families with many cases indicated that mortality from measles would be higher in large polygynous families. While this could reflect poor conditions in such families, in an African context, there may be a direct rather than an inverse relation between number of children in the family and socio-economic status. The size of family tends to reflect the power of the head of family. Thus it seemed natural to look for something different in the 'disease' rather than in the environment or socio-economic conditions of large families with many children. It was, therefore, hypothesized that secondary cases, i.e. those infected after prolonged contact within the home, were more severe than the index cases who had caught the infection from someone outside the home. This hypothesis made it essential for us to carry out a re-examination of the 1979 outbreak in Bandim with interviews of all the mothers to recover the missing information on exposure. This proposal was not acceptable to the funding organization, SAREC; it was considered methodologically unacceptable, since we had not had the hypothesis prior to the study. We could not do a new study to verify the hypothesis without vaccinating the children at the same time, thus limiting the possibility of observing the phenomenon. We therefore insisted on doing a re-examination of the outbreak in Bandim. However, we had to get funding elsewhere. All subsequent studies have confirmed the tendency towards higher mortality for secondary cases (Aaby 1995).

Infection from the opposite sex increases severity of infection. This is probably the most unexpected of the observations from Bissau (Aaby *et al.* 1986*a*). A problem of translation made this observation compelling. In a previous paper (Aaby *et al.* 1984*a*), an appendix had described the situation of contamination of the children who died of measles, stating, for example, that F. G., female, 2 years old, had been infected at home by a sibling. This report had to be translated into Portuguese for use in Guinea-Bissau. In Portuguese, there is no word for sibling, so this was always translated into the dead child having been infected by a brother (*irmão*). Since this was obviously not true, I had to review the records and thus it became clear that, in most instances when a girl had died, a boy had infected her, and vice versa. This observation was made on a small subgroup of children examined by a physician during the epidemic. It would have been difficult, not to say impossible, to obtain funding for a study examining this hypothesis. However, the data were already available from the outbreaks of measles in Bandim and Quinhamel. The tendency was clear in both data sets. Furthermore, case reports from the medical literature on measles supported the same trend (Aaby *et al.* 1986*a*). Subsequent studies from Senegal, Gambia, Copenhagen, and Greenland have confirmed the tendency (Aaby 1992). It seems likely that it may also apply to chickenpox and polio, whereas my data from whooping cough do not indicate any similar tendency. Thus, it may be a viral phenomenon. Studies of twins showing higher post-neonatal mortality for MF twins than for MM or FF twins suggest that it is a general phenomenon (Aaby and Mølbak 1990).

Measles vaccination has a much larger impact on mortality than predicted from the proportion of all deaths ascribed to acute measles deaths, suggesting that measles infection may have long-term negative consequences for survival which are also prevented by measles vaccination. If it was not 'weak' children who died of measles, and assuming that they would not die from other causes if they did not die from measles, a strong impact on survival could be expected after measles vaccination. Ethical consideration would have precluded a randomized study of this problem. However, before leaving Bissau we had vaccinated against measles all the susceptible children attending the re-examination, whereas the children who did not come in for re-examination had not been vaccinated. During the first year of the study, there was no difference in mortality between children who attended and children who did not attend the general examination. It was possible to examine whether vaccination against measles had a protective effect against mortality by examining the routinely collected deaths in relation to whether they had been present or not during the re-examination. A major effect of measles vaccination was not to be expected, since there had been little measles in Bandim. However, those who had been offered measles vaccination at the re-examination had 4–5 times lower mortality than the children who had not attended the re-examination (Aaby *et al.* 1984*b*). There had been no other intervention than measles vaccination specifically for the children attending re-examination. At this time, the *Lancet* published a study from Zaïre (Kasongo Project Team 1981) which had in fact attempted to examine whether the 'Darwinistic' model was correct in the sense that those saved from measles would be more likely to die of other causes and therefore the net impact of vaccination would be minimal. The paper concluded that in the long run there was no difference in survival between vaccinated and unvaccinated children, and that measles vaccination was not a priority. Fortunately, the Zaïre data did not support their own conclusion (Aaby *et al.* 1981). Before 3 years of age where most child deaths occur, the unvaccinated groups had twice the mortality of measles-vaccinated children. All subsequent studies have confirmed a similar or larger reduction in mortality after measles immunization (Aaby *et al.* 1995).

For girls, early vaccination with high doses of Edmonston Zagreb (EZ) measles vaccine is connected with reduced survival compared with girls who have received the standard schedule of Schwarz measles vaccine at 9 months of age. The impact of measles vaccination made it imperative to try to control measles also before 9 months of age. Had EZ measles vaccine not become available, we would have tried a two-dose strategy with Schwarz standard before 9 months of age. However, in 1983 the first reports appeared of successful immunization with EZ vaccination in the presence of maternal antibodies. The eventual decision in 1989 to recommend the use of high-titre EZ from the age of 6 months was based on demonstration of a satisfactory antibody response. However, our experience with Schwarz standard measles vaccine suggested that it would be desirable to study the impact on morbidity and possibly mortality. Studies were therefore initiated in 1985 in both Bissau and The Gambia. Based on the previous experience with Schwarz vaccine, it was hoped that EZ would have an equally pronounced effect, thus enabling us to show an impact on mortality. In Bandim, two trials were organized with children born August 1984 to September 1985, using medium-titre vaccine, and born May 1986 to April 1987, using both medium- and high-titre vaccine. While the first assessment in the first trial (Aaby *et al.* 1988) was positive in the sense that EZ was protective against measles and that EZ children had lower mortality (6.3 per cent) to the age of 2 years than the control children (9.5 per cent), subsequent follow-up in the second trial showed reduced survival among girls who had received the EZ vaccine (Aaby *et al.* 1993*a*). Mortality was 1.31 times higher in the combined analysis of both trials for the EZ children compared with the controls. The difference in vaccine titre may have been part of the reason for the difference in result in the first and second trial. Though increased mortality was not observed in areas such as The Gambia and Mexico with a low background mortality, similar trends of reduced survival for female recipients of high-titre vaccines were observed in Niakhar, Senegal (Aaby *et al.* 1991; Garenne, Leroy, and Sene 1991), and later in Haiti (Halsey 1993). This was clearly not a planned observation. It had to be made in a longitudinal study area. Few researchers would have thought of the need for following the population for three to five years to obtain a proper assessment of the impact, and no research council is likely to have funded a proposal arguing for the need to do so.

The data from Bissau and Senegal were presented at a consultancy meeting at the EPI in Geneva in February 1991 (EPI 1991). The experts found the data insufficiently convincing to change the official policy. Subsequent to the EPI consultancy in Geneva, a re-examination was carried out of all the children included in a seroconversion study on Haiti (Halsey 1993). The same tendency with increased mortality for female recipients of high-titre vaccines was found again and EPI/WHO was obliged to hold a second consultancy. At the meeting in Atlanta in June 1992, the experts recommended rescinding the recommendation of high-titre measles vaccine. Even though a plausible biological mechanism had not been found, the observation had turned out to be repeatable (EPI 1992).

There is no clear explanation of the surprising observation of increased mortality among female recipients of high-titre vaccines. The effect has been interpreted as a result of the vaccine doing harm possibly through a mechanism of persistence of vaccine virus (Halsey 1993). However, this hypothesis does not fit the facts that increased mortality was not found in areas with low mortality and not in comparison with unvaccinated children. In a subsequent study from Senegal when high-titre EZ was used routinely, the EZ-vaccinated children had significantly lower mortality than the children who had not attended vaccination sessions.

12.8 Conclusions

This description of the Bissau project has focused on how observations are made. If methodological rules had been adhered to, probably none of the observations from Bissau would have been made or pursued. Research methodology in epidemiology and public-health research is becoming increasingly standardized. The emphasis is on the testing of specific hypotheses. No one is going to obtain funding for a project merely stating the intention to elucidate everything possible about measles or diarrhoea. Since creativity is hard to evaluate before it occurs, the tendency will be to evaluate research proposals in terms of methodological standards in verifying the obvious. However, what makes research important to society and exciting to scientists are the new observations. It would, therefore, seem worthwhile to pay more attention to the question of how one allows for new observations in research organization. Longitudinal studies may have a particular role in this respect.

Since some data on survival, morbidity, and social conditions are collected within a longitudinal set-up even though they may not be the primary objective of the study, reality is allowed to contradict assumptions that had not been questioned in the study design. This happened several times in the Bandim project. Furthermore, longitudinal studies makes it easier and cheaper to verify hypotheses which had not been planned in the beginning. It is possible to go back and complement data if missing information is essential to a certain hypothesis or interpretation. The cost of setting up a new study would often be prohibitive for testing a new and 'unlikely' hypothesis. Ethical considerations may also preclude the testing of a hypothesis because the mortality problem studied can be prevented. In this situation, reanalysis of existing data or retrospective data may be the best that one can hope for. In Bissau, there were several instances where data to test unplanned observations were already available or could be complemented with little extra cost and with better validity than would be possible if a purely retrospective study had had to be carried out. In the case of the measles studies, this process was taken even further because other longitudinal studies were asked for data which could be used for verifying the observations from Bissau. Thus, collaboration about the verification of clustering, exposure, cross-sex transmission of infection, and the impact on mortality of measles immunization has been carried out in Keneba (Lamb 1988; Aaby and Lamb 1991); Bandafassi (Pison and Bonneuil 1988; Pison, Aaby, and Knudsen 1992); Niakhar (Garenne and Aaby 1990; Aaby 1992; Aaby *et al.* 1991); Machakos (Aaby and Leeuwenburg 1990, 1991); and Matlab (Koster 1988; Aaby *et al.* 1995).

While many of the observations were derived as deduction from other hypotheses, there were several important ones which were 'seen' accidentally or reported by the mothers. The process in these cases is difficult to describe, but depends partly on having a problem and therefore being willing to 'see'. It was characteristic that several observations occurred out of context while doing routine work such as interviewing, coding, or translating. Such routine activities undertaken for other purposes may force one to see patterns which had not been envisioned. While we mostly see reality through already exist-ing cultural/scientific categories, the context may present a new pattern which fundamentally breaks those categories. This is probably more likely to occur in longitudinal studies because there is simply more context than in a specific short-term study. Another important condition is, of course, that one is brought into situations where one's categories may be contradicted by 'reality'. One reason that focus-groups have become so popular in social-science research is probably that such groups open the possibility of people speaking between themselves around a given subject and in the process they are likely to come to contradict your assumptions. The varied experience in a longitudinal study may easily contradict project assumptions, thus producing new insights. In this connection it is important to emphasize the inherent danger if researchers become too specialized, only analysing information collected by assistants according to the researcher's categories about reality. In such a situation, there is little risk that new patterns will be observed. If they do present themselves, they are likely to be interpreted as 'noise' due to the poor performance of the field assistants or the small sample size.

There is a remarkable resistance towards seeing something new. We are apparently likely to interpret most contradictions we experience as acciden-tal: in a larger 'sample', things would be as we assume them to be. The first rule for seeing something new may be to pursue all contradictions between experience and our own assumptions. The tendency is usually to try to explain an unexpected observation as 'due to something else'. While one should obviously disprove the most simple forms of confounding, trying to disprove that a phenomenon is not due to something else is a limitless process providing no new insight. Trying to verify deductions from an observation/hypothesis is much more likely to produce assurance that the pattern is real than the attempt to disprove 'that it could be something else'. In this context, the longitudinal study is important because it facilitates the testing of new deductions.

Thus in conclusion, the longitudinal study if utilized to its full extent is more likely to produce new observations, since it allows for reality to present unimagined results which would not be visible in a short-term, highly focused study. Furthermore, the longitudinal study may provide both spatial and temporal contexts on the research issue in a way which facilitates the experience of contradictions, of something new. Finally, it is far easier, within a longitudinal study, to test deductions from a new hypothesis. This latter benefit may not be limited to the individual project, as collaboration between different longitudinal studies may greatly increase the possibility for using already existing data.

References

Aaby, P. (1988), 'Observing the Unexpected. Nutrition and Child Mortality in Guinea-Bissau', in J. C. Caldwell, A. Hill, and V. J. Hull (eds.), *Micro Approaches in Demographic Research*, Kegan Paul, London, pp. 278–96.

——(1992), 'Influence of Cross-Sex Transmission on Measles Mortality in Rural Senegal', *Lancet*, 340: 388–91.

——(1995), 'Assumptions and Contradictions in Measles and Measles Immunization Research: Is Measles Good for Something?' *Social Science and Medicine*, 41/5: 673–86.

——and Lamb, W. H. (1991), 'Sex and Transmission of Measles in a Gambian Village', *Journal of Infectious Diseases*, 22: 287–92.

——and Leeuwenburg, J. (1990), 'Patterns of Transmission and Severity of Measles Infection. A Reanalysis of Data from the Machakos Area, Kenya', *Journal of Infectious Diseases*, 161: 171–4.

————(1991), 'Sex and Patterns of Transmission of Measles Infection. A Reanalysis of Data from the Machakos Area, Kenya', *Annals of Tropical Pediatrics*, 11: 397–402.

——and Mølbak, K. (1990), 'Siblings of Opposite Sex as a Risk Factor for Child Mortality', *British Medical Journal*, 301: 143–5.

——Bukh, J., Lisse, I. M., and Smits, A. J. (1981), 'Measles Vaccination and Child Mortality', *Lancet*, 2: 93.

————————(1983), 'Measles Mortality, State of Nutrition, and Family Structure: A Community Study from Guinea-Bissau', *Journal of Infectious Diseases* 147: 693–701.

————————(1984a), 'Overcrowding and Intensive Exposure as Determinants of Measles Mortality', *American Journal of Epidemiology*, 120: 49–63.

————————(1984b), 'Measles Vaccination and Reduction in Child Mortality: A Community Study from Guinea-Bissau', *Journal of Infectious Diseases*, 8: 13–21.

————————(1986a), 'Cross-Sex Transmission of Infection and Increased Mortality due to Measles', *Review of Infectious Diseases*, 8: 138–43.

——————Leerhøy, J., Lisse, I. M., Mordhorst, C. H., and Pedersen, I. R. (1986b), 'Vaccinated Children get Milder Measles Infection: A Community Study from Guinea-Bissau', *Journal of Infectious Diseases*, 154: 858–63.

——Bukh, J., Hoff, G., Lisse, I. M., and Smits, A. J. (1987), 'Humoral Immunity in Measles Infection: A Critical Factor?' *Medical Hypotheses*, 23: 287–302.

——Jensen, T. G., Hansen, H. L., Kristiansen, H., Thårup, J., Poulsen, A., Sodemann, M., Jakobsen, M., Knudsen K., da Silva, M. C., and Whittle, H. (1988), 'Trial of High-Dose Edmonston-Zagreb Measles Vaccine in Guinea-Bissau: Protective Efficacy', *Lancet*, 2: 809–11.

——Samb, B., Simondon, F., Whittle, H., Coll Seck, A. M., Knudsen, K., Bennett, J., Markowitz, L., and Rhodes, P. (1991), 'Child Mortality after High-Titre Measles Vaccines in Senegal: The Complete Data Set', *Lancet*, 338: 1518.

——Knudsen, K., Whittle, H., Thårup, J., Poulsen, A., Sodemann, M., Jakobsen, M., Brink, L., Gansted, U., Permin, A., Jensen, T. G., Lisse, I. M., Andersen, H., and da Silva, M. C. (1993*a*), 'Long-Term Survival after Edmonston-Zagreb Measles Vaccination: Increased Female Mortality', *Journal of Pediatrics*, 122: 904–8.

——Samb, B., Simondon, F., Knudsen, K., Coll Seck, A. M., Bennett, J., and Whittle, H. (1993*b*), 'Divergent Mortality for Male and Female Recipients of Low-Titre and High-Titre Measles Vaccines in Rural Senegal', *American Journal of Epidemiology*, 138: 746–55.

————Coll Seck, A. M., Knudsen, K., and Whittle, H. (1995), 'Non-Specific Beneficial Effect of Measles Immunization. Analysis of Mortality Studies from Developing Countries', *British Medical Journal*, 311: 481–5.

EPI (Expanded Programme on Immunization) (1991), 'Safety and Efficacy of High Titre Measles Vaccine at 6 Months of Age', *Weekly Epidemiological Records*, 66: 249–51.

——(1992), 'Safety of High-Titre Measles Vaccines', *Weekly Epidemiological Records*, 67: 357–61.

Garenne, M., and Aaby, P. (1990), 'Pattern of Exposure and Measles Mortality in Senegal', *Journal of Infectious Diseases*, 161: 1088–94.

——Leroy, O., and Sene, I. (1991), 'Child Mortality after High-Titre Measles Vaccines: Prospective Study in Senegal', *Lancet*, 338: 903–7.

Halsey, N. (1993), 'Increased Mortality Following High Titer Measles Vaccines: Too Much of a Good Thing', *Journal of Pediatric Infectious Diseases*, 12: 462–5.

Høgsborg, M., and Aaby, P. (1992), 'Sexual Relations, Use of Condoms and Perceptions of AIDS in an Urban Area of Guinea-Bissau with a High Prevalence of HIV-2', in T. Dyson (ed.), *Sexual Behaviour and Networking: Anthropological and Socio-Cultural Studies on the Transmission of HIV*, Ordina, Liège, pp. 203–32.

Kasongo Project Team (1981), 'Influence of Measles Vaccination on Survival Pattern of 7–35-Month-Old Children in Kasongo, Zaïre', *Lancet*, 1: 764–7.

Koster, F. T. (1988), 'A Review of Measles in Bangladesh with Respect to Mortality Rates among Primary versus Secondary Cases', *Review of Infectious Diseases*, 10: 471–3.

Lamb, W. H. (1988), 'Epidemic Measles in a Highly Immunized Rural West African (Gambian) Village', *Review of Infectious Diseases*, 10: 457–62.

Lisse, I., Poulsen, A. G., Aaby, P., Kvinesdal, B. B., Mølbak, K., Dias, F., and Knudsen, K. (1990*a*), 'Immmunodeficiency in HIV-2 Infection. A Community Study from Guinea-Bissau', *AIDS*, 4: 1263–6.

——Whittle, H., Aaby, P., Normark, M., Gyhrs, A., and Ryder, L. P. (1990*b*), 'Labelling of T-cell Subsets under Field Conditions in Tropical Countries. Adaptation of the

Immuno-Alkaline Phosphatase Staining Method for Blood-Smears', *Journal of Immunological Methods*, 129: 49–53.

Mølbak, K., Højlyng, N., Ingholt, L., Silva, A. G. J., Jepsen, S., and Aaby, P. (1990), 'An Epidemic Outbreak of Cryptosporidiosis. A Prospective Community Study from Guinea-Bissau', *Journal of Pediatric Infectious Diseases*, 9: 566–70.

——Aaby, P., Ingholt, L., Højlyng, N., Gottschau, A., Andersen, H., Brink, L., Gansted, U., Permin, A., Vollmer, A., and da Silva, A. P. J. (1992), 'Persistent Diarrhoea as a Leading Cause of Child Mortality. An Analysis of Deaths among Children in Guinea-Bissau', *Transactions of the Royal Society of Tropical Medicine*, 86: 216–20.

——Højlyng, N., Gottschau, A., Ingholt, L., Silva, A. G. J., and Aaby, P. (1993), 'Cryptosporidium in Infancy: A Major Cause of Childhood Mortality in Guinea-Bissau, West Africa', *British Medical Journal*, 307: 417–20.

——Wested, N., Højlyng, N., Gottschau, A., Aaby, P., and da Silva, A. P. J. (1994*a*), 'The Aetiology of Early Childhood Diarrhoea. A Community Study from Guinea-Bissau', *Journal of Infectious Diseases*, 169: 581–7.

——Aaby, P., Højlyng, N., and da Silva, A. P. (1994*b*), 'Risk-Factors for Cryptosporidium Diarrhoea in Early Childhood: A Case-Control Study from Guinea-Bissau, West Africa', *American Journal of Epidemiology*, 139: 734–40.

——Gottschau, A., Aaby, P., Højlyng, N., Ingholt, L., and da Silva, A. P. (1994*c*), 'Prolonged Breastfeeding, Diarrhoeal Diseases, and Child Survival in a Community Study from Guinea-Bissau, West Africa', *British Medical Journal*, 308: 1403–6.

Pison, G., and Bonneuil, N. (1988), 'Increased Risk of Measles Mortality for Children with Siblings among the Fula Bande, Senegal', *Review of Infectious Diseases*, 10: 468–70.

——Aaby, P., and Knudsen, K. (1992), 'Increased Risk of Measles Mortality for Children with a Sibling of the Opposite Sex among the Fula Bande and Niokholonko, Senegal', *British Medical Journal*, 304: 284–7.

Poulsen, A. G., Kvinesdal, B., Aaby, P., Mølbak, K., Frederiksen, K., Dias, F., and Lauritzen, E. (1989), 'Prevalence of and Mortality from Human Immunodeficiency Virus Type 2 in Bissau, West Africa', *Lancet*, 1: 827–31.

——————Lisse, I., Mølbak, K., Dias, F., and Lauritzen, E. (1992), 'Lack of Evidence of Vertical Transmission of Human Immunodeficiency Virus Type 2', *Journal of Acquired Immune Deficiency Syndrome*, 5: 25–30.

——Aaby, P., Gottschau, A., Kvinesdal, B., Mølbak, K., Dias, F., and Lauritzen, E. (1993), 'HIV-2 Infection in Bissau, West Africa, 1987–1989: Incidence, Prevalences, and Routes of Transmission', *Journal of Acquired Immune Deficiency Syndrome*, 6: 941–8.

Appendix

Prospective Community Studies in Developing Countries:
A Survey of Surveys

MICHEL GARENNE AND EMILIA KOUMANS

A Survey of Surveys

This book presents in detail ten classic prospective community studies, some
more oriented towards public health and family planning, others more oriented towards demography. However, this is only a sample of all the similar
endeavours that have been conducted in the world since the 1930s. In this
appendix, we present the results of a systematic search on prospective community studies.

This 'survey of surveys' started by a search in *Medline* and *Popline*, two com-
puterized bibliographic databases, the first being more medical, the second
more demographic. A first set of seventy-two studies was identified. A questionnaire was sent to the principal investigators of the studies when possible.
The questionnaire included details on the location, the investigators, the duration and size, the sampling, the demographic surveillance, the epidemiological
surveillance the topics studied, the computer system, the human resources, the
sources of funding, and the major publications. This questionnaire was supplemented with readings from the studies.

Selection of studies

From this first set, we disregarded the studies that did not qualify as 'prospective community studies'. In particular, we excluded the very 'cohort studies',
familiar to epidemiologists, which do not include the total population but only
a sample of either young children or adults who are followed over time for a
specific study (physical growth, cardiovascular disease, cancer, etc.). We also
excluded the more 'anthropological studies' based on very small samples, such
as village studies. We also excluded the pure 'demographic studies', such as the
multi-round surveys, because their focus is more narrow and they are usually
conducted on short periods of time (two to four years) and are rarely geographically defined. Last, we excluded the studies for which too little information was available.

Our definition of 'prospective community study' included three elements:

1. The follow-up of a whole sizeable population, geographically defined, over a period of time of several years (at least four to five years). The size and the duration should combine to cumulate a relatively large total number of person-years, in the scale of at least 50,000 to 100,000 person-years, in order to provide meaningful demographic estimates.
2. The study is based on a census of the whole population, and includes a comprehensive record of vital events and migration (demographic surveillance system).
3. The study is multidisciplinary, and covers at least two fields among the following: demography, public health, epidemiology, anthropology, economics.

In the final list presented here we have introduced some flexibility in those strong requirements, and a few studies do not match totally all those criteria. In particular, we took into account the fact that a researcher or a small team of investigators devoted several years to the study and conducted multidisciplinary studies.

We present here a short comment on the results of this survey and a list of abstracts, one for each of the main studies analysed. We hope that this set will be useful for other researchers, since there was no comprehensive account of prospective community studies in developing countries. However, we do not pretend to have been exhaustive. We heard about many other studies which could have met most of our criteria. But they were out of reach, since we could not locate the persons in charge and we could not find any significant reports in the published literature. We do apologize for such omissions. The abstracts are short and therefore reductive. They should be taken only as a first introduction to the studies, not as a full account. We felt that this short presentation could be useful, for the other researchers who would like to have an idea of what has already been done, and for the users and funding agencies to show what can be achieved by prospective community studies.

For the abstract, most of the surveys are well identified in time and space. However, we have grouped some of the studies when they were conducted in approximately the same location, by the same institutions, even when there were significant changes in the sample size and in the focus. For instance, we have grouped together all the ORSTOM studies in Senegal, all the MRC studies in The Gambia, the studies that originated from Matlab (Teknaf and extension) with Matlab, and the various studies conducted in Bohol and in Cebu. However, we presented separately Khanna-I and Khanna-II, since the focus changed dramatically and the two studies were conducted thirty years apart from each other.

Results

1. Size and duration

The thirty studies investigated here had a wide range of size and duration. The size ranges from about 2,000 persons (Keneba) to about 200,000 (Matlab) and the duration from about four years (Malumfashi) to more than forty years (Keneba). An average study follows a community of about 30,000 persons for about eight years, and the total number of person-years cumulated exceeds 200,000: a typical example of this situation can be found in Machakos (Table A1).

Table A1. Size and duration

	Range	No. of surveys
Population size	<10,000	7
	10,000–29,999	12
	30,000–49,999	6
	≥50,000	5
Duration in years	<5	5
	5–9	17
	10–19	5
	≥20	3
Cumulated person-years	15,000–49,999	5
	50,000–149,999	11
	150,000–499,999	10
	500,000	4

Note: Some of the surveys are not yet completed. These values are only indicative of the situation at the end of 1991.

2. Demographic surveillance

The demographic surveillance almost always starts with a baseline census. Sometimes investigators use a national census recently taken as their baseline. Several options are then possible: a repeated census every six or twelve months, as done in many of the francophone surveys and in Khanna-I, or a census every four to nine years, as done in Matlab, or only a final census at the end of the study. Several options are also possible for the recording of vital events. Some studies use a very labour intensive approach, with visits to each household every one, two, or four weeks. Very frequent visits (one or two weeks) are usually justified for morbidity surveillance. Monthly visits are suitable to study pregnancy and menstruation. Other studies use a continuous

recording of vital events by people already living in the villages with a regular
check every two, three, four, six, or twelve months. In the multi-round survey
approach, events are usually updated only at the time of the yearly census
(Table A2).

Table A2.   DSS systems

	Yes	No	Unknown
Baseline census	28	1	1
Last census	19	3	8
Repeated censuses	18	4	8
"every year	7		
Vital events	28	0	2

3. Demographic events recorded

The priority of the demographic surveillance system is to record births and
deaths. Permanent migration comes next on the agenda of the DSS, whereas
short moves and seasonal migration are less frequently studied. The systematic recording of pregnancy is a very powerful tool for detecting live and stillbirths and is often used. Marriage, divorce, and widowhood are studied in
about half of cases. Studies focusing on fertility include the use of family planning and sometimes a systematic recording on menstruation. Special studies
of sexual intercourse are now conducted as a parameter of sexually transmitted diseases (Table A3).

Table A3.   Demographic events

	Yes	No	Unknown
Births	28	2	0
Deaths	28	2	0
Out-migration	22	8	0
In-migration	21	9	0
Pregnancy	21	9	0
Cause of death	18	9	3
Miscarriage	16	14	0
Marriage	14	16	0
Abortion	13	14	3
Contraceptive use	11	18	1
Divorce	10	19	1
Widowhood	8	19	3
Short move	6	24	0
Menstruation	5	24	1
Sexual intercourse	1	28	1
Circumcision	1	28	1

4. Socio-economic and anthropological data

Among the socio-economic and anthropological variables, a majority of studies records the housing conditions. Studies focusing on health often include some analysis of traditional knowledge and beliefs related to diseases. Precise data on assets, income, and agricultural production are less often asked and consumption patterns were reported in only two studies. Anthropological knowledge of kinship, inheritance, rules and genealogies are seldom included (Table A4).

Table A4. Socio-economic and anthropological data

	Yes	No	Unknown
Housing	12	10	8
Beliefs about diseases	7	15	8
Assets	7	15	8
Income	6	16	8
Agricultural	6	16	8
Kinship	5	17	8
Genealogies	2	20	8
Inheritance	2	20	8
Consumption	2	20	8
Environment	1	11	8

5. Epidemiologic surveillance

(*a*) *Diseases*

Outside the studies which focus on family planning or on very demographic issues, most studies have recorded one way or another morbidity, usually among children or among women in their reproductive ages. The diseases that are the most frequent causes of death (diarrhoeal diseases, measles, acute respiratory infections, malaria, tetanus, pertussis, and tuberculosis) are the most studied. This surveillance is usually done in special surveys, for selected cohorts and selected periods of time. Only a few studies include a systematic recording of some disease, such as measles in Niakhar (continuous since 1962). Among other diseases, epilepsy and poliomyelitis, typhoid, leprosy, varicella, and recently AIDS are also subjects of studies (Table A5).

(*b*) *Vaccination*

Another important aspect of epidemiologic studies is the monitoring of vaccines, their efficacy and their long-term effects on morbidity and mortality. Most of the EPI vaccinations are well represented, with emphasis on DPT, BCG, measles, and tetanus. The yellow fever vaccine applies only to Africa.

Table A5a.   Diseases

	Yes	No	Unknown
General morbidity	20	6	4
Diarrhoea	12	12	6
Measles	12	12	6
Acute respiratory	9	15	6
Malaria	9	14	7
Tetanus	8	16	6
Dysentery	7	17	6
Cholera	6	18	6
Pertussis	6	18	6
Poliomyelitis	5	19	6
Tuberculosis	5	19	6
Epilepsy	3	20	7
Typhoid	2	21	7
Leprosy	2	22	6
Syphilis	2	18	6
AIDS	1	21	8
Varicella	1	21	8
Hepatitis B	1	21	8
Trachoma	1	21	8

Table A5b.   Vaccines

	Yes	No	Unknown
Any vaccination	15	6	9
DPT	11	9	10
BCG	10	10	10
Measles vaccine	9	11	10
Tetanus toxoid	9	11	10
Oral polio vaccine	7	13	10
All EPI vaccines	7	13	10
Inactivated polio vac.	2	18	10
Yellow fever vaccine	2	18	10
Smallpox vaccine	2	18	10
Cholera vaccine	1	19	10

The issue of smallpox is no longer relevant since the eradication of the disease. Cholera vaccines have been mostly studied in Bangladesh.

(c) Growth and nutrition

Nutritional status, growth, and malnutrition are frequent objects of study. Among the most common indices of nutritional status are weight and height, recently arm-circumference, and more rarely the various skinfolds. Breast-feeding, food intake, and food supplementation have been studied in more than a third of all studies. A few studies focused on iron and vitamin A deficiency (Table A5c).

Table A5c. Growth and nutrition

	Yes	No	Unknown
Nutritional status	19	4	7
Weight	13	10	7
Breastfeeding	10	13	7
Height	10	13	7
Arm circumference	10	13	7
Food intake	8	15	7
Food	7	15	8
Deficiencies	2	15	13
Skinfolds	1	15	14

6. Other health topics

Many studies include some systematic analysis of the functioning of the health system and health services. Only a few have addressed the important issue of mental health. Although most would have included some kind of information on environmental factors, only two considered that sanitation was one of their research topics (Table A6).

Table A6. Other health topics

	Yes	No	Unknown
Health services	14	10	6
Mental health	3	19	8
Sanitation	2	20	8
Environment	1	21	8

7a. Topics studied

Among the topics studied, child survival comes as the most frequent. It is fol-lowed by health interventions, birth control, and health services. Most inves-tigators, however, felt that they addressed more general issues, at the intersection of several disciplines (interactions). Among other frequent topics are found: adult mortality, child growth, diseases (tropical or not), vaccines, migration, nuptiality, household dynamics. Table A7a also lists various other topics of interest in prospective community studies, although a prospective framework is rarely necessary for these. However, the presence of the research team, of the scientific and material infrastructure, as well as the necessity to understand the broader context of health make these studies possible and important for the whole study.

Table A7a. Topics studied

	Yes	No	Unknown
Child survival	24	5	1
Health intervention	15	14	1
Birth control	14	15	1
Health services	14	15	1
Interactions	11	16	3
Adult mortality	10	19	1
Tropical diseases	10	19	1
Child growth	10	17	3
Migration	9	20	1
Non tropical diseases	9	20	1
Vaccines	8	21	1
Nuptiality	7	22	1
Household dynamics	7	22	1
Medical	6	23	1
Parasitology	5	22	3
Cultural context	4	25	1
Social systems	3	26	1
Bacteriology	2	25	3
Human biology	1	28	1
Virology	1	26	3
Child mental	1	26	3
Adult nutrition	1	27	2
Rural economy	1	28	1

7b. Main focus

The main focus of the study can be grouped in three large categories: health, by far the majority, family planning, and more general demographic concerns (including mortality, migration, etc.). Before 1970, many studies focused on family planning, whereas after 1970 the majority of new studies focused on health. Two of the three new demographic studies after 1970 are Pison's studies in Senegal (Table A7b). Of course, health includes a wide variety of issues, from primary health care to tropical diseases, nutrition, vaccines, and other interventions.

Table A7b. Main focus, according to starting date

Main focus	<1970	1970–89
Health	5	12
Family planning	5	3
Demography and other	2	3

8. Human resources

The key disciplines for prospective community studies are medicine, demography, epidemiology, and sociology-anthropology. Some studies have also employed specialists in nutrition, biology, and economics, as well as groups of students and research assistants (Table A8a).

Table A8a. Research personnel

	Yes	No	Unknown	Average number
Physician	16	2	12	4.3
Demographer	15	2	13	1.7
Epidemiologist	12	6	12	1.5
Sociologist	9	8	13	1.2
Research assistant	9	8	13	2.4
Student	9	7	14	35.6
Anthropologist	6	11	13	1.1
Nutritionist	6	11	13	1.6
Biologist	5	12	13	1.4
Economist	3	14	13	1.0
Nurse, midwife	3	0	27	
Linguist	1	0	29	

The prospective community studies necessitate a large number of field-workers (1 per 1,000 to 2,000 persons), supervisors (1 per 4–6 fieldworkers), and drivers and mechanics for the vehicles. Computer work requires specialists for coding data, entering data in the computer, producing tables and statistical analysis. Studies doing more biological work also employ laboratory and nutritional technicians (Table A8b).

Table A8b.   Staff

	Yes	No	Unknown	%
Fieldworker	17	2	11	36.3
Supervisor	13	5	12	6.7
Coder	13	5	12	3.3
Programmer	10	8	12	1.3
Lab. technician	7	11	12	4.1
Analyst	6	12	12	2.0
Nutritional technician	3	15	12	1.3
Mechanic	3	15	12	2.0
Administration	2	0	28	

9. Sources of funding

The sources of funding have also been varied. The primary sources of financing have been governmental organizations and bilateral aid. Among the leaders in this group are USAID/NIH, the British MRC, the French agencies, CIDA/SAREC, IDRC, and various other European agencies. Private foundations also played a major role, in particular Ford, Rockefeller/Population Council, and other American foundations. Among the international organizations, the UN system contributed to a number of studies (WHO, UNICEF, UNFPA) and more recently the EEC invested in the field. Non-governmental organizations and pharmaceuticals more rarely participated as the main source of funding (Table A9). Of course, most of the studies that lasted for many years have received funds from various origins.

Table A9.   Main sources of funding

	Yes	No	Unknown
Government	13	12	5
Bilateral aid	11	14	5
Private foundation	11	14	5
International	10	15	5
Non-governmental	4	21	5
Pharmaceuticals	2	22	5

10. Discussion

Our survey of surveys is far from being perfect. First, it is certainly not exhaustive. Second, for some of the studies we had to complete the questionnaires from published literature and many of the questionnaires were incomplete for at least one of the questions asked. Furthermore, the questions were often so general that the answers could not reflect the complexity of the issues. For instance, some of the studies will have reported to have included pertussis among the diseases studied, but only a few of these would have developed a full scheme for monitoring this disease. Some of the topics studied may have been studied by only one student over a short period of time, whereas the same topic would have been the focus of a large survey in another setting. Because of these limitations, we did not pursue further the survey and did not attempt to get a full coverage for all the questions.

We hope at least to have given the reader a first idea about the diversity of the situations. If these prospective community studies vary in size, duration, focus, topics studied, and methodology, they share a common concern for improving our knowledge about health and population dynamics and have been extremely valuable in this respect.

Abstracts

List of studies analysed

Africa

[01] Three rural areas, Burkina-Faso
[02] Projet Recherche-Action, Burkina-Faso
[03] Sassandra, Côte d'Ivoire
[04] MRC studies, Gambia
[05] Danfa, Ghana
[06] Bandim and rural areas, Guinea Bissau
[07] Embu, Kenya
[08] Machakos, Kenya
[09] Saradidi, Kenya
[10] LEP, Malawi
[11] Garki, Nigeria
[12] Malumfashi, Nigeria
[13] Sine-Saloum, Senegal
[14] Bandafassi-Mlomp, Senegal
[15] Agincourt, South Africa
[16] Pholela, South Africa
[17] Kilombero, Tanzania
[18] Kasongo, Zaïre

Asia

[19] Matlab and extensions, Bangladesh
[20] Lower Yangtze, China
[21] Khanna-I, India
[22] Khanna-II, India
[23] Narangwal, India
[24] Singur, India
[25] Vellore, India
[26] Indramayu, Indonesia
[27] Karachi, Pakistan
[28] Lulliani, Pakistan
[29] Bohol, Philippines
[30] Cebu, Philippines
[31] Family-Planning Pilot Project, Sri Lanka
[32] Etimesgut, Turkey

Americas

[33] INCAP, Guatemala
[34] Projet Intégré de Santé et de Population, Haiti

[01] Three rural areas, Burkina-Faso

This study was supported by ORSTOM, UNICEF, and the Statistics Division of Burkina-Faso. It aimed at analysing the level and factors of mortality among preschool children in three rural areas of Burkina-Faso: Pissila, Niangoloko, and Yako-Gourcy. It started in 1985 and lasted until 1992 and was based on three samples totalling about 35,000 persons and 7,000 children age 0–5. The demographic surveillance system is based on a multi-round survey conducted every six months.

Topics studied
- Demography: mortality, fertility, migration, causes of death.
- Epidemiology: vaccination, water supply, malaria, diarrhoea, breast-feeding.
- Anthropology: perception of diseases.

Selected findings
Recent study.

Monograph
None.

[02] Projet Recherche-Action, Burkina-Faso

This project built on previous experience of the investigators on the primary health care systems in rural areas of Burkina-Faso. It is sponsored by the Ministry of Health, the University of Heidelberg, the German Co-operation Agency (GTZ), and the European Economic Community. It started in 1991 in a rural area of the Kossi and Sourou provinces. The study covers about 60,000 people in two distinct areas: a treatment area (Nouna) and a control area (Toma). The study is built on a comprehensive demographic surveillance system, with regular visits to villages and a yearly census. The emphasis of the treatment is on improving the functioning of the primary health-care system, its self-financing, and on community participation. The project is scheduled for at least three more years.

Topics studied
- Demography: birth, death, cause of death, migration.
- Epidemiology: chronic diseases, acute infections, diarrhoeal diseases, ARI, malaria, measles, pertussis, tetanus, tuberculosis, leprosy, epilepsy, EPI vaccinations, nutritional status.
- Anthropology: kinship, beliefs about diseases.

- Economics: income, assets, housing, agricultural production, consumption and health expenditures.
- Health system: health-care utilization and cost.

Selected findings
Recent study.

Monograph
None.

[03] Sassandra, Côte d'Ivoire

The study started in 1988, in an urban coastal area of Ivory Coast: Sassandra. It was still ongoing in 1993. The study is sponsored by ORSTOM and the National School of Statistics (ENSEA). It focuses on the impact on population dynamics and population health of recent changes in the terms of trade and in economic policies. Sassandra is an area of strong in-migration flows and of marked mixing of ethnic groups. The sample counted 6,594 persons in 1988.

Topics studied
- Demography: population dynamics, patterns of settlement, migration, fertility, mortality, family building patterns, reproductive health.
- Health systems: comparison of fixed-post strategy (dispensary) with mobile teams.

Selected findings
Recent study.

Monograph
None.

[04] MRC studies, The Gambia

The British Medical Research Council (MRC) has carried out numerous investigations and provided important health interventions in The Gambia for many years. The Keneba project started in 1949 and included two villages with a total population of 960, which was later extended to four villages of about 2,000 inhabitants and is still going on. The people of the villages underwent yearly medical exams, and all births and deaths were recorded. Special surveys, especially to determine the epidemiology of tropical diseases were carried out. Another project of a larger scale started in 1981 in Farafennie, for studying malaria, its prophylaxis, and its therapy. A third sample was started around 1987 in Basse for studies on ARI and pneumococcal vaccine. The same team, based in Fajarah has also conducted longitudinal studies in nearby urban areas (Sukuta).

Topics studied
- Demography: population dynamics, lactation, cause of death, and age and sex patterns.
- Epidemiology/nutrition: important epidemiological investigations in malaria, trypanosomiasis, schistosomiasis, filariasis, helminthiasis, measles, trachoma, diphtheria, polio, pertussis, haemophilus influenzae, meningitis, hepatitis B, gastroenteritis due to rotavirus, HIV, hypertension. Extensive nutritional studies, energy expenditure.
- Health care: a primary health-care post was provided to the population in Keneba, and its effects measured. It included a physician, a midwife, and some nurses. The effect of primary health care was also investigated in Farafennie.
- Interventions: trials included impregnated bednets, measles vaccination trials with high-titre Edmonston-Zagreb vaccine, a rotavirus vaccine, a hepatitis B vaccine and a pneumococcal vaccine. Dietary and iron supplementation trial, treatment and prevention of severe malaria.

Selected findings
- In a few years, the work of the health post reduced the level of mortality almost to that of England at the time, without any significant change in the socio-economic conditions.
- Impregnated bednets provided a good protection against malaria.
- High-titre Edmonston-Zagreb vaccine prevents measles even when given at 4–5 months of age.
- The rotavirus vaccine was not as effective as expected, and it inhibited the response to polio.
- Iron supplementation increased hemoglobin and hematocrit values, but also increased the number of febrile episodes in the people who received it.
- The T-cell response to malaria and the parasite's antigenic variability were described.
- *P. falciparum*-specific antibodies were described.
- The systematic treatment of fever with chloroquine had little effect if not combined with systematic chemoprophylaxis.

Monograph
None typical. Extensive list of publications and annual reports is available.

[05] Danfa, Ghana

The Danfa Comprehensive Rural Health and Family Planning Project of Ghana started in 1970 as a research programme to evaluate the feasibility and advantages of using an integrated approach to family planning, women's health care, and child health-care services. The Ghana Medical School proposed the project; through the co-ordinated efforts of private and governmental organizations in Ghana and the USA, the project emphasized service, training, and research, and ended in 1978. Four areas north-west of Accra were chosen as the test sites for the various intervention combinations; each had a population of approximately 16,000, with a total population of 60,000. The surveillance of the population occurred using various methods. A yearly census, after a baseline registration, started in 1972. Six months after the census, pretrained villagers undertook to visit all households to re-count the population, and to register any intervening births or deaths. In addition, there were a large number of other ongoing investigations which required selective and cross-sectional surveys in family-planning knowledge, child-care practices, etc.

Topics studied
- Demography: population dynamics, age and sex patterns, migrations, effect of birth intervals on women's and family health, maternal mortality, causes of death in children, causes and consequences of large family size, and family planning.
- Epidemiology: malnutrition, malaria, measles, respiratory infections, pertussis, diarrhoea, accidents, ascaris and other helminth infections, polio, tuberculosis, and anthropometrics. Adult infections studied included schistomiasis, Guinea worm (dracunculiasis), and others.
- Anthropology: specific aspects of life in rural Ghana were explored in order to assess the ability of the health posts and health-care workers to achieve their goals. These included attitudes towards health, traditional birth attendants, agricultural patterns, ethnicity, and religion.
- Economics: costs and effectiveness of providing care in the different modalities were calculated and measured, socio-economic variables were considered in the analyses.
- Health-care delivery: since this was a demonstration project, many outputs of the health care and education provided were monitored. Barriers to the use of the offered services were also explored.
- Interventions: the intent of the project was to compare an area with full family planning and maternal and child health-care services, with education, to three other areas with varying degrees of the same services. Outcome variables measured were fertility, mortality, and changes in knowledge and behaviour. Trial of oral (live) vs. intramuscular (killed) polio vaccine, malaria prophylaxis and treatment of fever in children, community sanitation measures, and agricultural improvements.

Selected findings
- The full intervention area had a probable reduction in mortality.
- Data collection problems, the transient nature of the population studied, and the deterioration of the economy made the above statement harder to verify.
- A malaria control programme by volunteers for children was feasible.
- Monthly pyrimethamine reduced the incidence of parasitemia in children.
- There seemed to be a distance beyond which most people would not travel for health care of 4–5 miles.
- Reasons for accepting family planning differed by sex and age.
- Training traditional birth attendants proved difficult.
- Primary health-care implementation needed a lot of planning, training, supervision, national morale, and national political will.
- Recommendations for implementing PHC included many familiar themes, i.e. integration of services (MCH and FP), local distribution of drugs and a reduced formulary of necessary drugs.

Monograph
Comprehensive final report (1979).

[06] Bandim and rural areas, Guinea-Bissau

The initial impetus to the Guinea-Bissau studies was the assumption that malnutrition caused higher mortality, which was to be investigated by a multidisciplinary team from Denmark, Sweden, and Guinea-Bissau (MISAS/SAREC). It started in 1978 in a neighbourhood of Bissau, when the population of Bandim was 6,072, which in 1980 had grown to 6,217. Five other rural areas were added to the study: Qinhamel, Cacheu, Oio, Tombali, and Bolama. Births and deaths were recorded continuously, and pregnancies monthly. The study in Bandim was still going on in 1993.

Topics studied
- Demography: the registration system collects data for population dynamics, infant and child mortality, and breast-feeding.
- Epidemiology/nutrition: while anthropometry was crucial to the beginning of the study, the investigators soon witnessed an epidemic of measles, which they then added to their investigations.
- Anthropology/economics: kinship networks, social structure, agricultural and housing patterns, sanitation, and ethnicity.

Selected findings
- Malnutrition was not an important factor in determining mortality in children.

- Measles was a large cause of mortality among children.
- Measles mortality was higher in polygamous households and among secondary cases infected at home.
- Standard measles vaccines had a relatively low efficacy, whereas the Edmonston-Zagreb vaccine was more efficient and reduced mortality of children.

Monograph
None. Extensive publications on measles and measles vaccines.

[07] Embu, Kenya

The Kenya Nutrition Collaborative Research Support Programme (CRSP) took place in the highlands of eastern Kenya, Embu district, from 1982 to 1986. It followed a subset of the population of the area (1,100 of 22,000) for four years, concentrating on the impact of nutrition on pregnancy, lactation, and child cognitive performance, morbidity, and growth. Extensive demographic and epidemiological data were collected by a census every three months (births were registered monthly).

Topics studied
- Demography: population dynamics, cause of death, nuptiality, pregnancy outcome, breast-feeding, menstruation, widowhood were all studied.
- Epidemiology/nutrition: all illnesses (weekly) and vaccinations (six monthly) were recorded, while anthropometric data were recorded for all children. A cross-sectional study was carried out on anxiety and depression. A survey of alcohol consumption was also done.
- Anthropology/economics: investigations on disease beliefs, as well as on income, assets, housing, agricultural production, and consumption took place to help support the nutritional study. Meteorological measurements and observations also took place.

Selected findings
Not specified.

Monograph
Not specified.

[08] Machakos, Kenya

The Machakos project of the Medical Research Centre, Nairobi, and the Royal Tropical Institute of Amsterdam arose out of the need for longitudinal, population-based data on morbidity and mortality, especially in women and children, in rural Kenya. It involved 23,000 people (*de jure*) from 5 areas/villages in the Northern Machakos district, about 80 km. from Nairobi, from October 1973 to April, 1981. They all belonged to one ethnic group. Since one of the founding goals of the study was demography, vital registration occurred biweekly after the first census in 1973 until August 1978, and then occurred monthly. Due to the original purpose of the study, accurate vital rates emerged quickly, which then lent the study area to further investigations using this unique data.

Topics studied
- Demography: population dynamics, age patterns, fertility, infant and child mortality, causes of death, breast-feeding, migration.
- Epidemiology: patterns of morbidity and mortality from measles, pertussis, diarrhoeal diseases, schistosomiasis, acute respiratory infections; birth weight, nutritional status, including the content of breast milk; periodontal diseases.
- Anthropology: traditional health-care behaviours, practices of traditional birth attendants.
- Economics: agricultural economists came to study land-use agricultural patterns, and income, and this was related to the daily household dietary habits among families and villages.
- Interventions: A pertussis vaccine trial, a polio vaccine trial, a nutrition rehabilitation programme, a training programme for traditional birth attendants, and a schistosomiasis treatment programme.

Selected findings
- The original emphasis on demography was justified, since it allowed so many other studies.
- Based on an epidemiological curve of measles, the optimal age for measles vaccination was determined to be 9 months.
- Two doses of pertussis vaccine, rather than three or more, was adequate based on antibody levels.
- Level of income and level of mortality were related.
- Determinants and risk factors for perinatal and infant mortality were identified, and a screening method developed to identify high-risk individuals.
- Obstetrical care and nutritional status of a mother relates to infant survival via risks for low birth weight.
- Family size influences *per capita* food consumption.
- Despite marginal nutrition during pregnancy and lactation, women gave birth to normal-weight infants and produced adequate breast milk.

Monograph
J. K. van Ginneken and A. S. Muller, *Maternal and Child Health in Rural Kenya*, Croom Helm, London, 1984.

[09] Saradidi, Kenya

The Saradidi Rural Health Development Programme had its roots in the 1970s, in Anglican congregations, with further impetus generated by Alma Ata, local health workers, and community leaders. Saradidi is located near the shores of Lake Victoria, in the District of Siaya, Nyanza Province, Kenya; the Rural Health Development Programme started in 1979, and included three scattered villages covering 225 km., with a population of 42,755 in 1980. When the project ended in 1988, the population had reached approximately 60,000. Demographic data were collected for all residents of the areas in 1980, 1981, 1982, and 1987, when censuses were carried out; in addition community health workers visited all households every six to nine months to collect demographic as well as morbidity data. Part of the programme included research, therefore some investigators from outside Saradidi carried out occasional sample surveys of the population. Major issues addressed during the programme grew out of both the wishes of the community and outside investigators.

Topics studied
- Demography: population dynamics, including births, deaths, and migrations, age patterns, marriage patterns, birth intervals, breast-feeding and family-planning practices, household composition, and education.
- Epidemiology: malaria, measles, ARI, diarrhoea, cholera, malaria in pregnancy. Other topics investigated epidemiologically were adverse events to chloroquine, sensitivity of *P. falciparum* to chloroquine, and anthropometric measurements of certain groups in the population.
- Anthropology: investigations into beliefs about diseases, health-seeking behaviour, factors determining the use of services and housing patterns all took place.
- Health-care delivery: the programme itself was an opportunity to study a community health-care organization and community participation. The programme applied knowledge from its own training programmes to improve them, and monitored vaccination coverage.
- Interventions: intervention in health and development was the primary impetus for the programme, and the many interventions cannot all be listed here. Many were local initiatives. Well-described and area-wide interventions included the Village Health Helper (VHH) programme, proliferation of family-planning services, chemotherapy and prophylaxis with chloroquine for the community and for pregnant women.

Selected findings
- Simultaneous community-based health care and research is possible, and problems were described.
- Health and medicine-seeking behaviour was transferred from shops to the VHHs.
- Chloroquine consumption varied by age and education, but not necessarily to those the most parasitemic.
- There was no describable difference in outcome for pregnant women with or without chloroquine prophylaxis.
- Malaria prevalence (by serology) did not change with increased chloroquine availability.
- Increasing chloroquine-resistant malaria was documented and described.
- Side-effects of chloroquine were made into incidence rates through the known population total.
- An individual's ability to recognize and diagnose locally occurring illnesses was evaluated.
- In an area of high fertility and mortality, demand for family-planning services was high.

Monograph
Special issue of *Annals of Tropical Medicine and Parasitology*, 1987.

[10] Lepra Evaluation Project, Malawi

The Lepra Evaluation Project on the shores of Lake Malawi (Karonga District) has been in progress since 1980. It initially started as a purely leprosy programme, but has since, given its unique set of data, included other diseases to be investigated, such as tuberculosis and HIV infection. The total initial population was 110,000. Phase I lasted from 1980 to 1984; Phase II from 1986 to 1989; a third phase started in 1990–1.

Topics studied
- Epidemiology: leprosy, tuberculosis, HIV.
- Intervention: BCG vaccination.

Selected findings
- Leprosy prevalence was higher than expected (1.5%).
- BCG protects somewhat against leprosy, but not against tuberculosis.

Monograpy
None.

318 Garenne and Koumans

[11] Garki, Nigeria

The WHO sponsored study of malaria in Garki District, Kano State, Nigeria took place from 1969 to 1976. The project was designed to elucidate previously unknown aspects of the ecology, epidemiology, biology, and medicine of malaria in a savannah region of Africa. It involved twenty-two villages, with a total population of 7,423. Vital statistics were collected through a yearly census and biweekly records of births, deaths, and migrations, while morbidity was recorded every ten weeks.

Topics studied
- Demography: population dynamics, and age and sex patterns of mortality were crucial for the completion of the study.
- Epidemiology: malaria was extensively studied, including immunology, serology, parasitology, entomology, and clinical manifestations. Other potential influences on malaria were also studied, including meteorology and nutritional status.
- Interventions that were evaluated during the project included pesticide spraying and mass malaria prophylaxis.

Selected findings
- There were large seasonal variations in mortality, perhaps due to malaria.
- There was no significant difference in mortality between mass-treated and untreated villages except for the infant mortality rate.
- The Hardy Weinberg law for sickle cell anemia was confirmed for neonates, but as would be expected, not for adults.
- Malaria antibodies were documented in people in both protected and unprotected (by spraying) environments.
- The level of parasitemia does not correlate at all with the level of antibodies except in infants.
- In the sprayed and mass-treatment areas, *P. falciparum* prevalence was reduced to 5 per cent in the wet season and 1 per cent in the dry season, but never eliminated.
- *P. malariae* and *P. ovale* were reduced at the same time as *P. falciparum*, but had slower rebound to pre-treatment levels after the interventions stopped compared to *P. falciparum*.
- There was a high level of both malaria transmission and vector capacity, neither of which were eliminated during the intervention.

Monograph
L. Molineaux and G. Gramiccia, *Le Projet Garki*, OMS, Geneva, 1980.

[12] Malumfashi, Nigeria

The Malumfashi project started in 1974 to collect accurate information on the epidemiology of endemic diseases, and was meant to evaluate the consequences for health after the construction of a dam near by. Seven villages were enumerated from 1974 to 1978, and from November 1977 to October 1978, all vital events and morbidity were recorded through home visits for 26,100 people. A total of 43,216 people were counted during different years. The main goal of the project was epidemiological, nevertheless many other investigations took place:

Topics studied
- Demography: mortality, fertility, age and sex patterns, birth spacing, causes of death, data collection techniques.
- Epidemiology/nutrition: malaria, effects of chronic malaria, schistosomiasis, meningitis, hookworm, and anemia were monitored.
- Anthropology/economics: religious beliefs were studied to try to understand local inhibitions toward co-operating with the programme.
- Interventions: A trial of rifampicin or sulpha was tested for the treatment of meningitis carriers, a trial of chloroquine for infants was carried out, and the effects of the construction and presence of the dam were monitored.

Selected findings
- Different indirect methods (widowhood, orphanhood) did not agree, nor did they agree with either of the surveillance methods, which called into doubt the results. This was most likely due to incomplete data.
- Births and deaths were seasonal.
- Mortality, fertility and age and sex structure typical for developing country.
- Transmission of *S. haematobium* was focal, with an age-specific peak prevalence consistent over the entire area, and men the most susceptible due to the time of day they came into contact with water.
- A drought reduced the prevalence of *S. haematobium* dramatically.
- The dam brought more water contact and increased the prevalence of *S. haematobium*.
- The species of snails changed with the construction of the dam.
- A test was developed to identify those with a high probability of infection with *S. haematobium*.
- The carrier rate of meningitis A was not predictive of epidemics.
- Rifampicin was more effective than sulpha in reducing carrier status.

- In children with chronic malaria, antibody response after immunization was adequate, but the decay of antibody levels was rapid.
- Chronic, seasonal malaria did not affect immunity, or ability to respond to immunizations, although the polysaccharide vaccines had a poor antibody response (given <15 months).

Monograph
None.

[13] Sine-Saloum, Senegal

The prospective studies in central Senegal started in 1962 and were organized by ORSTOM in collaboration with the National Census Bureau and the Ministry of Health of Senegal. The studies received support from numerous international organizations. The first phase, called Sine-Saloum: (1962–6) was based on two samples totalling about 50,000 persons. The second phase, called Ndemene-Ngayokheme (1967–82) was based on two sub-samples, totalling about 10,000 persons. The third phase, called Niakhar (1983–ongoing) was based on a single sample of about 25,000 persons. A complete demographic surveillance system was based on a yearly census and special surveys. It culminated after 1986, when weekly visits to each household were organized for a full monitoring of measles and whooping cough necessary for the vaccine trials.

Topics studied
- Demography: population dynamics, mortality, fertility, migration, nuptiality, household composition, age patterns, birth intervals, breast-feeding, causes of death, maternal mortality, data collection methods.
- Epidemiology: measles, whooping cough, tetanus, cholera, diarrhoea, epilepsy, poliomyelitis, mental health, nutrition status, EPI vaccines.
- Economics: agriculture, production system, income.
- Anthropology: kinship, inheritance, history, traditional medicine.
- Health interventions: vaccines (efficacy, safety, immunogenicity), food supplementation.

Selected findings
- Measles as a major cause of death.
- Outstanding age pattern of mortality in childhood.
- Birth intervals and breast-feeding as a determinant of child survival and fertility.
- Nutritional status as a risk factor of child survival.
- Arm-circumference as the best screening index for child survival.

- Negligible impact of food supplementation programmes.
- High effect of measles and pertussis vaccination on child survival.
- Excess mortality after high-titre measles vaccines.
- Hand-cleansing as a risk factor of neonatal tetanus.
- Pattern of measles transmission as a determinant of child survival.

Monograph
P. Cantrelle, 'Enquête démographique dans la région du Sine-Saloum; État-civil et observation démographique (Sénégal)', Travaux et Documents 1, ORSTOM, Paris, 1969.
A. Lericollais (ed.), *Les Paysans Sereer (Sénégal): Permanences et changements*, ORSTOM, Paris, 1995.

[14] Bandafassi-Mlomp, Senegal

The Bandafassi project in Eastern Senegal started as a research on population genetics conducted by the Musée de l'Homme, Paris, France and was part of a larger anthropological study of the Fula Bande people. The demographic surveillance started in 1970. The sample size was increased in 1975 and 1980 and accounts for about 7,000 persons. The Mlomp study is located in the southern part of Senegal (Casamance). It was started in 1984 and had a sample of similar size. Both studies have a primary focus on demography and anthropology, although the Mlomp study also includes an analysis of the health system. Both studies were still in course in 1993 and were sponsored by INED, CNRS, INSERM, and ORSTOM.

Topics studied
- Demography: birth, death, migration, nuptiality, polygyny, household structure, causes of death.
- Anthropology/genetics: genealogies, sexual behaviour, circumcision, DNA polymorphism.
- Epidemiology: blood-typing, sickle cell anemia, HIV, malaria.
- Health care: follow-up of the activity of the Mlomp dispensary.

Selected findings
- Data collection methods can be improved (age).
- Demography of polygamy.
- Measles may influence the sex ratio at birth.

Monograph
G. Pison, *Dynamique d'une population traditionnelle*, Cahier de l'INED 99, PUF, Paris, 1982.

[15] Agincourt, South Africa

The Agincourt study built on the long experience of the Health Services Development Unit of the Witwatersrand University, in the homelands of the Eastern Transval. The HSDU runs a comprehensive primary health care (Community Practice Project) centred around the Tinstwalo hospital. The longitudinal study started in 1991 with a census and is scheduled for several years. The sample size accounts for about 60,000 persons. The study is sponsored by the Ministries of Health, the Witwatersrand University, the European Economic Community, and the Kellog Foundation.

Topics studied
- Demography: mortality, fertility, migration, refugees, causes of death.
- Epidemiology: several diseases, latrines, sexual health: STDs, AIDS, chronic diseases (diabetes, hypertension), cancer registry in the hospital.
- Health systems: health education, service development (KK), community organization.
- Interventions: family planning, oral rehydration therapy, EPI, rehabilitation of physical handicaps, mental health, tuberculosis, mobile clinics, eye clinics.

Selected findings
Recent study.

Monograph
None.

[16] Pholela, South Africa

The experimental Pholela Health Unit among the Zulu at the foothills of the Drakensberg started in 1942 at the suggestion of the Union Health Department. The intention was to tackle some of the many health problems faced by blacks living in this 'Native Territory'. The first sample census was carried out among certain families on a hillside, 887 in total in 1942. Continuous vital registration seems to have continued for these families, and for others as they were added to the yearly census, which by 1950 had reached 7,481. The original investigators and the vital registration system seem to have stopped working in the area in 1956. During those fourteen years, a host of improvements in general health had occurred.

Topics studied
- Demography: the census and vital registration system did not function for the sake of research, but for the sake of improving the health of the

population. Population dynamics were particularly important because many men were migrant labourers, breast-feeding monitoring improved the health status of infants, etc.

- Epidemiology/nutrition: morbidity was recorded only in so far as when patients came to the clinic. Childhood infections, i.e. skin and diphtheria, as well as nutritional status, syphilis, and gonorrhoea were actively recorded.
- Anthropology/economics: The function and beliefs of traditional healers, traditional health practices, extent of sanitary facilities, number and size of gardens, and extent of soil erosion were all investigated.
- Interventions: maternal and child health, adult health reviews, educational programmes on disease prevention and health promotion, as well as typhoid vaccination constituted most of the important interventions.

Selected findings
- After some initial scepticism, people displayed increasing interest and co-operation, which led to further improvements in homes and health.
- The home visits and educational programme improved the growth of children.
- The longer families had been in the programme, the greater the reductions in mortality among them.
- Infant mortality was lower in families that had been in the programme for more than one year.
- Improvements in nutrition due to education, and larger and more diversified gardens probably led to the marked reduction in cases of pellagra and kwashiorkor.
- There were no epidemics of smallpox, typhoid, typhus, or diphtheria for eight years in the programme area, despite their presence in surrounding areas.

Monograph
S. L. Kark, *Epidemiology and Community Medicine*, Appleton-Century-Crofts, New York, 1974.
S. L. Kark, *The Practice of Community-Oriented Primary Health Care*, Appleton-Century-Crofts, New York, 1981.

[17] Kilombero, Tanzania

The ongoing Kilombero project is a collaborative effort between the Swiss and the Tanzanian governments. It covers a large sector of fifty villages along the Kilombero river. Its aim is to provide health care and study the interrelationships between nutrition, parasitic infections, immunity, environmental factors, and health. The study started in 1982 and has been continued since. However, the demographic studies cover only certain areas of the whole district of about 150,000 persons. Extensive surveys were conducted in the Kikwawila village.

Topics studied
- Demography (partial).
- Epidemiology: malaria, schistosomiasis, giardia, hookworm and other intestinal worms, and anthropometric status.
- Public health: water and sanitation, primary health-care system.

Selected findings
- Many data on prevalence of diseases and parameters of the health-care system.

Monograph
Special issue of *Acta Tropica*, 1987, 4 (2).

[18] Kasongo, Zaïre

The Kasongo Project has been a long-standing collaborative effort for health by the Prince Leopold Institute of Tropical Medicine of Antwerp and the Ministry of Health of the Government of Zaïre. It began in 1971, and serves a region of approximately 200,000 people in the administrative zone of Kasongo in the Kivu region. Its initial objective was to provide basic, affordable, and accessible health care to the area, along with research in tropical diseases, training of personnel, and management support. Experience and knowledge gained, which could be applied to other areas of the country, constituted a long-term goal. There was no regularized census or surveillance system for the entire area, although certain programmes, such as the measles vaccination programme, and the nutritional status survey, did collect information on morbidity, mortality, and vaccination status.

Topics studied
- Demography: population dynamics, age and sex patterns, and causes of death were studied in smaller sub-samples of the population.
- Hospital-based epidemiology covered the most prevalent tropical diseases, including malaria, schistosomiasis, trypanosomiasis, tuberculosis, etc. for adults, and many diseases afflicting children, such as measles.
- Nutritional surveys were also carried out on samples of children.
- Interviews on health-care access and utilization patterns were carried out as well.

Selected findings
- Accessible, quality health care could be provided at reasonable cost in rural areas, provided there was sufficient logistical and technical support.

- Measles vaccination increased survival for children up to 18 months after vaccination, but thereafter mortality increased.
- Children 'falling off' the growth curve under the age of 5 had increased mortality.

Monograph
Series of working papers.

[19] Matlab, Teknaf, extension area, Bangladesh

For the last thirty years, the International Centre for Diarrhoeal Diseases, Bangladesh, has operated a large research project and field station in rural Bangladesh. It was started initially for a cholera vaccination trial. The population covered by the project has fluctuated, but has generally remained above 200,000. One-half of that population is the control for the intervention group. A census and longitudinally collected data on births, deaths, and migrations constitute the basis for a host of other smaller research programme, and some larger ones that are applied project-wide. After 1978, the emphasis was on family planning and related issues. The mother project has been at the origin of two other projects: Teknaf, in south-eastern Bangladesh, which was conducted from 1976 to 1989 in a population of about 46,000 and the Extension Project, near Dhaka, which started in 1982 in a population of about 30,000 people. Due to their similarities, all three are treated together.

Topics studied
- Demography: population dynamics, age and sex patterns, mortality differentials, use of family planning, cause of death, components of the birth intervals, nuptiality, migration.
- Epidemiology/nutrition: while many diseases are routinely treated at the health posts, project-wide epidemiological surveillance has not generally taken place. Instead, certain diseases are investigated for shorter periods of time, such as diarrhoeal episodes in infants and children, dysentery, cholera, and tetanus. Anthropometry in children and adults was also performed.
- Anthropology/economics: kinship systems, income.
- Health care/interventions: several cholera vaccine trials, trial of home-based ORT administration, family-planning services, tetanus and measles immunizations.

Selected findings
The findings for this project are far too numerous to be listed here. See Chapter 2 by Aziz and Mosley as a first introduction.

Monograph
A comprehensive bibliography is available in: D. Habte and M. Strong, *Annotated Bibliography of ICDDR,B Studies in Matlab, Bangladesh*, Dhaka, Bangladesh, 1990.

[20] Lower Yangtze, China

In September 1931, a demographic surveillance project began in an agricultural area midway between Nanking and Shanghai, in the lower Yangtze river delta. The Scripps Foundation and the University of Nanking developed and directed the project, initially to understand the agricultural economy of the area. At the time, China's population was estimated to be 300 to 400 million; the population of the study area was about 20,000. Local villagers were recruited and trained to carry out vital registration of their villages, and reported the results monthly. A census was taken in 1932.

Topics studied
- Demography: the study emphasized population dynamics, i.e. births, deaths, and migration.
- Epidemiology: some epidemiological events were noted.
- Economics: land-ownership and agricultural production patterns were studied.

Selected findings
- The increase in population coupled with already small landholdings led to significant outmigration to the cities.
- The cholera and malaria epidemics that occurred during the study had a greater impact on male mortality than female mortality.
- These epidemics reduced the marriage rate.
- Female mortality was higher than male mortality from age 0–15, and from 24–55.
- Infant mortality was correlated with economic status.
- 'Rich' families had more living children and more land.

Monograph
C. M. Chiao, W. S. Thompson, and D. T. Chen, *An Experiment in the Registration of Vital Statistics in China*, Scripps Foundation for Research in Population Problems, Oxford, Ohio.

[21] Khanna-I, India

The Khanna Project intended to trace how births, deaths, migration, and changes in the environment affected population size, and how population size affected community health and social well-being. It was also intended as a family-planning project. The pilot project began in 1954, and the definitive study lasted from 1955 to 1960. Some villages did not enter the study until 1957, however. There were a total of eleven villages, with a population of 12,237. An annual census, and monthly records of births, deaths, and migration contributed to the strength of the demographic data. Investigators concerned themselves with many factors that could influence health and fertility.

Topics studied
- Demography: since the project was started to try to influence fertility, population dynamics, birth intervals, and breast-feeding were carefully monitored. Other topics of interest were the influence of the seasons, the effect of migration, and causes of death.
- Epidemiology/nutrition: diarrhoeal diseases, typhoid, measles, tuberculosis, pneumonia, and tetanus were monitored over time to calculate their incidence and prevalence.
- Anthropology/economics: detailed investigations of kinship, marriage, child-rearing practices, and castes were used to help the intervention. Local knowledge about sex and sexual patterns was also elicited from the population. Occupation and agricultural patterns were recorded.

Selected findings
- The concept of 'population pressure' was described, local response appeared to be an increase in agricultural production and emigration.
- Female mortality was higher than male, especially in the young.
- Increased mortality due to weaning diarrhoea was described.
- Breast milk was beneficial demographically, by reducing mortality and increasing the birth interval.
- There was marked differential mortality by caste.
- Increased child survival increased the chances of keeping family size low.
- Some principles for family-planning programme: reduce child mortality, promote community education, recognize the economic value of children, identify or create incentives for small family size and delaying marriage, ensure supplies of suitable and efficient contraceptives.

Monograph
J. Wyon and J. Gordon, *The Khanna Study*, Harvard University Press, Cambridge, Mass., 1971.

[22] Khanna-II, India

The project was a restudy of the eleven Khanna Study villages (see 22), and was conducted in 1984–8, after a gap of nearly thirty years after the original study. It was conducted from the National Council of Applied Economic Research, New Delhi, India, and funded by the International Development Research Centre, Ottawa, Canada. The data collection and editing were carried out from the nearby town of Khanna, by a team of thirty-six women from the district. The sample size was approximately 18,000 people in the study villages.

Topics studied
The demographic topics studied were fertility, child survival, birth intervals, nutritional intake, morbidity, income, consumption, and old-age support. The anthropological topics studied covered several areas, with a special focus on kinship issues. The analysis focused on (i) the causes of fertility decline; (ii) the relationship between women's status and women's and children's health; and (iii) identifying the children at highest risk of dying in the population, and the factors underlying their elevated risk of dying, and how simple selective health interventions can reduce child mortality.

Selected findings
The main new findings on this related to:
  1. The clustering of child deaths in a small proportion of households, even after controlling for several socio-economic and biological factors, such that targeting a small proportion of households can effect substantial reductions in child mortality.
  2. The concentration of excess female child mortality amongst higher birth order children, and the sharpening of this parity-specific gender discrimination with fertility decline.
  3. The poorer child survival and women's health outcomes resulting from low female autonomy during their peak reproductive years.
  4. Traditional mechanisms for regulating population growth and the effect of specific development policies in triggering fertility decline.

Publications
Monica Das Gupta, 'Selective Discrimination against Female Children in Rural Punjab, India', *Population and Development Review*, 13(1) 1987; 'Death Clustering, Mother's Education and the Determinants of Child Mortality in Rural Punjab, India', *Population Studies*, 44(3) 1990; 'What Motivates Fertility Decline? A Case Study from Punjab, India', in B. Egero and M. Hammarskjold (eds.), *Understanding Reproductive Change*, Lund University Press, 1994; 'Fertility Decline in Punjab, India: Parallels with Historical Europe', *Population Studies*, 49/3, 1995; 'Life Course Perspectives on Women's Autonomy and Health Outcomes', *American Anthropologist*, 97/3, 1995; 'Socio-economic Status and Clustering of Child Deaths in Rural Punjab', *Population Studies*, forthcoming; Monica Das Gupta and Sara Millman, 'Family, Gender and Nutrition in Punjab, India', mimeo, 1994.

[23] Narangwal, India

The project built on the experience gathered in Khanna and was conducted in the same Ludhiana District of Punjab state. It was conducted with the support of the Indian Ministry of Health and Family Planning. The Indian Council of Medical Research became responsible for its supervision, and carried that responsibility from the pretrial investigations that started in 1961, through the commencement in 1967, to the end in 1974. The project took place in a total of twenty-six villages (ten had various nutrition interventions, sixteen had various family-planning interventions) with a total population of 35,000. A census was carried out three times, in 1967, 1971, and 1973. A number of different people collected vital statistics, which from 1969 to 1973 included births, deaths, and marriages, every two weeks. Child morbidity was collected weekly, and anthropometric data monthly (or greater interval depending on age of child).

Topics studied
- Demography: population dynamics, age and sex patterns, pregnancy and its outcome, breast-feeding, family planning, maternal mortality, and child survival.
- Epidemiology/nutrition: diarrhoeal diseases, respiratory infections, skin and eye infections in children, and nutritional status.
- Anthropology/economics: housing, kinship networks, caste, education, occupation, income, possessions, land-holding and agricultural patterns, as well as health-care costs and cost effectiveness.

Selected findings
- Integrated services, including maternal and child health plus family planning, increased the use of family planning and probably reduced fertility and mortality.
- Integrated services were more efficient and two to three times more cost-effective than vertical programmes.
- Nutrition supplementation alone or with health care significantly increased weight and height in children over the age of 17 months.
- Mortality from 0–2 was significantly reduced in nutritional supplementation and in health-care villages.
- Perinatal mortality was significantly reduced by nutritional supplementation.
- Sex and caste of a child were independent modifiers for increases in weight and height.
- Psychomotor tests showed that the combination of nutritional support and health care had a synergistic effect in children.
- Health equity was obtainable through weekly surveillance and preferential care.

- Preventative and curative care for children increased contraceptive use among never-users.
- Family health workers were effective in training, support, and supervision.

Monograph
Child and Maternal Health Services in Rural India: The Narangwal Experiment: i. Integrated Nutrition and Health Care (eds. A. A. Kielmann *et al.*); *ii. Integrated Family Planning and Health Care* (eds. C. E. Taylor *et al.*), Johns Hopkins University Press, Baltimore, 1983.

[24] Singur, India

The Singur Study took place in a number of villages near the town of Singur, about 30 km. north of Calcutta, in west Bengal, India, and was initially conceived in 1954. The first census was completed in 1957 at the start of the programme. Researchers at the All-India Institute of Hygiene and Public Health set up, planned, and directed this family-planning study, which involved a population of 7,500 in the intervention area and 13,000 in the control area. Both areas had continuing surveillance, repeated about every six months, until at least 1963.

Topics studied
- Demography: population dynamics, pregnancy, abortion, miscarriage.
- Intervention: implementation of a family-planning programme in the intervention area, using either rhythm, coitus interruptus or foam tablets, plus education.
- Anthropology: the cultural context of the family-planning programme was also studied.

Selected findings
- the birth rate declined significantly, and this study appeared to be the first to demonstrate such an effect of a family-planning and educational programme.
- A family-planning programme should be well thought out and appropriate culturally.
- Quality of field staff is crucial.
- Findings should be generalizable.
- Men will participate in such a programme if supported by male fieldworkers.
- 'Difficult' contraceptive methods can be adopted by rural people with a low literacy rate.

- Personal contact with the population appeared to be the most effective.

Monograph
None.

[25] Vellore, India

Two large prospective studies have originated in Vellore, Tamil Nadu, India, from the Christian Medical College. The first, from 1969 to 1974, followed two stratified cluster samples of 40,000 in the urban Vellore area, and 50,000 in the surrounding rural area. The second, from 1989 to 1994, follows a cohort of the children born during the first study, and includes 45,000 in the urban area and 55,000 in the rural area. There is a yearly census of the study population, and morbidity and pregnancy surveillance occurs every five weeks. Children are monitored monthly during their first year, then every six months thereafter.

Topics studied
- Demography: population dynamics, nuptiality, menstruation, family planning, pregnancy and its outcome, cause of death, and widowhood were investigated.
- Epidemiology/nutrition: diarrhoeal diseases, dysentery, cholera, typhoid, acute respiratory infections, malaria, measles, pertussis, tetanus, polio, tuberculosis, leprosy, epilepsy, and all EPI vaccinations were monitored.
- Health care/interventions: the use of prenatal care services were monitored, and adolescents had a yearly check-up.

Selected findings (first study)
- There was a marked seasonal fluctuation in perinatal mortality.
- Results were replicated for India that infants experienced greater mortality with low gestational age and birth weight, elder mothers and multiparas of >6, and a short birth interval.
- Inbreeding in the area had no noticeable effect on rates of congenital anomalies, stillbirths, abortions, or mortality.

Monograph
Series of monographs from the Dept. of Biostatistics, Christian Medical College, Vellore.

[26] Indramayu, Indonesia

The Indramayu Project is an ongoing prospective surveillance study, the result of the collaboration between USAID and the Government of Indonesia. It is taking place in the Indramayu Regency on Java, in two *kecamatans* (areas) one of which is a control area. Two samples of 5,000 people each are being followed monthly or every three months, depending on the study. Other surveys take place within this framework as well. The aim of the project is to study family planning using population-based data, and to do programmatic research. It started in 1988. The sample registration system is based on that of the extension area of Matlab.

Topics studied
- Demography: births, deaths, birth intervals, menstruation, pregnancy, abortion, migration, nuptiality.
- Public health/epidemiology: drug consumption, vaccination, breast-feeding, food intake.
- Intervention: information, education and communication (IEC), family planning.
- Anthropology: knowledge and beliefs about birth control and health services, kinship.

Selected findings
Recent study.

Monograph
None.

[27] Karachi, Pakistan

The Aga Khan University in Karachi, Pakistan has developed an ongoing programme for teaching, research, and service in health care, with an emphasis on maternal and child health, in five squatter communities of Karachi (Katchi Abadi). The total population was 45,880 when the programme started in 1985 All clinical information is collected monthly by the health-care workers, and a specific cohort of children are followed monthly, but all other vital registration is collected quarterly.

Topics studied
- Demography: the registration system generates data on population dynamics, infant and child mortality, maternal mortality, fertility, contraceptive use, causes of death.

- Epidemiology/nutrition: diarrhoeal diseases, vaccinations and morbidity levels, malnutrition, malaria.
- Anthropology/economics: ethnicity, housing, and 'urban' amenities (water and electricity) are assessed.
- Interventions: the major intervention is the provision of primary health care, provided by health workers and traditional birth attendants, and including family planning.

Selected findings
Recent study.

Monograph
None.

[28] Lulliani, Pakistan

The Medical Social Research Project (MESOREP) at Lulliani was set up and carried out by the Population Council, the University of the Punjab, and the Ministry of Health of Pakistan, with technical help from the Johns Hopkins School of Hygiene and Public Health, from 1961 to 1965. Lulliani is twenty-five miles from the provincial capital of Lahore, and had a population of approximately 12,500 in 1961. The Medical Social Research Project was intended to evaluate the effectiveness of a family-planning programme integrated with a Primary Health Centre. Continuous registration of vital events by health workers made birth rate and fertility calculations possible. The intervention programme started in November 1962 and the principal outcomes of interest were demographic.

Topics studied
- Demography: population dynamics, including migration were monitored; emphasis on fertility variables.
- Epidemiology: epidemiological surveillance of trachoma, malaria, and malnutrition.
- Interventions: family-planning services and education.

Selected findings
- The major finding of the study was that the birth rate did not decrease, most likely due to the high removal rate of intra-uterine devices soon after insertion.

Monograph
None.

[29] Bohol, Philippines

The Bohol Maternal and Child Health-Based Family Planning Project was conducted in the island of Bohol, Philippines over a five-year period (1975–9). The family-planning project as a whole covered a population of 425,000 people. However, only a sample of about 8,000 households (Project Area) was studied prospectively. The demographic surveillance system was based on periodic household surveys and a continuous reporting of events. In the same island, another longitudinal project was conducted: the Bohol-ARI project.

Topics studied
- Demography: population dynamics, births, deaths, migration, contraceptive use, abortion, breast-feeding.
- Epidemiology/nutrition: nutritional status, birth weight.
- Intervention: family-planning services and education.

Selected findings
- Some decline in fertility was noticed.
- Rural health and family-planning programmes can be run at relatively low cost.
- More attention could have been given to men.

Monograph
None. Comprehensive final report.

[30] Cebu, Philippines

Investigations in Cebu, and on Cebu island, have covered a wide range of topics. The population of metropolitan Cebu is approximately one million. All of the studies have used some sample of children and/or mothers, and followed a cohort. The work has been carried out by the Medical School in Cebu, with other collaborators, in particular the Johns Hopkins School of Public Health and the University of North Carolina. A 1983 study followed 3,080 rural and urban births, and reported on the prenatal care, birth weight, and subsequent health of the children. Another study started in 1987 and was still going on in 1992. It was based on a census and periodic surveys every six months and included about 9,000 children.

Topics studied
- Demography: population dynamics, mortality of children, causes of death, breast-feeding.
- Epidemiology/nutrition: birth weight, anthropometry, vaccination.
- Interventions: primary care services, oral rehydration therapy, vaccination, management of acute respiratory infections.

Selected findings
- The quality of care, accessibility of care, and insurance available to the mother had important effects of prenatal patterns.

Monograph
None.

[31] Family Planning Pilot Project, Sri Lanka

The Sweden–Ceylon Family Planning Pilot Project started in 1959, after two years of negotiations, in two distinctive areas of the island. One area was a village, the other an estate; they had a combined population of 14,000. Both populations were followed with a yearly census, updated every four months, until 1965, in order to determine the impact of a family-planning programme.

Topics studied
Issues addressed by the study included population dynamics, the implementation of a family-planning programme within an already existing health-care structure, and the evaluation of the above which included education and various methods of contraception.

Selected findings
- In the village area where the birth rate was already lower, within two years it had fallen further, whereas in the estate area, the impact of the programme was slower to appear.
- When men became involved in family-planning education and decisions, they preferred to use condoms.
- The integration of family planning with health clinics was not perceived as beneficial.
- People hired to educate and visit families should have local language and cultural skills, and good interpersonal skills.

Monograph
None.

[32] Etimesgut, Turkey

The Turkish National Health Services set up an integrated health and family-planning programme in Etimesgut District in 1966 in order to test the feasibility of multipurpose health units which combined health and family-planning programmes. Etimesgut proper lies about 20km. from Ankara; the district encompasses 1,655 sq. km. and includes two large towns and eighty-four smaller villages. The population in 1973, at the end of the project, was 65,218. Records of vital events were kept and reported monthly by public health nurses, and various investigations took place during the study.

Topics studied
- Demography: population dynamics, including births, deaths, and migrations were studied, along with age and sex patterns, contraceptive prevalence, effective contraceptive use, and knowledge, attitude, and practice of contraception.
- Interventions: family planning.

Selected findings
- The total fertility rate declined, after a plateau, from 4.95 to 3.72.
- The percentage of contraceptive users did not change a lot, but the rate of effective contraceptive use rose dramatically.
- Infant mortality fell concomitantly with the fall in fertility.
- Integrated health and family-planning services were effective in Turkey.

Monograph
None.

[33] INCAP, Guatemala

The studies conducted in the Guatemalan highlands with the support of INCAP since the 1950s were some of the first to address the bi-directional nature of malnutrition and infectious disease causing morbidity and mortality with the use of population-based data. One of the first large studies coming from INCAP in this mode lasted from 1959 to 1964, and involved three villages, the most famous being Santá María Cauque. The total population in the villages was 3,039 in 1959; increases in population size were monitored through bimonthly visits (for the first two years), then quarterly visits to all homes, plus a yearly census. Another study involving only Santá María Cauque, had a census in 1963, 1967, and 1971, and weekly visits for vital statistics and morbidity. Although the main focus of the study originally concerned nutritional problems in children, the design of the study made it conducive to other topics, including anthropology, epidemiology, and demography.

Topics studied
- Demography: the recording of births, deaths, and migrations were integral to the understanding of population dynamics. Breast-feeding habits and determination of the cause of death, as well as infant and child mortality, were key aspects of the nutrition intervention arm of the field study.

- Epidemiology and nutrition: all children had anthropometric measurements taken, including weight, height, skin-fold thickness, and head circumference. Their physical and later, also mental development were monitored. Diseases recorded prospectively included (but was not limited to) kwashiorkor and other related nutritional diseases, diarrhoea, measles, tetanus, whooping cough, skin and eye diseases, and any illness befalling a child under the age of 5.
- Anthropology: many aspects of living in rural Guatemala were described, including household patterns, cooking, hygiene, ethnicity, economic status, and landownership.
- Interventions: the effect of food supplementation, health clinics, and vaccinations were compared between villages, and treatment for diarrhoea was evaluated.

Selected findings
- The infant mortality decreased at a rate greater than that which would have been expected from previous years in the nutrition supplementation village.
- Both the health intervention village and the nutrition supplementation village experienced reductions in mortality.
- There were no significant differences in anthropometric measurements between different villages after the interventions.
- The relative contribution of infection and malnutrition to child mortality remained unclear, although the burden of disease was better described epidemiologically.
- Mothers had a high rate of infections, and a poor a state of nutrition.
- The newborn's weight was correlated to the weight of the mother, to the length of the birth interval, and to survival.
- Weight increase in infants and children did not continue along the Harvard standard, but fell off the curve at 6 months.
- Mild chronic malnutrition was endemic.

Monograph
Not specified.

[34] Projet Intégré de Santé et de Population, Haiti

The PISP grew out of local initiative with outside support from the Harvard School of Public Health and private foundations. It started in 1967 with a series of health intervention, nutrition, and family-planning projects in two non-contiguous areas of south-eastern Haiti. A census was performed yearly among the population of 44,000, and volunteers paid monthly (or more frequent) visits to all homes for vital registration. They also performed quarterly surveys for morbidity. The same team conducted another study around the Albert Schweitzer Hospital, in another rural area of Haiti.

Topics studied
- Demography: population dynamics, mortality, fertility, contraceptive prevalence, migration, cause of death, age, sex, and marriage patterns, lactation, and birth spacing.
- Epidemiology/nutrition: the quarterly visits to households, as well as the health-care system and special surveys, allowed the investigators to assess the prevalence and incidence of diarrhoeal diseases, tetanus, tuberculosis, skin diseases, intestinal worms (Necatur sp. *Ancylostoma*, *Trichuris*, *Ascaris*), malaria, nutritional, and vaccination status for adults and children.
- Anthropology/economics: some investigations and information about housing, agricultural patterns, family structure, child-fostering, sanitation, religion, and the role of traditional healers played an important role in the overall investigation.
- Interventions: basic health clinics, adult as well as child vaccinations, a programme to increase community participation, child health, prenatal care, food supplementation, and family-planning programme.

Selected findings
- PISP reduced mortality below that expected from national levels.
- PISP dramatically reduced neonatal and adult tetanus mortality rates.
- Vaccination of pregnant women was efficient in controlling neonatal tetanus.
- Maternal mortality decreased.
- The family-planning programme had an uncertain effect on fertility.
- A very high proportion of the adult mortality rate was due to tuberculosis.
- Malnourished children who received food supplementation had a lower mortality rate.
- Age at menarche, age at first union, and age at first pregnancy were all related.
- Food supplementation did not affect mortality in those already receiving health care.
- The length of post-partum lactation, post-partum amenorrhoea, and birth interval increased with age, and are longer when the previous child survives.

Monograph
Series of monographs published by the Public Health Department of Haiti.

Index

Index 347